Jurisprudence of Jurisdiction

For much of the history of the western legal order, the question of jurisdiction – the question of the power and authority of law – has been the first question of law. This book investigates the difference that jurisdiction continues to make to the ordering of normative existence. It also follows the speculation that without an account of jurisdiction, jurisprudence would be left speechless, with no power to address the conditions of attachment to legal and political order.

The starting point of this book lies with the claim that a sharper focus can be given to normative legal ordering through questions of jurisdiction than can be through those of moral responsibility or social action. This is so because jurisdiction articulates both the potentiality of law and the conditions of its exercise. It provides the idiom of response to the fact that there is law and to the fact that law institutes, judges and addresses a form of life. From this viewpoint the contributors to this book examine the institution of human rights, the new global and national orders of sovereign power and of trade and information, the judgement and government of death and desire, and the address of colonial and postcolonial legal idioms. In doing this the contributors also provide for the elaboration of questions of jurisdiction as part of the resources and repertoires of jurisprudence.

This book provides a point of entry to an emergent genre of writing within doctrinal, historical and critical jurisprudence that has returned to questions of jurisdiction to think again about juridical order and change. In so doing, it also points to questions that must be asked for there to be any interdisciplinary study that addresses law.

Shaun McVeigh is a Senior Lecturer in the School of Law, Griffith University, Australia.

Jurisprudence of Jurisdiction

Edited by
Shaun McVeigh

Routledge
Taylor & Francis Group
LONDON AND NEW YORK

First published 2007 by Routledge-Cavendish

2 Park Square, Milton Park, Abingdon, Oxon OX14 4RN
711 Third Avenue, New York, NY 10017, USA

Routledge is an imprint of the Taylor & Franics Group, an informa business

First issued in paperback 2016

Typeset in Times New Roman by
Newgen Imaging Systems (P) Ltd, Chennai, India

British Library Cataloguing in Publication Data
A catalogue record for this book is available from the British Library

Library of Congress Cataloging in Publication Data
Jurisprudence of jurisdiction / edited by Shaun McVeigh. – 1st ed.
p. cm.
1. Jurisdication. 2. Jurisprudence. I. McVeigh, Shaun, 1947–

K235.J866 2006
340′.11–dc22 2006017522

ISBN 978–1–138–99286–3 (pbk)
ISBN 978–1–84472–032–3 (hbk)

Contents

Contributors

Shaunnagh Dorsett is a Senior Lecturer at the Victoria University of Wellington. Her research interests lie in the fields of legal history, property and jurisprudence. Her recent publications consider the colonial and postcolonial settlement of Australia and Aotearoa /New Zealand.

Costas Douzinas is Professor of Law and Dean of Arts at Birkbeck College, University of London. Over the part 15 years, his research with Ronnie Warrington has contributed to the creation of a distinct school of British critical legal thought and the turning of legal scholarship towards ethical and aesthetic concerns. Recent work has included an advanced alternative textbook in legal theory, *Critical Jurisprudence* (2005) (with A. Geary) and *Postmodern Just Wars* (2006), which proposes a postmodern theory of justice and analyses the metaphysics of humanity.

Maria Drakopoulou is a Senior Lecturer in Law at Kent Law School, the University of Kent. She is also a founding member and articles editor of the *Feminist Legal Studies* journal. Her main areas of research interest are Feminist Theory, Legal Theory and Legal History. She is currently working on a book whose subject is a genealogy of feminist legal thought.

Lee Godden is an Associate Professor in the School of Law, University of Melbourne. She has a range of interests in legal theory, environmental and property law, which intersect with questions of jurisdiction. These include an exploration of how property forms impose a jurisdiction over the natural world and indigenous peoples.

Bill Grantham is currently working as a media lawyer in Los Angeles. He has also been a consultant, publisher, writer and editor serving the film and television industries since 1983. He is the author of *Some Big Bourgeois Brothel: Contexts for France's Culture Wars with Hollywood* (2000) and has published extensively in the field of law and film.

Piyel Haldar is a Lecturer in the School of Law, Birkbeck College, University of London. Dr Haldar specialises in colonial history and postcolonial theory. He recently completed a book entitled *The Jurisdiction of the Lotus Eaters: Doctrines* *of Enjoyment and Fantasies of Pleasure in Colonial Rule* (2006). He has also published in the fields of legal history and evidence.

Mary Keyes is an Associate Professor in Law, Associate Dean (Postgraduate Studies) and Deputy Head of School at Griffith Law School. She researches in the field of private international law and is the author of the recently published *Jurisdiction in International Litigation* (2005), co-author of *Policy and Pragmatism in the Conflict of Laws* (2001) and co-editor of *Changing Law* (2005).

Shaun McVeigh is a Senior Lecturer in the School of Law at Griffith University. His research interests include the relations between jurisdiction and jurisprudence and the legal ordering of relations between the living and the dead.

Leslie J Moran is Professor of Law in the School of Law at Birkbeck College, University of London. He has published extensively on matters of sexuality and law. His most recent monograph, *Sexuality and the Politics of Violence and Safety* (with B Skeggs, P Tyrer and K Corteen, 2004), is a book based upon the UK's largest empirical study of lesbian and gay responses to homophobic violence. He also researches and publishes in law and popular culture and was the co-editor of *Law's Moving Image* (2004). He is currently writing a book on sexual diversity in the judiciary.

Stewart Motha is a Lecturer in the Kent Law School, University of Kent, Canterbury, United Kingdom. He has previously taught law at the Universities of Lancaster and Adelaide. He was a legal officer and case manager with the Aboriginal Legal Rights Movement in South Australia. He has co-edited a special issue of the journal *Law and Critique* and published articles in *Social and Legal Studies*, *Australian Feminist Law Journal*, *Griffith Law Review* and *Law and Critique*.

Nan Seuffert is an Associate Professor in Law and the Dean of Research and Graduate Programmes in the School of Law, University of Waikato. She researches in the fields of feminist and criticial jurisprudence and companies and securities law and has published in England, the United States, Canada, Australia and New Zealand. She has a forthcoming book titled *'Racing' and Engendering the Nation State* (2006).

John Strawson is Reader in Law at the University of East London. He works on law and postcolonialism with special reference to international law, Islam and the Middle East. He teaches law and Middle East studies at the University of East London, where he also directs the work of the Encountering Legal Cultures research group. His publications include (as editor) *Law after Ground Zero* (2002).

Preface

The contributors to this collection of essays were given a brief that was broad: it was to refresh the jurisprudence of jurisdiction. They were prompted to respond to the question 'What might be understood in jurisprudence by way of a return to questions of jurisdiction?' Behind this question lies the speculative claim that, without an account of jurisdiction, jurisprudence would be left speechless, left without the power to address the conditions of attachment to legal and political order. What was invited in this book was not so much a critique of the form of law, but an investigation of the modes or manners of coming into law and of being with law. Implicit in this is a refocusing of attention away from the litigious concerns of tribunals and fora towards an engagement with the inauguration, existence and practices of law.

Questions of jurisdiction have been central to Western legal and institutional thought, yet how to find a place within jurisprudence and the philosophy of law to pose such questions has not been obvious. At its broadest, the question of jurisdiction engages both with the fact that there is law and with the power and authority to speak in the name of the law. The encapsulation of jurisdiction involves consideration of the enunciation (or potentiality) of law, its technological and material modes of operation and its idiomatic expression. These concerns provide the frame of reference for the investigations into the jurisprudence of jurisdiction made in this book.

The approaches taken to jurisdiction in this book have not generally been limited to attempts either to justify existing accounts of jurisdiction or to reconcile the exercise of jurisdiction with state policy or party interests (important though these concerns are). Instead, two broad lines of investigation are pursued. In one direction, the contributions formulate and reconstruct jurisdiction as part of rival metaphysics of law; in another they perform as essays, or investigations, into the resources and repertoires of the jurisprudences of jurisdiction. In relation to the former, the essays consider afresh the ways in which philosophies of law and jurisprudence respond to questions of jurisdiction. They also serve as a reminder of the continuing importance of jurisdictional thought to both metaphysics and ethics. In relation to the latter, these contributions consider jurisdiction as exercise of a technology of law. As a question of technology, three themes are addressed: first, institutional relations between jurisdiction, state, sovereignty and territory; second, the governmental relations between jurisdiction, judgement and the technologies of law; and third, the idiomatic representation of jurisdiction to law. Taking up these topics, the contributors to this book examine the institution of human rights and the new global and national orders of sovereign power, the judgement and government of death and desire, and the address of colonial and post-colonial legal idioms.

The return to questions of jurisdiction forms part of an emergent genre of scholarship within doctrinal, historical and critical jurisprudence. Its address is primarily juridical, but it also raises questions for all disciplines enmeshed in questions of authority and authorisation as these concerns retain their juridical affiliations. Much of the impetus of the work in *Jurisprudence of Jurisdiction* is critical: the concerns of the contributors circulate around questions of belonging to law, of working within the idiom of law and what (if anything) can continue to be said about attachments of law and its orderings of time, space and place. Beyond this, a collection of essays on jurisdiction is as eclectic as the domains of the critical legal study of law.

Acknowledgements

There are many people who have helped one way or another in the production of this book. I would like to thank the Socio-Legal Research Centre at Griffith University for funding the symposium that initiated this book in June 2001, Susan Jarvis for editing the final text, and the staff at Routledge-Cavendish and UCL Press for bringing it to production. Thanks too to those who participated in the symposium and contributed in other ways including Geoffrey Airo-Farulla, Tarik Kochi, Marett Leiboff, Bill MacNeil, Desmond Manderson, Graeme Orr, David Saunders and many of the contributors to this book. Special thanks are due to Shaunnagh Dorsett, Costas Douzinas and Peter Rush, who have all at various stages collaborated in the production of *Jurisprudence of Jurisdiction*.

Part I

Introduction

1 Questions of jurisdiction

Shaunnagh Dorsett and Shaun McVeigh

Introduction

Questions of jurisdiction have been central to Western legal traditions, yet finding a place within jurisprudence and the philosophy of law to pose such questions has not been obvious. By contrast, the practice of the law is preoccupied with questions of jurisdiction and the arrangements of the authority to judge in matters of law. Despite this, the work of practitioners lacks anything but the 'thinnest' of descriptive accounts of what it means to engage with questions of jurisdiction. It is as if legal thought cannot, or can no longer, articulate the terms of its own existence. To introduce *Jurisprudence of Jurisdiction*, this chapter returns to some of the central topics of jurisdiction in order to investigate the modes or manner of coming into law and of being with law.

At its broadest, the question of jurisdiction engages with the fact that there is law, and with the power and authority to speak in the name of the law. It encompasses the authorisation and ordering of law as such as well as determinations of authority within a legal regime. Emile Benveniste has drawn out the inaugural character of the etymology of jurisdiction. The Latin *juris-dictio* links the Latin noun *ius* with the verb *dictio*. *Ius* is usually translated as 'law', and refers to the adjectival situation of conforming to law (*iustus*). Linked to the verb *dicere* – the saying or speech of law – *ius* becomes performative (and adverbial) (1973: 391). Within the institutional domain of the Roman courts, *ius* and *dicere* are linked to the office of the *iu-dex*, he who states the law, and *juris-dictio*, the saying or speaking of the law (*Digest* 2.1.1) (Benveniste, 1973: 392). In jurisdiction, then, might be found questions of the inauguration of law – its value and validity – and its articulation. It is with these concerns, and with the representation of the orders of law that are engendered through jurisdiction, that the contributions to *Jurisprudence of Jurisdiction* seek to engage.

The conceptual role that questions of jurisdiction play in legal thought has not received much attention in contemporary legal theory. At the risk of caricature, within the philosophy of law questions of jurisdiction fall for consideration somewhere between the concerns of philosophies of action and event, and those of moral responsibility. If located as a question of action and event, jurisdiction makes a brief appearance in relation to questions of sovereignty and of space but gives way to the evaluation of law in general or vacates law altogether for the fields of international relations and political geography. Perhaps this reflects a preference, predominant since the nineteenth century, for explanations of law framed in terms of social and not legal existence, state centred or otherwise (Kriegal, 2001). As a part of a discourse of moral authority, jurisdiction takes its place as an embodiment of value, or as a partial step towards value. Such approaches risk losing the questions of 'why law?' or 'why this law?' and with them the question of the authority and form of law. To address such questions ties jurisprudence back to the diction or speech of law and returns the process of jurisdiction both to a structure (or metaphysics) of law and to a history of the institutions that carry the meaning of legal life.

For some, tying questions of jurisdiction back into metaphysics and to the difficulties of staging a relation to law gives too much to a long tradition of thinking about law which has little hold on contemporary reality. Our present, whether viewed as modern, ultra-modern or postmodern, can no longer be considered capable of being structured or represented in fully legal or ethical form (Murphy, 1997). What is needed is a form of investigation that pays attention to the ways in which the authorisation of law is linked to its purposes or desire (Goodrich, 1996). For others, failure to pay attention to the difficulties of escaping from the metaphysics of law ensures only its repetition (Gadamer, 1979: 494; Rose, 1984: 3; Derrida, 1989). However, to think that it is possible simply to have done with questions of jurisdiction would be to forego the possibility of questioning the concepts of limit and structure in law as well as the links between speech and law and voice and authority. It is with these questions of jurisdiction, and not with those of morality and action, that first questions of law can be posed. This formulation of a metaphysics of law, together with the inaugural gestures of law itself, forms the first theme of this book.

There is also an insistent materiality to questions of jurisdiction that can initially be approached in terms of an institutional practice or pragmatics. At the centre of these practices are the various devices, techniques and technologies that make the enunciation and life of the law possible, and the investigation of these forms the second major theme of the book. It would be no great exaggeration to say that the institutional histories of Western law have been written in terms of jurisdiction. Questions of jurisdiction were central to the accounts of the protocols of government of imperial Rome just as much as they were to the accounts of the medieval ordering of the spiritual and temporal relations of church and state and to the rise of the modern nation-state. The history of the common law is also – and often is simply only – a history of jurisdiction. Holdsworth, for example, devoted much of his 16-volume *History of English Law* (Holdsworth, 1922–1972) to detailed accounts of particular and plural jurisdictions: those of common law, stannary, forestry, ecclesiastical law and so on. Likewise, the history of common law legal ordering of British colonisation, as with other imperial projects, was in many ways one of jurisdiction. It is through jurisdiction that the authority of the common and imperial laws have been asserted, and it is through questions of jurisdiction that the legal settlement of the colonies has been effected. Contemporary writings on international and universal jurisdictions are recent additions to this genre.

What is striking in the writing of the histories of jurisdiction is not so much the lack of substantive criticism but the lack of a language of analysis of jurisdiction. It is possible to develop ethical arguments about the moral value of universal jurisdiction or of the practical negotiations of the rival criteria of jurisdiction in the draft *Hague Convention on Jurisdiction and Judgments*, but there is as yet only a very limited discourse of jurisdiction itself (Macedo, 2005). Within legal doctrine, questions of jurisdiction are frequently merged with those of authority and its delimitation or, as in the case of private international law, figured in terms of justification (Whincop and Keyes, 2001). One consequence of this is that the technologies of law that establish authority are understood as descriptions of bare action or fact – technical commentary on the determination of forum and the recognition and enforcement of judgements. In all this, the character of jurisdiction as an instrument is frequently occluded. What is lost is the staging and representation of law as a work of figuration. A claim that the technologies of law do more than describe legal actions should raise no controversy within legal thought. Viewed as process, jurisdiction encompasses the tasks of the authorisation of law, the production of legal meaning and the marking of what is capable of belonging to law. If nothing else, the work of categorisation of persons, things, places and events; the procedures of summons, hearing, decision and sentence; and the forensic concerns of argument and proof serve as devices of attachment to law.

The analysis of the artefactual character of law has more recently been found in the domains of anthropology, sociology and cultural studies. In this book, these concerns are returned to law and addressed through jurisdiction. This allows for the consideration of the state, for example, as an assemblage of devices and techniques not only for the delimitation of relations of authority and the exercise of power, but also for their representation. In this book, rather than assuming a natural link between sovereignty, territory and land, the links between sovereignty, state and territory are studied in terms of techniques of authorisation and grounding. As a technology, jurisdictional practice institutes a relation to life, place and event through processes of codification or marking. It is through jurisdiction that a life before the law is instituted, a place is subjected to rule and occupation, and an event is articulated as juridical. In all this, of course, the long polemics of jurisprudence have disputed the representation and manner of being subject to a jurisdiction.

The concern with the diction, speech or idiomatic representation of law forms the third major theme of this book. The elaboration of how instruments give voice to law has been one of the tasks of jurisprudence. At issue are not so much the administrative aspects of government, but the broadly semiotic aspects of jurisdiction (Goodrich and Hachamovitch, 1991). The idiom of jurisdiction can be understood in terms of the interpretation and judgement of institutional meaning. However, to analyse the communication of law as jurisdictional enunciation, it is also necessary to consider what is passed on in the pragmatic performance of jurisdiction.

The contributions

The chapters presented in this book broadly follow the three lines of aspects of jurisdiction already outlined. In one direction, they formulate and reconstruct the metaphysics of jurisdiction and in so doing examine the inaugural gestures of jurisdiction. In another, they perform more or less as investigations into the resources and repertoires of the jurisprudences of jurisdiction and the technologies of government. In so doing, they investigate the attachments of jurisdiction. Finally, they direct attention to the idiom of jurisdiction and the representation of the symbolic or semiotic ordering of law.

Situations of jurisdiction

The metaphysics of jurisdiction addresses the speech of law and what allows the law to emerge or cohere as law. It seeks to formulate and respond to questions such as: 'How does jurisdiction (and so law) arise in its original form?' and 'What utterance inaugurates a jurisdiction and establishes a power to legislate in its act of speech?' Questions of jurisdiction address the relation between metaphysical and juridical thought and between the legal and the social domains. In this book, the two opening chapters are used to provide a point of entry into contemporary formulations of the relations between the metaphysical and juridical thought of law.

For Costas Douzinas and Maria Drakopoulou, questions of jurisdiction do not simply have answers in the history of law and practice, but rather form a part of the 'interior' sovereignty of law (Douzinas) or are statements that inaugurate law (Drakopoulou). Both authors, of course, make strong claims for the importance of jurisdiction to the conceptual formation of the political and legal domains. In the 'Metaphysics of Jurisdiction', Costas Douzinas engages the relationship between universal jurisdiction and the conflict of jurisdictions and sovereignty. For Maria Drakopoulou, in 'Of the Founding of Law's Jurisdiction and the Politics of Sexual Difference: The Case of Roman Law', the question is more morphological: 'what is engendered and given shape through jurisdiction?' Both draw questions of jurisdiction into the formation of the modern subject. For Douzinas, paying attention to the metaphysics of jurisdiction allows for the development of a critical, acoustic, subject. For Drakopoulou, the concern is more to reveal the synchronic morphology (the shape) of law's being, rationality and power – and the way sexual difference 'provides the conditions of possibility of the "visibility" of law's power'. The immediate objects of Douzinas' polemic are the claims to transcend sovereignty made in the name of universal jurisdiction. Against this, Douzinas posits conflicts of sovereignty as the presupposition of jurisdiction. The opening of political and legal thought is the coming together, or becoming common, of a community, which 'appears by expressing itself in a sovereign way by giving itself the law'. This initial gesture Douzinas names as *bare* sovereignty – the circumscription, or naming, of being in common. Insofar as there is a question of community at issue, there can be no escape from the metaphysics of sovereignty – and its accompanying institutionalisation. The sovereign giving of the law also invokes a law-maker and the enforcement of law or the recognition of the natural order of things. Within this scheme, jurisdiction marks the point of inauguration at which the community gives the law to itself, the most singular utterance offering up the most general law. Jurisdiction, then, is the speaking of the sovereign law of the community (*juris dicere*). If this is so, then the question of jurisdiction also grants a privileged point of location for thinking about political philosophy and philosophical politics (and law) as it is both the site and point of determination of political and legal decision.

Where Douzinas produces a chorography of the metaphysics of the sovereign subject of jurisdiction, Maria Drakopoulou can be said to produce a morphology of the metaphysics of the engenderment of jurisdiction. Where Douzinas draws on the linguistics of Benveniste to draw a distinction between enunciation and subject, Drakopoulou marks a similar distinction in terms of the statement and the narrative of sexual difference. Jurisdiction, for Drakopoulou, is not a structure but a 'function of existence' (Foucault, 1972: 86): it takes place. Her chapter in effect produces a semantics – and perhaps an ontology – of the enunciation of Western jurisdiction. In relating two accounts of sexual difference that shape the narrative of Roman law, the stories of Lucretia and Verginia examine the way in which the morphological power of jurisdiction is realised. Drakopoulou relates the story of the extortion of sex from Lucretia, the subsequent trial of Sextus for crimes relating to illicit sexual acts, and also relates her suicide to the founding of the new law of Rome. The radical transformation of time and space that inaugurated a new law was established by marking the feminine as sexual difference and as a referent outside of law. The other story of Rome that Drakopoulou relates is that of Verginia. Her story of sexual assault, honour, chastity and death is told as part of the relationship of the excluded legal relationship of the feminine to law.

The accounts of jurisdiction offered by Drakopoulou and Douzinas sit alongside, and can be counterposed to, two earlier broadly phenomenological accounts of jurisdiction by Goodrich and Cover. Together they flesh out the contemporary critical framing of jurisdiction. In the work of Peter Goodrich, jurisdiction is linked to the articulation or nomination of desire. It becomes a site of enunciation where affective desires become attached to law as person, place or event. Whereas Douzinas concentrates on the authorisation of jurisdiction, and Drakopoulou its shape, it is the ways in which law institutes life that are the central concern of Goodrich's pragmatics of jurisdiction. While jurisdiction is frequently described in terms of the posited laws of state law, Goodrich investigates those jurisdictions, or aspects of jurisdiction, that reveal the instituted common laws of desire. In *Law in the Courts of Love*, for example, Goodrich disinters a (possibly apocryphal) jurisdiction of the laws of love, in which the poetics of courtship and the conduct of love were subject to adjudication. Where the Christian tradition instituted a jurisdiction that encouraged a love of the divine and judged in the name of *lex caritas*, these courts of love followed the laws of erotic love (Goodrich, 1996: 217). The proceedings of the Courts of Love date back to the twelfth and thirteenth centuries and were related in the Troubadour traditions. For Goodrich, they emblematise an errant jurisdiction that pitches love and death into relation. They are not subject to church law but to a feminine jurisdiction where affect and desire are given due weight in an art of living. Where Goodrich finds a feminine jurisdiction in the interstices of law and a feminine politics within the law, Drakopoulou figures the feminine as outside the law. Accordingly, for Drakopoulou, the desires of law cannot recover a feminine voice within the genealogical ordering of law.

While somewhat different in idiom, Robert Cover's accounts of jurisdiction, bring out a fourth theme of a metaphysics of jurisdiction, the way that jurisdiction is bound to violence and justice. Robert Cover develops an account of jurisdiction that is more closely concerned to calculate or measure with the violence of law. To do this Cover elaborates something like a natural law of jurisdiction (Cover, 1995a,b,c).

What makes Cover's elaboration of jurisdiction distinct is the emphasis he places on linking his account of a jurisdiction of natural law committed to a justice 'yet to come' to an institutional account of the practical reasoning of the judge that restages a role-bound jurisdiction of violence. In this configuration the claim of jurisdiction is never simply a claim of present authority but invokes with it a commitment of a justice to come. The claim to judge and to actualise law and justice is never separate from the institutional force necessary to transform the contingent action into a meaningful event. This formulation also returns questions of jurisdiction to their point of ordering – their time and place (McVeigh, Rush and Young, 2001). This is so both for state law and for other normative orders (Roberts, 2005). Douzinas' chapter draws attention not just to the violence in law, but to the violence *of* law, a violence that can never simply be subordinated to the theological concerns of sovereignty and the aesthetic and ethical concerns of judgement. Drakopoulou's chapter displaces the fiction of the sovereign subject into the shape of law and finds violence in the separate and engendered form of violence that instantiates the law. At the risk of over-generalisation, it could be said that it has been the return to the problem of the time and place of law that has preoccupied critical legal theory in the last 10 years.

States of jurisdiction

The chapters in the third part of the book are relatively easy to situate. Two features have dominated modern Western formulations of jurisdiction: the significance of the state and its sovereignty; and the means through which the attachments of jurisdiction proceed. Conceptually and institutionally, they have been formulated in terms of a set of relations between jurisdiction, nation-state, sovereignty and territory.

Without pressing the issue too hard, at present, formulations of questions of jurisdiction dominate contemporary political and civil disputes. Questions of executive power, and the civil and military authority to try those held in Camp X-Ray, Guantanamo Bay, have returned issues of freedom and security to those of jurisdiction. Less publicly, and in many ways more farcically, the remnants of British colonial jurisdiction are being reassessed on Pitcairn Island, just as the legacy of the colonial jurisdictions is being effaced in the rest of the post-colonial domains [*R v 7 Named Accused* [2004] PNCA 1]. In a slightly different context, the new international orders of the commercial domain have pitched the complexities of the organisation of jurisdictions in private international law against the claims of a new *lex mercatoria* for global economies, universal jurisdictions of human rights and transmission systems of information such as the internet. What allows this array of jurisdictional questions to be connected is a concern with overstepping the territorial jurisdictions of nation-states. What inhibits thought about what this might mean is a relative lack of attention to the juridical and jurisdictional character of state sovereignty and its alternatives, and in particular to the homology of law and territory which still dominates contemporary accounts of the state.

If the contributions to the first part of the book seek to give conceptual order to questions of jurisdiction at the level of metaphysics, in this part the contributors engage with the particular jurisdictional formations of the modern sovereign nation-state. Where positivist jurisprudence has customarily represented jurisdiction in terms of a monologic of sovereign state power, the contributions to this book investigate both the natural law of jurisdictions and the plurality of state and non-state jurisdictions. While in some respects the influence of pluralism in the social and cultural study of law has pointed to the way in which legal practices are diverse in both production and reception of law, paying attention to questions of jurisdiction allows for these observations to continue to be phrased in terms of juridical ordering.

The overwhelming contemporary importance attached to the sovereign territorial jurisdictions of the nation-state should not obscure the variety of ways in which jurisdictional attachments can be, and have been, formed, as well as the different ways in which territory itself has been articulated. In medieval Europe, for example, territory was a term that referred to the district surrounding a city over which it had jurisdiction or exclusive authority. Roman and pre-modern sovereignty was conceptualised in terms of *imperium* and was connected to personal political denomination and office rather than land. In England, the feudal relation between Crown and subject was bound into a recognised system of rights and obligations (Ullman, 1975). While territorial jurisdiction was not unknown in medieval England, the most notable territorial jurisdictions were franchises. Franchises were grants of authority from the Crown to the territorial lord, who might be either lay or ecclesiastical. All these are some way from contemporary presuppositions of the fact of sovereignty and territory.

The modern sovereign territorial state as a particular form of jurisdictional organisation with a specific conceptual and institutional ordering owes much to the European political settlement consequent on the wars of confessional religion in seventeenth-century Europe. The Treaty of Westphalia in 1648 is credited with 're-spatialising' Europe in terms of bounded sovereign territories and specifiable populations (Schmitt, 1996). Its jurisprudence was the product of a self-conscious work, now recently revived, first of German political jurisprudence, then of English and French jurists in the seventeenth century (Hunter, 2001; Hunter and Saunders, 2003). Sovereignty, too, in the common law tradition might be viewed as a series of jurisdictional disputes. This is so from the early modern disputes over ecclesiastical, Royal and common law jurisdiction played out, for example, in the case of Prohibitions del Roy [(1607) 12 Co Rep 63], as well as the administrative battles for control of the government of the state in the nineteenth century and the present day reordering of the juridical orders of human rights.

The chapters in this part all address and complicate contemporary articulations of jurisdiction and sovereignty. Stewart Motha addresses the constitution of jurisdiction and the presence of the sovereign subject through the figure of the abandoned detainee at Guantanamo Bay. John Strawson and Nan Seuffert address the inheritance of colonial jurisdiction practices through analyses of contemporary 'experiments' in state formation: the absent state of Palestine and the 'bi-cultural' state of New Zealand. Finally, Mary Keyes addresses what is of interest to the state, as well as what interests the state has, in controlling jurisdiction and adjudication.

In 'Guantanamo Bay, "Abandoned Being" and the Constitution of Jurisdiction', the object of Stewart Motha's critical concern is those accounts of sovereignty and the rule of law that attempt to secure political community through a monistic account of sovereign and subject. Taking his cue from the work of Jean-Luc Nancy (2003), Motha argues that, far from being a unique exception to law, the 'abandoned' status of the detainees at Camp X-Ray, Guantanamo Bay, is central to the structure of sovereignty in general and to the neo-imperial American state in particular. Starting with the observation that the detainees at Camp X-Ray are not fully excluded from law, but are held in place by a law that excludes them from access to law, Motha draws out the way in which the condition of the life of the detainee unmediated by civil law is a product of a jurisdictional arrangement of the withdrawal of law. What is revealed in the 'abandonment' of the detainee is not a loss of law, but a structure that borders sovereign law and upholds both law and its withdrawal. For Motha, what is revealed is not so much a state of exception but a part of the working of the economy of sovereignty. The process of abandonment is one of reinscribing the limits of law by means of an inclusive exclusion. In this account, 'abandoned being' is neither inside nor outside the legal or political order of law, but is a possibility through which jurisdictional order proceeds and is constituted.

John Strawson considers absence of another kind in his chapter, 'Conjuring Palestine: The Jurisdiction of Dispossession'. Here what is at issue, in the context of Palestine, is the status of a jurisdiction that might appear to be expressing the authority of a self-determining sovereign state but is, for the time being, without state or territory. While Palestine possesses many of the trappings of statehood – walled borders, political representation, a national authority and so forth – what drives the formation of Palestine is not the logic of the possession of space and place but its dispossession. The institutional logic for this dispossession can be found, Strawson argues, in the continued use of the jurisdictional arrangements of the British colonial mandates over Palestine and Israel. Strawson elaborates that continuity in the meticulous legalism of subordination which characterises the contemporary politics of settlement.

Like Motha at Camp X-Ray, Strawson finds in Palestine a state of abandonment. Where Motha considers this abandonment as a question of being and of being a subject, Strawson elaborates it as a question of power and discourse. Nan Seuffert's chapter, 'Jurisdiction and Nation Building: Tall Tales in Nineteenth Century Aotearoa/New Zealand', is a companion piece to Strawson's account of Palestine. Like Strawson, Seuffert points to the way in which contemporary practices of dispossession in Aotearoa/New Zealand continue the jurisdictional practices that facilitated the dispossession of Maori in the nineteenth century. Seuffert draws out the ways in which the jurisdictional subordination of Maori law, and the displacement of Maori political and social structures, was also connected to a discourse of the ethnic nation and state. The state of New Zealand was constructed in the second half of the nineteenth century in conformity with the fantasy of an ethnically 'British' settlement. What Nan Seuffert's account drives home is how much of the aspiration of a 'bi-cultural' Aotearoa/New Zealand depends on structures of jurisdiction previously deployed to do precisely the opposite.

Where the earlier chapters in this part presume a central relation between state, jurisdiction and territory, in the final chapter, 'The Suppression of State Interests in International Litigation', Mary Keyes examines how state interests are represented in jurisdictional issues between private parties. Keyes shows that the criteria for determination of jurisdiction, such as the presumptions of territorial connection or compensation for personal injuries, are the product of a pragmatic formalism and the attempt to suspend or suppress overt reference to international political relations. In this way, jurisdictional arrangements are managed and a process of adjudication is practised that avoids direct involvement with questions of state policy or international relations. This, of course, does not stop a decision being made as to the choice of competing legal systems – and judgements being made that have effects on state interests.

In a way that resonates with the analyses provided by Strawson and Seuffert, Keyes shows the ways in which formal jurisdictional arrangements give shape to the understanding of the state. This should be no surprise given the history of jurisdictional practice. What may be a surprise, however, is the willingness of doctrinal scholars, practitioners and critics to overlook the difference jurisdiction makes to thinking about the state. One task of a critical jurisprudence would be to produce accounts of sovereignty and doctrine that no longer presuppose territory as fact – subject only to adjudicatory and administrative organisation. This is the concern of the third part of this book.

Technologies of jurisdiction

Jurisdiction, particularly in common law thought, is known through its acts and is elaborated through usage and practice. An exercise of a jurisdiction is always an exercise of a technology, or an assemblage of devices, that authorises law and in a general sense institutes a life – or at least a life before the law. In common law thought, this technical and material aspect might be characterised in terms of a technology or set of techniques that capture or attach its objects to law. One aspect of this has already been investigated in the elaboration of relations between sovereignty, territory and the state. It is the questioning of the relations between these three terms that allows for a more nuanced account of jurisdiction as an instrument of law. This is the concern of the third part of the book.

In this part, attention is turned to some of the devices of judgement, categorisation, government and administration that have dominated the processes of the attachment of persons, things, events and effects to the body of law. Consideration is given here to the ways in which space is instituted and demarcated through measurement (Shaunnagh Dorsett); place is organised through administration (Les Moran) desire is marshalled and distributed by planning regimes (Lee Godden); and the death of legal persons is delimited through status and role (Shaun McVeigh). In part, these contributions to the book are concerned with producing 'thick' descriptions of the techniques of jurisdiction, but they also help to redefine the ways in which the juridical can be thought in relation to technology.

One of the more striking revivals of jurisprudence has been the spatial turn taken in the elaboration of the links between law and political, cultural and social geography. In her chapter, 'Mapping Territories', Shaunnagh Dorsett explores cartography as an aspect of the inauguration of jurisdiction. As a technology of jurisdiction, a map enables space to become a jurisdiction, marked as the territory of a sovereign. It is this technology, Dorsett argues, that proved decisive in displacing the earlier jurisdictional arrangement based on status and dominion, as it provided for the possibility of a definitive delimitation of space. Where once a legal space might have been delimited by the amount of work done by an ox under plough, or the distance capable of being walked in a day, space could now be determined in relation to an abstract grid. In a more complex manner, cartography provided a device for the development of modern understanding of regulation since it allowed for the demarcation of boundaries to be determined by technical means and not local memory or custom. It rendered space abstract and knowable without particular knowledge of place or custom. As Dorsett notes, this technology provided a functional reference for the European and British colonial drive to gain possession of the world. Finally, a territorial jurisdiction based on mapping produces a particular way of understanding place and its relation to the ground or land. For the purposes of Western laws, all such relations must be capable of representation in terms of a grid.

Lee Godden and Les Moran investigate the space of jurisdiction through the contemporary orderings of bodies and desire. Where Dorsett considers geography, chorography and cartography as technologies of jurisdiction, Godden, in 'Jurisdiction of Body and Desire: Exploring the Boundaries of Bodily Control in Prostitution Law', positions jurisdiction between bodies and law, and Moran, in 'Placing Jurisdiction', figures jurisdiction in terms of a spatial ordering of bodies. For Godden, while the regulation of prostitution establishes the nexus – largely in terms of boundaries – between the body and law, how jurisdiction is understood and practised depends on a conception and practice of law. For Moran, the jurisdictional control of sexual bodies is set in the context of the creation of a queer domain of the 'Gay Village' in Manchester, England, and the maintenance of the homophobic political-legal order of the Queen's Peace.

In Australia, the regulation of prostitution has varied from the criminal regulation of a pre-existing sinful body that has transgressed moral values to the administrative regulation of prostitution that constrains, constructs and manages a 'form of life' of prostitution. Drawing on the work of Michel Foucault and Judith Butler, Godden shows how prostitution and planning laws in Queensland, Australia, shape prostitution in terms of place and a negative identity based on exclusion from both family and community. Jurisdiction in this account operates through the performance both of prostitution and of the regulatory technology that creates legal meaning both as a question of gendered sexual practice and as question of population control. Questions of jurisdiction emerge here to unify around the prostitute body a broad range of regulatory concerns relating to building use, planning, design, social hygiene, moral policing and so forth. However, in so doing, the prostitute body takes up a legal status (or a *de facto* legal status) that sets 'bounds for the prostitute's body and sexual activity by "identifying" the concurrent necessity for such bounding'.

In 'Placing Jurisdiction', Moran problematises the relation between space, language, the body and the law. In his analysis of the jurisdiction over male desire and homophobic violence, Moran voices these concerns in terms of a traditional civil jurisprudence: the safety and security of the Queen's Peace. In contrasting a police prosecution of seven men for sexual offences including sodomy in Bolton, Lancashire, with the construction of the 'Gay Village' in Manchester 15 miles away, Moran draws out the ways in which the jurisdictional arrangement of public and private space, natural and unnatural bodily activities, safe and unsafe sexual, social and commercial practices are brought into being and contested.

At the centre of Moran's analysis is the insistence that bodily–spatial arrangements should be thought of in political–legal terms. If the prosecution of seven men for consensual sexual activity provides a depressing reminder of the homophobic ordering of 'private' space, the spatial and bodily ordering of the 'Gay Village' provides a new and limited ordering of public space and bodies. However, as Moran's interviews highlight, both engage a politics of space and place. In Moran's account, the space of the 'Gay Village' does not offer the possibility of a jurisdictional solution to homophobic violence, since it organises only one aspect of public space. What it does reveal, however, are the different ways in which the sovereign body of the law is articulated through questions of jurisdiction.

In 'Subjects of Jurisdiction: The Dying', McVeigh returns the emergent jurisdiction over assisted suicide and euthanasia to the functional tasks of a dogmatic order and considers how a jurisdiction over the terminally ill might institute them as legal persons and bring them to their death. Many accounts of assisted suicide and euthanasia make appeals to a natural moral personality in order to judge legal regulation, whether it be in terms of the autonomous or sacred person of integrity. However, they have difficulty in accounting for the jurisdictional structures and techniques of regulation. As such, they leave untouched the means by which the state might express its interest in the terminally ill, or in assisting suicide or euthanasia. This chapter examines how these interests have been delimited by the status of legal personality and the available roles that give juridical shape to a dignified manner of dying for the terminally ill. More generally, the chapter explores a theme that runs throughout this book: the competition in legal thought between anti-legal regimes that are framed in terms of an escape from law in the name of a higher law (freedom, integrity or the sacred) and those political–legal orders that remain within a technically constructed (dogmatic) legal order.

To note that jurisprudence is transmitted through and must engage with the technologies of jurisdiction is to do no more than point out that coming to judgement in law – which is the task of jurisprudence – is neither just a matter of interpretation nor just a matter of consequential enforcement. What is at issue are the techniques of the inscription and institution of forms of life. The chapters in this part of the book can broadly be said to have investigated the attachment of bodies, things and events to the body of law. They also open up questions of jurisdiction to judgement and to the diction of jurisdiction (Rush, 1997).

Dictions of jurisdiction

The fifth part of the book takes up the idiomatic ordering, or diction, of jurisdiction. In this book, the elaboration of the inaugural character of jurisdiction and its topical and technical arrangement has been presented as double bound: it is distributed amongst the parts of law; and it is the point from which each of the legal parts are related and put into circulation. The voice of law – as well as the attendant thematics of enunciation, presence, authority and truth – owes as much to the inheritance of scholastic theology and canon law traditions as it does to formulations within contemporary legal thought (Helmholtz, 2004; Legendre, 1997). Equally, the status or standing of the technical understanding of jurisdiction can be traced both through the institutional inheritance of Roman law and the concerns of authorised government. How these two aspects might be articulated has been the subject on a long polemic between legal and anti-legal understandings of law (Schutz, 2005). While modern legal theory has often inaugurated its jurisprudence with the assertion or questioning of the sovereignty of the modern state, questions of jurisdiction become more readily visible as a concern of jurisprudence when they are not treated as homologous to sovereignty. This at least has been one of the persistent themes of the contributions to this book.

In this part, *Jurisprudence of Jurisdiction* reprises two moments of the meeting of laws at the frontiers of east and west in America and in India. In 'Embracing Jurisdiction: John Ford's *The Man Who Shot Liberty Valance*', Bill Grantham takes up the themes of idiom, authority and jurisdiction and examines them in terms of the 'forms of life' and consciousness represented in a John Ford Western. *Liberty Valance*, points out Grantham, was concerned with the clash of jurisdictions between the 'old' and 'new' laws of the West. On the one hand, there was the law of frontier based on the jurisdiction of personal authority (and the small arms and the self-interest of the property barons) and on the other hand, there was the new territorial jurisdiction of the state based on the rule of law (and federal arms, fundamental principles and the settled state).

The jurisdiction of the old law was founded on personal authority, that of the new law on principle. *Liberty Valence* re-tells the passing of one law to another. In this, *Liberty Valence* is unusual in the way that it self-consciously enacts its frontier story as one of rival jurisdictions and takes its interior drama of conscience as being that of the 'crisis of living with and without jurisdiction'. Stoddard, who narrates the story and is credited with establishing the new law by killing the dishonourable Liberty Valance in a shoot-out, discovers that he is not the man who shot Liberty Valance. The true killer was Doniphon who, as the last (honourable) representative of the old law of personal jurisdiction, died in the process. In doing this, Doniphon ushered in the new jurisdiction based on the rule of law. The crisis, of course, is that Stoddard – who is the hero of the film, the possessor of both the prize girl and the political life – does not have the personal authority to inaugurate the law. This is, as the jurisprudence of Robert Cover displays, the crisis of all thought of law that falls to be enforced. A valance, after all, is a drape used to hang over, cover or mask an underlying structure. Valence, a word that can be heard in the same way, is a measure of strength, capacity or attraction.

Against the tenor of some of the more structural accounts of the jurisprudence of jurisdiction presented in this book, Grantham captures the way in which the idiom of jurisdiction continues to reproduce a 'form of life' as a question of character, action and judgement – phrased in terms of the practical, physical knowledge of the procedures, conduct and manners of law. For Grantham, John Ford's filmmaking – or at least his account of it – proceeds through an empiricism of historical fact. No doubt it was an empiricism much influenced by American prudence and the sense that the factual narratives of the American West were epic and existed in some sense outside of time. Ford's was a kind of empirical Platonism to be found in the work of Ralph Waldo Emerson and in different form in the common law (Cavell, 1995; Deleuze and Guattari, 1994). In *Liberty Valance*, suggests Grantham, Ford mourns the passing of the old law of the West, not because this law was better (clearly, for Ford, it was not) but because the new jurisdiction of territorial law can offer no completion or redemption without the authority of a personal jurisdiction which no longer has a place.

In contrast, in his chapter, 'Jurisdiction and the Colonisation of Sublime Enjoyment', Piyel Haldar traces the idiomatic use of the sublime in the elaboration of the imperial aspirations of the British Crown and its common law in India.

The sublime directs attention not to the material presence of human laws, but to that which is beyond the domain of the human. As a motive to thought and action, it can open up the world to infinite pleasure and to awe or terror; subject to sublimation and appropriation, it can serve as the idiom of control and the extension of a territorial jurisdiction; and, as the invisible order of the law beyond law, it connects archaic jurisdictions to contemporary ones in order to invoke a universal jurisdiction. Perhaps in order to emphasise the affective character of the sublime, Haldar's investigation of India's colonisation proceeds at the level of biography and investigates the work and life of William Jones, seventeenth-century judge, Orientalist and colonial administrator in India.

For Haldar, the attempt to colonise what the mind cannot grasp in the sublime provides the shape of authority and desire in much eighteenth-century common law and contemporary legal thought. As a philologist, William Jones was a translator of the Laws of Manu; as a judge in Calcutta, he put those translations to use in the courts as a digest of indigenous law; and as a jurist–philologist, he speculated on the possible common origins of the English common law and the Laws of Manu. Readers of the work of Edward Said will no longer be surprised to find that the Romantic's' impulse to investigate Hindu and Muslim laws and literature was also put to imperial purposes. However, Haldar also examines the way that Orientalist romanticism has given a specific shape to the jurisprudence of jurisdiction. Jones' investment in the sublime as philologist can be registered in terms of pleasure. As a judge, such pleasure was sublimated and put to use to create an Indian subject of law governed now through the jurisdiction of English laws of Manu. As jurist seeking to justify the universal jurisdiction of the English common law and government through native law, the sublime was used to postulate a common origin of ancient laws. Finally, and perhaps inevitably, Jones was tempted to identify himself with the position of sublime legislator, joining the figures of Manu, Solon and Tribonian as both a passive recipient of a sublime law and a powerful conduit or mediator between the law and its subjects. With this, of course, colonial law obtains full force – although, for Jones and the common law, the sublime still remains an ungraspable idiom.

Concluding comments

The return to questions of jurisdiction forms part of an emergent genre of scholarship within doctrinal, historical and critical jurisprudence. In the *Jurisprudence of Jurisdiction* questions of jurisdiction and the institution, judgement and address of law have been directed to those of belonging to law, of working within the idiom of law, and what – if anything – can continue to be said in the name of the law. These might be taken as threshold concerns of exercising a jurisdiction.

References

Benveniste, E (1973) *Indo-European Language and Society*, London: Faber and Faber
Cavell, S (1995) *Philosophical Passages: Wittgenstein, Emerson, Austin, Derrida*, Oxford: Blackwell

Cover, R (1995a) 'Folktales of justice: Tales of jurisdiction', in M Minow, M Ryan and A Sarat (eds), *Narrative, Violence, and the Law: The Essays of Robert Cover*, Ann Arbor, MI: Michigan University Press

Cover, R (1995b) 'Nomos and narrative', in M Minow, M Ryan and A Sarat (eds), *Narrative, Violence, and the Law: The Essays of Robert Cover*, Ann Arbor, MI: Michigan University Press

Cover, R (1995c) 'Violence and the word', in M Minow, M Ryan and A Sarat (eds), *Narrative, Violence, and the Law: The Essays of Robert Cover*, Ann Arbor, MI: Michigan University Press

Davies, M (1996) *Delimiting the Law*, London: Pluto Press

Deleuze, G and Guattari, F (1994) *What is Philosophy?* London: Verso

Derrida, J (1989) 'Psyche: Invention of the other', in L Waters and W Godzich (eds), *Reading de Man Reading*, Minnesota, MN: University of Minnesota Press

Foucault, M (1972) *The Archeology of Knowledge*, trans A Sheridan Smith, London: Tavistock

Gadamer, H-G (1979) *Truth and Method*, 2nd edn, London: Sheed and Ward

Goodrich, P (1996) *Law and the Courts of Love: Literature and Minor Jurisprudences*, London: Routledge

Goodrich, P and Hachamovitch, Y (1991) 'Time out of mind: An introduction to the semiotics of common law', in P Fitzpatrick (ed), *Dangerous Supplements: Resistance and Renewal in Jurisprudence*, London: Pluto Press

Helmholtz, RH (2004) *The Oxford History of the Laws of England, Vol 1: The Canon Law and Ecclesiastical Jurisdiction from 597 to 1640s*, Oxford: Oxford University Press

Holdsworth, W (1922–1972) *A History of English Law, Vol. I–XV*, London: Methuen

Hunter, I (2001) *Rival Enlightenments: Civil and Metaphysical Philosophy in Early Modern Germany*, New York, NY: Cambridge University Press

Hunter, I and Saunders, D (2003) 'Bringing the state to England: Andrew Tooke's translation of Samuel Pufendorf's *De officio hominis et civis*' 24 *History of Political Thought* 218

Kriegal, B (2001) *The State and the Rule of Law*, trans M LePain, Princeton, NJ: Princeton University Press

Legendre, P (1997) *Law and the Unconscious*, P Goodrich (ed), London: Macmillan

Macedo, S (ed) (2003) *Universal Jurisdiction: National Courts and the Prosecution of Serious Crimes Under International Law*, Philadelphia, PA: University of Pennsylvania Press

McVeigh, S, Rush, P and Young, A (2001) 'A judgment dwelling in the law', in A Sarat (ed), *Law, Violence and the Possibility of Justice*, Princeton, NJ: Princeton University Press

Murphy, T (1997) *The Oldest Social Science? Configurations of Law and Modernity*, Oxford: Clarendon

Nancy, J-L (2003) 'Lapsus judicii', in Simon Sparks (ed), *A Finite Thinking*, Stanford,CA: Stanford University Press

Roberts, S (2005) 'After government? On representing law without the state' 68 *Modern Law Review* 1

Rose, G (1984) *Dialectic of Nihilism: Post-structuralism and the Law*, Oxford: Blackwell

Rush, P (1997) 'Deathbound legal doctrine: Scenes of murder and its inheritance' 16 *Studies in Law, Politics and Society* 71

Schmitt, C (1996) 'The land's appropriation of a new world' (translation of Chapter II, 'Die Landnahme einer neuen Welt' in *Der Nomos der Erde im Völkerrecht der Jus Publicum Europeaeum*, 1950, 2nd edn, Berlin: Duncker & Humblot) 109 *Telos* 29

Schutz, A (2005) ' "Legal critique": Elements for a genealogy' 16 *Law and Critique* 71
Ullman, W (1975) *Law and Politics in the Middle Ages: An Introduction to the Sources of Medieval Political Ideas*, Ithaca,NY: Cornell University Press
Whincop, M and Keyes, M (2001) *Policy and Pragmatism in the Conflict of Laws*, Dartmouth, VT: Ashgate

Part II
Situations

2 The metaphysics of jurisdiction

Costas Douzinas

In 1993, Belgium gave itself the jurisdiction to indict and arrest anywhere in the world and to try anyone suspected of having committed war crimes and crimes against humanity whenever and wherever these crimes may have been committed. Under this universal jurisdiction, the Belgian authorities issued an arrest warrant, in 2000, against Congo's Foreign Minister, Abdulaye Ndobasi. The Congo took Belgium to the International Court of Justice in the Hague, claiming that the warrant violated the Minister's immunity under international customary law. In February 2002, the Congo won and the court ordered Belgium to cancel the warrant.[1] The court accepted that Foreign Ministers cannot be brought before the criminal courts of a foreign state while in office, irrespective of the seriousness of the allegations, as they are protected by the immunity of sovereignty. However, three Western judges added that the court should have ruled that crimes against humanity can engage universal jurisdiction, even if it was not applicable in the current case, and a fourth argued that Belgium had the power to issue the warrant. As the three put it, while there may be no general rule specifically authorising the right to exercise universal jurisdiction, the absence of a prohibitive rule and the growing international consensus on the need to punish crimes regarded as most heinous by the international community indicate that the warrant for the arrest of Mr Ndobasi did not violate international law.

The question of universal jurisdiction is one of the most contested problems in the new times we live in after the collapse of communism. It is associated with the decline of the principle of sovereignty upon which international law was established in the post-Westphalian period. Ours is a period of proliferating jurisdictions, each positioning itself against the horizon of the universal. But every claim to universal jurisdiction soon becomes particular in relation to a wider claim (that of the International Court of Justice), and that again will be dwarfed by the greater universality of the International Criminal Court which will again be contested by the American exception with its implicit claim to an even wider de facto universality. The process of universalisation has a tendency to be reproduced

1 *Arrest Warrant of 11 April 2000* (*Democratic Republic of Congo v Belgium*), International Court of Justice, Judgment of 14 February 2002. Case report at http://212.153.43.18/icjwww/ipresscom/ipress2002/ipresscom2002-04bis_cobe_20020214.htm

ad infinitum as each universal becomes a particular against a new jurisdiction that claims even greater catholicity. But universal jurisdiction proclaimed by various particulars leads inexorably to a clash of jurisdictions: its proper field is the conflict of laws. This conflict appears to be external – a contest between different institutions and normative systems, each with its own priorities, procedures and scope of intervention. This essay argues, however, that the conflict of jurisdictions and the dialectic of universal, particular and singular is not just a contingency of contemporary jurisdiction, but a presupposition of jurisdiction *tout court* intimately linked with the metaphysics of sovereignty. Let us turn to this metaphysics.

A space, terrain or collection of people becomes community when this space gathers itself in common. By gathering in common, the terrain becomes territory, the collection, collectivity or community, the space of relationships, society. A community comes forth as *polis*, empire or state by circumscribing itself in its interiority and demarcating its proper from an outside. A community's outside may be seen as open space (the New World to old Europe), as uncircumscribed relations (the barbarians beyond the borders) or as another foreign community (Sparta to Athens or France to England). In all instances, this coming together or becoming common appears by expressing itself in a sovereign way by giving itself the law. In this minimal sense, sovereignty is the name of the appearance of a community, the expression of a decision to be in common. Sovereignty launches itself when it sets the origin and the ends of community, when a community gives itself to itself formally in self-jurisdiction. Community as coming together must gather itself by asserting the power of sovereignty as the outward expression and inner arrangement of its very facticity. While this assertion often presupposes the existence of commonality in the form of a mythical past, it is the declaration itself that brings it into existence. We can call this logical presupposition and historical expression of community, of any community, *bare sovereignty*.

For a community to be in common in its sovereignty, relationships amongst its members must be circumscribed – in other words, regulated. The maxim *ubi societas ibi jus* expresses the recognition that a collection becomes people in community when this or that law declares itself as the common law, and transforms relations from open and uncircumscribed to closed, encircled and ordered. But a law can become the common law and define community if someone, an ultimate instance decision-maker or decision decides with finality and sets the physical and spiritual borders of the common. The setting of the common law as the expression and organisation of community may take place through a long process of recognising a certain natural order of things, the *dike* of the world, or through the enunciation of a new law and constitution through an act of taking hold of the space and the people. But in all instances, a community gathers itself as common or sovereign in jurisdiction in *juris dicere*, the speaking of law.

Let me start with the etymology of the term. Jurisdiction speaks the law: it is juris diction – the diction of law, law's speech and word. As a double genitive, jurisdiction, law's speech, has two aspects, which are inescapably intertwined. It refers both to the diction that speaks the law – law's inauguration through words – and law's speech – what the inaugurated law says. And if the Romans believe that the law speaks, for the Greeks, the word for jurisdiction is *dikaiodosia, diken didonai*, the giving of *dike*, of order and of the law. Jurisdiction is the gift of law (but who gives this gift?) and law's gift (but what does the law donate?). Who speaks and gives the law (*dicere juris*), and what does the law give (*juris dictio*)? If we were to accept Ulpian's contested opinion in the Digest that the word for law *jus* derives from *justitia*, that is, justice, jurisdiction would be the diction of justice, that is, justice's talk.

The law speaks and the law gives; the law gives its talk and this law-talk is associated with justice. The common metaphysical structure that regulates jurisdiction follows a schema according to which the most particular, the singular – a speech or utterance – offers the most general, law. The universal as ratio, concept or law conjoins the most fleeting, the saying of a word or the happening of an event. But which speech establishes its power to legislate in its act of speaking? Which utterance brings about this formidable result while uttering mere words? How does jurisdiction arise in its original form? These ultimate questions of jurisprudence point to the proper boundary between law and politics, the political grounding of law and the legal foundation of the polity – in other words, to the heart of a political philosophy and of philosophical politics.

According to the French philosopher Jean-Luc Nancy, what is at stake in the articulation of the singular and the universal is the linking of the juridical and the political that brings law to existence, allows law's emergence as law (Nancy, 2003: 152–71). We are faced with the question of the nature of the decision or speech that makes law effective. This decision is an act of law. But, unlike law-making acts, which give effect to the generality of law, this act is singular and therefore belongs to the field of law's application. And unlike particular acts of law application, this is an act in which the law recognises itself as such, acts out its original right as law reflexively and, in doing so, institutes itself. The speech that gives law is a legislation or judgement. The nature of law-giving is most apparent in constitution-making, the inaugural act of the power to legislate. In all legislation, but particularly in constitution-making, the political as decision, act or judgement attaches itself to law as the precondition of law's coming into being. But for the law to come into existence, it must declare itself to be the law of a specific community and attach to a particular polity. The juridical too links itself to the political, to the *polis* as its constituting provision. We have a double linking of a judgement that singularly institutes the law, of a unique act that pronounces legitimacy in general: it is a particular judgement about the generality of law and a general judgement about the particularity of a polity and its sovereignty. Jurisdiction contains the motif of a declaration that gives now and prospectively reproduces the power of law as always linked with a polity and a politics.

In jurisdiction, legal speech both constitutes and states the law; it introduces the constitution (an act of utter singularity, indeed the very definition of the unique and unrepeatable event) and presents its principles and norms (a return to the universality of law and the uniformity of its application). Two axes are implicated here and are rolled into one: the universal and the particular as well as the performative and the constative. Their cohabitation helps confuse the four poles of the two dyads. To glimpse the structure of jurisdiction, we need to separate their respective positions.

Let me recall here a crucial semiotic distinction between two different speaking positions – that of the subject of enunciation and that of the subject of the statement. In literature, the subject of enunciation is the author of a novel, while the novel's fictional narrator is the subject of the statement, the one who tells the story. The lack of distinction between the two positions, the confusion of the distinct subjects of the diction, permeates jurisdiction and is at its most apparent in constitution-making. The French Declaration of the Rights of Man and Citizen, starts by claiming to derive from God and to speak on behalf of all humanity and its eternal and inalienable rights. It states: 'All men are born free and equal' but then proceeds to give the newly inaugurated rights to the only people it can legislate for – French citizens. The recently enacted South African Constitution begins: 'We the people of South Africa recognise the injustices of our past, honour those who suffered and adopt this constitution'. Now the subject of enunciation is the constitutional assembly – it is the body which creates the new institutions, structures and rights – but its statement is attributed to a totally different subject: God, humanity or the people. In both instances, the subject of enunciation – the constitutional legislator or the new sovereign – is utterly unique. It is the agent and result of revolution, the historical expression of triumphant political will – in other words, a singularity. The revolution and its agent form the essence, one could say, of eventness, of the utter unpredictability of a history-making event. And yet this representative of the event speaks the law, both creative and unique, as all creativity has to be, by referring it back to another speaker, a putative higher authority – God or the People – of which it presents itself as a particular instance. The particular and the universal are rolled together, as are the different subjects of enunciation and statement. One obvious explanation is that referral backwards or upwards to the universal acts as an ideological trope aiming to justify or legitimise the utter uniqueness of the action and diction. And yet, like many obvious explanations, I believe that it is not sufficient.

The confusion, the rolling together through the rhetorical figure of *metalepsis* (the part stands in for the whole), is implicit in the nature of all jurisdiction and not only in constitution-making after revolutionary upheavals. Enunciation is the general precondition for the existence of all discourse. Since Rome at least, the diction of *jus*, its public utterance, is the necessary prerequisite and constraint of all law. This constraint is not limited to law; enunciation is the general precondition of all discourse since, without its communication to at least one other person, discourse would remain a private matter. Discourse, in general, requires a speaking subject. Jurisdiction, following this constraint, demands:

> the existential positing of a *judex*, of an unique individual who says the right, and who is unique not because he takes this power to himself... nor because people have decided to give it to him [but because] only a single individual can speak.
>
> (Nancy, 1993: 132)

If the law must speak in order to exist, the law needs a mouth and voice. We, the law's addressees, must hear law's word and accept law's gift. But if the law needs a mouth, the mouth attaches to a face and a body. The law to speak must be one; only a unique individual can speak law. And it is because the law must have a mouth and a body that the great legislators – Moses, Solo, Lycurgus, Plato, Zarathustra – enter the stage. One could generalise: this is the entrance door for the great representatives of sovereignty, God, King, the People. Juris-diction is individual because it is indivisible. The legislator or *judex*, the sovereign himself, is a function of law's speech, of the speaking requirement of law.

The most extreme philosophical defence of the principle of monarchic sovereignty is advanced by Hegel (1967) in his *Philosophy of Right*. Hegel argues that the content and aim of the state is the union of all. The ethical state realises the principle of union as such. For Hegel, politics transcends collective life and other social relations established for the benefit of the partners; similarly, the citizen transcends the private individual of civil society. Sovereignty exists in the form of a subjectivity without foundation, a personality which enjoys complete self-determination. It is this transcendence, both metaphysical and empirical, that is incarnated in the monarch. He is 'the summit and base of everything' in the state (1967: 278), the truth of its truth, the truth of 'union as such' (1967: 279). The oneness and uniqueness of the monarch, the monistic *arche*, both presents the truth of the union of all in the state and embodies its empirical instantiation. The monarch is the superior individual of the state. He is the whole of the state, someone whose personal unity accomplishes the union of the state. The monarch is the state itself as individuality, an individuality which encloses both the utterly unique biological person of the ruler and the whole of the relations of the state. The monarch as a real person is the truth of the union, its very existence. The unity of the state is personal and the sovereign person is unitary. Indeed, the state has legal personality and exists only if it is identified with a single person: 'The personality of the State is real only if it is a single person' (1967: 278). The monarch incarnates the principle of sovereignty and affirms the essence of union by converting it into the unity of a real person.

But what creates the need for such a unique and universal person? What gives the monarch his two bodies and turns him into the secular simulacrum of Christ? It is the demand that the right be posited. '*Right is by its essence an actual positing* ... The actuality of right is its *sensible declaration* to the intelligence, and the exercise of its legitimate power' (Nancy, 1993: 119, italics in original). Hegel derives the need and nature of the singular, individual personification of sovereignty precisely from the requirement that law speaks. The position of law is jurisdiction. The right of the people, which is nothing other than the expression of the Spirit in the ethical state, must take empirical existence, speak through its positing in jurisdiction: 'The juris-*diction* of the monarch, on this account, is only the naming of right, of union as right' (Hegel, 1967: 131, italics in original). Right is the presupposition of the union of the people but to become real it must be pronounced. The monarch, the *monos archon* or unique sole ruler, comes into existence in order to voice this right. The long and tortuous metaphysical argument ends up with the same conclusion. The monarch is a function of jurisdiction, the historical mouthpiece of the Spirit as the announcer of the right of people. The sovereign person comes to existence because the Spirit as right must be actualised in the world. The 'signature, the name, and the mouth of the monarch who says "I will" constitute and are the decision that, even if it adds nothing to the content of the people's right, transforms the saying of the law and of the councils into the doing of subjectivity' (Hegel, 1967: 131).

Hegel believes in the union between the right(s) of people and the type of law a polity introduces through its sovereign (Douzinas, 2002). 'Concrete right is the absolute necessity of spirit' (Hegel, 1967: 28). Today we have to accept that rights are the effect and not the cause of law. If this is so, the figuration of king and right or of legislator and people takes a different inflection. It is the particular which speaks, the Constitutional Assembly, the legislator or the judge but their utterance is figured in the name of a silent partner for whom they speak – God, King, the People or law. The saying of law, juris-diction, is what brings together the universal and the particular and articulates their relation. Here we reach the original and basic structure of what one could call the theologico-political form of sovereignty. All legislators repeat the gesture of Moses in Sinai. Moses speaks and gives the law as a mouthpiece or a ventriloquist's dummy; in reality, it is God who speaks and dictates his words to Moses. According to theologico-political philosophy, the sovereign is he who declares the exception and metes out the excess and incalculability (Schmitt, 1985). The function of jurisdiction is to bring the sovereign to life and give him voice and then, by confusing the person who speaks and the subject who states, to conceal sovereignty by confounding its creative, performative aspect with the declaration of the law and by excepting or excluding the sovereign's power of exemption.[2] Even more importantly, the configuration of individual and universal creates a body politic which mirrors the individuality of the *juris-dictator* (he who speaks the law), a unified body which, while plural and therefore silent, wills the law singularly and speaks through its foil and representative, the sovereign, legislator or judge.

We can now understand a second crucial element of jurisdiction. As originary power or foil for sovereignty, it must both establish (perform) and confirm (state) the law. Both producer and witness, jurisdiction incorporates the contingent 'I' of the political agent (monarch, revolutionary or reformer) into the community of a deeply rooted or under construction 'We'. Nietzsche said that morality is the absolutisation and eternalisation of temporary relations of power. Could we not argue, similarly, that the diction of law and its constraint that it be spoken by an individual presents the social as individual – in other words undivided – as the mirror image of law's speaker? The distance between he who performs (the legislator) and he who states (the people or law) is where the One and All

2 For the difficulties of lawyers and political philosophers with the state of exception, see Agamben (2003).

are rolled together. But this confounding can also be unravelled. The particular claim to state a universal law is always an uncertain claim; uncertainty is its precondition. If the speaker – literally the *dictator* – was certain, jurisdiction would be asserted without anything else, without justifications and confusions, without confused reasons, like the robber who demands your money to spare your life. The need to justify, to offer reasons in order to *dicere juris*, shows insecurity – the fear that the claim can fail. It is because the claim of law can fail, because the gap between particular and universal or between performance and statement can be seen for what it is – as two separate moments that are not necessarily or automatically connected – that both violence and critique launch themselves in law.

Violence is the closing down or forgetting of the gap, critique the care for the distance, the cultivation of its memory and possibility. The closing down is violence *stricto sensu*, when the 'I' is forced to become part of the 'We', of a community or a communion where we find our essence through the identification with the spirit, the tradition or the history of the whole. All such violent identification can be called mythological. It asserts a common being in which the law speaks to its subjects as One and All or as All in One. In our liberal and democratic societies, forgetting the gap is the more common form: judicial interpretation and judgement are organised in a way that conceals the original performance of the law in favour of its reasoned and coherent statement. And yet this forgetting is at its most fragile when the jurisdiction of a court or judge is challenged. Both the Nuremberg and the Yugoslav war crimes tribunals resorted to the sheer fact of their establishment by the victorious or the powerful to get around the challenge to their jurisdiction. When jurisdiction is itself called into question, the original difference between creating and stating the law returns like the repressed. But the rare and exceptional challenges to jurisdiction, which make it take shelter in the political and violent act of its inauguration, should not fool us. Every trial explicitly or implicitly addresses the power of the court to judge. Jurisdictional acquiescence or challenge is the horizon against which all trials are conducted. It is in this sense that we should understand Benjamin's statement that there is something rotten in law (Benjamin, 1978). What is rotten in every legal act and in every judgement is the violence at law's inception, the original performative *dictio*, which established the law and predominantly takes the form in the modern nation-state of exclusion of other people, nations and races (Douzinas, 2000). This originary force is entombed in every legal act as a residue or excess, as the force which created law by cutting off an outside and mirroring itself as the proper or inside, as the normative power or will of community to live together, speaking its own law. This force shadows and guarantees the juridical most obviously when jurisdiction is contested. If jurisdiction tries to conceal its forceful creation of law and fake figuring of oneness, the repressed always returns and reveals the contingency of origins and the fragility of communal construction.

The transition from the contingency of the singular to the necessity of the universal is a detour always open to the possibility of mismatch. Jurisdiction as the mirroring of One and All, as the attempt to hypostasise a united people, law or community, or to limit or eliminate the effects of disunity, is subject to the disarticulation of not being One or the deconstruction of the mirroring effect. If law is not one, then critique is precisely the thinking of the not-One. As such, it will occasionally speak in favour of legal reformism and occasionally for a more permanent and structural kind of change, or even revolution. If the united speaker or subject of law is fake, an impostor, critique's job is to tend the distance between speaker and subjects, and to discern law's different aspects – conservative, destructive and creative.

But where does this ability to challenge law's force lie? How does the repressed return if such care has been taken to protect its metaphysical structure? We must move from the law's mouth to the subject's ear. If the law acts through speaking, law's addressees take the law through hearing. Law's word must pass through the ear; an acoustics regulates our relationship with the law. In one of the most influential essays of political structuralism, the French philosopher Louis Althusser argued that the subject comes to existence through the action of interpellation through a scene of hearing and responding to a call (Althusser, 1984). According to Althusser's theory of acoustic subjection, as someone walks in the street he is hailed from behind: 'Hey you'. He turns and sees that he is called by a policeman. He accepts the terms by which he is called; he accepts that the policeman, the law, has the power to call him to account and, in doing so, to give him identity and responds 'Here I am, officer'. In hearing law's word and accepting it as his true cause and vocation, the subject is called to existence both as free (he could have fled the scene, evaded the policeman or asserted his right not to respond to police inquiries) and as subjected. For Althusser, this acoustic scene is presented as an allegory for the way we come to identity through an ideological misrecognition: the institutions of ideology attribute to us a self-identical but false identity ('You the law's subject') and we accept it. Althusser, while mainly interested in religious and academic institutions, allegorises the social and ideological call that brings us to identity as legal as the demand to hear law's word and to align ourselves with it.

Hearing the word of law, juris-diction, brings us to identity – albeit a false one – in the same way that hearing the word of the sovereign performative gives social identity and political unity. But law's word is only one in a long list of jurisdictions that name and bring into existence. Althusser reminds us of the divine voice, logos or word which names Moses, Peter or light (let there be light) and thus brings them to life. God is the cause of Peter through a divine performative, by virtue of the continuing presence in the name of the one who names. Judith Butler (1997) complicates the scene: in hearing and turning around to face the law, the performative relies on a certain anticipatory attachment on the part of the addressee, a readiness to be compelled. One is already in relation to the voice before one responds, through an original acceptance of guilt, a desire to be reprimanded in order to gain purchase on identity, an original guilt upon which God, conscience and the law feed. Subjectivity is achieved through the guilty embrace of the word of law; guilt guarantees law's intervention and, through it, the subject's false and provisional totalisation that is identity.

In all these instances, an ear is opened and one passively hears law's word. This acoustic economy is a main characteristic of modernity's *nomophilia*. Before we hear it, the law has spoken. Our ears follow the law's mouth before we can know its contents; we obey the law before we know its demands; we are put under law's jurisdiction before we know what the law is or says. Consider two such cases. First, there is Kant's moral law. Every moral command involves an answer to the question of what I ought to do or to become in a particular situation. But before any formulation of an actual command, the fact that a moral command exists indicates that the law as a fact of reason has taken hold of me. To inquire about what I ought to do in a moral dilemma implies that I already feel that I ought to do something – that a feeling of being bound, of having been put under an obligation, comes before any particular obligation and command. Kant's law is the categorical imperative under which we must follow in each instance a maxim that can act as a principle of universal legislation. In following the law, we become autonomous, rational and free – rational by subjecting the multitude of chaotic representations and feelings to the coherence of concepts and categories; free, by obeying the moral law but acting as if we were the legislators of its commands. The confusion which characterised jurisdiction, the confounding of singular (passions, desires, needs), the particular (the sovereign legislator) and the universal (reason, the law) is reproduced fully. The modern subject is created in a double movement in which we hear and are subjected to the law but at the same time we imagine give it to ourselves as free moral persons. This is the meaning of autonomy, which we can transcribe as oto-nomy, the law of the ear, which brings *autos* (self) into being.

Freud, too, reminds us that we are subjected to the law and we obey it before any knowledge of its content. Our subjectivity, and thus our ideal ego, comes into being through our pre-Oedipal separation from the maternal object and our introduction to the symbolic order of language and paternal law. This originary separation opens and determines our destinies, but as it comes before the ego and before the scene of representation, it cannot be represented and remains repressed and forgotten. Entry to the law not only checks the absolute power of the 'other' but also introduces the subject to the realm of desire. Our *eros* obliges us before any particular obligation and subjects us to the law before we can know its demands. But conversely, our love confronts us as a necessity – as a fate pleasurable and painful, structured by the law. And, in a different context, Freud comments (in Derrida, 1985) that the ear is uncannily the only organ that the infant cannot close and therefore they are continuously exposed to the voice without defence. Butler's guilt, the voice of conscience that prompts our turning to the word of law and identity, is grounded on an earlier and inner law, a silent voice and an undefended but constitutive hearing.

Law's word comes before the ear has been opened or can be closed, before the scene of presence or representation. The word of law appears as the original gift; law's voice (juris-diction) turns us into subjects. The subject is always a hearing being, someone whose ears place them in a position of a hearing hierarchy, the creation of an oto-subjection or oto-subordination. Indeed, we can venture a general law: coming to subjectivity involves a relationship of obedience between a *sublimus* who speaks and *subditi* who turn towards them to hear the law. It is the great achievement of modernity to turn the mechanism of subjection from Lord and King to an inner voice, that of a transcendent, autonomous or unconscious authority which always already compels us to obey. The foundation of authority is not located outside the individual any longer but within them, in our very being as creature of the verb and extensions of the ear.

Ear's passivity is a well-known theme. For Nietzsche, who was proud of his small and nimble ears and even thought that they held a certain seductive attraction to women, the ear is the most dangerous of organs:

> For there are human beings who lack everything, except one thing of which they have too much ... 'An ear! An ear as big as a man!' I looked still more closely – and indeed underneath the ear something was moving, something pitifully small and wretched and slender. And, no doubt of it, the tremendous ear was attached to a small, thin stalk – but this stalk was a human being! ... The people however told me that this great ear was not only a human being, but a great one, a genius. But I never believed the people when they spoke of great men ... and I maintained by belief that it was an inverse cripple.
>
> (Nietzsche, 1976: 250)

But the greatest danger of the long ear is that it accepts the words of the state, believes the lies it hears and passes them for the word of the law:

> The state? What is that? Well then open your ears to me. For now I shall speak to you about the death of peoples. State is the name of the coldest of all cold monsters. Coldly it tells lies too; and this lie crawls out of its mouth. 'I the state am the people.' That is a lie ... And it is only the long eared asses and short-sighted who sink to their knees.
>
> (Nietzsche, 1976: 160–61)

Derrida comments on this text linking the ear to the educational system and the loss of autonomy. It is a question of turning to the law and accepting its call, opening the ear to take our marching orders:

> The hypocritical hound whispers in your ear through his educational systems, which are actually acoustic or acroamatic devices. Your ears grow larger and you turn into long-eared asses when instead of listening with small, finely tuned ears and obeying the best master and the best of leaders, you think you are free and autonomous with respect to State. You open widely the portals of your ears to admit the State ... having become all ears for this phonograph dog [called his master's voice] you transform

> yourself into a high-quality receiver, and the ear ... begins to occupy in your body the disproportionate place of the 'inverted cripple'.
>
> (Derrida, 1985: 34–35)

And again:

> How is the student connected with the university? ... By the ear as a listener. The student listens ... When he speaks, sees or takes up some art he is autonomous i.e. not dependent upon the educational institution. Very often the student writes as he listens and at these moments he hangs from the umbilical cord of the university. Eventually the ear grows huge as it nourishes itself with the brain's food and the brain atrophies.
>
> (Derrida, 1985: 35)

Can we defend ourselves against this most innocent and dangerous of organs? We must open our ears, prick up our ears, develop an active hearing, when listening to the law. What does it mean to have small, keen ears? As Derrida intimates, there is an imperceptible difference and a deferral, a time lag between the speaking and the hearing, even if I am only hearing the inner voice. In telling the story, I hear myself speak but in doing so, I hear myself through the ear of the other. It is the ear of the other through which I hear myself and constitute my own *autos* self. Again in hearing, recognition becomes effective not when the word is uttered but later when the ears have managed to receive the message. While the eye is given to permanence and to a fullness of presence, the phone, the voice and hearing belong to temporality, to a diachrony of moments and therefore the possibility of hearing otherwise. Whether hearing can transform whatever befalls it, the word of law and of the various jurisdictions is the crucial question of our times. And it is here that the clash of jurisdiction, of particular and universal, might give us some clue. If, according to the Greeks, law's diction is a gift, the gift of *dike* as order, and if the modern gift of the law is to call us to subjectivity and political identity (albeit one of freedom through subjection), our response could be to try to hear through the ear of the other and confront the community of the sovereign of the One and All with the plurality of many ears. In this sense, critique attaches itself today to the clash of sovereignties and the conflict of laws, to the breakup of unitary territories and laws, and against those who argue for universal jurisdiction and for the unitary logos (reason and speech) of law.

References

Agamben, Giorgio (2003) *Ėtat d'Exception*, Paris: Seuil

Althusser, Louis (1984) 'Ideology and ideological state apparatuses', in *Essays on Ideology*, trans G Locke and Brewter, London: Verso

Benjamin, Walter (1978) 'The critique of violence', in *Reflections*, trans E Jephcott, New York, NY: Schocken

Butler, Judith (1997) *The Psychic Life of Power*, Stanford, CA: Stanford University Press

Derrida, Jacques (1985) *The Ear of the Other*, trans Peggy Kamuf, New York, NY: Schocken

Douzinas, Costas (2000) *The End of Human Rights*, Oxford: Hart

Douzinas, Costas (2002) 'Rights, identity, recognition: What can Hegel teach us about human rights' 29 *Journal of Law and Society* 379

Hegel, Georg (1967) *The Philosophy of Right*, trans TM Knox, Oxford: Oxford University Press

Nancy, Jean-Luc (1993) 'The jurisdiction of the Hegelian monarch', in *The Birth to Presence*, trans Mary Ann and Peter Caws, Stanford: Stanford University Press

Nancy, Jean-Luc (2003) '*Lapsus Judicii*', in Simon Sparks (ed), *A Finite Thinking*, Stanford, CA: Stanford University Press

Nietzsche, Frederich (1976) *Thus Spoke Zarathustra*, in Walter Kaufmann (ed and trans), *The Portable Nietzsche*, Hardmondsworth: Penguin

Schmitt, Carl (1985) *Political Theology: Four Chapters on the Concept of Sovereignty*, trans George Schwab, Cambridge, MA: MIT Press

3 Of the founding of law's jurisdiction and the politics of sexual difference

The case of Roman law

*Maria Drakopoulou**

On defining jurisdiction

> ... For the progress of law consists in the destruction of every natural tie, in continual separation and isolation.
>
> (Jhering, 1907: 31)

The concept of jurisdiction designates the authority to speak the law – an authority presupposing a setting apart of the legal from the non-legal.[1] Without such acts of separation, law's existence can be neither adequately conceived nor materially manifested, since their very performance delineates its borders and time of reign.[2] These acts annunciate and bear the 'is' of law rather than being one of its products or functions. Yet, though at once both source of law's being and tangible evidence of its presence, the spatial and temporal boundaries defined by jurisdiction do not simply demarcate the legal empire. Any reference to law embodies designation of who and what occupies its 'space', where its limits lie and what exists beyond them, whilst evocations concerning time render an understanding of what can and cannot move or change within law, of what remains static, perennial or prohibited in its temporal domain. So jurisdictional acts of separation cohere specific structures of human existence – structures which, as well as providing organisational principles for social action, also configure the way in which the social world is understood.[3]

* I am deeply grateful to Shaun McVeigh for his support and endless patience, without which this paper would not be here.

1 The word 'jurisdiction' derives from the Latin verb *dicere*, to indicate, to speak, to tell, and *ius*, meaning law, right. *Iurisdictio* was defined as the office of saying right (*Digest*, 1973: II.i.1).

2 The significance of the principle of isolation for the establishment of law is acknowledged as one of the most important features of Roman law and hence of the Western legal tradition (Schulz, 1967: 19–39).

3 The temporal organisation of the social is expressed in the making of history and its importance in understanding and explaining of the social world. However, the significance of space is a relative newcomer. The broad position that the social and the spatial are inseparable and that the spatial form of the social has explanatory power – that 'geography matters' – is now increasingly accepted. See, for instance, Gregory and Urry (1985); Lefebre (1991); Soja (1990).

Jurisdiction here transcends the relationship between people and geographical place. It is more than territorial sovereignty, an attribute of political authority expressing the link between the *persona* (prince, emperor, king or legislator) with the power to lay down the law and the *res* (territory) within which this *persona* exercises the prerogative of *ius dicere*, the solemn declaration of law.[4] As the power to speak the law, jurisdiction is apprehended as the unfolding of law in pivotal acts of separation, isolation and delineation – a shift of emphasis from jurisdiction as a structural element of governance to jurisdiction as the birthplace of spatial and temporal forms in which humanity is substantiated. This shift deflects the focus of legal analysis away from the reach and nature of law's normative authority which, in its questioning of who has authority over whom, and what specific rules and commands this authority imposes, is firmly anchored in law's interiority. Taking its place is a morphological analysis whose gaze is directed at the very acts of separation themselves and the consequences of their performance. These consequences are not, however, measured at the level of the individual before the law or evaluated in terms of the implications they have for the construction of legal subjectivities or national and political identities. Instead, they are explored at the intersection between social life and its apprehension in law's imaging and imagining mind, where questions are raised about the forms of social being the founding of law's jurisdiction animates and the reading of the world it engenders.[5]

By privileging issues of separation and engendering, morphological inquiry into the nature of jurisdiction is fundamentally concerned with understanding difference and what it precipitates.[6] Exploration of difference can take many guises. It may spring from juxtaposition, the setting of the objects of inquiry against one another in oppositional, contrasting or disjunctive terms, or it can be based on mutuality, dependency or complementarity, where these objects presuppose, underpin or are implicated by one another. However it is articulated, difference is premised upon a duality wherein constitutive parts are considered in relation to each other, and where it can be either simply affirmed or engaged with through analysis of the objects of inquiry themselves. With foundational moments of law's jurisdiction, difference can be analysed as an outcome of a linear before-and-after comparison or in terms of co-existing 'geographical' distributions and forms of social relations. For the purpose of this paper, however, these dualities will be interrogated in terms of their fundamental reliance on a third parameter – that of sexual difference, which provides the site

4 The territorial conception of jurisdiction as developed in the Public Law of the Roman Empire and qualified by Christian doctrine was transmitted into the Middle Ages. For a discussion of this process see Ullman (1966, 1975: 33–36) and Perrin (1967). This conception of sovereignty still prevails in modern jurisprudence. See, for example, Picciotto (1984: 87–89) and, for a more comprehensive account, see Ford (1999).

5 This representation of law as *anima* is evident in the conception of the ruler as *lex animata*. For a general discussion, see Ullmann (1966: 35–40). For a discussion of this idea in the Roman Republic, see Born (1933).

6 For the etymological relatedness of the concepts of separation and engendering, see Lacan (1994: 213–14). I owe this reference to Julia Chrisostali.

of comparison. In adopting this approach, ways in which sexual difference is inscribed into the apparently innocent, neutral rationality of law's spatial and temporal order will be explored, both in relation to those forms instituted and those left 'outside' or 'behind'.[7]

In estimating law's time and space in terms of sexual difference, deductions based on factual observation of social reality or legal text do not suffice. Evidence is also sought in cultural captivations of the relationship between the legal and social encountered in legends concerning the generation of law and its jurisdiction. These stories have not been purposively thought up to sustain, explain or justify a true state of things. They do not act as mirrors to, or allegorical representations of, a once-existing truth; nor are they derivative or subordinate to an underlying reality. Although they are neither products of studious effort nor idle inventions of the storyteller's mind, they do not lack persuasive authority and their narrative enjoys a peculiar transparency and certainty that neither philosophy nor history can boast. There is never any doubt as to the who, what, when, how and why of their subject matter, for each story speaks and conveys reliable images, unambiguous pictorial representations, unique ways of seeing. They are narratives apparently free of contradictions, gaps or discrepancies, and so within them marks of sexual difference can readily be rendered visible and open to intellectual inquiry.

On Roman law and its jurisdiction

In Western legal culture, where foundational moments of law and its jurisdiction are far from scarce, the commentator is spoilt for choice. In exercising my right to choose the object of inquiry, I posit the foundational moment of the jurisdiction of the law of the Roman republic (451–427 BC) and stories that accompany it. In so doing, I raise questions about Roman law's spatial and temporal distributions, and the modes of social being they engender, both within and outside law's realm.

Lucretia or the story of separation

> The new liberty enjoyed by the Roman people, their achievements in peace and war, annual magistracies, and laws superior in authority to men will *henceforth* be my theme.
>
> (Livy, 1948: II.i)

Accounting for foundational moments almost invariably entails a search for delitescent beginnings wherein questions of 'whence' are followed by those of 'why' because for many, including Gaius himself, addressing these questions is an indispensable part of any fruitful attempt at explaining and understanding law (*Digest*, 1973: I.ii.1). The origin of Roman law is consistently accepted as the Twelve Tables, a legal code said to have been inscribed in bronze and placed

7 For a discussion of the association of space, time and gender, see Massey (1992: 71–76). Also, for the relationship of space and difference, see Sibley (1997: 3–31) and for the relationship of space, time and power, see Foucault (1980: 68–69, 1986, 1986a).

before the Rostra, the orators' platform in Rome's Forum, in 451 BC. Credited as the source of all public and private law, regarded as a comprehensive compendium of philosophical maxims and afforded the utmost respect by the Roman people, it was the subject of numerous encomiums delivered by jurists and historians alike, with every student of law obliged to thoroughly memorise its contents (Cicero, 1963: I.xliv; Livy, 1948: III.xxxiv.6). Its prelude is recounted in the second of the 142 books that comprise Livy's *History of Rome*, a monumental work, which sought to record for posterity Rome's inception, growth, triumphs and tribulations (Livy, 1948: I.9–10).[8] The opening lines mark a distinct break in the story told so far and that narrated thereafter. They boast of new beginnings, of a new order – the Roman Republic – signalling the key role law plays in Rome's rise to greatness, and are followed by an account honouring the most precious of all Roman possessions, the liberty of the Roman people and the political and legal institutions that guaranteed it. With law providing both foundation and safeguard of this liberty, law and liberty become almost indistinguishable in the Roman mind, and much of what subsequently unfolds is therefore interpretable as a narrative on law and its jurisdiction (Adock,1959: 13; Cicero, 1966: liii.146; *Digest*, 1973: I.v.4; Livy, 1948: II.i.7–11, II.viii.1–8, II.xviii.4–11; Radin, 1923; Schulz, 1967: 140–47; Wirszubski, 1950:1–30).

The meaning and limits of Roman liberty are articulated in the first jurisdictional acts of the new legal order. A twin consular magistracy is set up to replace the king and its bearers allowed to wield an authority embracing the military, the executive power and the right to create and enforce the law (Kunkel, 1966: 15). Yet, despite exercising this considerable authority, the consuls are not all-powerful.[9] They are subject to election by the people, in front of whom the fasces, bundles of rods symbolising the magistrate's authority to punish, are now lowered in acknowledgement that the people's power is ultimately the superior (Cicero, 1961a II.xxxi.53; Livy, 1948: II.vii.7–8).[10] This shift in the balance of power is furthered by the institution of the right of *provocatio*, whereby within the city boundaries citizens threatened with corporal or capital punishment can appeal to the people, and by the stipulation that a proportion of senators are to be appointed from outside the patrician class (Livy, 1948: II.i.9, viii).[11]

8 Livy's text has been the standard source for later writers, though of the 142 books only 32 survive intact, with only short summaries remaining of the others.

9 For a comparison of the position of consul and king, see Schiller (1978: 173–74). For a discussion of the consul's imperium as real *potestas regia* in Latin sources, see Henderson (1975).

10 The *lictors*, first appointed by Romulus, carried the fasces, bundles of rods with projecting axe-blades, which served as instruments as well as symbols of physical coercion. They are said to have terrified people, especially subjects of Roman domination abroad. Within the city, the axe-blades were removed (Cicero, 1961a: II.xxxi.55). For a discussion, see Kunkel (1966: 16) and Nippel (1995: 12–16).

11 The right to *provocatio* arose in the struggles between the plebs and the patricians. When these subsequently ended, it was formally recognised by a Lex Valeria. Roman tradition knows of three *Leges Valeriae de provocatione* (509, 445 and 300 BC) but only the last may be historically accurate. For a discussion, see Develin (1978); Kunkel (1966: 15); Nippel (1995: 5–7); Raaflaub (1986: 201–02).

Notwithstanding rank, all now swear the same oath that never again will they suffer a king in Rome.

In so speaking the liberty of the Roman people, the new law differs markedly from that of the past. The first act of Romulus was said to have been to assemble the people and give them laws, and all six subsequent kings reportedly did likewise (*Digest*, 1973: I.ii.2; Livy, 1948: I.viii.1–3). These earlier laws most likely commanded no less authority or respect, but in being the personal creations of Roman kings were enacted to suit particular requirements and were subject to regal vagaries. Thus Romulus, in seeking to maintain, enhance and control military and political power, appointed his own senate of councillors and legislated the composition, rights and obligations of noble and client classes (Dionysius, 1960: II.xxiii–xxx; Plutarch, 1959: XIII), whilst King Numa, favouring peacetime social cohesion and unity, used law to impose agricultural reform, redistribute land and protect the arts and trades (Dionysius, 1960: II.llxiv–lxxvi; Plutarch, 1959: VIII.1–4, XVI–XVIII).[12] Clearly, in stemming from the temper and character of their maker, said to bear his eyes and ears, a king's choice and exercise of law would likely reflect his feelings, passions and indulgences, and could equally well serve to return favours, seek revenge or dispense justice according to preference, mood or wisdom (Livy, 1948: II.iii.1–5). The new law, born of neither individual might, wisdom, will nor whim, contrasts sharply with the highly personal nature of kingly law. By advocating liberty and justice for all, not just 'the great', it can grant no favours to particular transgressors, whosoever they might be, for no personal feelings of sympathy, tenderness or hostility, no relationship to loved one, friend or foe, should influence or mediate its application.[13] This is law worded in the people's common will, reflecting its collective heart and mind, judgement and conviction, not the person of a king creator (Cicero, 1966: liii.146–47; Livy, 1948: II.iii.3–6). Now, as magistrates govern the people, the laws govern the magistrates and it could be said that, whilst the magistrate speaks the law, the law is a silent magistrate for all (Cicero, 1961b: III.i.3, 1975: II.xii.42). Formulated with the people's consent, law becomes 'true' law, grounded upon agreement and reason mediated by custom and the collective wisdom of common ancestors, and delivering its judgements as prudence, moral imperative and equity required (Gellius, 1927: VI.i; Cicero, 1961b: I.xxiii.60, 1975: I.xli.148; *Digest*, 1973: I.iii.20–40; Dumézil, 1996: 122).

This legal transformation radically altered an absolute space that had remained undifferentiated. Although made up of a variety of places – temples, palaces,

12 Debate has raged over the authenticity of the laws of the kings. The two main views are that the information encountered in the historical sources is either an invention of Roman historians or the law of a later period transported back in time. For a discussion, see Momigliano (1969) and Watson (1972).

13 The 'emotionless' character of this new law is epitomised in Brutus's condemnation of his own sons to death after they had been found guilty of conspiring to reinstitute the kingship (Livy, 1948: II.v.7–9).

abodes and commemorative or funerary monuments, each identified by shape and signifying objects – the overall texture and coherence of its vastness remained intact because differences were articulated in terms of religious significance rather than social function. Hitherto law had been concerned in establishing and protecting a harmonious relationship between Rome's human and divine inhabitants, and there were no distinct boundaries between law, magic and religion, with law-giving ascribed a divine origin, augury accepted as an integral part of judging and the act of punishment involving consecrations or offerings to gods (Fowler, 1911: 272–77; Scullard, 1981: 19; Watson, 1972: 103). When giving laws to the people, kings had claimed either to have received them from the gods, as did King Numa in citing Egeria, goddess of fountains and birth, or that they themselves were gods, as Romulus did. Sharing religion's space, law and law-giving had been part of the tradition of ancestral custom and secret rites, ceremonies and cults. It was shrouded in an aura of mystery and jealously guarded in colleges of pontiffs – 'lords spiritual' who, as custodians of all law, had been responsible for its preservation, interpretation and transmission. Law had inhabited a distinct enclosure, whether the 'house' of the king, the temple, the sacrificial altar, or the midst of the private house where the father, as 'priest' of the domestic cult, ruled on transgressions committed by family members (de Coulanges, 1955: 34–39, 85–86; Schulz, 1963: 6–12).[14] And even when spoken 'outside', as in cases concerning the adoption of free persons and in testamentary matters, this interiority had not been lost, for the assembly could only accept or reject the proposed legal arrangements as a whole, not meddle with their form, procedure or substance (Schulz, 1963: 19).

Born of elected magistracies and assemblies of free people, the new 'true' law was not only invested with high public visibility but, in promising an inexorable application of its rules, also became a measure against which people chose right from wrong in the interests of humanity rather than gods. Law thereby claimed a wholly secular existence (Cicero, 1961b: I.vi.19; *Digest*, 1973: I.i.1). Set out and exercised in easily accessible spaces – spaces that quickly achieved their own symbolic prominence and meaning – it entered the body politic and rendered itself known to all. It left religious ritual and priestly books behind, and acquired its own distinct way of communicating, its own language and jurisprudence, and its own class of professional experts to serve it. Gone were king as legislator and religious and political leader sitting at the head of a hierarchically organised sacerdotal order. Law's interpretation and doctrinal systematisation were now entrusted to the expert minds of jurists, its adjudication to praetors and private judges, its performance to the craft and skills of lawyers and orators, and its

14 The word *pater*, Latin for father, did not include the idea of paternity. In religious language it was applied to the gods, in legal language to everyone with property and his own ancestral worship, and in poetic language, to everyone attributed honour. The slave and client applied it to their master. It was synonymous with 'king' and embodied ideas of power, authority, majesty and dignity (de Coulanges, 1955: 90). For a comparison of the authority of father and king, see Lacey (1986).

exercise to the space of the Roman Forum, the dwelling place of Rome's greatest legal monument, the Twelve Tables (Cicero, 1961b: III.i.3).[15]

The jurisdictional acts of new legal beginnings also referenced silent endings; at a time of birth, they insinuated death and formed a temporal demarcation between the 'is' and 'was' of law (*Digest*, 1973: I.ii.2.3). Behind lay an uninterrupted, murky, primordial past where legend mingled with reality, the divine with the human, and where scarce evidence exposed accounts to questions of credibility, making this one of the least attractive periods for historians (Dionysius, 1960: I.viii; Livy, 1948: I.6–9).[16] Indeed, modern manuals, textbooks and sourcebooks of Roman law bear witness to the unreliability of information concerning this past by classifying the era as 'pre-history' and the period of the early law of the Republic as 'archaic', a term derived from the Greek *αρχή*, meaning 'beginning', when history and law began (Jolowicz 1961: 4; Schulz, 1963: 5; Sohm, 1907: 34; Stein, 1999: 128–30). Yet, once started, this history knew no temporal borders. At birth it already touched its future, nurturing Rome's grandeur and leading Her towards a glorious destiny. For, though war and force would win Rome the world, Her laws would bring peace and concord, and found the *pax romana*, ensuring Her *imperium* and future legacy. This was the promise the Gods had made to Aeneas, Romulus's Trojan ancestor, in luring him away from sweet Dido's embrace, and was what Anchises, his father, had foretold (Virgil, 1967: IV.224–31, VI.850–53).

The temporal order that the jurisdiction of the newborn law instituted, in contrast to that which preceded it, spoke to the present and a future life of uninterrupted growth and progress whose end is yet to be glimpsed. From its inception – its embodiment in the Twelve Tables – through its maturity as law of empire and transformation into the Justinian's *Corpus Iuris*, to its revival in the legal codes of modern Europe, Roman law would shine forth (de Zulueta, 1957: 173–76; Jolowicz, 1961: 4–6; Sohm, 1907: 42; Stein, 1999: 104–30). The opening lines of Book II of Livy's *History of Rome* therefore do not merely announce the beginning of Roman liberty and law. They also describe a clear spatial and temporal break from the narrative of Book I, the account of Rome's pre-history from its founding by Romulus in 753 BC to the fall of its last king, Tarquinius the Proud, in 509 BC. Posited at the juncture between Books I and II, the legend of Lucretia forms the bridge between the pre-historical period of kingship and the birth of liberty and law, providing 'one of the hinges on which the history of the Romans turns' (Bayle, in Donaldson 1982: 8). Over the years, following the notable renditions by Livy (1948: I.lvii–lx), Ovid (1931: II.717–852), Dionysius (1960: IV.lxiv–lxxxiv), and Dio (1961: II.13–20), her legend has attracted

15 The word 'forum' was applied to any place that formed the local centre of commerce and jurisdiction. In Rome, it was situated between the Palatine and Capitoline Hills. For a discussion of the spatial arrangement and function of the Roman forum, see Patterson (1992: 190–94). For a comparison of its function with that of the Greek agora, see Lefebre (1995: 237–38).

16 For a contemporary discussion on the problematic nature of the early history of Rome, see Dumézil (1996: 3–12), Fraccaro (1975) and Momigliano (1969).

considerable attention, firing many a creative imagination in art and literature, whilst classicists and historians debated its origin, meaning and truth, and its allegorical and symbolic value.[17] Within the field of law, however, Lucretia has – rather surprisingly – never enjoyed a similar level of interest. Her status has borne no resemblance to the iconic glory afforded Antigone or Portia and, despite her story being in essence one about law, she has attracted only sporadic references in legal commentary.

The curtain rises one night during the siege of Ardea, the capital of Rutili, some 25 miles south of Rome (Ogilvie, 1965: 220). A group of Roman noblemen, feasting in the quarters of the king's son, Sextus Tarquinius, are bragging about their wives, each boasting about the superior qualities of his own. Amidst this rivalry, Tarquinius Collatinus, kinsman of the king, insisting his wife Lucretia surpasses all others in chastity and beauty, proposes they return unannounced to see what their wives are doing in their absence. They discover all spouses revelling, save Lucretia, who sits spinning with her maids in the middle room of the matrimonial home. She is the inimitable winner of their wager. Lucretia graciously welcomes them, and on encountering such beauty and modesty, Sextus is overcome with desire for her. A few days later, he returns unexpectedly and, as the king's son and Lucretia's husband's kinsman, he is received with great courtesy, accorded the best hospitality and duly accommodated in a guest room. That night he enters Lucretia's bedchamber threatening to kill her if she cries out. Using all his wiles in trying to seduce her but finding her equally unmoved by declarations of love, entreaties or threats to her person, Sextus tells her that if she does not yield to him he will kill her, together with his slave, place both naked in her bed, and claim he discovered them together and put them to the sword which, as her husband's kinsman, he had full right to do. Fearing her reputation irrevocably and indefensibly sullied, Lucretia finally submits to Sextus, who then rides back to Ardea.

The next morning, Lucretia sends messages to her father, Lucretius, and husband asking each to bring a trusted friend. Lucretius arrives with Publius Valerius, and Collatinus with Lucius Brutus, a relative of both the king and himself. They find Lucretia inconsolable. She describes her ordeal, proclaims her innocence of mind and calls for vengeance. Then, despite those gathered seeking to appease and comfort her, she takes a knife concealed in her garments and stabs herself through the heart. Everyone is paralysed with grief except Brutus who, incensed by the tragedy that has unfolded before him, pulls the knife from her breast and vows by her blood to vindicate her by expelling the tyrannical house of Tarquinii from Rome. All swear likewise, and Lucretia's body is carried out and displayed in the Forum, where the hitherto timid Brutus, transformed into a

17 The heroine has been invariably represented as the Roman feminine ideal of virtue and seen as complicit with patriarchal values or as a model of resistance to patriarchy (Bromley, 1983: 210–11; Lee, 1953: 117–18; Ogilvie, 1965: 222; Pais, 1971: 203). Her story has also been regarded as an allegory for republican liberty or as one of the founding myths of patriarchy (Arieti, 1997: 213–14; Bryson, 1989: 163–64; Donaldson, 1982: 9–12; Joplin, 1990; Joshel, 1992; Kahn, 1997: 27).

dynamic, eloquent orator, urges the populace to help him make good his word. Mindful of the Tarquinii's many crimes, the people rise up and follow Brutus to liberate Rome. The monarchy is exiled, the Republic founded, and Collatinus and Brutus are elected as its first consuls.

In terms of its structure, setting and language, the legal 'credentials' of this story are clear (Philippides, 1983: 116; Watson, 1975: 35, 167–68). A serious crime is committed, the perpetrator identified and a court of law instituted to judge the case. Sextus's crime was the type the Romans called *stuprum*, an illicit sexual act, whether consensual or not, that imparted injury, corruption or fault to the body of the victim (Adams, 1990: 200–01; Livy, 1948: I.lvii.10, lviii.7–8; Robinson, 1995: 58–64).[18] Where one party had a prior bond of engagement or marriage, the *stuprum* was distinguished as *adulterium*, mainly because it might result in 'counterfeiting', a materialisation in offspring of suspect paternity (*Digest*, 1973: IIL.5.6i; Treggiari, 1991: 262–64). In early Rome, a family court dealt with these offences, and this begins to happen when Lucretia summons her father, husband and family friends to judge the events and participants (Ogilvie, 1965: 219; Pomeroy, 1976: 217–18; Treggiari, 1991: 264–66; Watson, 1975: 167).[19] Before them, she admits the *stuprum* and relates the details of the crime of which she is technically guilty, the issue of consent being relevant only in respect to her punishment, which could be divorce, loss of dowry, exile, even death (Corbett, 1930: 127–33; Robinson, 1995: 58, 66). Defending herself, she declares her lack of culpability but then, without apparent reason, stops this 'legal' process by taking her own life. Lucretia does not perish in compliance with any decision of the court. In fact, her 'evidence' is heard with great sympathy, and in one version she anticipates and dismisses the court's favourable stance towards her, declaring, 'the pardon that you give me I do refuse' (Ovid, 1931: II.830–31). Neither is her self-imposed fate sought in order to avoid punishment; it is equivalent to the harshest penalty awarded a woman found guilty of her crime. True, she must fulfil her victim status in order to provide the force that moves Brutus and the Roman people to revolt, but why could her violation alone not provide sufficient catalyst for this? Her death is problematic because it introduces the possibility that her suicide was the act of a guilty mind, and any suspicion that she might have consented would fundamentally undermine subsequent events. St Augustine (1984: 29–30) was possibly the first to write of the ambiguity surrounding Lucretia's demise, asking whether she should be judged as chaste or adulterous. If chaste, then why suffer a punishment much heavier than the exile imposed upon Sextus? If adulterous, then why praise her honour so highly?

18 Forcible intercourse was not a punishable offence in its own right and initially the verb *rapio*, the Latin ancestor of our own word 'rape', meant to seize and drag off into captivity, as the Romans had done with the Sabine women (Adams, 1990: 175). Rape was first legislated as a crime by Emperor Constantine, with a public criminal prosecution for sexual violation, first introduced at the time of Augustus under the Julian law of violence (Dixon, 2001: 51; Gardner, 1986: 118; Treggiari, 1991: 309–10).

19 This process of summoning first the father and then husband occurs in all principal Roman narrations of the story. Ovid's version of Lucretia closely follows Livy's (Lee, 1953: 108).

It seems as if her words and deeds before the family court are designed to obscure her status, for she accuses her abuser as if victim, protests her own innocence as if accused and condemns herself to death as if guilty. Within a single page of text, she is the victim, accused, judge and executioner, a rapid exchange of roles that seriously compromises her victim status.

The ambivalence surrounding the legend has encouraged commentators to treat it as having two distinct components: personal and public. Focusing on the personal embroils the reader in the nature of Lucretia's character, and the story becomes a tale of a woman's misfortune, injury, pride and vengeance. Adopting a public orientation tends to treat her as simply a vehicle for telling the story of radical political change, thereby ignoring St Augustine's questions altogether. In order to address the paradox of Lucretia's tale, the unity of the story must be maintained, with her death – that which unites these two components – forming the analytical starting point. Traditionally, Lucretia's death has been regarded as the trigger for Brutus turning against the monarchy and the subsequent institution of the Republic. Yet its most immediately significant consequence is to annul the function of the family court. Allowed to continue, it would have deliberated, judged the parties, and decided upon and imposed punishment, thereby making Lucretia's death unnecessary and removing cause for Brutus's decision. By passing and executing a capital sentence upon herself, Lucretia suspends existing law, rendering the court she herself asked to be convened incapable of pronouncing a verdict and meting out justice. In so doing, she opens a new dimension of critique of law, one that does not address the particular case, but which is directed at the kingly legal order, and which is necessary for the birth of the Roman liberty and law that follows. Her death now becomes justifiable. Although set outside the law she initially evokes, her suicide is an act of moral exaltation that transcends any historical, temporal or spatial continuum. If looked at retrospectively, it becomes intelligible, indeed interpretable and legitimate, as the enabling condition for the law that subsequently arises. Lucretia's suicide is neither a heroic act nor a brutal consequence of a rivalry between men that leads to self-sacrifice complicit with patriarchal values, as some have argued (Bromley, 1983: 210; Kahn, 1997). It does sit comfortably within the cultural ideology of her time, accepting the household as the centre of a woman's life, chastity as the most precious female quality and purity as fundamental to her husband's reputation and lineage. Lucretia herself does nothing to contradict this view. Contrary to what has been suggested (Belsey, 2001: 330–34), she is not driven by a wish for self-determination or a questioning of the values of her culture; nor does she take her own life to enlist the community to replace vengeance with submission to the will of people and thereby affirm a model of politics based on consent. Yes, her death *is* necessary to the politics of consent, the consummation of liberty and law, but not as a source of inspiration or active force of progress. It is necessary because it configures a female identity that is excluded from these politics. With her life erased along with the law of kings, there is no place for Lucretia in the latter part of the story. Banished from the space in which liberty and law come to reside, only her corpse – the enabling condition for the new law's jurisdiction – enters the Forum. And when revenge is taken in her name, when all those who are subjects of law, who establish laws and wield them, are present, she is not.

Lucretia has been exiled outside the time and space of the law to be. Yet her dead body, lying at its origin, irrevocably grounds it in sexual difference. Hence Lucretia's story is not merely one of law, it is one of law and sexual difference – a difference clearly voiced in the demarcations of time and space that form and inform the economy of the legend, and in the displacements these demarcations elicit. Her chastity spent, Lucretia cuts short her life and severs the continuity of time. The knife she uses is that by which Brutus makes his vow, puts out the 'eyes and ears' of laws serving kings and enables laws whose severity and impartiality are blind and deaf. In demarcating these separations, this knife also marks out the space in which her story begins and ends: that of the household. Here is she first encountered, found spinning in the *maedio aedium*, the middle room of the Roman house, and it is in her bedchamber that she suffers violation, 'trial' and death. Here is she the ideal wife set firmly within its interiority, the perfect Roman matron, her chastity and modesty (her *pudicitia*) symbolised by the making of wool.[20] The narrative continues, but does so elsewhere, in the open public space of the Forum, where Brutus 'cuts off' the tears and mourning of the Roman men, leads them to a revolution that bestows upon them their manliness (*virtus*),[21] and where they, in assembly, decide the first laws of the Republic. A double act of violence perpetrated upon Lucretia's body is thus followed by a series of displacements irreparably marked by sexual difference wherein her personal story is wholly displaced by the story of Roman liberty and law. Sextus's individual violence is displaced by the public, political violence of his father; Lucretia's modesty and self-inflicted violence by the revolutionary, liberating violence of Brutus and the Roman men; the space of the household by that of the Forum and finally, the 'lawlessness' of kingship manifested in Sextus's libidinal desire by the institution of the new legal order of the Republic.[22]

20 Roman brides carried a spindle and wool at their weddings, and the act of spinning wool was overseen by the goddess Pudicitia residing in the temple of Vesta, goddess of the hearth of the Roman household (Ogilvie, 1965: 222). Both were honoured in the temples of Juno, goddess of womankind, marriage and motherhood. For a discussion of the relationship of Juno and Pudicitia, see Mueller (1998: 224–27).

21 *Virtus* was the quality distinguishing men from women, which enabled them to perform lawful deeds in the service of the state (Earl, 1967: 70–78; Verro, 1958: V.75). During the period of kings, *virtus* was primarily associated with the pursuit of glory, courage and bravery in military affairs; during the Republic, it was associated with pre-eminence in statesmanship (Earl, 1967: 73–74).

22 In ancient historiography, it is not uncommon for sexual offences to be offered as justification for overthrowing tyranny. For a discussion, see Jed (1989: 3), Rudolph (2000: 159–61) and Shuger (1998: 529–32). However, in examples involving men, political change is not accompanied by a change of legal order. In fact, in the case of one commonly cited example, the overthrow of Pissistratide in Athens, Thucydides (1959: VI.liv.54) argues that the tyrannical laws benefited the city and should be maintained.

Verginia or the story of engendering

> Those who share Law must also share Justice; and those who share these are to be regarded as members of the same commonwealth.
>
> (Cicero, 1961b: I.vii.23)

The newly instituted law did not merely produce a separation of that previously unified. Its space and time, being more than creations of law's mind, of its images and imaginings, imparted their mark upon human relationships and action, and were directly expressed in the mode in which the social was organised – Roman law spoke them and the Romans lived them. Under the thrall of the divine order, social cohesion had been maintained by the dread of violating the *pax deorum*, peace with the gods. Kings, priests, heroes and ordinary people alike acknowledged no other social bond save that of religion, with neither birth nor intimacy providing the key foundation for domestic relationships since only worship could fulfil this function (Fowler, 1911: 273; Scullard, 1981: 19). Accordingly, the family constituted a religious rather than biological association, with blood ties deemed inferior to agnatic ones, those bonds deriving from the shared worship associated with a common patrilineal ancestry (Gellius, 1927: XV.xxvii; Cicero 1961c: XIII. 35–36; de Coulanges, 1955: 40–42, 54–59; Gaius, 1932: I.156; Jolowicz, 1961: 122; Sohm, 1907: 448–51). And, as the community of domestic deities defined kinship, so did common sacra, rites, gods and genii rather than political affiliation or generation define membership of the *curia*, Rome's earliest social and political unit.[23] With law gaining its own 'territory', this pre-existing unity was rent asunder. Beneath the sign of law there now operated a different unifying principle, law's prescriptive reason – its promises, announced in the first jurisdictional acts are fulfilled with clarity, brevity and simplicity in the code of the Twelve Tables, which mould and nurture a novel form of life and sociability. Upon all those it chose to inhabit its realm, those awarded the gift of Roman *civitas* (citizenship), law had bestowed a unique status, one embracing both person and property. Each and every citizen could own and administer property, enter valid contracts, make a will, be made a heir, legatee or guardian of other Roman citizens and possess paternal authority – rights which were enshrined in law – and each and every citizen was free to conduct their own affairs as they saw fit, provided they did so within the parameters set down by law (Schulz, 1967: 146, 158; Tables III–VIII). Subjects of law, all were subordinate to its rules and precepts, and, whenever it demanded, obliged to obey its 'protocols' of procedure (Tables I, II and VII).

23 King Romulus first instituted the curiae, dividing the people into 30 groups on the basis of common worship and allocating specific rites, gods and genii to each. These curiae were sacred brotherhoods under the presidency of the pontifex maximus, Rome's head priest. Each possessed its own priests (curiales), performed its own sacrifices, and ate in its own dining room at the curial hearth (Cicero, 1961a: II.viii.14; Dionysius, 1960: II.vii.3–4, xxiii.1–3; Plutarch, 1962: I.xx.1–3). For a discussion, see Kunkel (1966: 9–11) and Palmer (1970: 67–75, 80).

The novel form of humanity law engendered was not predicated upon a radical transformation of the individual's rights, duties and obligations, with law establishing first-time bearers of proprietary rights, voters, taxpayers or soldiers. They already existed and were called *Quirites*, a term betokening religious ties uniting members of the *curiae* and denoting entitlement of ownership, inheritance and adoption deriving from this membership (Palmer, 1970: 191–97). However, a hitherto unknown form of sociability had been born. Knowing no distinctions of wealth, rank or birth, all citizens participated in the *comitia centuriata*, the supreme, sovereign committee of the Roman people, and shared equally in the rights, freedoms and liberties their *civitas* afforded (Dionysius, 1960: IV.84; Table IX.v).[24] All were endowed with the right to appeal to their fellow citizens when life or liberty were threatened, were protected from punishment without formal trial and conviction, and, following the prohibition of laws granting personal privilege or exception, were shielded from the arbitrary wielding of power and authority (Cicero, 1961a: I.xxvii.43, 1961b: III.xix.44, 1961c: XVI.xvii.43, xxiv.77; Livy, 1948: II.i.7; Table IX.ii;). So, although *Quirites* remained the official term by which Romans addressed each other, the mode of being animated by the new law was by no means exhausted within the parameters defined by the word. Romans had become more than *Quirites*; they were also *cives* – an associative term meaning 'citizens', but which, most significantly, also meant 'fellow citizens'. Like its Indo-European ancestor *keiwos*, *civis* referenced the familiar, dear and friendly, the sentimental aspects of relationships uniting members of a group, be they political or personal, and distinguished these persons from different varieties of 'stranger' posited outside the alliance. Yet it was only in the Latin that such feelings of endearment and friendship binding people together gained a juridical meaning, stemming as they did from an equality of rights secured by law; only in the Latin did *cives* designate a sentimentally based alliance grounded upon a community of rights set in law (Benveniste, 1973: 273–75). Being a Roman citizen was not therefore primarily associated with the territorial space of Rome, for whereas other Italian languages made little or no distinction between *civitas* and *urbs* (city), using them interchangeably to denote a place or its people, the Latin *civitas* referred to the nature of the social relationships and functions that followed the city's foundation; it designated the inhabitants' *mode of being*.[25] Furthermore, because this *civitas* was etymologically linked to *civis*, this was a mode of social being befitting a community united by law. *Civitas* embodied a social partnership (*societas civilis*) wherein the common purpose shaping the partners' will was neither religion or family ties, nor political or military alliance but the desire to live equally under the same law.

24 The *comitia curiata*, the assembly at which the king's decisions on matters of tax, peace and military obligations were announced, survived as a religious vestige with the sole power to formally confirm the auspices and command of certain magistrates (Kunkel, 1966: 10; Palmer, 1970: 189, 276–81).

25 The noun of *civitas* in Latin was used for 'of a situation and a town, also of the rights of a community, and of a body of men' (Flaccus, in Gellius, 1927: XVIII.vii.5).

This new form of sociability was, for the Roman mind, the pinnacle of a developmental process wherein, through reason, language or experience of more primitive forms of association such as those of kinship or religion, humans had eventually come to regard the juridical community as the greatest manifestation of the common good (Cicero, 1949: I.1–3, 1961a: I.xxv, 1961b: I.v.16, 1975: I.iv.11–13, I.xvi.50, I.xliv.156–58; Lucretius, 1953: V.950–60). *Civitas*, posited as the supreme form of companionship and friendship, as the optimum form of humanity, thereby acquired a life and a value above and beyond the lives and qualities of individual citizens. It formed the tangible representation of the bond of law in which all citizens shared, the 'visible' object of their commonality, and as such became the *res publicum*, the common wealth belonging to all citizens, with its management entrusted to those pre-eminent in prudence, virtue and wisdom – the Roman magistracy (Cicero, 1961a: II.xxxiii.58, 1961b: III.i.5). Within this civic community – this 'paradise of freedom' as Cicero (1930: II.29) so fondly called the Roman commonwealth – a dual sense of selfhood was animated. Ordinary private citizens enjoyed a life of liberty under the rule of law, whilst the Roman magistrates engaged in a public life of honour and glory in the government and preservation of the Roman *civitas*, a position which, though open to anyone choosing the path of statesmanship, was awarded to those thought steeped in dignity, the sons of the most worthy families (Cicero, 1961a: I.xix.35).[26]

The story of the code of the Twelve Tables is the story of the Roman *civitas*. It tells us of the sociability law begets and of the balances required to sustain it (Cicero, 1961a: I.iv.8). Yet the codification of law in the Twelve Tables was not easily won. Demands for unambiguous, freely accessible law protecting the weak and limiting the power of the mighty had persisted ever since the early laws of the Republic had first ushered in law's new empire. The intervening period had seen considerable discord and unrest, with the Roman world repeatedly disrupted by social and political struggles between patricians and plebeians, and unsettled by frequent conflicts with external enemies. Finally, in 450 BC, after envoys had returned from studying Greek laws and institutions, the patricians gave way to plebeian demands and agreed the appointment of a board of 10 men (*decemvirs*) to be given one year and Draconian powers to frame the relevant law (Livy, 1948: III.xxxi–xxxiii). The patricians' influence was such that only they were elected to these posts. At first they acted impartially, presenting a draft code of ten tables that was widely accepted but deemed incomplete. So their authority was renewed for another year to allow them to fulfil their mandate (Livy, 1948: III.xxxiii–xxxv). With this second term, however, the picture of harmony suddenly changed when Appius Claudius, hitherto largely unnoticed amongst the *decemvirate*, took control of the committee and proceeded to run it as a tyranny directed against the plebeians (Livy, 1948: III.xxxvi). Amidst the renewed social

26 For discussions of the social, political and economic criteria for election to the Roman magistracy, see Jolowicz (1961: 43–55); Kunkel (1966: 14–22); Nicolet (1980: 206–26); Schulz (1967: 168–72; Wirszubski (1950: 17–24).

unrest this autocracy fermented, neighbouring tribes seized the opportunity to start plundering raids, forcing the *decemvirs* to make the Senate approve a levy to raise an army to defend Rome. However, the soldiers – predominantly plebeians – fought half-heartedly under the unwanted leadership of the *decemvirate*, preferring to hold rather than defeat the enemies approaching the city. And so, with the destruction of Rome imminent, and peace and concord seeming more hopeless a dream than ever before, it was the death of another woman – the plebeian maiden Verginia – that enabled Rome to overcome the threat to its survival and finally institute a code of law.

The story of Verginia, like that of Lucretia, is one of female chastity and death, male sexual desire, freedom and law, and one whose outcome is a new social cohesion for Roman citizens.[27] Verginia, a young maiden betrothed to Icilius, becomes the object of Appius Claudius's unbridled lust. Failing to seduce her with promises and riches, and with her father Lucius Verginius absent defending Rome, he sets his client, Marcus Claudius, to take possession of her by claiming she is the daughter of one of his slaves, accosting her one morning as she enters the Forum. The crowd attracted by her nurse's cries defends her, but Claudius summons her before Appius's tribunal, promising to prove his case and demanding the court grant him his right to hold her until the case is decided. Her uncle pleads that in Verginius's absence Appius must grant them custody so that her honour is not jeopardised before her status is adjudicated but Appius awards custody to Claudius. Icilius protests vehemently and, as the *lictors* attempt to eject him from the hearing, delivers a passionate, rousing speech accusing Appius of coveting his wife-to-be, and the *decemvirate* of stealing the people's liberty and their right to appeal to their fellow citizens. Calling upon the assembled *Quirites* to protect his bride, he pledges his lifeblood to prevent the decree being enacted, and the crowd, deeply moved, turns on Appius who, skilfully retreating, asks Marcus to allow the girl to remain at large until the next day. This he does, and messengers are dispatched to fetch Verginius, who arrives at dawn and, accompanied by a crowd of supporters, leads his daughter to the Forum. Here, in a fit of temper and ignoring proper procedure, Appius summarily finds in favour of Marcus Claudius. When Verginius, Icilius and their fellows try to prevent Claudius from claiming his 'prize', Appius accuses them of promoting sedition, and orders armed men to implement his judgement. Seeing his allies thwarted, Verginius apologises to Appius and, granted leave to question Verginia and her nurse as to how he has been deceived into believing himself her father, snatches a knife from a butcher's stall and stabs Verginia to the heart, exclaiming: 'Thus my daughter, in the only way I can, do I assert your freedom!' devoting her blood to Appius's destruction. Verginius, safeguarded from arrest by his allies, escapes the city, returns to camp and explains his action to his fellow soldiers, warning that Appius's lust might now turn upon any of their own daughters, sisters or

27 The story of Verginia is narrated in Livy (1948: III.xliv–lviii). Other accounts include those by Dio (1961 in Zonaras 7:18) and Dionysius' (1960: XI.xxviii–xxxix).

wives. As those assembled declare loyalty to his cause, news arrives that, in the wake of Appius's latest act of tyranny, the outraged people of Rome, inspired by Icilius, have taken over the Forum, forced the Senate to convene, and are demanding the *decemvirate* immediately abolished. Abandoning the enemy, Verginius's army marches on Rome, seizes the Aventine hill, elects its own military council and demands the election of plebeian tribunes. The senators are in disarray, bickering over how best to respond, so the army, followed by plebeian citizens, marches out of Rome leaving it undefended. Finally goaded into action, the senators force the *decemvirs* to resign and reinstate the former constitutional order significantly strengthened in favour of plebeian–patrician equality (Livy, 1948: III.liv–lv). With the power and liberty of the plebeians now firmly established, the *decemviral* laws, the Twelve Tables, are engraved in bronze and displayed in the Forum, thereby sealing a new civic unity and partnership (Livy, 1948: III.lvii.10). Finally, the army – reconstituted to fight 'for the first time as free men fighting for a free Rome' (Livy, 1948: III.lxi) – marches out of the city to lay waste to Her enemies.

It has been suggested that Livy adapted Verginia's story from Lucretia's in order to further dramatise his narrative (Ogilvie, 1965: 477; Pais, 1971: 186–87; Watson, 1975: 168) and they do exhibit notable similarities. However, the person of Verginia contrasts markedly with Lucretia, being accorded nothing like as much attention, admiration and praise, and being the subject of few, predominantly passing, references in the wider literature – feminist or otherwise.[28] She exhibits no courage and performs no acts of heroism, attracting only pity and sympathy as 'the sweetest maid in Rome' (Ogilvie, 1965: 476), and throughout her lacklustre performance, not only does she not say a single word, she makes no sound at all. No proud, brave speech, no appeal, no call for revenge, passes her lips. When Marcus Claudius grabs her in the Forum, when Appius twice delivers a judgement condemning her to slavery and defilement; even when her father pierces her breast with the knife, she utters no bold declaration, no cry for help, no plea for mercy, no scream or sob, not even a sigh. Neither is she seen to move on her own account; one or other of the male protagonists places her in custody, brings her to court, leads her to death, takes her life, and parades her corpse. Even the trait apparently so crucial to her story, her plebeian social class, is questionable, with some sources presenting her as a patrician (Pais, 1971: 198). Perhaps, as Ogilvie (1965: 477) suggests, she is a hypostatisation of the virgin maiden, for in some texts she is not even named (Cicero, 1961a: II.xxxvii.63; Diodorus, 1945: IX.xxiv). In all accounts she is but an empty name; lacking characteristics, feelings and presence distinguishing her as an individual, she passes invisibly through her own story as if a mask any woman can wear.

It is not just the prosopographical that distinguishes Verginia's from Lucretia's drama; the stages upon which each unfolds also differ radically. No bedchamber

28 For example, see the accounts by Joshel (1992) and Vasaly (1987).

or spinning wheel placed symbolically at the heart of a home to which the heroine is confined is encountered here. Verginia's story starts and finishes in the public space of the Forum, the centre of the city, where men assembled, swore their oath against tyranny, heard speeches from the orator's platform and decided the first laws of the Republic. It was here that law would reside; here the prison would be built; here that the *praetor*, attired in his purple-bordered robe, would convene his semi-circular court; and here that Rome's greatest legal monument, the Twelve Tables, would come to dwell. Though likewise precipitated by sexual desire, the nature of the case differs markedly from that which entangled Lucretia. It involves no sexual offence, concerning instead the maiden's loss of status as free person and Roman citizen, and 'the legal details are stressed and lingered over' more than in any other of Livy's tales (Watson, 1975: 169).[29] In condemning Verginia to slavery, Appius redefines her as a commodity to be owned, possessed and used as her master wishes. No longer a person in the eyes of law, she becomes but 'a mortal thing' – the term the *Digest* employed to define slaves (Crook, 1967: 56). A terrible and unambiguous fate awaits her. Yet those champions leaping to her defence do not address this issue. Their brave speeches castigate Appius's tyranny and speak emphatically and repeatedly of liberty and freedom, but do so in the name of the Roman people, not in Verginia's name (Dionysius, 1960: XI.xxxi.3–4; Livy, 1948: III.l.10–li.8). Even when they finally bring down the *decemvirate*, they vindicate plebeian freedom, not hers. There is only one rhetoric spoken in her name, that of chastity. So when uncle and fiancé elicit the crowd's resistance to her initial surrender to Marcus Claudius's keep, they plead her virginity otherwise jeopardised; when opposing the claimant's attempt to reclaim his 'slave', her father protests on her honour and his having not raised her to gratify men's lust; and, as he plunges the butcher's blade through her heart, proclaiming to thereby assert her freedom, his sole reference is to the loss of her pure, chaste life (Livy, 1948: III.xlv.6–7, xlvii.7, l.6).[30] Vivified on the minds and lips of male protagonists, the association of Verginia with chastity is also evidenced in other details of the plot. Her death occurs by the shrine of Cloakina, deity protector of virgin modesty and purity, and is thought to have initiated a cult honouring the chastity of plebeian women (Livy, 1948: III.xlviii.5, X.xxiii; Ogilvie, 1965: 487; Pais, 1971: 196–99). Yet, most indicatively, at no point do either her defenders or the story's narrator recognise that, in losing her freedom, control of her body would pass to her owner and the issue of chastity would thereby become irrelevant. Neither is there any moment of superimposition or displacement between liberty and chastity, as happened in Lucretia's story. The two remain firmly separated, with liberty associated with the brave men and their fellow citizens – those effecting revolution – and chastity assigned to Verginia and their womenfolk (Dionysius, 1960: XI.xxxv.3; Livy, 1948: III.xlv.9, l.8–9).

29 It is mainly Dionysius's (1960: XI.xxxiv) account that provides details of the trial and the arguments put forward by Verginius.

30 In Dionysius's account (1960: XI.xxxvii.6), Verginus does make passing reference to his daughter's liberty as he kills her.

The assault on Verginia's freedom is not therefore, as has been argued, an attack on the liberty of all plebeians (Vasaly, 1987: 219–20). Verginia bears no measure of this liberty because she falls outside it, with her story and the dual rhetoric that characterises its plot serving to delimit two distinct domains and modes of being. One is occupied by liberty, firmly ensconced in the time and space of law and enjoyed by the civic brotherhood. In the other sits chastity, 'immersed' in the sacred, living fire of the domestic hearth, which, tended by chaste women, was residence of the virgin goddess Vesta and symbol of the household's preservation and prosperity (de Coulanges, 1955: 26–33; Dumézil, 1996: 353–55; Orr, 1978: 1560–61; Pomeroy, 1975: 210–14). First drawn with the blood of a patrician matron, this division is consolidated with that of a plebeian maiden, their stories united by the same rhetoric – that of chastity – and adorned with its insignia. Chastity was their crowning virtue, and both had been sacrificed upon its altar.

To satisfy his libido, Appius could simply have abducted Verginia or tricked his way into her home or her into his. By disguising his lust with a question of law, he transforms a personal sexual matter into a public legal one, a displacement that points to the true nature and significance of the narrative. In posing and adjudicating the legal question of Verginia's status, Appius also poses and adjudicates the question of the feminine and its relationship to law, a question that must be set before law if Her right to inhabit its domain is to be recognised. In the event, his judgement erases the mark of *civitas* from Verginia and her sex, and with it their right to stand before the law. Whilst Lucretia never drew breath in its space and time, Verginia, though a free Roman citizen, has her right to inhabit this realm questioned, adjudicated and negated, cut out by the hand of men. Hereafter, neither they nor their ilk can live the Roman *civitas* as equal partners in law, and enjoy the crowning liberty of the right of *provocatio.*[31] Nor will their names appear in the Roman census, that cornerstone of civic life providing the sole means by which people could prove themselves citizens.[32] Their fate thus sealed, their person has no place in law and therefore no place in the Twelve Tables, even though it was Verginia's passing that brought about their institution. This text bears no legal category that befits the presence of the feminine, and affords it just two references: the first stipulating ownership of the 'fruit of Her loins' (Table IV.iv); the second that women, like chattels, pass under their husband's authority after residing in his house for an uninterrupted year (Table VI.i).

Verginia's story is therefore the story of the codification of the Twelve Tables *and* the story of how law configured the feminine mode of being. Denied residence in law's empire, banished outside its gates and text, She is relegated to the Roman household 'inviolably hedged by all kinds of sanctity' and across

31 The prevailing view among Romanists is that *provocatio* was not available to women as of right, though some argue that it was granted in practice. For a discussion of both views, see Strachan-Davidson (1913: 141–44).

32 Unless widowed, women were assumed under their husband's declaration that he was married. For a discussion of the significance and function of the Roman census see Nicolet (1980: 49–88).

whose threshold law cannot pass.[33] Law has no say on the personal relationships of its inhabitants, the ways and types of marriage, or the reasons for divorce (Cicero, 1961c: xl.106, xli.109, xlix.128; Nevett, 1997: 289; Schulz, 1967: 147; Watson, 1975: 20, 33, 39).[34] Yet this is not, as has been suggested, because its 'humane face' acknowledged its subjects' individuality and respected the freedom of their private lives (Schulz, 1967: 146–63). Such interpretations are premised upon a modern apprehension of public and private as designating distinct, incompatible spheres of life. For Romans, these categories represented co-existing juridical modes of being available to law's subjects only, both being clearly prescribed in the Republic's first laws and the Twelve Tables (IX.i.ii.iv). Whilst the word *publicus* signified a life dedicated to the service of the people, one spent governing and managing the common wealth, a life *privatus* emphasised, as the word suggests, a sense of deprivation distinguishing ordinary private citizens not involved in affairs of state (Cicero1961a: I.iv.7–8; Ernout and Meillet, 1979; Koumanouthis, 1972; Wirszubski, 1950: 15). The sustained mode of being of the Roman *familia* was therefore neither private nor public. Caring nothing about deliberations in popular assemblies, magistracies, or the triumphs and spoils of war, alien to the civic brotherhood whose language of equality and liberty brought strangers together, its concern was with immediate material life. It had originated in the primordial condition of human beings when, under nature's dictate, 'Venus joined their bodies in the woods', created the first human bond – that of the union between husband and wife – and thereby softened the human race to enable subsequent unions of family and kinship (Cicero, 1975: I.iv.11, I.xvii.54; Lucretius, 1953: V.1011–27). Centred on each family's living hearth and religious cult, the domestic mode of being spoke a language of affectionate duty and respectful obedience (de Coulanges, 1955: 26–27; Saller, 1991: 146–51, 1999: 24). It claimed no independent existence beyond those who 'lived' it; it only existed for as long as they, together with the hearth's fire, were alive; and it boasted to be neither the product of intentional activity nor the achievement of human reason. It simply followed from the course of nature.

Just as it was for the order of the household, so too was the life of the feminine ruled and measured by nature alone – not because She, like all beings, originated at birth and terminated at death, but rather because Her person signified the materiality of human existence. Her body provided the source of new life. Her duties and obligations embraced the care of offspring, the elderly and the deceased, and Her right conduct – Her *pudicitia* – resided in Vesta's hearth and

33 The term *familia* in its widest sense refers to all persons and property under the control of the oldest male. More often, however, it denoted the conjugal family, dependents, slaves and freedmen living in the house (*Digest*, 1973: 50.16.195.1–4; Rawson, 1986: 7–9). *Domus* was used to designate the physical space of the house, but also included family, slaves and the broad kinship group – agnates and cognates, ancestors and descendents. For a more detailed discussion of these definitions, see Martin (1996) and Saller (1984, 1994: 71–95).

34 The only interference of law in marriage was Table VI.x, requiring a man to give reason when repudiating rather than divorcing his wife, and, the soon-to-be-abolished Table XI.ii, prohibiting marriage between plebeians and patricians (Dionysius, 1960: XI.xxviii.4).

was responsible for the maintenance of the family's ethical life. It was *Her* guardian goddesses who were called upon to preserve the household's physical and spiritual well-being, and *Her* personhood, which was rooted in the particularity of the household.[35] As if the feminine had remained untouched by law's beginning, She continued to live under a male head of family exercising absolute power over free persons and slaves alike. She could still be married or divorced without legal formality and, as previously, upon marriage had to either join Her husband's domestic cult under his control, or remain tied to Her father's authority (Corbett, 1930: 68; Gardner, 1986: 44–50, 84–85; Treggiari, 1991: 32–36; Watson, 1975: 17–19, 31). Now, as before, She could, on the death of Her male head of family, be called on intestacy as his immediate heir and continue to own this property until She came under a husband's authority (Corbett, 1930: 108–14; Gardner, 1986: 71, 169–71; Jolowicz, 1961: 123–25). And now, as before, whether under the authority of a father or husband, having committed a sexual or other criminal offence, She would, as Lucretia had done, appear before and be punished by the family court, even when, as in later times, She became entitled to a public trial (Pomeroy, 1976: 219; Strachan-Davidson, 1913: 32–35; Treggiari, 1991: 265–75; Watson, 1975: 36–38).[36]

As daughter, wife or mother to be, She of the body, earth and abyss below, She, the most natural person of all, thus emerged as if confined to law's past, to what the Romanists describe as law's pre-history and what Mommsen called 'the original order of things' (Mommsen, in Strachan-Davidson, 1913: 32–33). Although the life of the feminine continued seemingly undisturbed by jurisdictional acts of separation and engendering, in delimiting law's mode of being, these acts also set the interpretative planes through which Her space, time and mode of being would be read. No longer would She inhabit the vast and uncharted space in which Lucretia had dwelt, for this had stopped being an undifferentiated place wherein the social, natural and supernatural were conflated. Redefined in juxtaposition to law's spatial order, it now occupied law's exteriority, forming a domain ruled by nature (*Digest*, 1973: I.i.1.3, 4). There was She exiled as a creature of nature clearly distinguished from the juridical 'animal' (*civis*) who in entering the partnership in law denounced the primacy of His natural existence. Not only was her persona now seen as a gift of nature, but also Her entitlement to property ceased to be akin to that of her male siblings. Theirs became a legal right to own and alienate property;

35 The main goddesses protecting women were Tellus, the earth mother, Ceres, goddess of productivity in the fields, procreation in marriage, and of death and guardian of the *mundus*, the sacred passage to the underworld, and Vesta, goddess of the family hearth (Dumézil 1996: 374–77; Pomeroy, 1975: 214–17). The Penates were tutelary deities of the food supplies, whilst Juno, goddess of birth and fecundity, of the moon and monthly cycles – queen goddess of womankind and protector of her *pudicitia* – measured her right conduct (de Coulanges, 1955: 34–39; Dumézil, 1996: 291–303, 341–43; Orr, 1978: 1559–63).

36 When in 331 BC two women were accused of poisoning their husbands, they were strangled by the decree of their kinsmen, while the women involved in the secret cult of Bachanalia in 186 BC, despite standing trial in public, were executed by their own families (Livy, 1948: VIII.18, XXXIX.xviii.6). Even following the lex Julia, which made adultery a public offence, it was the family council that designated and executed punishments.

Hers remained a material relationship grounded upon agnatic ties and activated on the death of the paterfamilias, a claim to what was already naturally Hers, and that which proved Her unyielding ties to the family – the homestead, burial ground, spring, garden and fields (de Coulanges, 1955: 70–72; Diosdi, 1970: 38–39, 44–46; Gaius, 1932: II.157, 159; Table V.i.ii; D. 28.2.11).

As law's jurisdictional acts reconfigured the space and mode of being of the feminine, so too did they redefine the time of Her being. Her life spent servicing material needs was not born out of rational understanding and reflection, not part of a temporal process motivated by a search to achieve the common good. Clearly distinguished from and immune to progressive moves in which the life of law unfolds, the time of the feminine had no linear, progressive continuity, but like that of nature was ruled by repetition, the cycles of the moon, changes of season, recurrence of birth and death. It was exhausted within its own present and claiming neither past nor future, remained timeless. Thus would Her life and acts never fall within the time of law and unity of history. Unlike those of Brutus, Icilius or Verginius, they could never be cast in the grand spectacle of human activity as forces of change, progress and civilisation shaping the intellectual forms by which our present – the heir of Rome and Roman law – renders its past legible and intelligible. In Appius's court, the question of the feminine before the law was set, and in the same court, it was laid to rest. There would be no place for Her in the Roman law of persons and those legal systems founded upon it; She would hold no public office or perform other civic functions; and She would neither be able to act upon her own property, alienate it, leave it to heirs of her choosing, nor enter commercial contracts – not even when free of the authority of a male head. She would always need a father, husband or male guardian to mediate Her standing before the law (*Digest*, 1973: XVI.1.1; Gaius, 1932: I.iii; Cato in Livy, 1948: XXXIV.ii.11).[37]

On the politics of sexual difference

> ... some overtures have been made to the world of women. But these overtures remain partial and local... Has an erosion of the gains won in women's struggles occurred because of the failure to lay foundations different from those on which the world of men is constructed?
>
> (Irigaray, 1993: 6)

The story of Roman law I have narrated here is one not told by historians, jurists and feminists, and is perhaps one to which many might take exception. In asserting the feminine to lie outside the realm of law, I did not intend to nurse a belief in a 'golden' age preceding law when a matriarchal order held sway.[38] Neither did my

37 For a detailed discussion of the guardianship and property ownership of Roman women, see Gardner (1986: 5–29, 163–203).

38 For a discussion of whether a matriarchy existed in pre-historic Italy, see Briffault (1927: 343–50), Hallett (1984: 14–28) and Thompson (1949: 92–101, 171–77). It is commonly accepted, however, that the Twelve Tables, in instituting the principle of agnatic guardianship, substantially strengthened the power of the father (Hallet, 1984: 23; Watson, 1972: 102–03).

analysis merely seek to explore the past; in so doing, I hoped to shed light on current concerns about law, power and sexual difference. To this end, the choice of Roman law might appear anachronistic, contemptuous of time and context, and even if accepted as appropriate – even assuming the tales of Lucretia and Verginia have real contemporary significance – my analysis is still difficult to reconcile with most modern feminist critiques of law. To claim that an ousting of the feminine from law's empire constitutes part of the bedrock of our legal tradition seems, to say the least, forgetful of the struggles of our nineteenth-century foremothers in which our rights and liberties, our personhood and standing before the law, were so obviously won, and our place in the modern *civitas* so clearly secured. Furthermore, its conclusions, so readily interpretable as gloomy and pessimistic, appear at odds with the optimism that the quest for legal change, so dominant within modern feminist legal scholarship, sustains. I admit no great enthusiasm for law-making activities, nor do I share the belief in their potential for instituting significantly positive changes for women; 'better' legal norms have been replacing older ones for almost 200 years, but the promise law once held for us has yet to be fulfilled. In fact, it was my questioning of the transformative aspirations of feminist legal scholarship which first fuelled my interest in notions of stasis rather than change and led me to a morphological analysis of the concept of jurisdiction and my choice of Roman law – both of these appearing so amiable to stasis *and* to change.

The founding of law's jurisdiction always annunciates a discontinuity with, and rejection of, the past. Yet, despite this demarcation, it remains closely linked with this past because the conditions of its possibility lie in the *a priori* positing of a time, space and mode of being that existed without this law, so that the axiom of non-law (or corrupt law) founds the new law's jurisdiction. Here, change embraces a diachronic comparison of the 'before' and 'after' articulated in the statement: the 'B' of then differs from the 'A' of now, wherein analysis indicates the extent of this difference.[39] However, the forms of space, time and life, which jurisdictional acts beget cannot be known through diachronic analysis alone. They can only be properly apprehended by synchronic comparisons whose objects are contemporaneous to one another. This is because the identity of these forms is premised upon their antithesis, relying on a dichotomy wherein the one can only be conceptualised in terms of the absence of the other and articulated as: 'A' and that which is not 'A'. When law claims an interiority, there is an exteriority against which it is defined; if there is a time of law, there must be one which does not belong to law; if there is a juridical mode of being, there must be a non-juridical one as well. So, whilst the diachronic comparisons morphological inquiry employs interrogate jurisdiction's historicity, its synchronic comparisons care little about history and change. Locating their origins in law's 'beginning', they

39 For a discussion of the themes of change and stasis in the founding of law's jurisdiction, see Gordley (1994) and Varga (1978). For a general discussion of the past as the condition of possibility of the present, albeit from different theoretical positions, see Boorstin (1941), Goodrich (1992) and Krygier (1986).

instead point to that which is static in law, its morphological power. This is a constant feature of its nature, a structural element of law's being from which it is unable to liberate itself without being destroyed, for in speaking the law jurisdictional acts do not merely bear law's being, they also bear law's power of separation and engendering. This power is, however, not a mimetic one, with law – like an artist – carving its forms to reflect, translate or reproduce 'true' forms arising from social conditions within its empire. Neither is it the power to enforce these norms – that wielded by a ruling elite, class, order or state controlling the legal institutions. It is an inherent power residing in jurisdictional prescription itself, a power silently deployed in law's displacements and demarcations, in its ordering of domains, spheres and sites of social life.

Merely accounting for the permanence and constancy of this power does not in itself render it visible and open to analysis or critique; the forms of space, time and life that substantiate it can neither find their positive statement nor empirical manifestation in simple juxtaposition of opposing categories. Entwined around the polarity of a binary structure, they cannot be made tangible through the drawing of lines between home/exile, own/alien, same/different or reason/feeling; they appear as little more than abstractions of law's language and logic, and thereby obliterate both the function of law's power and its morphological implications for the social. It is only by introducing a third parameter, one that performs as a comparator against which these binaries can be measured, that the power of law gains social meaning and hypostasis. In my analysis of Roman law, it is sexual difference that fulfils this role. However, sexual difference is not methodologically equated with norms regulating the conduct of men and women.[40] It provides the referent that convokes scattered and seemingly trivial 'evidence' that would otherwise go unrecognised or assume the guise of historical fact or self-evident truth. Unravelling the manner in which the bipartite divisions law institutes map the feminine/masculine dichotomy testifies to law's tactics and strategies of power, forms of domination and its opaque instances of exclusion. The 'legend' of the social being law narrates is thereby exposed and the sexuated nature of law's power laid bare. Carefully surveyed, hitherto 'innocent' evidence can thus yield a common point of reference; they comprise the empirical manifestation of law's morphological power, a power no longer merely juridical, mental or conceptual but now tangible, social and real.

Ingrained in the dichotomies law institutes, sexual difference is evidenced as a systemic element of its power and thereby shares its peculiar affinity to stasis. Permanently attached to law's being, structuring the cultural images that acts of separation and engendering elaborate and transmit, sexual difference becomes integral to the way law images and reads the world, and thus highly resistant to change.[41] It also means that my analysis of Roman law may not be so historically

40 For such an analysis of Roman law, see Thomas (1992).

41 For a discussion of binaries, their relation to the dichotomy feminine/masculine and their resilience to change, see Jay (1981: 47) and Massey (1992: 73).

specific because, though belonging so obviously to our distant past, it is also very much part of our present. For us unwilling heirs to its legacy, much has changed in the years since the Twelve Tables were first displayed in the Forum, yet I would argue that much has remained essentially untouched. For how is it that law and its agencies still recoil at the idea of crossing the domestic threshold when violence is perpetrated against its female inhabitants (Douglas, 2003)? How is it that woman's work in the family continues to be seen as a natural task or labour of love, and Her time not able to be measured against that spent in the workplace (Bottomley, 1994; Conaghan, 2006)? And why does the question of female personhood still occupy us feminists of the postmodern era (Naffine, 1990)?

Establishing linkages across time and raising questions about the constancy of sexual differentiation in law's normative patterns gives credence to feminist ontological knowledge claims identifying law's nature as male, patriarchal or phallocentric and, like my own claims, points to its resistance to change. Yet trans-historical accounts of legal norms, in collapsing the permanent in law into the persistence of norms that discriminate against women, offer little when it comes to understanding the function of law's power and its fundamental reliance upon sexual difference. In employing sexual difference to interrogate law, my approach has argued for a critical inquiry which, unhitched from the chariot of normative analysis, poses as its object law's own language and logic of divisions, and the manner in which these found and shape its relationship to the social world. Here, sexual difference not only provides the condition of possibility of the 'visibility' of law's power, and consequently of its critical analysis but emerges as a critical standpoint thereby opening up a discursive space wherein a feminist rereading of law may take place. This paper, in raising questions concerning law's being, the nature of its rationality and the sexual economy of its power – questions that resist law's own self-representation and thus critical questions of legal ontology – may be seen as a first attempt, however incomplete, to engage in such a rereading.

References

Adams, JN (1990) *The Latin Sexual Vocabulary*, London: Duckworth

Adock, FE (1959) *Roman Political Ideas and Practice*, Ann Arbor MI: University of Michigan Press

Arieti, J (1997) 'Rape and Livy's view of Roman history', in S Deacy and K Pierce (eds), *Rape in Antiquity: Sexual Violence in Greek and Roman Worlds*, London: Duckworth

Belsey, C (2001) 'Tarquin dispossessed: Expropriation and consent', in *The Rape of Lucrece* 52 *Shakespeare Quarterly* 315

Benveniste, E (1973) *Indo-European Language and Society*, London: Faber and Faber

Boorstin, D (1941) 'Tradition and method in legal history' 54 *Harvard Law Review* 424

Born, L (1933) 'Animate law in the Republic and the laws of Cicero' 64 *Transactions and Proceedings of the American Philological Association* 128

Bottomley, A (1994) 'Production of a text: *Hammond v Mitchell*' 2 *Feminist Legal Studies* 83

Briffault, R (1927) *The Mothers: A Study of the Origins of Sentiments and Institutions*, New York, NY: Johnson Reprint Co.

Bromley, L (1983) 'Lucrece's Re-creation' 34 *Shakespeare Quarterly* 200

Bryson, N (1989) 'Narratives of rape in the visual arts: Lucretia and the Sabine women' in S Tomaselli and R Porter (eds), *Rape: An Historical and Cultural inquiry*, Oxford: Basil Blackwell

Cicero (1930) *De Lege Agraria*, Loeb Classical Library, Cambridge, MA: Harvard University Press

Cicero (1949) *De Inventione*, Loeb Classical Library, Cambridge, MA: Harvard University Press

Cicero (1961a) *The Republic*, Loeb Classical Library, Cambridge, MA: Harvard University Press

Cicero (1961b) *Laws*, Loeb Classical Library, Cambridge, MA: Harvard University Press

Cicero (1961c) *De Domo*, Loeb Classical Library, Cambridge, MA: Harvard University Press

Cicero (1963) *De Oratore*, Loeb Classical Library, Cambridge, MA: Harvard University Press

Cicero (1966) *Pro Cluentio*, Loeb Classical Library, Cambridge, MA: Harvard University Press

Cicero (1975) *De Officiis*, Loeb Classical Library, Cambridge, MA: Harvard University Press

Conaghan, J (2006) 'Time to dream? Flexibility, families and the regulation of working time', in J Fudge and R Owen (eds), *Precarious Work: A Challenge to Legal Norms*, London: Hart Publications

Corbett, PE (1930) *The Roman Law of Marriage*, Oxford: Clarendon Press

Crook, JA (1967) *Law and Life of Rome*, London: Thames and Hudson

de Coulanges, F (1955) *The Ancient City*, New York, NY: Doubleday Anchor Books

de Zulueta, F (1957) 'The science of law', in C Bailey (ed), *The Legacy of Rome*, Oxford: Clarendon Press

Develin, R (1978) '*Provocatio* and *Plebiscites*' 31 *Mnemosyne* 45

Digest (1973) in SP Scott (ed), *The Civil Law*, Cincinnati: The Central Trust Co.

Dio Cassius (1961) *Roman History*, Loeb Classical Library, Cambridge, MA: Harvard University Press

Diodorus Siculus (1945) *Library of History*, Loeb Classical Library, Cambridge, MA: Harvard University Press

Dionysius of Halicarnassus (1960) *The Roman Antiquities*, Loeb Classical Library, Cambridge, MA: Harvard University Press

Diosdi, G (1970) *Ownership in Ancient and Pre-classical Roman Law*, Akademiai Kiado: Budapest

Dixon, S (2001) 'Rape in Roman law and myth', in *Reading Roman Women*, London: Duckworth

Donaldson, I (1982) *The Rapes of Lucretia*, Oxford: Clarendon Press

Douglas, H (2003) 'Prosecutions of Intimate Partner Violence in Queensland's Higher Courts', Paper presented at the annual workshop of the Gender and Law Group of ISA, University of Oxford

Dumézil, G (1996) *Archaic Roman Religion*, Baltimore, MD: Johns Hopkins University Press

Earl, D (1967) *The Moral and Political Tradition of Rome*, London: Thames and Hudson

Ernout, A and Meillet, A (1979) *Dictionaire Etymologique De La Langue Latine*, Paris: Editions Klincksieck

Ford, RT (1999) 'Law's territory (a history of jurisdiction)' 97 *Michigan Law Review* 843
Foucault, M (1980) 'Questions of geography', in C Gordon (ed), *Power/Knowledge*, London: Harvester Wheatsheaf
Foucault, M (1986) 'Space, knowledge and power', in P Rabinow (ed), *The Foucault Reader*, Harmondsworth: Penguin Books
Foucault, M (1986a) 'Of other spaces' 16 *Diacritics* 22
Fowler, WW (1911) *The Religious Experience of the Roman People*, London: Macmillan and Co
Fraccaro, P (1975) 'The history of Rome in the regal period' 47 *Journal of Roman Studies* 59
Gaius (1932) *Institutes*, in SP Scott (ed), *The Civil Law*, Cincinnati, OH: The Central Trust Company
Gardner, JF (1986) *Women in Roman Law & Society*, London: Croom Helm
Gellius, A (1927) *Attic Nights*, Loeb Classical Library, Cambridge, MA: Harvard University Press
Goodrich, P (1992) 'Critical legal studies in England: Prospective histories' 12 *Oxford Journal of Legal Studies* 195
Gordley, J (1994) 'The myths of the French Civil Code' 42 *American Journal of Comparative Law* 459
Gregory, D and Urry, J (1985) *Social Relations and Spatial Structures*, Basingstoke: Macmillan
Hallett, J (1984) *Fathers and Daughters in Roman Society*, Princeton, NJ: Princeton University Press
Henderson, MI (1975) '*Potestas Regia*' 47 *Journal of Roman Studies* 82
Irigaray, L (1993) *An Ethics of Sexual Difference*, London: The Athlone Press
Jay, N (1981) 'Gender and dichotomy' 7 *Feminist Studies* 38
Jed, S (1989) *Chaste Thinking: The Rape of Lucretia and the Birth of Humanism*, Bloomington: Indiana University Press
Jhering, R (1907) *Die Geist des römischen Rechts Auf den verschiedenen Stufen seiner Entwicklung*, Leipzig: Breitkopf & Hartel
Jolowicz, HF (1961) *Historical Introduction to the Study of Roman Law*, Cambridge: Cambridge University Press
Joplin, P (1990) 'Ritual work on human flesh: Livy's Lucretia and the Body Politique' 17 *Helios* 51
Joshel, S (1992) 'The body female and the body politic: Livy's Lucretia and Verginia' in A Richlin (ed), *Pornography and representation in Greece and Rome*, Oxford: Oxford University Press
Kahn, C (1997) 'The sexual politics of subjectivity in *Lucrece*', in *Roman Shakespeare: Warriors, Wounds and Women*, London: Routledge
Koumanouthis, S (1972) *Latin–Greek Dictionary*, Athens: Gregoris Publications
Krygier, M (1986) 'Law as tradition' 5 *Law and Philosophy* 237
Kunkel, W (1966) *An Introduction to Roman Legal and Constitutional History*, Oxford: Clarendon Press
Lacan, J (1994) *The Four Fundamental Concepts of Psycho-Analysis*, London: Penguin
Lacey, WK (1986) 'Patria *Potestas*', in B Rawson (ed), *The Family in Ancient Rome*, London: Croom Helm
Lee, AG (1953) 'Ovid's Lucretia' 22 (66) *Greece & Rome* 107
Lefebre, H (1995) *The Production of Space*, Oxford: Basil Blackwell
Livy (1948) *The History of Rome*, Loeb Classical Library, Cambridge, MA: Harvard University Press

Lucretius (1953) *De Rerum Natura*, Loeb Classical Library, Cambridge, MA: Harvard University Press

Martin, D (1996) 'The construction of the ancient family: Methodological considerations' 86 *The Journal of Roman Studies* 40

Massey, D (1992) 'Politics and space/time' 96 *New Left Review* 65

Momigliano, A (1969) 'The origin of the Roman Republic', in C Singleton (ed), *Interpretation: Theory and Practice*, Baltimore, MD: John Hopkins University Press

Mueller, HF (1998) 'Vita, pudicitia, libertas: Juno, gender, and religious politics in Valerius Maximus' 128 *Transactions of the American Philological Association* 221

Naffine, N (1990) *Law and the Sexes: Explorations in Feminist Jurisprudence*, Sydney: Allen & Unwin

Nevett, L (1997) 'Perceptions of domestic space in Roman Italy', in B Rawson and P Weaver (eds), *The Roman Family in Italy*, Oxford: Clarendon Press

Nicolet, C (1980) *The World of the Citizen in Republican Rome*, London: Batsford Academic & Educational Ltd

Nippel, W (1995) *Public Order in Ancient Rome*, Cambridge: Cambridge University Press

Ogilvie, RM (1965) *A Commentary on Livy*, Oxford: Clarendon Press

Orr, DG (1978) 'Roman domestic religion: The evidence of the household shrines' II.16.(2) *Aufstieg und Niedergang der Romischen Welt* 1557

Ovid (1931) *Fasti*, Loeb Classical Library, Cambridge, MA: Harvard University Press

Pais, E (1971) *Ancient Legends of Roman History*, New York, NY: Books for Libraries Press

Palmer, R (1970) *The Archaic Community of the Romans*, Cambridge: Cambridge University Press

Patterson, JR (1992) 'The City of Rome: From Republic to Empire' 82 *The Journal of Roman Studies* 186

Perrin, JW (1967) '*Legatus*, the lawyers and the terminology of power in Roman law' 11 *Studia Gratiana* 461

Philippides, SN (1983) 'Narrative strategies and ideology in Livy's "Rape of Lucretia"' 10 *Helios* 113

Picciotto, S (1984) 'Jurisdictional conflicts, international law and the international state system', in D Massey and J Allen (eds), *Geography Matters*, Cambridge: Cambridge University Press

Plutarch (1959) *Parallel Lives: Theseus and Romulus Lycurgus and Numa Solon and Publicola*, Loeb Classical Library, Cambridge, MA: Harvard University Press

Plutarch (1962) *Roman Questions*, Loeb Classical Library, Cambridge, MA: Harvard University Press

Pomeroy, S (1975) *Goddesses, Whores, Wives and Slaves*, New York, NY: Shocken Books

Pomeroy, S (1976) 'The relationship of the married woman to her blood relatives in Rome' 7 *Ancient Society* 215

Raaflaub, KA (1986) 'From protection and defense to offense and participation: Stages in the conflict of orders', in KA Raaflaub (ed), *Social Struggles in Archaic Rome*, Berkeley, CA: University of California Press

Radin, M (1923) 'Roman concepts of equality' 38 *Political Science Quarterly* 262

Rawson, B (1986) 'The Roman family', in B Rawson (ed), *The Family in Ancient Rome*, London: Croom Helm

Richlin, A (ed), *Pornography and Representation in Greece and Rome*, Oxford: Oxford University Press

Robinson, OF (1995) *The Criminal Law of Ancient Rome*, London: Duckworth

Rudolph, J (2000) 'Rape and resistance: Women and consent in Seventeenth Century English legal and political thought' 39 *The Journal of British Studies* 157

Saller, R (1984) '*Familia*, *domus* and the Roman conception of the family' 38 *Phoenix* 336
Saller, R (1991) 'Corporal punishment, authority, and obedience in the Roman household', in B Rawson (ed), *Marriage, Divorce, and Children in Ancient Rome*, Oxford: Clarendon Press
Saller, R (1994) *Patriarchy, Property and Death in the Roman Family*, Cambridge: Cambridge University Press
Saller, P (1999) 'Roman kinship: Structure and sentiment', in B Rawson and P Weaver (eds), *The Roman Family in Italy*, Oxford: Clarendon Press
Schiller, A (1978) *Roman Law: Mechanisms of Development*, The Hague: Mouton Publishers
Schulz, F (1963) *History of Roman Legal Science*, Oxford: Clarendon Press
Schulz, F (1967) *Principles of Roman Law*, Oxford: Clarendon Press
Scullard, HH (1981) *Festivals and Ceremonies of the Roman Republic*, London: Thames and Hudson
Shuger, D (1998) 'Castigating Livy: The rape of Lucretia and the old Arcadia' 51 *Renaissance Quarterly* 526
Sibley, D (1997) *Geographies of Exclusion*, London: Routledge
Sohm, R (1907) *The Institutes: A Textbook of the History and System of Roman Private Law*, Oxford: Clarendon Press
Soja, EW (1990) *Postmodern Geographies: The Reassertion of Space in Critical Theory*, London: Verso
St Augustine (1984) *City of God*, London: Penguin Books
Stein, P (1999) *Roman Law in European History*, Cambridge: Cambridge University Press
Strachan-Davidson, JL (1913) *Problems of the Roman Criminal Law*, Oxford: Clarendon Press
Thomas, Y (1992) 'The division of the sexes in Roman law', in P Pantel (ed), *A History of Women I From Ancient Goddesses to Christian Saints*, Cambridge, MA: Belknap Press
Thompson, DG (1949) *Studies in Ancient Greek Society: The Prehistoric Aegean*, New York, NY: Lawrence & Wishart
Thucydides (1959) *History of the Peloponnesian War*, The Loeb Classical Library Cambridge, MA: Harvard University Press
Treggiari, S (1991) *Roman Marriage*, Oxford: Clarendon Press
[Tables] 'The laws of the Twelve Tables' (1973), in SP Scott (ed), *The Civil Law*, Cincinnati: The Central Trust Company
Ullmann, W (1966) *Papst und König*, Salzburg: Verlag Anton Pustet
Ullmann, W (1975) *Law and Politics in the Middle Ages*, London: The Sources of History Limited
Varga, C (1978) 'Utopias of rationality in the development of the idea of codification' 55 *Revista Internationale di Filosofia del Diritto* 21
Verro, MT (1958) *On the Latin Language*, Loeb Classical Library, Cambridge, MA: Harvard University Press
Vasaly, A (1987) 'Personality and power: Livy's depiction of the Apii Claudii in the First Pentad' 117 *Transactions of the American Philological Association* 203
Virgil (1967) *Aeneid*, Loeb Classical Library, Cambridge, MA: Harvard University Press
Watson, A (1972) 'Roman private law and the *Leges Regiae*' 62 *Journal of Roman Studies* 100
Watson, A (1975) *Rome of the XII Tables Persons and Property*, Princeton, NJ: Princeton University Press
Wirszubski, C (1950) *Libertas as a Political Idea at Rome During the Late Republic and Early Principate*, Cambridge: Cambridge University Press

Part III

States

4 Guantanamo Bay, abandoned being and the constitution of jurisdiction

*Stewart Motha**

> [U]nder the [US] Government's theory, it is free to imprison Gherebi indefinitely... without acknowledging any judicial forum in which its actions may be challenged. Indeed, at oral argument, the government advised us that its position would be the same even if the claims were that it was engaging in acts of torture or that it was summarily executing the detainees.
>
> (*Gherebi v Bush and Rumsfeld* at 46)[1]

The detention of persons in Guantanamo Bay is potentially indefinite, contingent on the duration of the 'war on terror', a 'war without end'. There is mounting evidence that detainees are being tortured (for evidence of torture in Guantanamo Bay and Abu Ghraib Prison, Baghdad, see Hersh 2004a,b). The decision on whether the 'life' of a detainee in the 'camp' will be mediated by civil law is ostensibly determined by whether US Federal Courts have jurisdiction to grant the writ of *habeas corpus*.[2] This chapter considers the abject condition of the detainee as part of the complex relation between an 'emergency' or 'exception' determined by a sovereign at 'war', and the juridical structure of a 'life' mediated by law. In several *habeas corpus* cases brought on behalf of the detainees in Guantanamo Bay, this relation has been reduced to a question of jurisdiction.

* Earlier versions of this paper were presented at the Centre for Law and Society, Edinburgh Law School, January 2003; at the Law Culture and Humanities conference, Benjamin Cardozo Law School, New York, March 2003; and at the Critical Legal Conference, Westminster University, September 2004. I am grateful for the critical engagements with my arguments at each of those gatherings. Brenna Bhandar, Beverley Brown, Pablo Ghetti, Emilios Christodoulidis and Peter Fitzpatrick have made invaluable suggestions on previous drafts. Shaun McVeigh supplied several incisive suggestions that ultimately shaped an otherwise sprawling discussion. All errors are mine.

1 *Falen Gherebi v George Walker Bush and Donald H Rumsfeld* (2003) United States Courts of Appeals for the 9th Circuit, California, 18 December.

2 By 'life' in the 'camp', I am referring not only to detainees in Guantanamo Bay but also to persons held indefinitely without trial in other US military bases within the United States, and in Diego Garcia, and Bagram Airport, Kabul. The term 'life' connotes a being who is 'outside' political and juridical space, distinct, for instance, from a 'subject' whose life is mediated by right. The distinction is drawn from Agamben who explains this as the difference between *zoē* and *bios* (Agamben, 1998: 1).

By reviewing the *habeas corpus* cases,[3] I argue that it is the figure in the 'camp' – in Jean-Luc Nancy's (1993a) terms, 'abandoned being' – who marks the limits of the juridical and political order. I explore a number of ways in which the condition of the 'life' in the camp is fashioned by law's self-inscribed withdrawal in the face of the sovereign exception.

My argument is structured as follows. Consideration of decisions to grant the writ of *habeas corpus* reveal that courts are far more concerned with delimiting and affirming the province of sovereignty than securing the liberty of the subject. A court's decision on whether it has jurisdiction which is a precursor to granting the writ, first affirms a mode of 'governance' and 'governmentality' before deciding whether to admit the 'life' of the 'camp' into the juridical order. The 'form of life' in the camp is then always already exposed to being interpolated through governmental concerns – and is not merely rendered 'bare' when law accepts the imperative to withdraw in the face of the sovereign exception. Giving an account of the (legal) subject in the 'camp' who is at once inside/outside the juridical order thus follows from the courts' refusal to bring the detainee 'before the law'. This is why the theorisation of 'abandonment' is so essential to revealing the constitutive role of the inhabitant of the 'camp'. We will see that 'life' in the 'camp' is in fact saturated with political and juridical significance. 'Abandoned being', I will argue, reveals the constitution of jurisdiction.

My intention is also to problematise Giorgio Agamben's influential treatment of the relation between the sovereign decision on the exception which constitutes the juridical order and 'life' in the 'camp' (Agamben, 1998). For Agamben, the 'camp' marks the juridical paradigm of modernity, the *nomos* of the political space in which we now live (Agamben, 1998: 166, 174–75). The 'camp' localises a matrix of politics where the distinction between a factual decision on the 'enemy' ('*quaestio facti*') and the legality of detention in the camp ('*quaestio iuris*') become indistinguishable (Agamben, 1998: 170). Contrary to Agamben, I do not consider it possible for a 'form of life' to emerge which is not touched by governmental, biopolitical or exceptional manifestations of power. Agamben's anti-nomian stance seeks to constitute a 'form of life' which is 'wholly exhausted in bare life' (Agamben, 1998: 188). The distinction between 'bare life' and a 'political subject' would then cease to matter. It is not clear how such a life would be less exposed to the contingencies of biopolitical power – for he acknowledges that this 'life' continues to take the form of a 'biopolitical body' (Agamben, 1998). It may be that Agamben loads too many of his anti-nomian ambitions on the figure of 'bare life'. The fact remains that a subject-of-right is contingent on the complex relation between sovereignty and law. It is this relation that is disclosed in the concept of 'abandonment' outlined below.

3 In particular, *Rasul and Odah v Bush* 215 F. Supp. 2d 55 (DDC 2002); *Falen Gherebi v Bush* (2003a) (US District Court for the Central District of California, 13 May 2003); *Rasul v Bush* (Supreme Court of the United States, decided 28 June, 2004) (hereafter '*Rasul v Bush* (2004)'); and *Hamdi v Rumsfeld* (Supreme Court of the United States, decided 28 June, 2004) (hereafter *Hamdi v Rumsfeld* (2004)).

Jurisdiction and the indefinite 'War on Terror'

Around 600 detainees from 40 nations have been held without charge or trial at the US naval base in Guantanamo Bay since January 2002. The land on which the naval base is situated was leased to the United States by Cuba for the purpose of coaling and naval stations in 1903. The individuals labelled 'enemy combatants' were detained by the US military and security agencies in the course of 'military operations' commonly termed the 'War on Terror'. Following the 9 September 2001 attacks on the World Trade Center in New York City and the Pentagon in Washington, Congress authorised the President of the United States to use all 'appropriate force' against nations, organisations or persons who may have planned, authorised or committed the attacks.[4] The Authorisation for the use of force was also directed at nations, organisations or persons who might harbour terrorists or who may commit 'international terrorism' in the future. On 13 November 2001, the President of the United States as Commander in Chief of its Armed Forces issued a 'Military Order' authorising the 'Detention, Treatment, and Trial of Certain Non-Citizens in the War Against Terrorism'.[5] According to s 2 of this Military Order, an 'individual subject to this order' means 'any individual who is not a US citizen with respect to whom I [the President] determine from time to time in writing' that, *inter alia*, an individual is or was a member of Al Qaida, or the person aims to cause 'adverse effects' to US citizens, security, foreign policy or economy (s 2(1)). There is also a catch-all provision in the Military Order: an individual can be so detained if 'it is in the interests of the United States that such individual be subject to this order' (s 2(2)). Section 4 provides for a Military Commission to try such individuals. Such a Commission may punish such individuals with 'life imprisonment or death' (s 4(a)). The President also declares the limits of all 'other law'. According to s 7(b)(1) and (2), military tribunals shall have exclusive jurisdiction with respect to offences by the individual subject to an order.

This Military Order authorised the indefinite detention of persons in Guantanamo Bay. US citizens such as Hamdi and Padilla have also been detained without trial in military bases within the United States. A Military Commission has been established to try, and potentially order the execution of, persons captured during the 'War on Terror'. To challenge the legality of these detentions, lawyers acting on behalf of the detainees sought the writ of *habeas corpus* from US Federal Courts. The ancient writ is famously supposed to protect the liberty of the individual from the abuse of state power. Where a person is detained, so the mythic story goes, the state authorities can be compelled to produce the prisoner's body in court. But the story of the writ of *habeas corpus* is more complicated. In *The Jurisprudence of Emergency: Colonialism and the Rule of Law* (2003), Nasser Hussain provides a stunning demystification of the celebrated writ by arguing that:

> Whether in its origin as a facilitation of sovereign power or its subsequent and modern guise as a check on the executive, whether used to intern or to

4 Authorisation for Use of Military Force (AUMF), Pub. L No. 107–40, 115 Stat 224 (2001).

5 *Presidential Documents, Federal Register*, 16 November 2001, Vol. 66, No. 222: 57831–57836.

> free, habeas corpus is a mode of binding subjects to the law and to its economies of power.
>
> (Hussain, 2003: 70)

As Hussain emphasises: 'Capias enforces the writ (Latin: "that you take") by literally capturing the body and bringing it into the law' (Hussain, 2003: 69). As Hussain points out, this is an irony regarding the 'Writ of Liberty' (Blackstone's grand embellishment) that was realised with embarrassment by Edward Jenks: 'Whatever may have been its ultimate use, the writ of *Habeas Corpus* was originally intended not to get people out of prison but to put people in it' (Jenks, 1902: 65, cited in Hussain, 2003: 69). As we will see when we consider the *habeas corpus* cases in relation to Guantanamo Bay, it is the 'custodian' rather than the detainee who is ultimately brought before the law (see *Rasul v Bush* (2004) discussed below).

The availability of the writ to the detainees in Guantanamo Bay in fact consolidates the sovereign's power by determining where the sovereign's 'writ runs'. The province of law is determined by the extent of a court's 'jurisdiction', and which 'subject' will be governed by law. The relevant 'subject-of-law' over whom jurisdiction is ultimately asserted is not the detainee in the 'camp' but the 'official' who imprisons him. Moreover – and this reinforces the point about the writ facilitating sovereign power – the US courts remain heavily deferential to the exigencies of a sovereign at war when determining the extent of 'due process' available to the detainee. In what follows I will consider, through a discussion of the *habeas corpus* cases, how a particular kind of 'abandonment' in the 'camp' discloses the nature of the relationship between sovereignty and jurisdiction.

There are multiple approaches to conceptualising jurisdiction in the *habeas corpus* cases. The first approach, from the US Federal Court for the District of Columbia, is set out in *Rasul and Odah v Bush* (2002) (this decision dealt with multiple *habeas corpus* applications). *Rasul and Odah* treated jurisdiction as a concomitant of a state's sovereignty over 'territory'.[6] Sovereignty over a territory is delimited in time and space, and attributed to one sovereign. The courts of a state can have no jurisdiction over a territory unless the state also has formal sovereignty over that territory. Whether the United States has sovereignty over Guantanamo Bay is determined by the meaning given to the words 'ultimate sovereignty' in the 1903 Lease Agreement between the United States and Cuba in relation to Guantanamo Bay. According to the DC Federal Court's reading of the Lease Agreement in *Rasul and Odah*, Cuba retains 'ultimate sovereignty' and the United States has

6 *Rasul and Odah v Bush* 215 F. Supp. 2d 55 (DDC 2002), two applications heard together, was the first *habeas corpus* application to be brought on behalf of the Guantanamo detainees in a US Federal Court, the District Court for the District of Columbia. The first was for the writ of *habeas corpus* by two British and one Australian national. In the second, *Odah v United States*, 12 Kuwaiti nationals sought a permanent injunction prohibiting the government from refusing to allow them to meet with their families, be informed of the charges against them, consult with counsel of their choice and have access to impartial courts or tribunals. The US Government moved the court to dismiss both actions on jurisdictional grounds.

'jurisdiction and control'.[7] For the court in *Rasul and Odah*, a finite sovereignty over Guantanamo Bay, which cannot be divided, shared or qualified, is attached to the nation-state of Cuba. Thus the court concluded that jurisdiction does not extend to Guantanamo Bay and the writ of *habeas corpus* is not available.[8]

The approach of the Federal Court and Court of Appeals in *Rasul and Odah* transposes the question of jurisdiction into a question of sovereignty over territory. It is an approach that was ultimately retained in the Supreme Court decision in *Rasul* (2004)[9] – with the alteration that the territorial question of jurisdiction relates to the location of the custodians rather than to the location of the detainees (I will say more about the Supreme Court decisions shortly).

The second approach was developed by the majority decision in *Gherebi v Bush and Rumsfeld*.[10] Their approach is multifaceted. On the one hand, 'jurisdiction' is regarded as a notion which can exist without sovereignty. In a circular formulation, the majority argued that jurisdiction follows from the exclusivity of 'control and jurisdiction' exercised over a territory. On the other hand, the majority also tied jurisdiction to sovereignty. Unlike the earlier decisions in *Rasul and Odah* (2002), the majority in *Gherebi v Bush and Rumsfeld* found that the US exercises sovereignty over Guantanamo Bay.[11] The United States–Cuba Lease Agreement of 1903 in relation to Guantanamo Bay states that Cuba retains 'ultimate sovereignty'. The discussion of the concept of 'sovereignty' in *Gherebi* thus turned on the meaning of the term 'ultimate' rather than on 'sovereignty' as such. If 'ultimate' is the key 'modifier' of sovereignty in the Lease Agreement, as the majority put it, should it be construed as a 'temporal' or 'qualitative' modifier?[12] 'Ultimate sovereignty' in the 'temporal' sense would suggest that Cuba's sovereignty over Guantanamo Bay is a 'residual' interest, akin to a reversionary interest that substantively vests in Cuba once the United States 'abandons its physical and absolute control of the territory'.[13] The 'qualitative' meaning of 'ultimate' sovereignty connotes 'basic, fundamental or maximum' sovereignty.[14] The majority conclude that 'ultimate

7 *Rasul and Odah v Bush* 215 F. Supp. 2d 55 (DDC 2002) at 23.

8 In formulating the condition for granting the writ, the court in Rasul applied the Supreme Court decision in *Johnson v Eisentrager* 339 US 763 (1950). The Supreme Court in *Johnson* had held that, although aliens – whether friendly or enemy – may be extended the privilege of litigation when they are in the United States because their presence in the country implied protection, no such basis can be invoked when 'prisoners at no relevant time were within any territory over which the United States is sovereign, and the sentence for their offence, their capture, their trial and their punishment were all beyond the territorial jurisdiction of any court of the United States' (*Johnson v Eisentrager* 339 US 763 (1950) at 777–78, emphasis added). The District Court in *Rasul*, citing Johnson as authority, declared that a court was unable to extend the writ of *habeas corpus* to 'aliens held outside the sovereign territory of the United States' (*Rasul v Bush* (2004) at 72–73, emphasis added).

9 *Rasul v Bush* (2004).

10 *Falen Gherebi v George Walker Bush and Donald H Rumsfeld* US Courts of Appeals for the 9th Circuit, California, 18 December 2003) (hereafter *Gherebi*).

11 *Gherebi* at 14–24.

12 *Gherebi* at 25–26.

13 *Gherebi* at 26.

14 *Gherebi* at 26.

sovereignty' as used in the Lease 'can only mean temporal and not qualitative sovereignty':[15]

> Under the preferred construction of 'ultimate', the use of the term in the Lease establishes the *temporal* and *contingent* nature of Cuba's sovereignty, specifying that it comes into being only in the event that the United States *abandons* Guantanamo: in such case, Guantanamo reverts to Cuba and to Cuban sovereignty rather than being subject to some other actual or attempted disposition. Most important, under the *preferred temporal construction*, Cuba does not retain any *substantive sovereignty* during the term of the US *occupation*, with the result that, during such period, sovereignty vests in the United States.[16]

There are a variety of meanings attributed to sovereignty in the court's formulation. Sovereignty is at once divisible, temporal and contingent. It is capable of being divided and held by an 'occupying power'. Sovereignty is also capable of being abandoned or disavowed. The fact that the Lease refers to the '*continuance* of the ultimate sovereignty of the Republic of Cuba' is dealt with by treating the Lease as if it were a 'standard land disposition' where 'bundles of rights' are partitioned into present and future interests.[17] Thus what 'continues' as the 'ultimate sovereignty' of Cuba is sovereignty as a 'reversionary interest' which must await the discontinuance of the substantive sovereignty currently indefinitely vested in the United States. Notably, the court supports its conclusion by stating that the 'division or sharing of sovereignty is commonplace. Sovereignty is not an indivisible whole'.[18]

Gherebi v Bush and Rumsfeld demonstrates the extent to which the ambit of jurisdiction is heavily tied to the territorial, temporal and qualitative character of sovereignty. Jurisdiction, far from being enlivened by the indefinite deprivation of the liberty of individuals by US military authorities, is instead articulated as a function of the quality and character of sovereignty. Through the dubious analogy drawn between sovereignty and the temporal quality of a lease, the court turns the capacity of the United States to control territory as an 'occupying power' into the juridical basis for expanding the court's jurisdiction to the occupied territory. In this formulation, it is the construction of sovereignty as a divisible 'temporal interest' rather than the abject 'life' of the detainee that enlivens the court's jurisdiction. As we will see, this economy of sovereign power is more explicitly at stake in the way the Supreme Court dealt with the *habeas corpus* applications.

15 *Gherebi* at 26–27. The key source for this conclusion is the trusty *Black's Law Dictionary*, which defines 'ultimate' to mean: 'At last, finally, at the end. The last in the train of progression or sequence tended toward by all that precedes; arrived at as the last result; final'.

16 *Gherebi* at 29 (emphasis added).

17 *Gherebi* at 31.

18 *Gherebi* at 31.

On 28 June 2004, the Supreme Court of the United States in *Rasul v Bush* (2004), *Hamdi v Rumsfeld* (2004) and *Rumsfeld v Padilla* (2004)[19] decided appeals from the Federal District Court decisions. The issue to be decided in *Rasul* was whether US Federal Courts have jurisdiction to consider the legality of the detention of foreign nationals captured abroad and being held in the US naval base in Guantanamo Bay. The court decided this issue on the very narrow basis that Congress had granted Federal Courts jurisdiction in a statute[20] to hear applications for *habeas corpus* 'within their respective jurisdictions' by persons who claim to be 'in custody in violation of the Constitution or laws or treaties of the United States'. The question that emerged in interpreting the *habeas* statute was the meaning of 'within their respective jurisdictions'. The material question – a matter of statutory construction – was whether it was the 'custodian' or the 'detainee' who was required to be 'within the respective jurisdiction' of the Federal Court. The majority resolved this question on the basis that it was adequate for the 'custodian' of the prisoner to be within the court's jurisdiction. I will go on to argue this discloses that the determination of jurisdiction for the purposes of the *habeas* writ is a function of the court's regulation of government officials within an economy of governmental power in the sense described by Foucault (1991 [1978]).

Previous Supreme Court decisions in *Ahrens v Clark* (1948) and *Johnson v Eisentrager* (1950) had interpreted the *habeas* statute and its words 'within their respective jurisdictions' as requiring the petitioner's presence within the district court's 'territorial jurisdiction'.[21] This interpretation created a 'statutory gap' whereby, if the petitioner was not present within the court's territorial jurisdiction, the court would not be able to grant the writ. In *Rasul*, the majority elected to follow the authority of *Braden v 30th Judicial Circuit Court of Ky*[22] which held, contrary to *Ahrens*, that the prisoner's presence within the territorial jurisdiction is not necessary because the writ of *habeas corpus* 'does not act upon the prisoner who seeks relief, but upon the person who holds him in what is alleged to be unlawful custody'.[23] The 'custodian can be reached by service of process'. The writ of *habeas corpus*, according to this approach, governs the 'custodian' as a means of granting the relief sought by the prisoner. The person made subject to the law (of the court granting the writ) is not the detainee but the custodian. Indeed, if the status of being a 'subject' is dependent on the law applying to you – on life being mediated by law – the 'subject' here is not the detainee but the custodian. The implications of this formulation for the character of the *habeas* jurisdiction is significant. Is it the 'life' of the detainee that is being mediated by law, or rather is it the authority of the custodian that is being regulated? The answer to this question is quite significant

19 *Rasul v Bush* (2004); *Hamdi v Rumsfeld* (2004); *Rumsfeld v Padilla* (Supreme Court of the United States, decided 28 June, 2004) (hereafter '*Rumsfeld v Padilla*, 2004').

20 28 US.C §§ 2241(a), (c)(3).

21 *Rasul v Bush* (2004) at 8–11, esp 8.

22 *Braden v 30th Judicial Circuit Court of Ky* 410 US 484, 495 (1973).

23 *Braden* at 494–95; *Rasul v Bush* (2004) at 10.

because it discloses that *habeas corpus*, at least as it operates through the US Federal Statute 28 US.C § 2241, contrary to the laudatory claims made about the writ, is not the source of a 'subject' whose 'life' is mediated by right.

Is the 'life' of the detainee 'bare', in Giorgio Agamben's terms, until and unless the custodian of this 'life' is part of a system of governance that regulates the custodian's authority? Or instead, is the 'bare life' of the 'camp' caught in a network of power and governmentality elaborated by Foucault (1991 [1978]). In this latter scenario, it is not the archaic sovereign power over 'life and death', or the juridical status of being a 'subject-of-law' that matters but rather whether the law is made to appear (Foucault and Blanchot, 1987). In these *habeas corpus* cases, the law shows itself in order to regulate the custodian. It is a law called forth by the potential transgression of norms by government officials.[24]

The question of 'jurisdiction' at a time of 'war' complicates the matter even further. War marks the return of an archaic sovereign whose appearance makes the law withdraw. Schmitt's *Political Theology* (1985) and Agamben's *Homo Sacer* (1998) tell us that the sovereign exception in fact makes the law possible. I want to argue that it is precisely this dialectical movement of appearance and withdrawal of both law and sovereignty that we observe in the *habeas corpus* cases which have determined the jurisdiction of US Federal Courts in relation to persons detained at Guantanamo Bay and other military bases.

The Supreme Court in *Rasul*[25] answered the question of whether the Federal District Court's jurisdiction extended to Guantanamo Bay in the following way: the prisoners are in federal custody and alleging the violation of the laws of the United States. As no one disputes that the District Court has jurisdiction over the petitioners' custodians, the court held that '§ 2241 confers on the District Court jurisdiction to hear petitioners' *habeas corpus* challenges to the legality of their detention at the Guantanamo Bay naval base'.[26] While this is a welcome result, I would urge very strongly that it cannot be assumed that the prisoners are likely to have their detention reviewed by civil courts which will apply the normal measures demanded by due process. The law may be called forth, it may be coaxed to make a cameo appearance, but it will not hamper the sovereign at war. Thus an examination of the character of jurisdiction must also consider law's withdrawal in the face of the sovereign exception. The Supreme Court's lengthy and complex decision in *Hamdi* would sustain my contention.

Hamdi[27] involved the detention of a US citizen who was captured during military operations in Afghanistan. The question addressed by the court was

24 These are insights offered by Blanchot's discussion of Foucault (see Foucault and Blanchot, 1987). I cannot expand on this here – but in brief, the account Blanchot gives of the character of law in Foucault's thought is that of a 'limit' that must be transgressed in order to make the law appear. Law is a horizon, a limit that must be transgressed. The space of this limit is the place of law.

25 *Rasul v Bush* (2004).

26 *Rasul v Bush* (2004) at 15–16. This was the line of argument in the Court of Appeals decision in *Gherebi* – but the more complex issues of 'territorial jurisdiction' discussed in *Gherebi* were not canvassed in the Supreme Court decision in *Rasul*.

27 *Hamdi v Rumsfeld* (2004). The references below are to this judgement.

whether the Executive had the authority to detain citizens who were 'enemy combatants'. The court agreed that Congress had authorised Hamdi's detention under its Authorisation for Use of Military Force (AUMF), granted to the President.[28] The court confirmed that Hamdi was validly detained under this authorisation:

> We conclude that detention of individuals falling into the limited category we are considering, for the duration of the particular conflict in which they were captured, is so fundamental and accepted an incident of war as to be an exercise of the 'necessary and appropriate force' Congress has authorised the President to use.[29]

The capture of lawful and 'unlawful combatants' is an important incident of war. Detention is fundamental to waging war and thus falls within the AUMF as 'necessary and appropriate force'.[30] Can detention be 'indefinite' or 'perpetual'? The court recognised that the 'War on Terror' was 'unconventional' and may be prosecuted for several generations.[31] But indefinite detention for 'interrogation' is not authorised by AUMF.[32] However – and this is the key element that will impact on the future judicial assessment of detention in Guantanamo – the AUMF is interpreted as including the 'authority to detain for the duration of the relevant conflict, and this is based on long-standing law-of-war principles'.[33] The court recognised that the conflict was ongoing in Afghanistan. To the extent that the Executive claims to be prosecuting a 'war' that may be indefinite, individuals may be detained for the duration of that conflict. Detention for the duration of the conflict is only permissible once it is established that the detainee is in fact an 'enemy combatant' – 'whether this is established by concession or by some other process that verifies this fact with sufficient certainty seems beside the point'.[34] This criteria must be viewed in light of the ample evidence that torture is used as a means of extracting intelligence and confessions in Guantanamo and Iraq (see Hersh, 2004a,b).

In relation to the duration of detention, Hamdi contended that Congress had not authorised indefinite detention. The Geneva Convention requires that those detained be released and repatriated on the cessation of hostilities.[35] The court recognised that the 'War on Terror' underpinned national security in ways that were 'broad and malleable'.[36] Demonstrating its deference to government concerns,

28 AUMF, Pub. L No. 107–40, 115 Stat 224 (2001).
29 *Hamdi* at 10.
30 *Hamdi* at 12.
31 *Hamdi* at 12–13.
32 *Hamdi* at 13.
33 *Hamdi* at 13.
34 *Hamdi* at 16.
35 Article 118 Geneva Convention III Relative to the Treatment of Prisoners of War, 12 August 1949 [1955] 6 UST 3316, 3406, TIAS No. 3364.
36 *Hamdi* at 12.

it pointed out that the current conflict was unconventional and was not likely to end with a formal ceasefire.[37] The court recognised that the government's consistent position was that this 'unconventional war' may not be 'won for two generations'.[38] Hamdi's detention could thus last for the rest of his life. As long as the United States is engaged in active combat in Afghanistan, detention is recognised to be part of the 'necessary and appropriate force' authorised by Congress.[39] The exception, as far as it concerns Hamdi's life, has become the norm.

If Hamdi is entitled to 'due process' while he is detained under the AUMF, what should this involve? In deciding this, the court balances Hamdi's 'private interest' to liberty with the 'governmental interest' of ensuring that the enemy does not return to the battlefield (the reasoning now slipping back to the scenario of a 'conventional' war).[40] The court recognised that strategic matters in 'warmaking' were in the hands of the Executive. In arriving at what it thought the content of due process ought to be, the court drew particular attention to the fact that Hamdi had the 'privilege' of American citizenship.[41] With these elements in mind – particularly that the government was prosecuting ongoing military operations and that Hamdi was a citizen – the court set out the following elements of due process:

- A 'citizen-detainee seeking to challenge his classification as an enemy combatant must receive notice of the factual basis for his classification, and a fair opportunity to rebut the Government's factual assertions before a neutral decision-maker'.[42]
- A 'properly constituted military tribunal' could meet this requirement of a neutral decision-maker.[43]
- Aside from the first core element of knowing the factual basis of detention in a timely fashion, 'enemy-combatant' proceedings can be tailored to alleviate the potential to burden the Executive at a time of military conflict.
- Hearsay may have to be accepted as the most reliable form of evidence in proceedings that determine the factual basis of detention.[44]
- The Constitution will not be offended by a presumption in favour of the government's evidence – that is, once the government puts forward its evidence, the onus will shift to the alleged 'enemy combatant' to prove that they are not.[45]
- Initial capture in the battlefield will not require this extent of due process. It is only when a determination is made to *continue* to hold the person who has been seized that the due process requirements cut in (original emphasis).[46]

37 *Hamdi* at 12.
38 *Hamdi* at 12.
39 *Hamdi* at 14.
40 *Hamdi* at 17.
41 *Hamdi* at 25.
42 *Hamdi* at 28.
43 *Hamdi* at 31.
44 *Hamdi* at 27.
45 *Hamdi* at 27.
46 *Hamdi* at 27–28.

Will it be necessary for such a 'decision' to 'continue to detain' to be taken before review by an independent tribunal is available? This is an open question yet to be determined by Federal Courts.

- The court emphasises, several times, that it is dealing here with the *citizen's* core right to challenge the government's case.[47]

Although *Rasul v Bush*[48] extends access to US courts to citizens and aliens, what this actually amounts to for the non-citizen detainees at Guantanamo Bay is far from certain. The detainees in Guantanamo Bay will now have the right to ask a District Court to grant the writ of *habeas corpus*, and thus review the decisions and procedures of the Military Commissions in Guantanamo Bay. But it remains uncertain what 'due process' concessions will be made to those whom the government insists are 'unlawful combatants'. The distinction between 'lawful/unlawful combatants' and 'enemy combatants' has not been determined. The Military Commissions which will now consider the factual basis of detention will also determine the nature and status of the prisoner. Jurisdiction of the Federal District Courts remains territorially specific and the detention of (un)lawful combatants will continue for the duration of a conflict which the court in *Hamdi* acknowledged may be for the rest of Hamdi's life (two generations).

The decisions in *Rasul*[49] and *Hamdi*[50] demonstrate that the *habeas* jurisdiction is not a function of law's capacity to intervene to guarantee that an individual has not been illegally deprived of their liberty. Rather, jurisdiction is enlivened by the court's capacity to reach the government official. Once jurisdiction is established, it is 'governmental' imperatives such as a concern not to hamper the sovereign at war or preventing the 'enemy's' return to the battlefield that are balanced with the detainee's 'private' right to liberty. The content of due process is contingent on a governmental calculation. The decision in *Hamdi* also disclosed how the governmental concern to ensure neutral decision-making does not amount to determination of the factual basis of detention by civil tribunals. 'Military tribunals' are adequate to determine the factual basis of potentially indefinite detention. The task now is to explain how the sovereign exigencies at a time of emergency or war come to so heavily dominate whether 'life' is mediated by civil law. What is the relationship between sovereignty and jurisdiction disclosed in these cases?

In discussing the cases, I have identified the various instances where 'governmental' concerns and deference to sovereign power impact on the judicial determination of jurisdiction. In what follows, I will consider what the 'life' abandoned beyond the calculations of civil law can tell us about the constitution of jurisdiction. Is the 'life' indefinitely abandoned in the camp a figure who marks

47 *Hamdi* at 24, 25, 26, 30.
48 *Rasul v Bush* (2004) at 12–13.
49 *Rasul v Bush* (2004).
50 *Hamdi v Rumsfeld* (2004).

the 'permanent exception' in which we all live, or is it rather a sacrificial figure in the economy of sovereign distributions? I will argue that the figure abandoned in the camp does not mark the arrival of a 'permanent state of exception'. Rather, as we observed through Hussain's claims about the writ of *habeas corpus*, it is law's deference to the economy of sovereignty, and its capacity to appear and withdraw within a governmental mode of power, that explains the relation between sovereignty and law in the context of indefinite detention.

In making this argument, I will invoke Agamben's (1998) seminal work on the juridical structure of the 'camp'. According to Agamben's discussion of the juridical structure of the concentration camp, the 'camp' is not an anomaly of the past, but 'the hidden matrix and *nomos* of the political space in which we are still living' (1998: 166). I will distinguish Guantanamo Bay from the indistinction between 'fact' and 'right' which Agamben asserts is central to the 'permanent state of exception' marked by the 'camp': 'the camp is a hybrid of law and fact in which the two terms have become indistinguishable' (1998: 170). The modest contention confirmed by my analysis is that the judiciary cannot be exempted from responsibility for the ongoing detention and abject condition of the detainee. To characterise indefinite detention in Guantanamo Bay as a permanent state of exception where fact has collapsed into right too readily absolves the judiciary and the US Congress of responsibility (recall the AUMF and its central role in the court's reasoning in *Hamdi*).[51]

Law's exception or exception as law?

Is 'abandonment' in the 'camp' a condition where 'life' is utterly bereft of mediation by law? How are we to decide whether indefinite detention in the 'camp' at Guantanamo Bay is a juridical event where the question of fact and the question of right have become indistinguishable? Engaging with Agamben (1998) and one of his key antecedents, Carl Schmitt, will help us to address this question. The distinct contribution made by Agamben for the study of modern power and sovereignty is to bring Schmitt's thought on the sovereign exception to bear on Foucault's genealogy of modern power and characterisation of 'biopolitics' (see Gregory, 2004: 62–63, 282–83, n 43). For Agamben, the decision to 'abandon' life, to place it beyond the calculations of law, is the decision on the exception which constitutes the law (Agamben, 1998: 18). The 'relation of exception' involves the 'inclusive-exclusion' of the 'life' which is 'taken outside' the 'normal juridical order' (1998: 170). The question of whether a person is inside or outside the law is not only a question of law's 'application' but also a more complex case of being 'abandoned', 'inclusively excluded' by the law. For Agamben, it is not the decision to 'apply' the law but the decision to 'abandon' life that constitutes the juridical order: '*The originary relation of law to life is not application but Abandonment*' (Agamben, 1998: 29, original emphasis).

51 *Hamdi v Rumsfeld* (2004).

As Agamben puts it, Foucault attempts to de-emphasise the questions 'What legitimates power?' and 'What is the state?' (Agamben, 1998: 5). But if this theoretical privileging of sovereignty is removed, what explains the point of intersection between 'techniques of individualization' and 'totalizing procedures' (1998: 6)? Agamben attempts to address the nature of power as it is manifested at the point of intersection between 'juridico-institutional' and 'biopolitical' models of power (1998: 6). Before moving to consider whether the 'original activity of sovereign power is the production of the biopolitical body' (1998: 6) and its implications for understanding the relationship between law and its exception, I wish to briefly consider Carl Schmitt's thought on the exception. The 'exception' – its complex position inside/outside the juridical order – is central to attempts by courts to position the actions of the 'sovereign at war' beyond the purview of law. For instance, in cases like *Gherebi*[52] and *Hamdi*,[53] the US Government relied on the 'emergency' and 'state of war' as the grounds for claiming that the judicial branch of government could not interfere with the actions of the 'sovereign at war'. Although the question of jurisdiction has been 'territorialised' – that is, jurisdiction is determined on the basis of whether the custodian is within the 'territorial' jurisdiction of a court – the US Government's rationalisation for 'indefinite' detention, and the possibility of the death penalty being administered by officials who are part of the Executive arm of government, continues to rely on the exceptionality of war asserted by the sovereign and acknowledged by the courts.

Let us look more closely at the sovereign exception. Not every emergency or sovereign decree is necessarily an exception. As Carl Schmitt puts it in *Political Theology* (1985), an 'exception is different from anarchy and chaos, order in the juristic sense still prevails even if it is not of the ordinary kind' (Schmitt, 1985: 12). Not only does order in the juristic sense prevail but also the potential for the exception can be prefigured or anticipated by the law that recedes. This is evidenced by the possibility of such a 'withdrawal': 'the legal system itself can anticipate the exception and can "suspend itself" ' (1985: 14). Indeed, this is assumed by liberal constitutional models that attempt to regulate the exception by enumerating the conditions or criteria by which law would suspend itself (1985: 14; see also Schmitt 2004). However, this capacity of law to suspend itself troubles Schmitt, who asks (without providing any clear response): 'From where does law obtain this force, and how is it logically possible that a norm is valid except for one concrete case that it cannot factually determine in any definitive manner?' (1985: 14). The fact or instance of the exception, according to this account, cannot be determined by law. However, law can anticipate the exception and suspend itself or withdraw. The juridical order is (always already) divided by law's potential to withdraw and the sovereign's capacity to declare an exception.

52 *Falen Gherebi v Bush* (2003a) (US District Court for the Central District of California, 13 May 2003).
53 *Hamdi v Rumsfeld* (2004).

A concrete treatment of the sovereign exception can be observed in Schmitt's discourse on the decision on the 'political' developed in *The Concept of the Political* (Schmitt, 1996). This discourse is reflected in the judicial determinations on both sides of the Atlantic which I will shortly discuss. According to Schmitt, the 'specific political distinction to which political actions and motives can be reduced is that between friend and enemy' (1996: 26). The 'enemy', is the limit figure of the political for Schmitt. The enemy is:

> … the other, the stranger; and it is sufficient for his nature that he is, in a specially intense way, existentially something different, an alien, so that in the extreme case conflicts with him are possible. These can neither be decided by a previously determined general norm nor by the judgment of a disinterested and therefore neutral third party.
>
> (1996: 27)

The extreme case Schmitt is referring to is war – for a world in which 'war' is eliminated is, for Schmitt, a world without politics (1996: 35). The centrality of the figure of the enemy is expressed thus:

> Words such as state, republic, society, class, as well as sovereignty, constitutional state, absolutism, dictatorship, economic planning, neutral or total state, and so on, are incomprehensible if one does not know exactly who is to be affected, combated, refuted, or negated by such a term.
>
> (1996: 31)

The principal authority discussed in the US *habeas corpus* cases in relation to the detainees at Guantanamo Bay, *Johnson v Eisentrager*,[54] reflects Schmitt's assertions. Justice Jackson, who delivered the opinion of the majority, stated:

> Citizenship as a head of jurisdiction and a ground of protection was old when Paul invoked it in his appeal to Caesar. The years have not destroyed or diminished the importance of citizenship nor have they sapped the vitality of a citizen's claims upon his government for protection.[55]

Time has not dimmed the significance of membership in a particular political community. The UK Court of Appeal has recently confirmed that the character of being a subject of law is a direct function of nationality: 'In short, the nationality of an individual is his quality of being a subject of a certain state. In historical terms, the concept of nationality has its origins in the oath of allegiance owed by the subject to his king.'[56] The nationality centred qualifier for being a subject of

54 *Johnson v Eisentrager* 339 US 763 (1950).

55 *Johnson v Eisentrager* 339 US 763 (1950) at 769.

56 *A v Secretary of State for the Home Department* (2002), para 112. This proposition was not endorsed by the House of Lords in *A v Secretary of State for the Home Department* [2005] 2 AC 68.

law would not be all that surprising if it were not for the rhetoric of universal human rights that is propounded by the courts and governments of the United Kingdom, Europe and the United States. The subject-of-rights is universal, a concomitant of the triumph of liberal democracy (see Fukuyama, 1992). But being a subject whose life is mediated by law is conditioned on being a member of a particular 'nation' (a point made long ago by Hannah Arendt (1958: Chapter 9)). It is within the limit of being included as a member of a 'nation', and thus within law's jurisdiction, that the sovereign excess is apparently checked. But, as we observed in *Hamdi*,[57] the 'enemy' is now also 'within'. Citizenship is no guarantee of a life mediated by civil law. Crucially, it is the withdrawal of legal protections that creates the appearance of an indistinction between 'fact' and 'right'. The exception is a factual decision of which law is cognisant. The 'indistinction' between fact and right proposed by Agamben seems to turn law's suspension – indeed, its self-authored withdrawal – into a complete disappearance: 'a permanent state of exception'.

We have now considered the nature of the sovereign limit, the character of the exception and the manner in which sovereignty and law mark the 'limit' of the juridical order. But what of the 'subject' abandoned in the 'camp'? The detainee in the camp is the figure that is compelled to occupy the limit. Indeed, it is the question of whether life at the limit will be mediated by civil law which gives rise to many of the debates about the relationship between sovereignty and law. I shall now turn to examine the role of 'abandoned being' in the constitution of jurisdiction.

'Abandoned being' and the constitution of jurisdiction

For Agamben, the 'life' exposed to a sovereign exclusion and thereby included in political calculations is *homo sacer*, or 'bare life' (Agamben, 1998: 85). This is the life that can be 'killed with impunity' but cannot be sacrificed (1998: 81–82). That is, 'bare life' is beyond the calculations of profane and divine law (1998: 72, 82–83). Though law is not utterly absent, its presence – if this formulation can be strained – is as an absence. The figure of 'bare life' discloses the character of law when law is in a state of privation. Recall Schmitt's query, 'With what force does the law withdraw in the face of the exception?' (1985: 14). There is a 'potentiality' in law to prevent itself from becoming actualised – its 'im-potentiality', as Agamben calls it in his collection of essays *Potentialities* (1999: 177–84). This im-potentiality corresponds to the *force* which enables law to withdraw in the face of the exception. *Homo sacer*, or 'bare life', is thus the figure that discloses law's self-privation or im-potentiality. The question is whether the detainee, a figure whose incarceration is based on the assertions of a sovereign at war, and is in any event captured within a sovereign economy of power where detention may be indefinite, is a 'bare life' produced by law's self-inflicted privation. To address this question, we must consider what Agamben calls the 'relation of exception'.

57 *Hamdi v Rumsfeld* (2004).

The 'relation of exception' is the core insight of Agamben's theory on the structure of sovereignty, and the constitution of the juridical and political order. The relation of exception demonstrates the potentiality of law to maintain itself as an absence:

> If the exception is the structure of sovereignty, then sovereignty is not an exclusive political concept, an exclusive juridical category, a power external to law (Schmitt), or the supreme rule of the juridical order (Hans Kelsen): it is the originary structure in which law refers to life and includes it in itself by suspending it. Taking Jean-Luc Nancy's suggestion we shall give the name *ban*... to this potentiality (in the proper sense of the Aristotelian *dynamis*, which is also always *dynamis me energein*, the potentiality not to pass into actuality) of the law to maintain itself in its own privation, to apply in no longer applying.
>
> (Agamben, 1998: 28)

What is useful for my purposes (and Butler, 2004; and Gregory, 2004 have made similar use of Agamben) is that the figure of *homo sacer* is a symbol of the irresolution of the 'limit' between sovereignty and law. It is a figure through which the 'limit' can be understood as a relation – the relation of 'inclusive exclusion'. It is in this way that the detainee in the 'camp', the 'unlawful combatant' captured during the indefinite 'War on Terror', can be regarded as inhabiting a zone of indistinction inside and outside the calculations of the sovereign and the juridical order. It is *law* that refers to life and suspends its juridical and political status as a bearer of rights in Agamben's formulation of the structure of the 'ban'. As we have seen time and again now, law has the 'force' to engage in a withdrawal. It has the capacity to be cognisant of the governmental imperatives of a sovereign at war. For instance, in *Hamdi* (2004), we observed that the Supreme Court was more than willing to be cognisant of the 'exception' – the fact that the Executive was prosecuting a war, and that any intervention made by the judicial branch of government must not overly hinder the exigencies of the 'War on Terror'. The formulation of watered-down 'due process' reflects law's self-privation in the face of the exception. The limit between sovereignty and law is thus wrought through the positioning and treatment of the life of the 'enemy combatant'. The 'enemy combatant' whose life is differentially mediated by civil law marks the 'limit' of jurisdiction. This argument can be developed further by considering Nancy's conception of 'abandoned being'.

The figure of 'abandoned' life harbours the antinomies of sovereignty and law. The etymological root of 'abandon' is *bandon* (*a-bandon*) – and *bandon* means 'jurisdiction and control' (OED). To be abandoned is to be taken 'beyond', cast 'outside' jurisdiction. But to be abandoned is also to be free from constraint or convention, to relinquish to the control of another, or to desert – that is, to leave behind or leave without help. To abandon, then, is to be relieved of certain modes of control and protection. Another way of putting it is to say that abandonment involves being banished from a particular jurisdiction. But to be cast outside a certain order is in another sense to be subject to an order. Abandonment is a point of ambivalent inter-relation that takes the form of an inclusive-exclusion which Agamben has explored in *Homo Sacer* (1998: 28–29). This is why abandonment cannot be conceived as an instance of absolute sovereignty, or as the condition of a being entirely unmediated by law. As Agamben argues, it is not possible to say whether abandoned being is inside or outside the juridical order. The 'limit' of law is fashioned on the body (that may not be) brought before it. This is what qualifies abandoned being as the figure who lies at the foundation of the political and the juridical:

> The banishment of sacred life is the sovereign *nomos* that conditions every rule, the originary spatialization that governs and makes possible every localisation and every territorialization.
>
> (1998: 111)

Abandoned life thus lies at the limit-point of jurisdiction. Thus the courts administering the 'rule of law' of a particular political community cannot exempt themselves from responsibility for the figure of the abandoned detainee because the detainees' abandonment by judicial decision defines the limits of the 'rule of law'. There is nothing more proximate to 'jurisdiction' than the figure 'abandoned' in the camp. Let me develop this assertion of a link between 'abandonment' and the limits of jurisdiction.

To be abandoned from law is (as we have seen in the cases examined above) also to be abandoned *by law*. That is, the condition of a life 'unmediated' by civilian courts is a function of variable judicial constructions of the notions of 'territorial jurisdiction', 'ultimate sovereignty', 'within jurisdiction' and 'jurisdiction and control' (these are the determinants of jurisdiction in the *habeas* cases examined above). But to be abandoned by law, understood through Nancy's extensive exploration of the question, is to be abandoned to a law: 'one always abandons to a law' (Nancy, 1993b: 44). But what is this *law* that one abandons to? In his essay 'Abandoned Being', Nancy names 'sovereignty' as this 'other law':

> The origin of 'abandonment' is a putting at *bandon*. *Bandon* (*bandum*, *band*, *bannen*) is an order, a prescription, a decree, a permission, and the power that holds these freely at its disposal. To *abandon* is to remit, entrust, or turn over to such a sovereign power, and to remit, entrust, or turn over to its *ban*, that is, to its proclaiming, to its convening, and to its sentence.
>
> (1993b: 44)

To abandon to the law of a sovereign power is also to abandon to the law of a community. That is, to be abandoned is not to be utterly 'bare', entirely alone at the mercy of a 'singular' sovereign. To be abandoned is to be given over, to be remitted and entrusted by an authority with the force and power to perform this act. What we see in the *habeas corpus* cases is that the decision on jurisdiction and the determination of the content of due process is the event of this 'abandonment'. The limits of jurisdiction are wrought on the body of 'abandoned being'. Abandonment constitutes the legal order:

> Turned over to the absolute of the law, the banished one is thereby abandoned completely outside its jurisdiction. The law of abandonment requires that the law be applied through its withdrawal. The law of abandonment is the other of the law, which constitutes the law.
>
> Abandoned being finds itself deserted to the degree that it finds itself remitted, entrusted or thrown to this law that constitutes the law, this other and same, to this *other side of all law that borders and upholds a legal universe*: an absolute, solemn order, which prescribes nothing but abandonment. Being is not entrusted to a cause, to a motor, to a principle; it is not left to its own substance, or even to its own subsistence. It is-in abandonment.
>
> (Nancy, 1993b: 44, emphasis added)

The abandonment of being produces the law. It is in this way that the abandoned subject is before the law (and the political) in the starkest possible way. It is not possible to determine whether the condition of abandonment is one of fact or right. It is always already both. Fact and right in relation to the 'life' of the 'camp' thus do not occupy a zone of indistinction, as Agamben has claimed. Rather, 'abandoned being' discloses the reciprocal constitution of fact and right – a process that produces the abject 'life' of the 'camp'.

Conclusion

The detainees being held at the US Naval Base in Guantanamo Bay bear the sovereign *ban* of a neo-imperial nation-state. Though they have now been given access to US courts, their detention will be subject to the exigencies of a war that may be 'without end'. Such an illimitable sovereign power, I have argued, manifests the 'im-potentiality' of law. The courts, by varied and contradictory pronouncements on the limits of jurisdiction have placed 'enemy combatants' at the mercy of diminished requirements of 'due process'. In the face of what is claimed to be an illimitable sovereign war, the courts are indeed in a state of 'withdrawal' anticipated by Schmitt. This withdrawal paradoxically delimits the plenitude of the illimitable sovereign by enunciating the sovereign event.

A different approach to the question of jurisdiction must seek to overcome the governmental concerns which have featured so heavily in the courts' deferential enunciation of jurisdiction. The decision on jurisdiction, including one that is cognisant of governmental concerns, inevitably contains an account of the (legal) subject. The constitutive centrality of the 'abandoned' subject to the over-heralded triumph of democracy and the 'rule of law' offers another point of entry to a critical understanding of jurisdiction. Decisions on jurisdiction must confront the fact that the juridical and political order is constituted through the abandonment of the (legal) subject refused entry by the law.

The discussion of the *habeas corpus* cases in this chapter should provoke a wider enquiry. 'Abandoned being' marks the limit-point of a juridical order and political community that celebrates the triumph of liberal democratic values and the 'rule of law' (see generally Fukuyama, 1992; Ignatieff, 2003a, b). The person 'abandoned' in the camp is emblematic of the ever-proliferating 'enemies' who must be contained and, if necessary, eliminated in order to sustain 'democracy' and the 'rule of law'. If 'abandonment' in the 'camp' has now become a condition-precedent to securing 'democracy' and the 'rule of law', then 'abandoned being' is a figure that should inform and inspire critical engagements with the character of 'democracy' and the 'rule of law' as they are currently taking shape in a neo-imperial era.

Bibliography

Agamben, G (1998) *Homo Sacer: Sovereign Power and Bare Life*, trans Daniel Heller-Roazen, Stanford, CA: Stanford University Press

Agamben, G (1999) *Potentialities: Collected Essays in Philosophy*, Stanford, CA: Stanford University Press

Arendt, H (1958) *The Origins of Totalitarianism*, San Diego, CA: Harcourt Brace and Co

Arendt, H (1973) *On Revolution*, Harmondsworth: Penguin

Bartelson, J (1995) *A Genealogy of Sovereignty*, Cambridge: Cambridge University Press

Bataille, G (1993) *The Accursed Share: An Essay on General Economy, Volume III, Sovereignty*, trans Robert Hurley, New York, NY: Zone Books

Bauman, Z (2002) 'Reconnaissance wars of the planetary frontierland' 19(4) *Theory, Culture, Society* 81

Benjamin, W (1968) 'Theses on the philosophy of history', in *Illuminations*, London: Pimlico

Bennett, H (1930) 'Sacer esto' lxi *Transactions of the American Philological Association* 5

Bobbitt, P (2002) *The Shield of Achilles: War, Peace and the Course of History*, London: Penguin

Bodin, J (1992) *On Sovereignty: Four Chapters from The Six Books of the Commonwealth*, Cambridge: Cambridge University Press

Bush, George W (2002) *National Security Strategy of the United States of America*, Washington, DC: White House

Butler, J (1997) *The Psychic Life of Power: Theories of Subjection*, Stanford, CA: Stanford University Press

Butler, J (2004) *Precarious Life: The Powers of Mourning and Violence*, London: Verso

Dallmayr, F (2002) 'Lessons of September 11' 19(4) *Theory, Culture, Society* 137

Derrida, J (2002) 'Force of law: The "mystical foundation of authority" ', in Gil Anidjar (ed), *Acts of Religion*, trans Mary Quaintance, London: Routledge

Derrida, J (2003a) *Without Alibi*, trans Peggy Kamuf, Stanford, CA: Stanford University Press

Fitzpatrick, P (2001) *Modernism and the Grounds of Law*, Cambridge: Cambridge University Press

Fitzpatrick, P (2003) ' "Gods Would be Needed… ": American Empire and the Rule of International Law' 16 *Leiden Journal of International Law* 429

Foucault, M (1977) 'Preface to Transgression', in *Language, Counter-Memory, Practice: Selected Essays and Interviews*, trans Donald Bouchard and Sherry Simon, Ithaca, NY: Cornell University Press

Foucault, M (1991 [1978]) 'Governmentality', in P Burchell, C Gordon and P Miller (eds), *The Foucault Effect: Studies in Governmentality*, London: Harvester Wheatsheaf

Foucault, M (1984) *The History of Sexuality, Vol. I*, in Paul Rabinow (ed), *The Foucault Reader*, Harmondsworth: Penguin

Foucault, M (1997) 'Truth and Juridical Forms', in James Faubion (ed), *Essential Works of Foucault 1954–1984, Vol. III*, trans Robert Hurley *et al.*, New York, NY: New Press

Foucault, M (2003) *'Society Must be Defended': Lectures at the Collège de France: 1975–1976*, trans David Macey, New York, NY: Picador

Foucault, M and Blanchot, M (1987) *Foucault/Blanchot*, trans Brian Massumi and Jeffrey Mehlman, New York, NY: Zone Books

Fowler, W Warde (1920) *Roman Essays and Interpretations*, Oxford: Clarendon Press

Fukuyama, F (1992) *The End of History and the Last Man*, New York, NY: Free Press

Gordon, C (1997) 'Introduction', in James Faubion (ed), *Essential Works of Foucault 1954–1984, Vol. III*, New York, NY: New Press

Gregory, D (2004) *The Colonial Present: Afghanistan, Palestine, Iraq*, Oxford: Blackwell

Hardt, M and Negri, A (2000), *Empire*, Cambridge, MA: Harvard University Press

Hersh, S (2004a) 'The gray zone', *The New Yorker*, 24 May

Hersh, S (2004b) 'Rumsfeld's Dirty War on Terror', *The Guardian*, 13 September, pp. 2–4

Hussain, N (2003) *The Jurisprudence of Emergency: Colonialism and the Rule of Law*, Ann Arbor, MI: University of Michigan Press

Ignatieff, M (2003a), 'The burden', *New York Times Magazine*, 5 January

Ignatieff, M (2003b), *Empire Lite: Nation-Building in Bosnia, Kosovo and Afghanistan*, Toronto: Penguin

Jenks, E (1902) 'The story of *habeas corpus*' 18 *Law Quarterly Review* 65

Lefort, C (1988) *Democracy and Political Theory*, trans David Macey, Oxford: Polity Press

Loughlin, M (2003) 'Ten tenets of sovereignty', in Neil Walker (ed), *Sovereignty in Transition*, Oxford: Hart Publishing

Motha, S (2002) 'The Sovereign Event in a Nation's Law' 13 *Law and Critique* 311

Nancy, J-L (1991) *The Inoperative Community*, trans P Connor, Minneapolis, MN: University of Minnesota Press

Nancy, J-L (1993a) *The Experience of Freedom*, trans B McDonald, Stanford, CA: Stanford University Press

Nancy, J-L (1993b) 'Abandoned being', in *The Birth to Presence*, trans Brian Holmes, Stanford, CA: Stanford University Press

Nancy, J-L (1993c) 'The jurisdiction of the Hegelian monarch', in *The Birth to Presence*, trans Brian Holmes, Stanford, CA: Stanford University Press

Nancy, J-L (1997) 'Politics II', in *The Sense of the World*, trans Jeffrey Librett, Minneapolis, MN: University of Minnesota Press

Nancy, J-L (2000a) *Being Singular Plural*, trans RD Richardson and AE O'Byrne, Stanford, CA: Stanford University Press

Nancy, J-L (2000b) 'Of being singular plural', in *Being Singular Plural*, trans RD Richardson and AE O'Byrne, Stanford, CA: Stanford University Press

Nancy, J-L (2000c) 'War, right, sovereignty – technē', in *Being Singular Plural*, trans RD Richardson and AE O'Byrne, Stanford, CA: Stanford University Press

Nancy, J-L (2000d) 'Eulogy for the mêlée', in *Being Singular Plural*, trans RD Richardson and AE O'Byrne, Stanford, CA: Stanford University Press

Nancy, J-L (2003a) *A Finite Thinking*, trans Simon Sparks, Stanford, CA: Stanford University Press

Nancy, J-L (2003b) 'The confronted community', trans Amanda Macdonald, 6 *Postcolonial Studies* 23

Nancy, J-L (2003c) 'Deconstruction of monotheism', trans Amanda Macdonald, 6 *Postcolonial Studies* 37

Nancy, J-L (2003d) 'The war of monotheism', trans Amanda Macdonald, 6 *Postcolonial Studies* 53

Norris, A (2003) 'The exemplary exception: Philosophical and political decisions in Giorgio Agamben's *Homo Sacer*' 119 *Radical Philosophy* 6

Sassen, S (2002) 'Governance hotspots: Challenges we must confront in the post-September 11 world', 19(4) *Theory, Culture, Society* 233

Schmitt, C (1985 [1922]) *Political Theology: Four Chapters on the Concept of Sovereignty*, trans George Schwab, Cambridge, MA: MIT Press

Schmitt, C (1996 [1932]) *The Concept of the Political*, trans George Schwab, Chicago, IL: University of Chicago Press

Schmitt, C (2004 [1932]) *Legality and Legitimacy*, trans Jeffrey Seitzer, Durham: Duke University Press

Strachan-Davidson, JL (1912) *Problems of the Roman Criminal Law, Vol. 1*, Oxford: Clarendon Press

Urry, J (2002) 'The global complexities of September 11th' 19(4) *Theory, Culture, Society* 57

Cases

A v Secretary of State for the Home Department (Court of Appeal, October 2002)

A v Secretary of State for the Home Department [2005] 2 AC 68

Ahrens v Clark 335 US 188 (1948)

Braden v 30th Judicial Circuit Court of Ky 410 US 484, 495 (1973)

Cuban American Bar Association v Christopher 43 F. 3d 1412 (11th Cir. 1995)

Coalition of Clergy v Bush 189 F. Supp. 2d 1036 (CD Cal 2002)

Eisentrager v Forrestal 174 Fed Rep, 2nd S 961 (1948)

Falen Gherebi v Bush (US District Court for the Central District of California, 13 May 2003)

Falen Gherebi v George Walker Bush and Donald H Rumsfeld (United States Courts of Appeals for the 9th Circuit, California, 18 December 2003)

Hamdi v Rumsfeld (US Court of Appeals for the 4th Circuit, No. 02–6895, 12 July 2002)

Hamdi v Rumsfeld (Supreme Court of the United States, decided 28 June, 2004)

Johnson v Eisentrager 339 US 763 (1950)

Khaled AF Al Odah v United States of America (US Court of Appeals for the District of Columbia Circuit, No. 02–5251, 11 March 2003)

Ex Parte Quirin 317 US 1 (1942) 31

Ralpho v Bell 569 F. 2d 607 (DC Cir. 1977)

Rasul and Odah v Bush 215 F. Supp. 2d 55 (DDC 2002)

Rasul v Bush (Supreme Court of the United States, decided 28 June, 2004)

Rumsfeld v Padilla (Supreme Court of the United States, decided 28 June, 2004)

Zadvydas v Davis 533 US 678 (2001)

5 Conjuring Palestine

The jurisdiction of dispossession

John Strawson

Colonialism's embrace

Colonialism employs the most rigorous legalism to effect the subordination of the colonised. For the Palestinians, a form of late colonialism has ensured that the process has continued into the twenty-first century. Despite the much referred to 'peace process' since the signing of the Oslo Agreements in 1993,[1] Israel's primary colonisation of the West Bank through land acquisition and settlement has rapidly increased. At the moment when legal texts appeared to grant Palestinians a measure of jurisdiction over their own lives, growing areas of the land of Palestine were vanishing beneath the bulldozer and the tank. This chapter suggests that law's collusion with colonialism has been a powerful factor in the dispossession of the Palestinians. Israel has been the beneficiary of a British legal bequest.[2]

When Palestine appeared before the International Court of Justice in February 2004 to argue the case that the wall the Israelis were building in the West Bank was illegal, there was a sense of unreality to the event.[3] What was this 'Palestine', represented by eminent lawyers from Britain, Belgium and the Middle East? After all, was not the existence of a Palestinian state the subject of the negotiation of the Oslo Agreements[4] and the Road Map to Peace?[5] Had Palestine arrived before it had been created? The World Court's hearing was to determine an advisory opinion on the issue requested by the United Nations General Assembly (UNGA).[6]

1 Palestine Liberation Organisation (PLO) and the State of Israel, Declaration of Principles on Interim Self-Government Arrangements, 13 September 1993, 32 *International Legal Materials* 1525.

2 The argument that is developed here is indebted to Said's (1978) use of Foucault. Said suggestively takes Foucault's use of discourse and the imagery of archaeology (as in Foucault, 2003) and engages in a contextualisation of discourse analysis. In this piece, the sense of archaeological site in the Saidian sense is useful as legal texts and discourses crumble into each other as foundations of buildings are often reliant on earlier remnants.

3 For the statement on the end of the oral pleadings see: http://212.153.43.18/icjwww/idocket/imwp/imwpframe.htm

4 For a comprehensive discussion on the Oslo Accords in international law see Watson (2000).

5 For the text of the road map see: www.state.gov/r/pa/prs/ps/2003/20062.htm

6 The 10th Special Session of the General Assembly adopted Resolution A/RES/ES-10/14 on 8 December 2003. It requested an advisory opinion on the legality of the wall being built by Israel in Occupied Palestinian Territories.

The very subject of the wall goes to the heart of whether or not a Palestinian state can be established on viable territory. The 700 kilometre wall cuts through the Israeli-occupied West Bank, dividing communities and people from their land and slicing Palestine into even smaller units of land surrounded by Israeli control. The 'Palestine' that appeared at the International Court of Justice is the nomenclature accorded to the Palestine Liberation Organisation's observer delegation at the United Nations. Since 1974, the UNGA has recognised the Palestine Liberation Organisation (PLO) as 'the sole legitimate representative of the Palestinian people' (UNGA resolution 3210 [XXIX]) and accorded the organisation observer status (UNGA resolution 3237 [XXIX]) (see Sybesma-Knol, 2002). This process has granted the PLO a degree of international legal personality and has allowed it to participate in the UN bodies and UN-sponsored international conferences. This form of legal personality is, however, not connected to the characteristics of state, and does not necessarily imply that any temporal jurisdiction exists (for a discussion of international legal personality, see Higgins, 1994).

Palestine entered the concerns of the international community during the First World War (for a discussion of this period, see Fromkim, 1989). The British occupation after 1917 and the subsequent League of Nations Mandate for Palestine are the two key and related moments. General Allenby's army of occupation arrived with more than the normal military agenda. The Balfour Declaration, issued only a month earlier (2 November 1917) contained the commitment that the British Government 'viewed with favour the creation of a national home for Jews in Palestine'. In the diplomatic arrangements with the French, the British from 1916 (Sykes-Picot Agreement) had decided on an inter-imperial division of the Middle East. Syria and Lebanon would be allocated to the French, while Palestine (with Jordan) and Iraq would pass to British control. However, this was accompanied by a novel addition in the form of the allocation of an as yet unspecified scope of 'national home' for the Jews within one of the areas of British influence. In 1917, there were fewer than 85,000 Jews in Palestine, less than 10 per cent of the total population – most Jews lived in Europe and in the Arab world. Britain thus arrived to create neither a plantation colony nor a settler colony, but with the idea of a unique colonial project for the creation of a national space for a people yet to be assembled. In the British narrative, the Jewish people were awaiting the protective embrace of the Empire (on the way in which the British governed, see Shepherd, 1999). This political policy was transformed into legal norms with the creation of the Mandate for Palestine by the League of Nations in 1922 (for a discussion of Mandate Palestine, see Segev, 2000).

During the Mandate years, immigration created a significant Jewish population amounting to about a third of the total by 1948. British policy wavered through its three decades of rule, at times resisting both Palestinian Arab and Jewish nationalisms. However, the legal infrastructure that Britain established provided for robust institutions for a Jewish proto-state. At the same time, Britain's military policies crushed Palestinian resistance, especially in the mid-1930s, which undermined Palestinian nationalism.

In 1947, the British authorities announced that they would terminate their responsibilities under the Mandate and turned the matter over to the United Nations. As a result, the Special Committee on Palestine recommended that Palestine should be partitioned into a Jewish state and an Arab state, with Jerusalem coming under international supervision (for a discussion on the UN partition plan, see de Waart, 1994). According to UN procedures General Assembly resolutions must be adopted by a two-thirds majority which endows them with a high degree of legitimacy and adds weight to their implementation. In November 1947, the General Assembly adopted resolution 181 by such a majority and the partition plan at that time appeared to be the will of the international community. The currently occupied territory of the West Bank and Gaza was assigned to the Arab State. East Jerusalem was assigned to the international regime, together with West Jerusalem.

While the plan was accepted by the Zionist movement, it was rejected by the Palestinians and the Arab world. It was controversial, not least in the fact that at the time the Jewish population of Palestine constituted only a third of the entire population yet was awarded 54 per cent of the land. More fundamentally, perhaps, the majority of the population had sought to gain self-determination in a unitary state.

Israel's acceptance of the resolution went beyond political rhetoric, as the legal narrative of its Declaration of Independence (14 May 1948) demonstrates. The grounds cited for the legitimacy of the state were the historic claim of the Jewish people and the UN resolution:

> On the 29th of November, 1947, the United Nations General Assembly passed a resolution calling for the establishment of a Jewish State in Eretz-Israel; the General Assembly required the inhabitants of Eretz-Israel to take such steps as were necessary on their part for the implementation of that resolution. This recognition by the United Nations of the right of the Jewish people to establish their state is irrevocable.
>
> (quoted by de Waart, 1994: 227)

The phrasing of this paragraph is significant. First, it should be noted that in the Israeli text the resolution is 'required' to be implemented. This implies the acceptance of an obligation. Second, it is 'irrevocable'. On the latter point, the argument could be raised that irrevocability applies to the creation of the Jewish state. The Declaration relies on the resolution as a key source of legitimacy for the Israeli state and logically this must imply that all of its provisions are equally valid, including the establishment of the Arab State. Indeed, the decisive part of the Declaration makes it clear that the whole of the resolution is being relied on:

> Accordingly we, members of the People's Council, representatives of the Jewish community in Eretz-Israel and of the Zionist movement, are here established on this day of the termination of the British Mandate over Eretz-Israel and by virtue of our natural and historic right and on the strength of the resolution of

the United Nations General Assembly, hereby declare the establishment of a Jewish state in Eretz-Israel, to be known as the State of Israel.

(de Waart, 1994: 227–28)

This legal and foundational reliance on the UN partition plan indicates that Israel formally accepted that its jurisdiction did not extend to territories outside those allocated to it. In the 1948 war, the new state was able to expand its territory by conquest to some 78 per cent of the total of what had been British Mandate Palestine. Jordan occupied the West Bank and East Jerusalem and Egypt took control of the Gaza Strip. While Jordan unilaterally annexed the West Bank and East Jerusalem (see Shlaim, 1988) and integrated it into the Kingdom, Egypt left the status of the Gaza Strip unchanged. It was these territories that Israel occupied in the 1967 war (Oren, 2002). As the occupation took root, Israel began to refer to the West Bank and Gaza as 'disputed territories', and unilaterally annexed East Jerusalem in 1980. This slippage in language and the purported change of status of Jerusalem needs to be contrasted with Israel's state practice between 1948 and 1967 of never making any formal claims to any territory beyond the armistice line established in 1949, known as the 'green line' (see Golani, 1999).

By the time these territories were subject to the Oslo Agreements, the Israeli occupation had been in existence for a quarter of a century. The construction of settlements, military installations and road systems, combined with the presence of large numbers of Israeli military forces, transformed the life of the Palestinians. The PLO–Israel Agreements represented the first time that either side had agreed to a formula for discussing the resolution of the conflict. While some Palestinians argued that this represented a shift from occupation to an independent sovereign state, others thought to the contrary that they were a new form of consolidating the occupation – with a new element, Palestinian consent.[7]

The Palestinian National Authority

The Palestinian National Authority is the creation of two agreements between the PLO and the State of Israel, and subsequent instruments emanating from the Authority itself (see Brown, 2003: 12–13). The first agreement, often known as the Cairo Accord,[8] is formally entitled the 'Agreement on the Gaza Strip and the Jericho Area' and dates from 4 May 1994. The purpose is the implementation of the 'interim self-government arrangements' in the context of the 1993 Declaration of Principles. The second is the 1995 Interim Agreement.[9]

7 This can be seen in the differences of approaches by Palestinian contributors to Cotran and Mallat (1996). The argument that the agreements represent a consolidation of the occupation are most forcefully put by Edward Said – see, in particular, Said (1995).

8 Israel–PLO Agreement on the Gaza Strip and the Jericho Area, 4 May 1994: 33 *International Legal Materials* 622.

9 Israel–PLO Agreement on the Gaza Strip and the Jericho Area, 4 May 1994: 33 *International Legal Materials* 650.

The Cairo Accord provides under Article IV for the Authority, which is designated as 'one body of 24 members' that will be 'responsible for all the legislative and executive powers and responsibilities transferred to it' (Article IV (1)). The composition of the Authority will be decided by the PLO and it will inform the Government of Israel of the initial personnel and any subsequent changes. The Authority is thus conceived as a body that is subordinate to the PLO although distinct from it. Article V provides for the jurisdiction of the Authority which is described as 'territorial, functional and personal' (Article V (1)). These types of jurisdiction are explained as:

> (a) The territorial jurisdiction covers the Gaza Strip and the Jericho area territory, as defined in article I, except for the settlements and the Military Installation Area. Territorial jurisdiction shall include land, subsoil and territorial waters, in accordance with the provisions of this agreement.
> (b) The functional jurisdiction encompasses all powers and responsibilities as specified in this agreement. This jurisdiction does not include foreign relations, internal security and public order of Settlements and the Military Installation Area and Israelis, and external security.
> (c) The personal jurisdiction extends to all persons within the territorial jurisdiction referred to above, except for Israelis, unless otherwise provided in this agreement.

These provisions are thus highly conditional. Not only does jurisdiction only extend to tiny areas of land in Gaza and the Jericho Area (carefully defined in maps that form an annex of the agreement) but it is also severely limited in scope (for a critical review of the agreements, see Said, 1995, 2000). Most of the description of jurisdiction is exclusory to prevent the Authority from exercising power over any of the Israeli security needs, its military installations or the settlements, and to ban international relations. In addition, and significant, is the removal of any Israeli from the provenance of the Authority. The scope of Israel's powers in respect of 'internal security and public order of Settlements and the Military Installation Area and Israelis, and external security' is not detailed. This has been interpreted by the Sharon Government (elected in 2001) very widely as meaning that the Israeli Defence Force is able to carry out major military operations, incursions and targeted assassinations on the basis of securing the settlements or in the interests of general Israeli security. This appears to fatally undermine Palestinian control over its territory and people (see Kimmerling, 2003).

The ban on external relations is curiously expressed when it is further elaborated in Article VI of the agreement. The sphere of foreign relations is specified as 'the establishment of abroad of embassies, consulates or other type of foreign missions and posts, or permitting their establishment in the Gaza Strip or the Jericho Area, and the appointment of or admission of diplomatic and consular staff, and the exercise of diplomatic functions' (Article VI (2) (a)). However, the next clause demonstrates the neat division of labour between the Authority and the PLO as it outlines that:

> Notwithstanding the provisions of this paragraph, the PLO may conduct negotiations and sign agreement with states or international organizations for the benefit of the Palestinian Authority in the following cases only:
>
> (1) economic agreements...
> (2) agreements with donor countries for the purposes of implementing arrangements for the provision of assistance to the Palestinian Authority;
> (3) agreements for the purpose of implementing the regional development plans detailed in ... the Declaration of Principles or in agreements entered into in the framework of the multilateral negotiations; and
> (4) cultural, scientific and educational agreements.

The agreement thus carefully redefines activities that would normally fall within international relations as being consistent with the prohibition on such relations providing the PLO acts on behalf of the Authority. It is interesting that the text is silent on the precise manner in which the Authority and the PLO relate to each other in order to effect these relations. In practice, the personnel have been much the same, Yasser Arafat was the head of both the Authority and the PLO as is his successor, Mahmoud Abbas. However, it is significant that, in the negotiations of the agreement, both Israel and the Palestinians found it useful to keep the PLO distinct from the Palestinian Authority. It permits the Palestinians to use the international legal personality of the PLO to carry out international relations while, for the Israelis, the Palestinian Authority in the occupied territories is deprived of a decisive power associated with statehood.

In 1995, the Israeli–Palestinian Interim Agreement on the West Bank and the Gaza Strip transformed the Authority from one body into a series of institutions. The institutions took on a state-like character, with an elected 'Ra'ees' as the head of the Executive Authority, the 20 appointed members of this executive and an elected Palestinian Council of 88 members. The use of the term Ra'ees is instructive of the studied ambiguities that stalk all the documents of the Oslo process. It is the Arabic term for the 'head' of an organisation and can be variously translated as 'head', 'chairperson' or 'president'. This allows the Israelis to talk of the chairperson of the Authority while Ra'ees retains the flavour of a president for the Palestinians. When these sections of the agreement were implemented by the Palestinians, there were many terminological shifts: not only was the Ra'ees very definitely the president but the executive also became the cabinet and the Council assumed the title of Palestinian Legislative Council (for a discussion of these developments in the early period, see Mahler, 1996 and generally Brown, 2003). These internal changes took place through executive decisions and then appeared in the many drafts of the Basic Law for the Authority, the final version of which was promulgated by 'President Arafat' and published in the *Gazette* in July 2002.

The text provides for the creation of institutions intended to be of a transitional nature for both sides. However, whereas the Israelis attempted to limit their powers to internal self-government, the Palestinians sought to use them as a basis for laying the foundations of an independent state. The shift in nomenclature is symbolic of a struggle for self-determination carried on by institutional means.

The question of the territorial jurisdiction of the Authority also underwent significant changes as the result of the Interim Agreement which, while leaving the arrangements in Gaza unchanged, assigned three different categories to territory in the West Bank. Area 'A' was to be under exclusive Palestinian control, whereas area 'B' would be a joint responsibility of Israelis and Palestinians, although the Authority would be responsible for civil administration. Area 'C' was to be under Israeli control. These area designations became central in the allocation of jurisdiction. The complexity of the arrangements was increased due to the transitional character of the agreement, and as 'jurisdiction will extend gradually to cover West Bank and Gaza Strip territory…through a series of redeployments of the Israeli military forces' (Article XVII (2) (8)). It should be noted that ambiguity continues in this section, as there is no specification of what territory will be redeployed from, with the absence of the definite article before 'West Bank and Gaza Strip territory'. The extent of territorial jurisdiction is far from clear. Although the redeployments will take place in the West Bank, the text obfuscates whether or not the intention is to redeploy from all of 'the' West Bank in three manoeuvres. This is only an apparent imprecision as this formula carefully transfers to Israel the active voice of the text. It continues: 'Further redeployments of Israeli military forces to specified military locations will commence immediately upon the inauguration of the Council and will be effected in three phases' (Article XVII (2) (8)). It appears from this and similar formulations that it will be Israeli authorities alone who will determine the scope of the redeployments. Palestinian territorial jurisdiction is dependent on Israeli military considerations and is not a result of any independent conception of rights – linked, for example, to the doctrine of self-determination.

This conditional character of jurisdiction is compounded by the difference between the Cairo Agreement, which refers to Israeli 'withdrawal' from the Gaza Strip and the Jericho Area, and the Interim Agreement, which refers only to 'redeployment'. This implies a less permanent state of affairs than withdrawal does. As Raja Shehadeh (1997) points out, Article XIII (2) affirms that 'Israel shall retain overriding responsibility for security for the purpose of protecting Israelis and confronting the threat of terrorism.' This reinforcement of similar provisions of the Cairo Agreement is made absolutely clear in Annex I, which deals with the details of redeployment: 'nothing in this article shall derogate from Israel's security power and responsibilities in accordance with this agreement' (Article 1.7). Shehadeh (1997: 63) is correct when he says 'the security arrangements agreed upon substantially limit the jurisdiction of the Palestinian

Council in all respects including in area A where it is agreed that that the Palestinian Council can exercise territorial jurisdiction'.

The consequence of these agreements was to create the Palestinian Authority and to endow it with a degree of jurisdiction limited to internal affairs while territorially limited to tiny tracks of land. When the elections for the Ra'ees and the Legislative Council took place (in January 1996), area A, over which the Palestinians exercised exclusive control, amounted to only 3 per cent of the West Bank. Area B, where the Palestinians ran education, social services, health and cultural affairs, was about 20 per cent of the area. By the time of the failed Camp David talks in the autumn of 2000, area A amounted to 22 per cent and area B to about 18 per cent. While 90 per cent of the Palestinian population fell under the civil administration of the Palestinian Authority, they were far from empowered. The designation of categories A, B and C was portrayed as temporary zones to effect the redeployments. However, it should be borne in mind that area C contained all Israeli settlements with a population of about 130,000 in 1995. In addition, the areas under Palestinian administration were not contiguous but scattered areas that could only be reached by passing through areas of Israeli control. During the period of the negotiations, the population of the Israeli settlements grew dramatically, reaching 240,000 in 2003. In addition, Israel had acquired significant amounts of occupied land to construct a system of highways linking the settlements to each other and to Israel. As a result of these developments, the designated areas A, B and C began to gain a degree of permanence. This gave rise to the occupation culture of the checkpoints, established along the lines demarcating the zones. These military installations which are sometimes permanent and sometimes episodic, dominate the everyday life of the population. At times, there have been as many as 200 for a population of little more than two million. Permission to move from one area to another within the West Bank, to occupied East Jerusalem, to work in Israel or to Ben Gurion International Airport is regulated through an intricate series of passes reminiscent of apartheid South Africa. The hope of empowerment rapidly gave way to the reality of imprisonment.

Since its establishment, the Palestinian Authority has increasingly come to resemble a state. The amendments to the Basic Law in 2003[10] demonstrate how the language about the institutions has changed since the Cairo and Interim Agreements. The use of the terms 'Council of Ministers' and 'cabinet' are significant, as is the designation of the post of prime minister. Reading the amendments gives an impression of the emergence of a mature constitutional order. This is further reinforced by the presence in the cabinet of a Minister of Foreign Affairs. Yet this apparent widening and deepening of the jurisdiction of the Authority has been accompanied by the effective reoccupation of the West

10 I am working from the Draft Amendment moved by the Council of Ministers to the Palestine Legislative Council on 8 March 2003 (Draft Bill No. 111/2003/M), contained in 'Draft Amendment to the Basic Law for the Palestinian National Authority' Jerusalem: Jerusalem Media and Communications Centre, Occasional Document Series No 10, July 2003.

Bank by Israel and regular incursions into Gaza since the beginning of the second intifada in the fall of 2000.

The Authority exercises no effective control over any of 'its' territory, and its jurisdiction appears ephemeral. This situation is the result of a change in Israeli policy on the creation of the Palestinian state (see Pape, 2004: 232–68; Rubinstein, 2000: 111–272). The opposition to a Palestinian state was common to both major political parties, Labor and Likud, until the mid-1990s. At the 1996 election, the Labor Party changed its policy to support the creation of a state as one of the possibilities for resolving the conflict. Likud appeared to oppose this and went on to win the elections. However, little noticed at the time was the subtle shift in tone from one of the Likud leaders, Ariel Sharon, who argued that in reality the Palestinian state had come into existence with the establishment of the Palestinian Authority (Strawson, 1998). While he was opposed to that development, he saw the advantage that the Authority was weak and confined to relatively little territory. If this weak entity could be called a state, then perhaps there would be fewer objections to it. By the date when the 'permanent status' talks were to have been completed (4 May 1999), there was great speculation that Yasser Arafat would unilaterally declare a state in the absence of a signed agreement. Many in Israel hoped that he would, thus confining Palestine to its existing territory – towns and villages surrounded by Israeli settlements and the rest of area C. The Sharon faction in Likud thought this would be a green light to annex the rest of the West Bank to Israel. It was highly significant that when Sharon assumed the premiership in February 2001, he pursued a military policy rather than a negotiations strategy. The aim of the then newly announced policy was of unilateral disengagement from Gaza – including dismantling the settlements – and from some areas of the West Bank. That offered the Palestinians the poisoned chalice of a society devastated by Israeli attacks, fenced in by the wall yet in need of administration. In this sense, Ariel Sharon becomes the father of the Palestinian state – small, weak, territorially discontinuous, and at the mercy of Israel's economic and military policies.

This walk through the texts of the Oslo Agreements is, however, treading an older path constructed by the British Mandate for Palestine. The trajectory of marginalising the Palestinians began at that time, through legal instruments approved by the League of Nations (Strawson, 2002).

The British Mandate

Reading the Mandate at a distance of 80 years, one is struck by the overwhelming weight given to the Balfour Declaration and its implications. The preamble and the first part of the actual provisions are taken up with this objective (Articles 2, 4, 6, 7 and 11). The Palestinian population is referred to, variously, as the 'existing non-Jewish communities', 'other sections of the community' and 'natives' but remains with an identity undisclosed. These references are *inter alia* in provisions covering issues such as the principle of non-discrimination, the Arabic language and religious freedom.

In his intriguing article on the impact of British Mandate law on Israel, Assaf Likhovski (1995) argues for the development of a relational historical narrative for Israelis and Palestinians. Despite the success of the article in plotting critical aspects in the history of the cultural–legal form of the Mandate – and neatly exposing the racism and cultural superiority of the judiciary to both Jews and Palestinians (Likhovski, 1995)[11] – no relational narrative emerges. Rather, we are confronted with a British legal policy that secretes itself into two societies which are themselves being radically constructed or reconstructed. Rather than a relational narrative, the history of contemporary Israelis and Palestinians has been negotiated through an existential conflict in which space – land – has been at the core. The centrality of the 'Jewish National Home' and the marginality of the unnamed plural 'existing non-Jewish communities' results in the jurisprudential privilege of the former over the latter. The construction of the proto-Israeli legal personality as central is striking, as the people who gain such identity are largely absent. The tiny Jewish population of Palestine is thus not the only intended beneficiary, but rather takes its place within a wider category: the Jews. With the Palestinians, the opposite process takes places as their new legal personality – the result of the general provisions of the Mandate system – is systematically undermined by the terms of the particular Mandatory instrument.

The text of the Mandate does not merely reinscribe the terms of the Balfour Declaration in its preamble, but fleshes out the objective and institutional means of establishing a Jewish National Home in the body of the document. Article 2 places the obligation on the Mandatory to 'be responsible for placing the country under such political, administrative and economic conditions as will secure' its establishment. Almost as a second thought, it adds: 'the development of self-governing institutions, and for safeguarding the civil and religious rights of all the inhabitants of Palestine irrespective of race and religion'. There are the outlines of the legal agenda of the Mandate which, first, create the condition for a Jewish National Home; second, develop self-governing institutions and third, safeguard the rights of all the inhabitants. This drafting of provisions that appear to grant rights, yet are subject to an overriding norm that entirely changes their content, is a familiar technique in the Israeli–Palestinian conflict's legal discourse. It should be added that it is a common feature of international law in general.

In Article 4 of the Mandate, we see the grant of international legitimacy to the legal privileging of the Jewish National Home. It provides:

> An appropriate Jewish agency shall be recognized as a public body for the purpose of advising and co-operating with the Administration of Palestine in such economic, social and other matters that may affect the establishment of the Jewish national home and the interests of the Jewish population in Palestine and subject always the Administration, so assist and take part in the development of the country.

11 See the discussion of the book: Mustard and Cress, *Palestine Parodies: Being the Holy Land in Verse and Worse* (privately published, 1938).

> The Zionist organization, so long as its organization and constitution are in the opinion of the Mandatory appropriate shall be recognized as such agency. It shall take steps in consultation with His Britannic Majesty's Government to secure the cooperation of all Jews who are willing to assist in the establishment of the Jewish national home.

This article is significant in several respects. First, it creates a state-like administrative body out of a civil society organisation – the Zionist organisation becomes the Jewish agency. Second, that organisation will be the key element on 'advising and cooperating' with the Mandatory authority on the creation of the conditions necessary for the creation of the Jewish National Home. Third, the Zionist organisation/Jewish agency will not only operate within the jurisdiction of the Mandate but will also have an obligation to 'secure the cooperation of all Jews' willing to engage in the project. In this way, the Jewish agency becomes the institutional link with the absent population. Interestingly, the implication is that the Mandate confers on Jews outside Palestine 'willing to cooperate' an elementary *locus standii* in Palestine itself.

In the 1920s and 1930s, Palestinian Arab lawyers began to argue that the Mandate was itself illegal. Wissam Boustany made the case in his book published in 1936:

> The Palestine Mandate is invalid in the presence of Article 16 of the Treaty of Lausanne, and Article 20, and the fourth paragraph of Article 22 of the Covenant of the League of Nations. It is not formulated as an 'A' Mandate. Great Britain as a party to the Covenant should have procured her release from the Balfour Declaration.
>
> (Boustany, 1936)

This argument essentially rests on interpretations of the Covenant of the League of Nations. Article 20 has some similarities with Article 103 of the UN Charter in that it wants to create the legal regime of the League as superior to all other sources of international law. Reflecting the character of the times, Article 20 is somewhat more discrete about sovereignty as it requires members to act to invalidate any previous obligations that are inconsistent with the League. Article 20 reads:

> 1 The Members of the League severally agree that this Covenant is accepted as abrogating all obligations or understandings inter se which are inconsistent with the terms thereof, and solemnly undertake that they will not hereafter enter into any engagements inconsistent with the terms thereof.
>
> 2 In the case of any Member of the League shall, before becoming a Member of the League, have undertaken any obligations inconsistent with the terms of this covenant, it shall be the duty of the Member to take such immediate steps to procure its release from such obligations.

Boustany, in his argument, links this article with Article 22 (para 4) which deals with the Mandate system. This reads:

> Certain communities formerly belonging to the Turkish Empire have reached a stage of development where their existence as independent nations can be provisionally recognised subject to the rendering of administrative advice and assistance by the Mandatory until such time as they are able to stand alone. The wishes of these communities must be a principal consideration in the selection of the Mandatory.

In his account, these two provisions mean that their effect:

> . . . by no means constitute a justification or a legalization of an infringement and a violation so long as the provisions of the fourth paragraph of Article 22 and those of Article 20 of the Covenant are not abolished or amended to exclude Palestine or to make the special exception of a policy in favour of 12–16 million Jews in the presence of hundreds of millions of Moslems and Christians.
>
> (Boustany, 1936: 32–33)

In his opinion, therefore, the inclusion of the terms of the Balfour Declaration in the Mandate is:

> . . . ultra vires and entirely foreign to the principles laid down in Article 22 of the Covenant of the League cannot supply any justification of any departures from those principles, namely: (a) the well-being of the community and development of the people of the mandated area, and (b) the recognition of the community of the territory of an 'A' mandate as an 'independent nation'.
>
> (Boustany, 1936: 18)

This interpretation of Articles 20 and 22 of the Covenant is problematic, as Boustany has overlooked the elliptical and rather indeterminate drafting of the provisions. Article 22, para 4 (on the Mandate system) does not refer to all the 'communities formerly belonging to the Turkish Empire' but more enigmatically to 'certain communities formerly belonging to the Turkish Empire'. This implies that some 'communities' may not be treated in the same manner. Nor is it the case that there is an emphatic recognition that such communities are to be recognised as independent nations. Article 22 is ringed around with caveats on this point. It suggests that 'certain communities' that have reached a certain 'stage of development' 'can be provisionally recognized' as such. Article 22 therefore leaves open entirely which communities are being referred to. Nor does it define what is meant by the 'stage of development'. Finally, the article merely says that such entities can be recognised clearly, meaning that equally they might not be. In any event, the recognition is provisional and further subject to the terms of 'advice and assistance' of the Mandatory. The latter must refer to the exact terms of each individual mandate. Boustany also makes much of the wishes of the relevant community in the selection of the Mandatory power. However, again the article is more carefully written than Boustany assumes. While appearing as an example of democratic consultation – if that can be used to describe the right of a people to select their own colonial power – it is less than it appears. The wishes of the people are only '*a* principal consideration' and not '*the* principal consideration' (italics added). This implies that there are other 'principal considerations' that would be weighed up in making the selection – these conveniently remain unspecified.

The creation of the League of Nations Covenant, mainly by the then great powers, reflected a world fundamentally divided into imperial and colonial states. The flexibility contained in Article 22 necessarily benefited the imperial powers. It was they who dominated the Council of the League, especially after their victory in the First World War, and thus it is they who were the active element in interpreting and applying the Covenant. All the elliptical phrases offered them the power to decide how to draft the mandates and what their exact terms would be. In addition, the provisions of Article 20 would be used to reinforce their legality.

The 1929 Hague Academy of International Law lectures were delivered by Norman Bentwich, then the Attorney General of Palestine. His topic was the Mandate system. In the preface to the subsequent publication, Bentwich was described by his editor Angus McNair as 'one of the few international lawyers to whose lot it has fallen to be intimately responsible for the actual working of a Mandate' (Bentwich, 1930: v). McNair also cogently sums up the purpose of the Mandate system as:

> introducing a new code of mixed law and morality into the dealings of colonising Powers with the peoples inhabiting their dependent possessions. It has also introduced into the colonial administration a defined objective, namely, the gradual preparation of the dependent peoples for the independent management of their own affairs and for the ultimate growth into statehood.
>
> (Bentwich, 1930: v–vi)

McNair is right to point out that the Mandate system is a new form of colonial policy, and he quite accurately identifies the colonising powers as those who will hold the mandates and that the peoples they govern will be 'inhabiting their dependent territories'. Imperial powers and their surrogates alone, it is assumed, will be given the mandates.[12] In his lectures, Bentwich explains the novel features of the system as introducing into political science and international law two principles:

> 1 A System of national responsibility for the government of a country under the control of an international body
> 2 A system of guardianship of peoples, similar the guardianship by individuals of minor persons.
>
> (Bentwich, 1930: 17)

12 Britain and France are the main beneficiaries. The Union of South Africa, created on the basis of a racist constitution in 1910 (according to the terms of the *British Union of South Africa Act* 1909), was awarded the Mandate for the former German colony of South West Africa, now Namibia. This decision indicates quite clearly how the 'welfare' of the peoples of these territories was viewed.

Whether the idea of 'guardianship' is a new concept in the context of the colonial world of the 1930s could be disputed, but the formal international regulation of the system through the Permanent Mandates Commission certainly is a new concept. Bentwich deals head on with the particular character of the Palestine Mandate, as he discusses the features of class A mandates:

> Class A is limited to territories detached from Turkey which are populated by civilized peoples and it was thought, were unable for a time to stand on by themselves. There the function of the Mandatory is to render Administrative advice and assistance, tough as we shall see, this position in Palestine does not conform to this character. There were special features of the Mandate over that country which put it in a class by itself, as the government of Palestine has been frequently of old. The wishes of the peoples were to be considered in the choices of the Mandatory: but this proved to be a *pious voex* than a practical counsel, because the Arab peoples concerned were opposed to the basic idea of the Mandate and desired complete independence.
>
> (Bentwich, 1930: 12–13)

Bentwich exhibits a great deal of candour in explaining the reason for this situation:

> Of the Palestine Mandate it may be said that, if the Mandate system had not been evolved for other purposes, it would have had to be created for the government of this little land... For Palestine, by its history, its geography, its population and its destiny is an international country, and its well being and development form, in the nature of things, a sacred trust of civilization.
>
> (Bentwich, 1930: 21)

This was a striking admission of the particular role that the Mandate system was to play in Palestine. The use of the term 'international country' indicates a reified existence that requires special governance, the specific features of which will be the Balfour Declaration. The function of the Mandate in transforming this policy into law is quite explicit in Bentwich's account:

> The Palestine Mandate recognizes the historical connection of Jewish people with the territory as giving national rights to which the Mandatory in the first place, and the League of Nations ultimately, has pledged itself to give effect. It is the application in law of the idea that 'memory also gives a right'.
>
> (Bentwich, 1930: 23)

It is ironic to find this early evocation of a now much discussed issue in the context of law and postcolonialism: the problem of restitution for past wrongs committed in the colonial period. It is much discussed, for example, in relation to land (see Fischbach, 2003; Hussein and McKay, 2003). The role of memory is often seen as a vital part of the possibility of legal recovery. It is all the more ironic in the context of Palestine and the dispossession of Palestinian land, which is a contemporary rather than merely historical issue (see Holme, 2003). Bentwich is quite frank about the implications of this legal situation for Palestine:

> The principle of self-determination had to be modified because of the two national selves existing in Palestine: and the majority Arab population could not be allowed to prevent the fulfilment of the Mandate in relationship to the minority Jewish population.
>
> (Bentwich, 1930: 27)

British policy deploys international law through the application of the Mandate. The Palestine Order in Council which creates the legal basis for British rule includes the Balfour Declaration in its preamble. The order thus created affords the Jewish National Home and its institutions a further degree of legal personality. In Bentwich's terms, 'it signifies a territory in which a people, without receiving rights of political sovereignty, has nevertheless, a recognized legal position and the opportunity of developing its moral, social and intellectual ideas' (Bentwich, 1930: 24).

Boustany's argument that the Mandate is legally defective thus appears entirely problematic. The characters of the Covenant and the Mandates themselves seem doctrinally part of the then existing international law. The proof of this is also demonstrated not so much in the power of Bentwich's arguments but in the prestigious forum in which he delivers them – The Hague Academy of International Law. These summer lectures were, and remain, a seminal event in the life of international legal discourse.

Conclusion

Reading legal texts rarely offers the pleasure of uncovering a kernel of emancipation or of justice. Rather, they encode the power relations in sometimes elegantly composed technical prose. In the case of the Palestinians, international law appears as a chimera offering the dignity of self-determination in a sovereign state. Yet international law's origin in colonial conquest reasserts itself in a particularly aggressive manner in the texts of the Israeli–Palestinian conflict. This is done not in some general way but takes the form of specific documents and discourses that are devoted to legal arguments for the marginalisation and dispossession of the Palestinians. Colonialism and the postcolonial collude to create a legal lineage that reaches Israel through the British experience. Palestinian rights are often referred in this discourse, but are always conditional on a more central obligation: the creation of the Jewish National Home or Israeli security interests. A decade of the jurisdiction of the Palestinian Authority has poignantly evidenced this. For many years the president of the Authority operated from a building surrounded by rubble[13] after a sustained Israeli siege, all Palestinian police stations were destroyed – mostly bombed by F16's – while the Israeli authorities increased control over the civilian population particularly through the checkpoints.

Palestine, however, is not unique. The great tragedy of the situation is that we have seen this all before – albeit before the television age. Colonial conquest and international law have been aggressive allies in the making of the contemporary world built on 350 years of European colonialism and the attendant ethnic cleansings, genocide, slavery, theft of territory and subjugation of peoples. Colonialism reassigned identities and created boundaries, then international law 'granted' rights to the peoples left within this dispensation and dignified them with the doctrine of self-determination. Palestine should remind the international conscience of this history – indeed, perhaps it is because it represents such a history that its significance is repressed.

As the wall is built in the West Bank, the scene is set for the next manoeuvre of marginalisation of Palestine. Israel rejected the International Court's advisory opinion that the wall is illegal. However, even this opinion is a two-edged one for the Palestinians, as it provides legal recognition for the first time of Israel's conquest of territory allocated for the Arab State in Palestine by the United Nations in the 1948 war. Israel can undoubtedly draw comfort from this, believing that persisting with settlements in the West Bank might in the long run win legal recognition too. The April 2004 Bush–Sharon plan for Israeli disengagement from Gaza provides the precise contours of Israeli hopes.[14] Disengagement from Gaza with the removal of settlements and Israeli military installations means permanent control of much of the West Bank as Israeli settlements become, in President George W Bush's new parlance, 'existing major Israeli population centers'. The election of the Kadima-led government in March 2006 indicated that despite the furore around the Gaza disengagement, there is a major consensus in Israel on the plan. Gaza is already fenced in, and the West Bank wall will complete the process of creating a society that is literally captive in a cage. It is this entity, no doubt, that Israeli Governments will wish to present to the world as a Palestinian state and the realisation of the right to self-determination. Given the current plans for the wall, this would mean that the Palestinians would gain 15 per cent of British Mandate territory. This small area, combined with five million refugees living outside the country, would effectively mean not only an unviable state but also one which would be unable to address this pressing problem. The Balfour Declaration has produced a persistent legal inheritance, and international law, despite the mantra of self-determination, might sanctify another jurisdiction of dispossession.

13 The Mukata became a symbol of the actual situation of the Palestinian National Authority: at once legally significant and politically enfeebled. After the election President Mahmoud Abbas in 2005, the rubble was removed and the buildings restored. Perhaps his sense of irony was less pronounced than his predecessor.

14 The plan was published on 18 April 2004 after Ariel Sharon had returned from securing agreement to the plan from Washington. For the text, see 'The Disengagement Plan', at www.mfa.gov.il

References

Bentwich, Norman (1930) *The Mandates System*, London, New York, NY, Toronto: Longman, Green and Co.

Boustany, F (1936) *Palestine Mandate: Invalid and Impracticable*, Beirut: American Press

Brown, Nathan J (2003) *Palestinian Politics After the Oslo Agreements: Resuming Arab Palestine*, Berkeley, AL: University of California Press

Cotran, Eugene and Mallat, Chibli (eds) (1996) *The Israeli–Arab Accords: Legal Perspectives*, London: Kluwer Law International

de Waart, Paul JIM (1994) *Dynamics of Self-Determination in Palestine: Protection of Peoples as a Human Right*, Leiden, New York, NY and Koln: EJ Brill

Fischbach, Michael R (2003) *Records of Dispossession: Palestinian Refugee Property and the Arab–Israeli Conflict*, New York, NY: University of Columbia Press

Foucault, Michel (2003) *The Archaeology of Knowledge*, trans AM Sheridan Smith, London: Routledge

Fromkim, David (1989) *A Peace to End All Peace: Creating the Modern Middle East 1914–1922*, London: Andre Deutsch

Golani, Motti (1999) 'Jerusalem's hope lies only in partition: Israeli policy on the Jerusalem question, 1948–67' 31(4) *International Journal of Middle East Studies* 577

Higgins, Rosalyn (1994) *Problems and Process: International Law and How We Use It*, Oxford: Oxford University Press

Holme, Robert (2003) 'An irreversible conquest? Colonial and postcolonial land law in Israel/Palestine' 12(3) *Social and Legal Studies* 291

Hussein, Hussein Abu and McKay, Fiona (2003) *Access Denied: Palestinian Land Rights in Israel*, London and New York, NY: Zed Press

Khalidi, Radid (1997) *Palestinian Identity: The Construction of Modern National Consciousness*, New York and Chichester: Colombia University Press

Kimmerling, Baruch (2003) *Politicide: Ariel Sharon's War Against the Palestinians*, London and New York, NY: Verso

Likhovski, Assaf (1995) 'In our image: Colonial discourse and the Anglicanization of law in Mandatory Palestine' 29(3) *Israel Law Review* 292

Mahler, Gregory S (1996) *Constitutionalism and Palestinian Constitutional Development*, Jerusalem: Palestinian Academic Society for the Study of International Affairs

Mustard and Cress (1938) *Palestine Parodies: Being the Holy Land in Verse and Worse* (privately published)

Oren, Michael B (2002) *Six Days of War: June 1967 and the Making of the Modern Middle East*, Oxford: Oxford University Press

Pape, Ilan (2004) *A History of Modern Palestine: One Land, Two Peoples*, Cambridge: Cambridge University Press

Rubinstein, Amnon (2000) *From Herzel to Rabin: The Changing Image of Zionism*, New York, NY, London: Holmes & Meier

Said, Edward W (1978) *Orientalism: Western Conceptions of the Orient*, Harmondsworth: Penguin

Said, Edward W (1995) 'The morning after', in Edward W Said (ed), *Peace and Its Discontents: Gaza–Jericho 1993–1995*, London: Vintage

Said, Edward W (2000) *The End of the Peace Process: Oslo and After*, London: Granta Books

Segev, Tom (2000) *One Palestine Complete: Jews and Arabs Under the British Mandate*, trans Haim Watzman, London: Little Brown

Shehadeh, Raja (1997) *From Occupation to Interim Accords: Israel and the Palestinian Territories*, London, The Hague, Boston: Kluwer Law International

Shepherd, Naomi (1999) *Ploughing Sand: British Rule in Palestine 1917–1948*, London: John Murray

Shlaim, Avi (1988) *The Politics of Partition: King Abdullah, the Zionists and Palestine, 1921–1951*, Oxford: Oxford University Press

Strawson, John (1998) 'Netanyahu's Oslo: Peace in the slow lane' 8 *Soundings* 49

Strawson, John (2002) 'Mandate ways: Self-determination in Palestine and the "existing non-Jewish communities"', in Sanford R Silverburg (ed), *Palestine and International Law: Essays in Politics and Economics*, Jefferson and London: McFarland

Sybesma-Knol, Neri (2002) 'Palestine and the United Nations', in Sanford R Silverburg (ed), *Palestine and International Law: Essays on Politics and Economics*, Jefferson and London: McFarland

Watson, Geoffrey E (2000) *The Oslo Accords: International Law and the Israeli–Palestinian Peace Agreements*, Oxford: Oxford University Press

6 Jurisdiction and nation-building

Tall tales in nineteenth-century Aotearoa/New Zealand

*Nan Seuffert**

Introduction: jurisdiction and nation-building

Questions of jurisdiction involve the determination of the boundaries of the law. Notions of modern territorial jurisdiction emerged with the development of the modern nation-state as the bounded territory in which a particular set of laws applied. These modern notions of both nation-state and jurisdiction facilitated colonisation by determining the territorial boundaries in which colonial law applied, by opposing the national space to other nations, and by producing difference within national and jurisdictional boundaries. The production of internal difference, the creation of differences between distinct groupings through the law's jurisdictional speech, is arguably the most important work that jurisdiction performs (Ford, 1999: 908).

Jurisdiction determines the boundaries of legal space in at least three ways: through territorial boundaries; by defining what is law and what is non-law; and by subject-matter (Dorsett, 2000: 34; Rush, 1997: 150). Subject-matter jurisdiction is the determination of what is included in the law of property, or contract. Territorial jurisdiction contributes to the construction of political subjectivity by tying individuals to the fixed boundaries of the modern nation-state (Ford, 1999: 905). Power is consolidated within the nation-state in part through a centralised jurisdiction that represses and excludes difference through homogenisation and assimilation (Dorsett, 2000: 35).

As part of the process of New Zealand's colonisation, jurisdiction operated as a tool of the state, one that consolidated and centralised power, and participated in nation-building, producing ideas about the identity of the emerging modern nation. Nations are ideas – stories that are told about the collective past and current cohesion of groups of people (Renan, 1990: 19). In the nineteenth century, the prevailing stories of nations revolved around a fiction of unity

* I would like to thank Shaun McVeigh for inviting me to the Jurisprudence of Jurisdiction symposium at Griffith University in 2002 which spurred me to think through this history in a new light, and for his patience and skill in editing this collection.

through kinship and culture (1990: 19), as summarised by New Zealand's famous jurist, John Salmond:

> A nation is a society of men united by common blood and descent . . . speech, religion and manners. A state . . . is a society of men united under one government.
>
> (Salmond, 1907: 103)

Salmond went on to suggest that in every nation there is an impulse to develop into a state. In his fictional story, states grew out of nations. Where a state encompassed cultural differences, it tended to become a nation:

> The unity of political organization eliminates in course of time the national diversities within its borders, infusing throughout all its population a new and common nationality, to the exclusion of all remembered relationship with those beyond the limits of the state.
>
> (Salmond, 1907: 103)

Salmond's language provides a tie between nineteenth-century notions of jurisdiction and nation-building. Modern nation-states are territorially bounded, as opposed to 'primitive' notions of states as ruling over a group of people (Salmond, 1907: 102). As part of the process of colonisation, jurisdiction contributes to nation-building by extending a centralised power system for the homogenisation of individual and political identity within contested territorial boundaries (Ford, 1999: 906–08). This centralisation facilitates the erasure, violent elimination and assimilation of jurisdictional and legal diversity within national boundaries while it simultaneously determines those boundaries.

Salmond's reference to the exclusion of remembered relationships, and Benedict Anderson's more recent work on nations as imagined communities (Anderson, 1991: 6), provide tools for analysing jurisdiction's nation-building work. Anderson argues that nations are imagined political communities. A nation is *imagined* because no member can ever know all of those who make up the nation, and therefore each carries a fictional image of the nation. It is an imaged *community* in the sense that all members of the nation are imaged as part of a fraternity. This part of the fiction typically masks various forms of exclusion, inequality and exploitation. As imagined communities, nations are the stories that are told about collective identities. Cases and legislation participate in nation-building by presenting stories of imagined communities that remember some relationships and exclude others (Harris, 1996: 214). In these stories, the nation is defined in part through its limits and in opposition to its others:

> Because the nation is constitutively finite, it is through the articulation of its limits that nation defines itself. But in a seemingly contradictory

> maneuver, the nation is constructed as the universal in opposition to what appears other to it, an other that is defined in terms of particularity.
>
> (Stychin, 1998: 4)

A nation is defined by its boundaries, or limits, at the same time that the excluded 'other' resides within it. Defining the nation in opposition to external and internal foes, both real and imagined, is integral to the production of national identity (Ford, 1999: 908). In the context of colonisation, the emerging modern nation-state is often defined in universals in opposition to primitive particularities.

This chapter traces the ways in which jurisdiction, the law's speech, participates in telling stories of inclusion in and exclusion from the boundaries of the nation-state, producing difference within the nation, and internal foes to the nation. Throughout the nineteenth-century colonisation of New Zealand, the jurisdiction of the colonial courts over the indigenous Maori people and their land was contested. Stories of the jurisdiction of the colonial courts, in cases, legislation and other historical materials, reveal its role in the contested process of nation-building, or colonial attempts to produce, in nineteenth-century terms, 'one people' who were a 'better Britain'. Maori were excluded from and produced as internal foes within an emerging nation that was also in the process of defining itself in relation to Imperial Britain.

This chapter traces these contested attempts to centralise jurisdictional power in the colonial courts through the exclusion and erasure of Maori laws and customs. Integral to this process was the production of difference within the emerging nation. The creation of a sub-jurisdiction in the Native Land Courts provides an example of jurisdiction's production of difference. As colonisation continued throughout the nineteenth century, the 'remembered relationships', in Salmond's (1907) terms, between colonial laws and Maori laws and customs were violently erased. The resulting tall tale that Maori laws and customs had never existed in New Zealand facilitated both stories of Maori assimilation to a nation increasingly defining itself as a 'better' and 'purer' (whiter) Britain and the production of Maori as internal foes of the emerging nation. This tale was buttressed by stories of Maori as descendants of the same 'Aryan' ancestors as the Anglo-Saxons, creating a common blood descent line for all New Zealand, and one imagined community, or nation.

However, the elaborately constructed story of the progress of colonisation in producing one nation in New Zealand – in part through the extension of jurisdiction – was a fiction. Throughout the nineteenth century, many Maori continued to live under their own laws and customs, sometimes selectively incorporating ideas from Britain, sometimes not. The colonial story of the production of one nation is a story of anxiety and insecurity on the part of the British and the settlers. This chapter reveals the ways in which ideas about jurisdiction, and the creation and application of jurisdictional boundaries, contributed to the myth of nation-building in New Zealand.

Clashing jurisdictions

In New Zealand's dominant founding story, the indigenous Maori people freely agreed in the Treaty of Waitangi (the 'Treaty'), signed on 6 February 1840, to cede their sovereignty to the British Crown in return for its protection, for a guarantee of 'full exclusive and undisturbed possession of their Lands... ', and for the rights of British citizenship. This story is constructed using the official English version of the Treaty. Consistent with this story, upon the signing of the Treaty at Waitangi, Governor Hobson declared 'We are one nation' (see Frame, 1995: 109), making New Zealanders all British subjects, and all one community.[1]

This dominant story coalesced at the turn of the century, facilitating the emergence of a modern nation while repressing and excluding Maori understandings of these events (Binney, 1981: 16). The Maori versions of the Treaty, signed by most Maori leaders, who never saw the English version, did not cede sovereignty to the British (Ross, 1972: 136). Rather, Maori retained their traditional control over their land and people, explicitly recognised in the guarantee in the Maori versions of the Treaty of *te tino rangatiratanga* (Williams, 1989: 79), and in oral guarantees of Maori laws and customs (see Colenso, 1890: 32; Durie, 1996: 460–61; Frame, 1981: 106; Law Commission, 2001; Williams, 1999: 116–19). In this story, Maori simply agreed to allow the 'lawless' British to establish a government to govern themselves.[2] Maori laws and customs would continue to apply to Maori through their established practices. The dominant story of the fusion of Maori and settlers into one nation contrasts with the guarantee of protection of Maori sovereignty, laws and customs, and the parallel legal jurisdictions envisioned by the Maori versions of the Treaty (Frame, 1995: 109).

The story of power-sharing through parallel jurisdictions is buttressed by the early denial by the British Colonial Office of any intention of ruling over Maori (see Normanby, 1968: 38, disclaiming any intention of seizing New Zealand without the consent of Maori; and Gipps, 1968: 200, stating that the British Government 'interferes' in New Zealand against its will). The British were reluctant to colonise New Zealand right up until 1840 (Hight, 1940: 46, 90–92). The proclamation of British sovereignty over Maori may have been

1 For the extent to which this dominant story still prevails, see Moon (2002: 10): 'I assumed – like most other people – that there were certain facts about the Treaty that were beyond the reach of challenge even by the most incorrigible historian or analyst... One fact in particular stood out clearly... that the purpose of the Treaty was for the British Crown to assert sovereignty over Maori. Yet the more I considered this assertion in the light of evidence I was uncovering, the less it seemed to stand up to close scrutiny.'

2 Moon (2002: 10): 'The central argument of this book... is that the British Crown never intended to rule, preside over, or govern Maori... the evidence suggests that the Treaty was intended by the colonial office to allow Crown rule to apply solely to British settlers in the fledgling colony'; Adams (1977: 156): 'Hobson was not definitely instructed to seek cession of the whole country... Hobson was told to try and acquire sovereignty of the lands where British subjects were already located first, but to accept the whole lot if the Maoris wished to cede it.'

more the result of British officials and missionaries in New Zealand acting in their own self-interests than the result of official policy (Seuffert, 1998: 73–77):

> It was only after the Treaty was signed, and Hobson's dubious Proclamations of Sovereignty had arrived at London, that the possibility of British sovereignty applying to Maori emerged as a serious consideration.
>
> (Moon, 2002: 185)

This 'dubious' status of the British in New Zealand subsequent to the Treaty is reflected in early British policy. Much of this early policy recognised that Maori retained their right to govern themselves, and that Maori law and custom would continue to apply at least to Maori (Adams, 1977: 210–37; Frame, 1981: 105–09). For some colonial actors, this policy was consistent with continued Maori self-governance and parallel legal systems. For others, it was a temporary measure in the assimilation of Maori to British laws and customs – or, in Salmond's terms, the fusion of two cultures into one nation. In any case, lack of money and resources meant that in the early years the British could at most pretend to govern Maori, a position that induced contempt in Maori who did have contact with the British (Adams, 1977: 236–37; Boast, 1993: 136–39). During these years, the simple fact was that most Maori continued to be governed by their own laws and customs, applied by their own people through established procedures, and were outside the jurisdiction of the colonial courts. British laws and customs simply did not extend to many Maori (Adams, 1977: 225–37).

An 1842 editorial in the *Bay of Islands Observer* provides a contemporaneous statement reflecting the two governing and legal systems operating with parallel jurisdictions:

> *The Maoris (sic) are not and cannot be governed by the Crown* [emphasis in original]. Those who signed it [the Treaty] and those who didn't alike disregard it, as far as the Government is concerned... The sovereignty over them on the part of Great Britain is entirely nominal... Thus, there are really two distinct communities in this country, living and more or less mingling with each other, governed on different principles, and by different laws and customs, and acknowledging a totally different authority.
>
> (Quaife, in Moon, 2002: 149–50)

This quote records the position of many Maori – the idea that they had ceded the power to apply their laws and customs was simply incomprehensible (Walker, 1989: 266; see also Swainson, 1859) and, initially at least, the Treaty signing had little or no impact on their lives or actions. According to Salmond's nineteenth-century notions of nation, fusing the two cultures in New Zealand into one nation would require eliminating diversities and creating a common nationality by excluding relationships to those beyond the limits, or boundaries, of the dominant nation.

Early British policy recognising continued Maori self-governance was implemented through colonial laws excepting or exempting Maori from their application and through laws declaring the recognition of Maori laws and customs (Adams, 1977: 230). Both of these approaches participated in defining the nation. Exempting Maori from the application of colonial laws defined the limits of the colonial jurisdiction, and positioned Maori outside the jurisdictional boundaries determining the emerging modern nation. Soon after his arrival in New Zealand in 1843, Governor Fitzroy, in a speech to 200 Maori leaders, assured them that he did not want to interfere with customs that affected only Maori (Adams, 1977: 223). He secured the passage of the Native Exemption Ordinance 1844, which provided for European interference with, or responses to, crimes between Maori only upon Maori request (Pratt, 1992: 42). This approach positioned Maori outside, but in parallel to, the emerging colonial nation, implicitly recognising the existence of two legal systems and two nations. The Ordinance was critiqued on the basis that it allowed Maori to maintain 'their nationality' (Adams, 1977: 223).

Statutory recognition of Maori laws and customs brought them within the subject-matter jurisdiction of the colonial courts, and provided the courts with the power to define and reshape those laws and customs.[3] This dynamic produced difference within the subject-matter jurisdiction of the courts and within the nation. The *New Zealand Government Act 1846* provided for Maori laws, customs and usages to be observed within certain districts in New Zealand. The Royal Instructions accompanying the *Act* provided for the setting aside of such districts, and for the application of Maori laws to both Maori and non-Maori inside the districts and between Maori outside the districts (Frame, 1981: 106–07).[4] With respect to jurisdiction, the 1846 proposal provided:

> The jurisdiction of the Courts and magistrates...shall extend over the said aboriginal districts, subject only to the duty...of taking notice of and giving effect to the laws, customs, and usages of aboriginal inhabitants.
>
> (Frame, 1981: 106–07, citing Chapter. 14 in 'Draft Instructions')

The creation of local districts, or sub-territorial units of difference, is one of the ways that jurisdiction may operate to produce difference within the nation. In the colonial context in New Zealand, where British governance was dubious, this proposal simultaneously extended jurisdiction, providing for the fusion of Maori into the emerging modern nation, and provided for the determination of difference within that jurisdiction by giving effect to Maori laws. This *1846 Act* was suspended, and the districts were never set aside.

The *New Zealand Constitution Act 1852* made New Zealand a self-governing colony with a General Assembly (the Crown, through a Governor, maintained imperial control over Maori affairs until 1861). The *1852 Act* remained in force

3 Hohepa and Williams (1996: 46): 'Whilst it is true that Maori custom is supposed to have been the basis for decisions of the Maori Land Court from 1865 to 1967 and 1974 to the present day, it has to be said that the "Maori custom" applied in that Court derives from rules laid down by Land Court judges which often bear but a remote resemblance to tikanga Maori.'

4 *Rira Peti v Ngaraihi Te Paku* (1888) 7 NZLR 235 at 239; s 6 was repealed by Royal Instructions of 1848.

until 1986, and also provided for districts to be set apart in which Maori laws, customs and usages would apply between Maori:

> It may be expedient that the laws, customs, and usages of the aboriginal or [Maori] inhabitants of New Zealand, so far as they are not repugnant to the general principles of humanity, should for the present be maintained for the government of themselves, in all their relations to and dealings with each other, and that particular districts should be set apart within which such laws, customs, or usages should so be observed.
>
> (s 71)

The language here is couched in the qualifiers 'may', 'expedient' and 'for the present'. This type of recognition of indigenous laws and customs was often part of the process of the creation and containment of difference in constructing a colonial nation:

> Custom...was 'recognised' solely in subordination to the law of the colonist and denied such recognition where it was 'repugnant to natural justice, equity, and good conscience', or 'contrary to the general principles of humanity' to take two standard and revealing formulations.
>
> (Fitzpatrick, 2001: 180)

'Recognition' of Maori laws that are not 'repugnant' to 'general principles of humanity' aligns the emerging modern nation with universalist notions of civilisation and subordinates Maori laws as particularist, producing difference within that nation (Fitzpatrick, 2001: 120–25). This language creates a site for the determination of which Maori laws would be recognised and applied, and which would be declared 'repugnant' to humanity, or civilisation, marking the boundary of inclusion within the jurisdiction of the colonial courts, and the nation. However, no districts were ever set aside; instead, Maori were to be violently assimilated to the centralised jurisdiction.

Boundary anxieties

By the 1860s, the form and boundaries of the nation were still debated. Debates regarding the meaning and effect of the Treaty still raged, with Maori, the Crown and the colonial governments still holding views ranging from power-sharing with Maori self-governance and parallel legal systems to absolute sovereignty of the British and complete control by the colonial administration.[5] Continued Maori demands for autonomy and self-governance, based on the Treaty, were reflected in developments such as the King Movement, in which substantial sectors of

5 See Orange (1987: 159–75) – for example, at p 168, quoting Sewell (1864: 5, 9, 40–41). Sewell, a member of the Legislative Council, perceived New Zealand as at a crossroads, with the essential question to be resolved 'what are the respective rights and obligations of two races placed in political relation to each other'.

North Island Maori came together in an effort to retain Maori self-governance, restrict sales of Maori land and reassert Maori values and culture (Firth, 1890: 32–51; Orange, 1987: 142; *Te Kingitanga*, 1996). In response to these types of co-ordinated Maori resistance to selling land and demands for parallel governing systems (Belich, 1986: 303), the British and colonial governments, in attempts to fix the boundaries of the nation-state, waged wars of sovereignty on Maori (Orange, 1987: 137–78). Although it is often assumed that Maori lost the wars, the wars were not successful in abolishing the King Movement, Maori demands for self-governance or centres of Maori autonomy (Belich, 1986: 305–10; *Maori History*, 1995: 555; *Te Kingitanga*, 1996: 50). James Belich writes that, even as late as 1884, the King Country encompassed 7,000 square miles:

> In the late nineteenth century an independent Maori state nearly two-thirds the size of Belgium existed in the middle of the North Island. Not all historians have noticed it.
>
> (1986: 306)

The King Movement and King Country represented an ongoing challenge to the centralised jurisdiction of the colonial courts and the determination of fixed national boundaries. In 1865, the King issued his own war honours (Orange, 1987: 173). The King Country both harboured fugitives from the colonial courts and killed Europeans who entered the area without permission, indicating the failure to extend colonial jurisdiction over it.

In light of the continued existence of centres of Maori autonomy it is not surprising that by 1865, it was still unclear, even to the colonial legislators, whether the general jurisdiction of the colonial courts extended to Maori. The *Native Rights Act 1865* expressed this anxiety explicitly in its preamble, which stated:

> An *Act* in response to doubts about whether the colonial courts have jurisdiction in all cases touching the persons and property of the Maori people.

This *Act* anxiously declared that the colonial courts had jurisdiction over Maori in an attempt to amalgamate Maori into colonial governing structures (Orange, 1987: 177–80). It simultaneously recognised jurisdiction over the determination of interests in land where native title had not been extinguished according to 'the ancient custom and usage of the Maori people' in the newly established Native Land Courts. The split in jurisdiction between the two court systems reflected ongoing anxiety about jurisdictional and national boundaries.

This boundary anxiety was revealed in a case in which the Supreme Court was required to determine whether all of the owners of a piece of land held under Maori title were capable of entering into a contract with respect to that land. The Court stated that it was 'quite at sea upon such questions – at sea without chart or compass…helpless to do anything but refer'[6] to the Native Land Court.

6 *Horomona & Others v Drowner* (1878) Vol IV NS 104, Supreme Court, at 107.

The requirement to refer a question of Maori law and custom to the Native Land Court results in the Court's acute anxiety; the language provides a dramatic image of the Court's discomfort with a limit to its ability to speak the law for the entire territory bounded by the sea. This lack of power leaves the Court at sea, outside the bounded territory, suggesting that Maori law and custom occupy the territory. The split in jurisdiction alone provides a challenge to the fiction of the emerging colonial nation.

In the context of the wars of sovereignty and ongoing Maori demands for autonomy, the establishment of Native Land Court jurisdiction performed two aspects of nation-building. It consolidated power in the colonial jurisdiction, buttressing the fiction of one nation. It also performed some of jurisdiction's most important work: the production of local difference within the territory of that jurisdiction 'by dividing society into distinctive local units that are imposed on individuals and groups' (Ford, 1999: 908), which also produced 'others' within the nation.

The function of the *Native Lands Act 1865* was to identify the 'ownership' of land held according to Maori proprietary customs, 'to encourage the extinction of such proprietary customs', replacing those customs with ownership of land in Crown-derived titles, and to regulate the succession of land with Crown titles (Preamble, s 23). The process was designed to enable potential buyers of land to identify the owners and to provide purchasers with certain title to land. The *Act* was intended to enable the British to more easily colonise the North Island by facilitating the sale of land, and to bring an end to 'tribal' Maori practices by destroying communal ownership, which was seen as part of a type of communism (Parsonson, 1998: 190–91). The Native Land Court jurisdiction therefore assimilated Maori to a centralised colonial jurisdiction by requiring its use for confirmation of their land ownership. It assimilated Maori to the nation by converting Maori laws and practices in relation to property into common law ownership.

The Native Land Court jurisdiction also produced Maori as different within the centralised colonial jurisdiction by creating a body of 'Maori law and custom' that often bore little relationship to the rules and practices used by Maori. The extent to which the courts shaped and created Maori law and custom in the process of applying it was recognised in 1910:

> A body of law has been recognized and created in that Court which represents the sense of justice of its judges in dealing with people in the course of transition from a state of tribal communism to a state in which property may be owned in severalty, or in the shape approaching severalty represented by tenancy in common.
>
> (*Willougby v Waihopi* at 149)[7]

As the quote suggests, the judges of the Court were much more interested in eliminating Maori customary tenure than in determining ownership according to Maori law (Williams, 1999: 165). This jurisdiction subordinated Maori law and

7 *Willougby v Waihopi* (1910) 29 NZLR 1123 at 149.

custom to the colonial courts while simultaneously reproducing it as inferior within that jurisdiction, with the goal of destroying it.

For example, the *Native Lands Act 1865* provided in s 23 for the court to issue certificates of title specifying the names of the persons or the tribe who, 'according to native custom', own or are interested in land, and provided that no certificates be issued to more than ten owners.[8] The provision for tribal title was under-utilised because applicants tended to name representative owners of the land rather than asking for tribal title. Despite the representative status of these people, the court frequently made grants to the named people as individual owners of undivided one-tenth shares in a whole block of land, insisting that the ten-person rule under s 23 was part of Maori custom, which clearly could not be the case (Williams, 1999: 162–64). In addition, the *Act* provided that any one of a number (sometimes hundreds) of communal owners of a block of land, regardless of their status as decision-makers in the *iwi* or *hapu* (people, 'tribe', 'subtribe') could bring the block in front of the court for a determination of title, forcing the rest of the *iwi* or *hapu* to participate. The jurisdiction thus facilitated land hungry settlers and speculators in persuading individual Maori into forcing the rapid individuation of title to Maori land, and the contemporaneous or subsequent alienation of the land, at great cost to Maori.

A 'bewildering succession' of *Acts* applying to the Native Land Court were passed in a manner that made it extremely difficult to ascertain the applicable law. The 'ridiculous' number of *Acts*, which were sometimes contradictory, may have resulted from attempts to deal with Maori land as though it were English land 'owned in severalty under a title of freehold'. The resulting system was 'expensive, complicated, slow and inefficient; nor did it even produce certainty of title' (Parsonson, 1998: 192). The system resulted in many Maori spending months away from home at locations where the court sat, often with disastrous affects on their health, funding the exorbitantly expensive court process with loans that ate into the proceeds of subsequent sales – transactions which were not in the interests of the *iwi* or *hapu* and against the wishes of many of the participants (Banner, 2000: 82–88). The Native Land Court jurisdiction's 'recognition' of Maori law and custom operated both to amalgamate Maori to a centralised system and to ensure their subordination within that system. The Chief Judge of the Native Land Court at the time stated: 'It is beyond the power of man to transfer the entire land of a country from one race to another without suffering to the weaker race' (Banner, 2000: 71, quoting Fenton, 1871). Indeed, the purpose of the court was to respond to colonial anxiety by attempting to create or produce Maori as a weaker, inferior race. Participation in the Court facilitated this by identifying Maori as a distinctive and particular local group within the centralised colonial jurisdiction.

The views of colonial officials and judges also reflect the fact that the Native Land Court and Maori were treated as 'different' from, and inferior to,

8 Section 23 allowed the court to issue certificates in the name of a tribe only with respect to pieces of land in excess of 5,000 acres.

the colonial norm. In *Wi Parata v The Bishop of Wellington*, discussed below, the Court characterised the Native Land Court jurisdiction as 'new and peculiar' (at 80). The Native Land Courts were said to be required to determine the ancient custom of the Maori people 'by methods known only to itself', positioning the jurisdiction, as well as Maori law and custom, as particular and peculiar in opposition to the universal principals of the common law. One early judge labelled Maori 'damned Cannibals', lamenting his entire tenure on the court. Other judges, who increasingly as time went on knew nothing about Maori language or culture, developed a dislike for Maori in general. Many officials were not interested in achieving justice through the court, and carelessness and the desire to facilitate land sales often prevailed over attempts to ascertain the true owners of Maori land. Maori were well aware of this dynamic. By 1868, the Native Land Court was already labelled the 'land taking court' by Maori; it has also been called an engine of destruction and a government 'weapon' of land confiscation (Banner, 2000: 71–82).

In the face of the ongoing claims to self-government represented in the King Movement, the combination of the *Native Rights Act* and the *Native Land Court Acts* anxiously extended the jurisdiction of colonial courts over Maori and Maori land, attempting to assert control. The land tenure revolution effected through the jurisdiction of the Native Land Court assimilated the ownership of Maori land to colonial title, while the *Native Rights Act* asserted jurisdiction over land after it passed through the Native Land Courts, and over the persons of all Maori. The two pieces of legislation operated as major mechanisms of centralisation of power in the colonial courts, consistently feeding more power through those courts. Maori in some areas, such as the King Country, resisted use of the Land Courts, and managed to maintain autonomy. Other Maori, attempting to work with the government, were more likely to end up in the Land Courts with a resulting further loss of autonomy (Belich, 1986: 308). By breaking *iwi* and *hapu* control and authority over land, the Land Court 'revolution' was an integral part of the war on sovereignty, interfering with Maori leadership and decision-making. Simultaneously, the jurisdiction of the Native Land Courts divided society into two groups: those whose land was dealt with in these Courts and those whose land was dealt with in the mainstream colonial courts. It was ownership of land with Maori title, or Maori ownership of land, which landed one in the Native Land Courts, where particular rules – and not those of Maori law or custom – applied. This process facilitated the production of Maori as different and of 'Maori law and custom' as particular and inferior to the 'general' common law that was defined as encompassing universal principals of humanity.

Tales of jurisdiction and nation

The establishment and operation of the Native Land Court reflected a tidal change in colonial policy regarding jurisdiction away from even sporadic recognition of any meaningful self-governance for Maori. While it nominally recognised the existence of Maori law and custom, it shaped that recognition in the interests of colonisation, assimilating Maori to a centralised jurisdiction that participated in producing them as assimilated political subjects of Britain. In 1877, in *Wi Parata v The Bishop of Wellington*,[9] Chief Justice Prendergast was to tell a story of New Zealand as a nation that violently ended any remaining uncertainty of the courts with respect to the recognition of Maori laws and customs, and the jurisdictional boundaries of the courts.

The context in which the case was decided is important to an understanding of its implications for nation-building. During the first decades after the signing of the Treaty, Maori people gifted many pieces of land to churches in trust for the purpose of building schools for the local *iwi*. Few schools were built. The government wanted control over these lands. Gaining control required wresting control from the churches, and eliminating any reversionary rights to the land in the original Maori donors (Hackshaw, 1989: 109). Further, the land gifted to church-held charities was only one piece of a bigger puzzle. By the early 1870s, it was clear to Maori that the British were using any means possible, including war and the jurisdiction of the Native Land Court, to prise land from their hold. In response to their dissatisfaction, Maori were encouraged to use the courts. This suggestion was vigorously followed throughout the 1870s, and by the 1880s more than 1,000 Maori petitions were presented, with the Treaty figuring prominently in many of them (Orange, 1987: 186).

Wi Parata was a leader of Ngati Toa who claimed original ownership of one of the pieces of land; this piece had been given to Bishop Selwyn in 1848 for the purposes of educating the Ngati Toa children (*Wi Parata v The Bishop of Wellington* at 72). In 1850, a Crown grant of the land was made to Bishop Selwyn. Wi Parata applied to the Supreme Court for a declaration that the Crown grant of the land was void, and that the land should revert to Ngati Toa as it had not been used for the purposes for which it had been given (at 73–74). It was argued that the Crown grant was void, as the only way the Crown could obtain land from Maori was through purchase (at 74). The implications of Wi Parata's claim were therefore far-reaching: if he succeeded, a precedent for return of other land would be set, and a precedent for other claims based on the Treaty's guarantee of undisturbed possession of Maori land might also be created – a possibility of which the government was fully aware (Orange, 1987: 186). Chief Justice Prendergast concluded that, in New Zealand, the Court had no jurisdiction to avoid a Crown grant on the basis that it did not conform with the intention of the original owners (at 76–77), and therefore the land could not revert back to Ngati Toa.

In the course of its decision, the Court rewrote the story of New Zealand as a colony and emerging nation, violently erasing the power-sharing agreement in the Treaty and in Maori laws and customs (Fitzpatrick, 2001: 178), and unequivocally excluding those laws and customs from the boundaries of jurisdiction, and from the nation. The Court categorised Maori as uncivilised barbarians, and the land

9 *Wi Parata v The Bishop of Wellington* (1877) 3 NZJR (NS) 72.

they inhabited as 'thinly peopled by barbarians without any form of law or civil government' (at 77). Any guarantees to exclusive and undisturbed possession of land in the English version of the Treaty were irrelevant to the outcome of the case since the Treaty was a 'simple nullity... [because] No body politic existed capable of making cession of sovereignty' (at 78). According to Justice Prendergast, Maori people were uncivilised, primitive barbarians, and therefore could not constitute an independent political society with a sovereign capable of ceding sovereignty.

The Court relied on this characterisation to ignore and erase early colonial policy recognising Maori law and custom:

> Had any body of law or custom capable of being understood and administered by the Courts of a civilized country, been known to exist, the British Government would surely have provided for its recognition, since nothing could exceed the anxiety displayed to infringe no just right of the aborigines. (at 73)

Yet, as discussed above, a number of statutes *had* explicitly recognised Maori law and custom. The explicit recognition by the *Native Rights Act 1865* of the 'ancient custom and usage of the Maori people' was dismissed: 'As if some such body of customary law did in reality exist. But a phrase in a statute cannot call what is non-existent into being' (at 79).

In response to the 'doubts about whether the colonial courts have jurisdiction' over Maori in the preamble to the *Native Rights Act 1865*, the Court asserted that 'we do not understand what could be the doubt' (at 79). The Court adamantly – and incorrectly[10] – concluded that the British Government had never recognised Maori law and custom because it did not exist. It also erased 38 years of the continued application of those laws and customs to Maori outside of the colonial court system.

The Court's tall tale of early colonial policy violently erased Maori law and custom, and simultaneously created a fantasy of an emerging modern nation. Maori are positioned as uncivilised, dispersed barbarians without law, in opposition to the civilised unified nations of the world. Where there is a 'cession of territory by one civilised power to another', the laws of the ceding country are administered by the Courts of the new sovereign (at 78); the Court found however that Maori were not a civilised power, and therefore could not cede sovereignty and had no laws for the courts to apply.

The court also defined what is meant by civilisation in opposition to the slippery and ill-defined words 'barbarian' and 'savage'. Peter Fitzpatrick has argued that terms such as 'savage' operated in the colonial period in opposition to modernity as 'cohering, "quilting" point[s], bringing together the disparate dimensions of modern

10 Frame (1981: 109) – see discussion of *Nireah Tamaki v Baker* (1901) NZPCC 371; Hackshaw (1989: 93): '[I]nstead of reflecting established law, *[Wi Parata]* reflected untested positivist-inspired legal theories...'; Brookfield (1989: 10): 'the work done recently by academic writers... appears to leave no doubt that since the late 1870s successive New Zealand judges have misunderstood the law... on the whole they did indeed get it wrong'.

identity' (Fitzpatrick, 2001: 18, 65). In order to operate in this manner, these concepts had to be both apart from modern identity and yet recognisably related to it, and had to provide opposites to the aspects of modern identity that they were to 'quilt' together. Aspects of modernity might be 'quilted' in opposition to a degenerate or 'savage and barbaric' past, which modernity must guard against (Stychin, 1998: 4).

The Court's use of the term 'primitive barbarians' (at 78) illustrates this quilting effect well. 'Primitive' invokes the pre-modern past, and 'barbarians' connotes inferiority, 'lack of refinement, sensitivity, learning or artistic or literary culture; uncivilised' (Longman, 1984). The emerging nation-state is defined in opposition to its own pre-modern past, providing the crucial link necessary to quilt modern identity. Opposition to 'barbarian' positions this modern national identity as an intricate quilt of refinement, sensitivity, artistry, culture and civilisation. The Court's reference to a past where New Zealand was 'thinly peopled', at a time when there was an influx of settlers to New Zealand, also positions high-density population, and colonisation, as aspects of civilisation. Defining Maori as without law or civil government allows the existence of those institutions alone, regardless of their processes or capacity to achieve justice, to count as civilised. In this context, the Court's refusal of jurisdiction to avoid the Crown grant protects the Court from tainting by its pre-modern, or uncivilised, past.

In Salmond's (1907) terms, the decision in *Wi Parata* operates to eliminate diversities within the nation's borders by excluding 'all remembered relationship with those beyond the limits of the state'. Justice Prendergast's decision literally remembers the nation by telling a tall tale erasing or cutting off not only any recognition of Maori laws and practices in colonial law but also any existence at all of those laws and practices. Prendergast's decision, by disclaiming jurisdiction to hear Treaty claims and Maori property rights, and by erasing the entire body of Maori law and custom, violently assimilates Maori to the subject-matter jurisdiction of the colonial courts, the colonial laws and the emerging modern nation-state of New Zealand.

In practical and political terms, Justice Prendergast's conclusion that, in New Zealand, a Crown grant extinguished native title and therefore the land could not revert back to Ngati Toa legitimated the Crown in extinguishing Maori title to land without purchasing it. The case also emphasises that Maori will have no recourse to the courts, the proclaimed arbiters and protectors of justice within the imposed system, for Treaty breaches. The decision in *Wi Parata* facilitated the ongoing confiscation of Maori land, legitimating over 100 pieces of legislation to 'legalise' Maori dispossession from Maori land. It has been argued that all of these pieces of legislation were enacted in breach of the Treaty (Jackson, 1993: 77).

Internal foes within the nation

The extension of criminal jurisdiction over Maori was an integral part of the use of jurisdiction as a tool of nation-building. I have noted that early colonial policy, such as the Native Exemption Ordinance 1844, provided for colonial interference in crimes between Maori only at Maori request. Until at least the early 1860s, specific attempts to extend criminal jurisdiction over Maori were often ignored or subverted (Hill, 1986: 856–64; Pratt, 1992: 43–58). Prendergast's 1878 *Wi Parata* fantasy, in which the jurisdiction of the colonial courts extended unequivocally to all Maori, both facilitated and buttressed the progressive extension of criminal jurisdiction over Maori, increasingly positioning them as internal foes within the nation.

It is argued that, by the mid-1860s, the sovereignty war, combined with the extension of civil administration such as roads and health systems, broke down some resistance to colonial penal jurisdiction over Maori (Pratt, 1986: 56). This extension of jurisdiction meant that some Maori customs and practices integral to Maori law would be punished as criminal acts, criminalising Maori and branding their practices as different within the emerging modern nation. However, in many areas Maori laws and customs still prevailed, and the extension of jurisdiction often came only with Maori acquiescence (Pratt, 1986: 56–58).

In 1863, in the midst of the sovereignty war, a raft of legislation targeted at criminalising the behaviour of Maori, both extending the courts' jurisdiction over Maori and positioning them as internal foes within the nation, was passed. It included the *New Zealand Settlements Act 1863*, which authorised the confiscation of whole districts of land where 'any considerable number' of Maori were believed to be in 'rebellion' – effectively meaning those who were acting consistent with the Treaty guarantees of autonomy (Miller, 1966: 109–10; Orange, 1987: 167). This measure was directed in part at the King Movement but could apply in any district of the country. The *Suppression of Rebellion Act 1863* authorised the arrest and detention without trial of anyone suspected of complicity in the 'rebellion' (Orange, 1987: 169–70).

As resistance to the attacks on Maori sovereignty through land confiscation, and in particular the *New Zealand Settlements Act*, continued through the 1870s and 1880s, other pieces of legislation were also passed. For example, in the 1870s, at the same time that *Wi Parata* was being decided, Maori disputed the confiscation of land in Taranaki and the failure to create reserves promised as part of land sales. They peacefully ploughed and fenced the 'confiscated' land in protest, putting up no resistance to arrest. If charged with trespass, the protestors would be likely to receive little if any gaol term. The *Confiscated Lands Inquiry and Maori Prisoners' Trials Act 1879*, rushed through with all three readings in one day, allowed Maori to be held in gaol without bail until the Governor in Council fixed a date for their trial (s 6). The *Maori Prisoners Act 1880* provided that all of those awaiting trial or held in custody were deemed to have been lawfully arrested and in lawful custody until the Governor ordered their release (s 3), indicating that 'large numbers' of Maori were detained under these measures.[11] *TheMaori Prisoners Detention Act 1880* again extended the length of time that the Maori protestors could be held without trial. The *West Coast Settlement*

11 *Confiscated Lands Inquiry and Maori Prisoners Trial Act 1879* (NZ), parenthetical from long title of Act; Sinclair (2000: 152).

(North Island) Act 1880 allowed the arrest without a warrant of anyone who might be suspected of being about to commit an offence such as unlawfully ploughing or fencing, or interfering with a survey. The possible punishment included 2 years of imprisonment with hard labour (Parsonson, 1998: 188–89). The government's own inquiry promised by the *1879 Act* found that promises to set aside reserves for Maori had been repeatedly broken (AJHR, 1881: G-1), suggesting that the protests were justified. The *Acts* therefore criminalised the activities of Maori who were generally simply living consistent with the terms of the Treaty or attempting to peacefully focus attention on to grievous Treaty breaches. The only justification for imprisonment without trial was the perception that the release of these Maori 'would endanger the peace of the colony, and might lead to insurrection'[12] – they were treated quite literally as internal foes of the nation.

Producing a 'better Britain'

Prendergast's *Wi Parata* fantasy of the unequivocal supremacy of the Crown in New Zealand, and of a superior British civilisation in opposition to a primitive and savage indigenous people, was consistent with the emerging national identity of New Zealand – an identity focused on racial purity and embracing British culture as the peak civilisation. Aspirations to racial purity were facilitated by the erasure of Maori laws and customs, allowing the assimilation of 'good' Maori into a fiction of a unified nation, while Maori who insisted on recognition of the Treaty agreements were positioned as internal foes to the nation. In the late nineteenth century, fantasies of Maori as an Aryan race, descended from the same people as the Britons (although not as advanced as the Britons) emerged. These fictions positioned Maori as suitable candidates for quick amalgamation into the idea of a better Britain aspired to by many colonials who were coming to think of themselves as 'New Zealanders'.

By the end of the century, New Zealand was in the process of emerging from residual British control as a Dominion. However, it considered itself the English colony that remained most faithful to the mother country, and many New Zealanders were proud to identify as British, both culturally and racially (Gibbons, 1998: 309, 314). New Zealand was seen as a laboratory for the production of a 'better Britain'. This experiment was founded on the idea of the careful selection by the 'systematic' colonisers in the 1840s and 1850s of the 'pick' of British stock to colonise New Zealand (Reeves, 1899: 404). The history of selection on the basis of quality was opposed to Australia's convict immigration. Immigration was strictly limited by an unwritten 'whiter than white' policy that maintained a largely homogenous British population: 'New Zealand was viewed by successive governments as a utopia for a few, preferably white, Protestant Britons' (Brooking, 1995: 23).

12 *Maori Prisoners Act 1880*, preamble.

The image of New Zealanders as having a 'special destiny as the vanguard of British civilisation', the finest of all civilisations, resulting in New Zealand being dubbed 'God's own country', was strong. The ranking of civilisations was explicitly racial, and the subjugation of non-Europeans by the British was imagined as inevitable (Gibbons, 1998: 309–16; Stocking, 1987: 133–37). New Zealand's national identity was promoted as separate from imperial identity while deriving its coherence and stability from its flexible incorporation of Imperialist ideologies – 'primarily racism and cultural superiority' (O'Neill, 1993: 24). These sentiments are captured in this turn of the century passage:

> 'Home' means that we have transplanted to these alien lands and seas the national ideals of the North, the racial vigour and aspirations of our sires. It means that we have tried and are trying to be true to type, to keep our blood clean and pure, to preserve our past traditions, to be worthy of our great history, to progress undeviatingly and steadily along the lines instinctively taken by the heroes and leaders of our ancestral people. In a word, we seek to make of New Zealand a Better Britain.
>
> (Sinclair, 1986: 79, quoting *New Zealand Herald*, 26 March 1910)

The emphasis was on the purity of racial descent and the fiction of New Zealand as originally British – and potentially even more British than Britain itself. Aspirations to a 'better Britain' incorporate the recognition that British civilisation is at the top, as high as one can go in the hierarchy of civilisations that was so prevalent in the late nineteenth century; it was an idea that served the purposes of colonisation and imperialism well (Stocking, 1987).

Maori were incorporated into aspirations to a better Britain with flimsy arguments (Hanson, 1989: 892) that they were descended from the same common stock as the Anglo-Saxon (Gibbons, 1998: 313; Reeves, 1899: 417). The classic text for this viewpoint was Edward Tregear's *The Aryan Maori* (1885), which argued that Maori were descendants of the same Aryan people from whom the settlers came. As great explorers and migrants of the Pacific, the Maori were 'ennobled' in European eyes (O'Neill, 1993: 231). Maori were also positioned as the 'Vikings of the Sunrise' (Wanhalla, 2002: 18). It was argued in 1889 that 'the Maories [sic] are a branch of the Aryan race, and in their language, customs, characteristics, and traditions, possibly present better glimpses of our Aryan ancestors than any nation now in existence' (Firth, 1890: v). This quote positions Maori as providing, in the present, 'better' glimpses of British ancestors than any other nation. Maori were therefore 'pure' examples of settlers' pre-modern ancestors, without the progress to modernity that the great civilisation of Britain had provided.

These texts of 'hyperbolic admiration' (O'Neill, 1993: 232) both justified the inclusion of Maori in the story told about New Zealand as a better Britain, and simultaneously positioned Maori as pre-modern, and therefore as inferior to the settlers. Maori were therefore perceived as potential, and deserving, beneficiaries of the higher British civilisation. Maori were positioned as outside of the *modern* nation, but clearly recognisable to it, and capable of being incorporated into it as 'long lost Aryan siblings' (Ballantyne, 2002: 76–77). At a time when Maori were again clarifying demands for self-governance based on the Treaty, these stories supported policies of amalgamation into one nation in opposition to recognition of the right to self-governance.

The idea of New Zealand as a laboratory for the development of a 'better Britain' involved quilting that identity, partly in opposition to a number of strands of ideas regarding Maori. The idea of Maori as sharing pre-modern but superior origins with the British was just one of these. Another was the myth that Maori were, in any case, a 'dying race', superseded by the superior British who, while they may have had shared origins, had progressed far beyond the Maori (Belich, 1986: 299; Firth, 1890: v; Reeves, 1899: 398; Stenhouse, 1999: 81–86). This popular nineteenth-century brand of Darwinism was 'a basic axiom of nineteenth-century racial thought... Europeans in contact with lesser races would inevitably exterminate, absorb, or, at the very least, subordinate them' (Belich, 1986: 323). The inevitability of these ideas helped to contain the threat that Maori posed as other to the emerging modern nation. As a dying race, with falling numbers, Maori would lose any political power and any ability to threaten the cohesion of one pure nation or demand fulfilment of the Treaty and be forced to assimilate. In fact, from 1896 the Maori population in New Zealand was increasing rather than decreasing, highlighting the mythical aspect of these ideas (King, 1998: 286).

In contrast to fantasies of a unified 'better Britain', many Maori were still demanding that the government honour the Treaty and give effect to its vision of power-sharing. The King Country was still operating largely independently. It was exercising its own jurisdiction, collecting taxes, administering justice and discouraging land sales through the 1890s (Belich, 1986: 307). In the 1870s and 1880s, great *hui* (gatherings) were held to formulate strategies for seeking government recognition of Maori grievances. Major chiefs throughout the North Island pledged themselves to union and setting up a Maori government under the Treaty, known as the *Kotahitanga* parliaments, which began to meet in 1892. The chiefs also sought the grant of a constitution for Maori, which would allow them to pass laws governing themselves and their lands, consistent with the Treaty. They sought equal rights for Maori with British settlers, who became known as *Pakeha* (Parsonson, 1998: 197). The reality was that, by the late 1890s, it had become clear that Maori 'had resisted the first great push of the British to assimilate them' (O'Malley, 1998: 241; Parsonson, 1998: 197).

Conclusion

Jurisdictional boundaries, like ideas of nation and national boundaries, are contested. In the process of colonisation in New Zealand, tall tales and fantasies were told about both jurisdictional and national boundaries. These tales were told in legislation and cases, highlighting the operation of jurisdiction as a tool for the creation of a myth of colonial progress in which Maori were subordinated to the colonial courts. This fantasy required ignoring and erasing ongoing Maori authority and self-governance. In fact, many Maori successfully resisted colonial assimilation throughout the nineteenth century. This analysis suggests close scrutiny of the extent to which current dominant assumptions of 'one nation' continue to erase Maori autonomy and self-governance.

References

Adams, Peter (1977) *Fatal Necessity*, Auckland: Oxford

Anderson, Benedict (1991) *Imagined Communities: Reflections of the Origins and Spread of Nationalism*, London: Verso

Ballantyne, Tony (2002) *Orientalism and Race: Aryanism in the British Empire*, New York, NY: Palgrave

Banner, Stuart (2000) 'Conquest by contract: wealth transfer and land market structure in colonial New Zealand' 34 *Law & Society Review* 47

Belich, James (1986) *The New Zealand Wars and the Victorian Interpretation of Conflict*, Auckland: Auckland University Press

Binney, Judith (1981) 'Maori oral narratives, *Pakeha* written texts: Two forms of telling history' 21(1) *New Zealand Journal of History* 16

Boast, Richard (1993) 'Maori and the law, 1840–2000', in P Spiller, J Finn and R Boast (eds), *A New Zealand Legal History*, Wellington: Brookers

Brookfield, FM (1989) 'The New Zealand constitution: The search for legitimacy', in IH Kawharau (ed), *Waitangi: Maori and Pakeha Perspectives on the Treaty of Waitangi*, Auckland: Oxford University Press

Brooking, Tom and Rabel, Roberto (1995) 'Neither British nor Polynesian: A brief history of New Zealand's other immigrants', in SW Greif (ed), *Immigration and National Identity in New Zealand*, Palmerston North: Dunmore

Colenso, William (1890) *The Authentic and Genuine History of the Signing of the Treaty of Waitangi*, Wellington: np

Dorset, Shaunnagh (2000) ' "Since time immemorial": A story of common law jurisdiction, native title and the case of Tanistry' 26 *Melbourne University Law Review* 32

'Draft Instructions' to 1846 Constitution, CO 881/1, XXXIII, London: Public Records Office

Durie, ET (1996) 'Will the settlers settle? Cultural conciliation and law' 8 *Otago Law Review* 449

Fenton, Francis (1871) Letter to Donald McLean, 12 August, MS-Copy-Micro-0535–052, Turnbull Library, Wellington

Firth, JC (1890) *Nation Making: Savagism and Civilization*, London: Longman, Green, and Co.

Fitzpatrick, Peter (2001) *Modernism and the Grounds of Law*, Cambridge: Cambridge University Press

Ford, Richard (1999) 'Law's territory (a history of jurisdiction)' 97 *Michigan Law Review* 843

Frame, Alex (1981) 'Colonising attitudes towards Maori custom' *New Zealand Law Journal* 105

Frame, Alex (1995) *Salmond: Southern Jurist*, Wellington: Victoria University Press

Gibbons, PJ (1998) 'The climate of opinion', in GW Rice (ed), *The Oxford History of New Zealand*, 2nd edn, Auckland: Oxford University Press

Gipps, Governor Sir George (1968) to Lord John Russell, 16 August 1840, in BPP, *Correspondence and Other Papers Relating to New Zealand 1835–42, Colonies, New Zealand, Vol. 3*, Shannon: Irish University Press

Hackshaw, Frederika (1989) 'Nineteenth century notions of Aboriginal title and their influence on the interpretation of the Treaty of Waitangi', in IH Kawharau (ed),

Waitangi: Maori and Pakeha Perspectives on the Treaty of Waitangi, Auckland: Oxford University Press

Hanson, Allan (1989) 'The making of the Maori: Culture invention and its logic' 91 *American Anthropologist* 890

Harris, Angela P (1996) 'Comment: Seductions of modern culture' 8 *Yale JL & Human* 213.

Hight, J and Bamford, HD (1914) *The Constitutional History and Law of New Zealand*, Christchurch: Whitcombe and Tombs

Hill, Richard S (1986) *Policing the Colonial Frontier, Part Two*, Wellington: VR Ward, Government Printer

Hohepa, Pat and Williams, David (1996) 'The taking into account of Te Ao Maori in relation to reform of the law of succession', Law Commission Working Paper, Wellington: New Zealand Law Commission

Jackson, Moana (1993) 'Land loss and the Treaty of Waitangi', in Witi Ihimaera (ed), *Te Ao Marama 2: Regaining Aotearoa*, Auckland: Reed

King, Michael (1998) 'Between two worlds', in GW Rice (ed), *The Oxford History of New Zealand*, 2nd edn, Auckland: Oxford University Press

Law Commission (2001) 'Maori custom and values in New Zealand law' Study Paper 9, March, Wellington: Law Commission

Longman Dictionary of the English Language (1984) Essex: Merriam-Webster

McDonnell, Lieutenant Colonel (1997) *Maori History: Being a Native Account of the Pakeha-Maori Wars in New Zealand*, Auckland: H Brett

Miller, Harold (1966) *Race Conflict in New Zealand 1814–1865*, Westport: Greenwood Press

Moon, Paul (2002) *The Path of the Treaty of Waitangi: Te Ara Ki Te Tiriti*, Auckland: David Ling Publishing

Normanby, Marquis (1968) to Captain Hobson, RN, 14 August 1839, BPP, *Correspondence and Other Papers Relating to New Zealand 1835–1842, Colonies, New Zealand, Vol. 3*, Shannon: Irish University Press

O'Malley, Vincent (1998) *Agents of Autonomy: Maori Committees in the Nineteenth Century*, Wellington: Huia

O'Neill, Phillip Raymond (1993) 'Unsettling the Empire: Postcolonialism and the troubled identities of settler nations', unpublished PhD thesis, New York University

Orange, Claudia (1987) *The Treaty of Waitangi*, Sydney: Allen & Unwin

Parsonson, Ann (1998) 'The challenge to Mana Maori', in GW Rice (ed), *The Oxford History of New Zealand*, 2nd edn, Auckland: Oxford University Press

Pratt, John (1992) *Punishment in a Perfect Society*, Wellington: Victoria University Press

Quaife, Barzillai (1842) Editorial, *Bay of Islands Observer*, 10 March

Reeves, William Pember (1899) *The Long White Cloud: Aotearoa*, London: Horace Marshall & Son

Renan, Ernest (1990) 'What is a nation?', in H.K. Bhaba (ed), *Nation and Narration*, London: Routledge

Report of the Royal Commission appointed under the *Confiscated Lands and Maori Prisoners Trials Act 1879* (1881) AJHR, G-1

Ross, Ruth (1972) 'Te Tiriti o Waitani: Texts and translations' 6(2) *New Zealand Journal of History* 129

Rush, Peter (1997) 'An altered jurisdiction: Corporeal traces of law' 6 *Griffith Law Review* 144

Salmond, John W (1907) *Jurisprudence or the Theory of the Law*, 2nd edn, London: Steven and Haynes

Seuffert, Nan (1998) 'Colonising concepts of the good citizen: Law's deceptions and the Treaty of Waitangi' 4.2 *Law Text Culture* 69

Sewell, H (1864) The New Zealand Native Rebellion, Letter to Lord Lyttleton, Auckland, pp 5, 9, 40–41

Sinclair, Keith (1986) *A Destiny Apart: New Zealand's Search for National Identity*, Wellington: Unwin

Sinclair, Keith (2000) *A History of New Zealand*, Auckland: Penguin

Stenhouse, John (1999) 'Darwinism in New Zealand, 1859–1900', in R Numbers and J Stenhouse (eds), *Disseminating Darwinism: The Role of Place, Race, Religion and Gender*, Cambridge: Cambridge University Press

Stocking, George W Jr (1987) *Victorian Anthropology*, New York, NY: Free Press

Stychin, Carl F (1998) *A Nation by Rights*, Philadelphia: Temple University Press

Swainson, William (1859) *New Zealand and its Colonisation*, London: Smith, Elder and Co.

Te Kingitanga: The People of the Maori King Movement (1996) Essays from the *Dictionary of New Zealand Biography*, Auckland: Auckland University Press

Tregear, Edward (1885) *The Aryan Maori*, Wellington: Government Printer

Walker, Ranganui (1989) 'The Treaty of Waitangi as the focus of Maori protest', in IH Kawharau (ed), *Waitangi: Maori and Pakeha Perspectives on the Treaty of Waitangi*, Auckland: Oxford University Press

Wanhalla, Angela (2002) 'Maori women in *Waka* traditions', in L Fraser and K Pickles (eds), *Shifting Centres: Women and Migration in New Zealand History*, Dunedin, FL: University of Otago Press

Williams, David (1989) 'Te Tiriti o Waitangi – unique relationship between Crown and Tangata Whenua?', in IH Kawharau (ed), *Waitangi: Maori and Pakeha Perspectives on the Treaty of Waitangi*, Auckland: Oxford University Press

Williams, David (1999) *'Te Kooti Tango Whenua': The Native Land Court 1864–1909*, Wellington: Huia

Cases

Horomona & Others v Drowner (1878) Vol. IV NS 104, Supreme Court, 107

Nireah Tamaki v Baker (1901) NZPCC 371

Rira Peti v Ngaraihi Te Paku (1888) 7 NZLR 235, 239

Wi Parata v The Bishop of Wellington (1877) 3 NZJR (NS) 72

Willougby v Waihopi (1910) 29 NZLR 1123

Legislations

Confiscated Lands Inquiry and Maori Prisoners' Trials Act 1879 (NZ)

Constitution Act 1986 (NZ)

Maori Prisoners Act 1880 (NZ)

Maori Prisoners Detention Act 1880 (NZ)

Native Lands Act 1865 (NZ)

Native Rights Act 1865 (NZ)

New Zealand Constitution Act 1852 (NZ)

New Zealand Government Act 1846 (NZ)

New Zealand Settlements Act 1863 (NZ)

Suppression of Rebellion Act 1863 (NZ)

West Coast Settlements (North Island) Act 1880 (NZ)

7 The suppression of state interests in international litigation

Mary Keyes

Introduction

This chapter considers the role state interests play in the resolution of international jurisdictional disputes. Judicial jurisdiction, in Australian law, is composed of two inquiries. First, does the court regard itself as competent to hear and determine the dispute? I refer to this as the 'existence' of jurisdiction. Second, assuming the first requirement to be satisfied, will the court in the exercise of its discretion decline to hear the dispute? I refer to this as the 'exercise' of jurisdiction. It is difficult to refute the proposition that jurisdiction, which determines the extent of state authority and when it ought to be exercised in the context of international litigation, fundamentally involves problems of state interest. Remarkably, in international litigation it is rare to find an express acknowledgement of this fact. It is more likely – although still rare – to find judges expressly disavowing the relevance of state interests.

In *Lubbe v Cape*, the House of Lords had to determine whether it ought to exercise its jurisdiction. This was a group action in which a very large number of plaintiffs, almost all resident in and citizens of South Africa, sought damages in the English courts for personal injuries against an English corporation, essentially for its responsibility over its South African subsidiary companies. Lord Hope wrote that the relevant principles for determining this issue 'leave no room for considerations of public interest or public policy which cannot be related to the private interests of any of the parties or the ends of justice' in the particular cases.[1] Other members of the House of Lords agreed.

While this may not seem particularly noteworthy in a normal instance of international commercial litigation, this case clearly implicated state interests. The South African Government made submissions to the House of Lords, arguing that this dispute ought to be heard in the English courts and that for public policy reasons the defendant ought not be permitted to manipulate the forum (Muchlinski, 2001: 18). The South African Government argued that its own substantive laws on workplace negligence applicable at the time of the alleged

1 *Lubbe v Cape plc* [2000] 1 WLR 1545 at 1566.

torts were unconscionable as they were racially discriminatory and therefore that they should not be applied to resolve the dispute (Muchlinski, 2001: 21). One might have thought that these submissions, especially when expressed by the government of a foreign state, were quite a clear indication that issues of state interest were live in this dispute.

State interests, both of the legal system providing a forum and of foreign legal systems, are relevant and often influential in determining whether jurisdiction exists and whether it ought to be exercised. Both foreign and state interests are usually suppressed, although for different reasons. This suppression is unnecessary and makes the law uncertain and confusing. It would be preferable for the courts explicitly to acknowledge the role that state interests play (Fawcett, 1989: 226–27), which would permit a consideration of the legitimacy of those interests.

This chapter is presented in three sections. The first identifies how state interests may impact on jurisdictional principles and practices, giving some examples of the state interests which may be discerned from the relevant principles and the courts' practices. In my discussion of the courts' practices, I refer to empirical research I undertook which analysed all published decisions of the Australian superior courts between January 1991 and September 2001 in which the courts decided whether to exercise their jurisdiction (Keyes, 2005). The second section of the chapter suggests why state interests are suppressed, while the third section argues that they ought *not* to be suppressed.

State interests in jurisdiction

State interests are evident – although seldom articulated in those terms – in many aspects of jurisdictional law and the practices of the courts in resolving international disputes. The state interests may be those of the state in which the dispute is being heard (the forum), or those of other states. If the court perceives that the forum state's internal interests are at stake in the litigation, it may take the view that it is bound to uphold these interests. If the court perceives that a foreign state has some interest in the resolution of the dispute – which is inevitable to a greater or lesser degree in international litigation – it is likely not to give weight to that interest except in extreme cases. If the court perceives that the forum state and the foreign state both have interests in the resolution of the dispute, it will in most cases prefer the interests of the forum state. But, almost invariably, these questions are suppressed under the seemingly neutral language of international litigation.

The forum state's interests

When the forum court apprehends that there is an issue of state interest at stake in the litigation and that the court is obliged to ensure that interest is protected, this may influence and sometimes determine the outcome of a dispute.

The clearest example of such a case is where the litigation concerns the application of substantive mandatory forum legislation. If the legislation appears to apply to the dispute, the court may hold that it is constitutionally obliged, under the doctrine of parliamentary sovereignty, to apply the legislation,[2] irrespective of the usual jurisdictional principles. In *Akai v The People's Insurance Co*, a bare majority of the High Court took this view. On their interpretation of the *Insurance Contracts Act 1984* (Cth), this legislation was applicable to the dispute, although the parties had expressly negotiated a choice of English courts and English law, and the legislation said nothing about its intended effect in a jurisdictional dispute. The majority thought the court was constitutionally obliged to ensure the application of this legislation.[3] Because the defendant had not proven that the English courts would apply the Australian legislation (an impossible task), the court retained its jurisdiction (for criticism, see Whincop and Keyes, 1998).

The courts seldom explicitly take this approach. In my study of the Australian courts' practices in exercising jurisdiction referred to in the introduction to this chapter, I did not find any case in the five years following the decision in *Akai* in which the court applied the same analysis. But the potential application of 'mandatory' forum legislation appears to influence decisions. Section 52 of the *Trade Practices Act 1974* (Cth) prohibits misleading and deceptive conduct, and has mandatory effect in domestic Australian litigation. It is silent as to its intended effect in international litigation. In my study I found that, in every case not involving a contractual submission to jurisdiction in which the plaintiff claimed for breach of s 52, the court retained jurisdiction (Keyes, 2005: 170). In disputes in which there was no claim for breach of s 52, the court retained jurisdiction in 74.2 per cent of cases (Keyes, 2005: 170). While the courts do not state that they are retaining jurisdiction because of their constitutional responsibility to ensure application of this legislation, its potential application appears to assert a decisive influence.

Other kinds of local state interests are evident in the rules on establishing jurisdiction. Consistently with the division of authority between states in public international law, the forum state is taken to have authority to regulate local persons, property and activities, and these are common bases of determining the existence of jurisdiction. However, public international law imposes a requirement that any territorial connection be substantial in order to warrant the assertion of authority (Mann, 1984: 29). Some of the rules on the existence of jurisdiction based on territorial connections do not satisfy this criterion and do not otherwise identify the state interest in claiming jurisdiction on which they are based. One infamous basis of jurisdiction in international disputes permits the court to hear cases where a plaintiff has suffered a tort anywhere in the world, as long as some damage is felt in the forum.[4] While this basis of jurisdiction can be used in cases in which the state has a legitimate interest in providing a forum – such

2 *Compagnie des Messageries Maritimes v Wilson* (1954) 94 CLR 577 at 585.

3 *Akai v The People's Insurance Co Inc* (1996) 188 CLR 418 at 447.

4 *Federal Court Rules 1979* (Cth), O8 r 2 item 5; *Uniform Civil Procedure Rules 1999* (Qld), r 124(1)(l).

as where a dangerous product has been intentionally exported to Australia by a foreign manufacturer – it would be preferable if the rules articulated such interests more clearly.

Other types of interest motivate jurisdiction, but are much more obscure. For example, the rules on establishing jurisdiction and the courts' practices in exercising jurisdiction demonstrate a particular concern to protect personal injuries plaintiffs. The rule of establishing jurisdiction commonly relied on in such cases require the plaintiff only to show that they have suffered some damage within the jurisdiction, a condition which is easily satisfied. In my study of the courts' practices in exercising jurisdiction, the court retained jurisdiction in 100 per cent of personal injuries cases, whereas it retained jurisdiction in only 71.4 per cent of non-personal injury cases (Keyes, 2005: 173). It is very unusual to find any explicit acknowledgement that this factor is relevant, let alone decisive. Indeed, Kirby J recently stated that 'natural sympathy' for the predicament of the plaintiff who had become a paraplegic in an accident that occurred abroad was 'legally illegitimate'.[5] The majority in that case did not say whether they were sympathetic or not, but the plaintiff succeeded. There are acceptable justifications for the special treatment of such plaintiffs, including a concern for their financial and physical abilities to participate in foreign litigation, particularly when this is relative to the abilities of large foreign or multinational corporations to participate in litigation in Australia.

The courts have occasionally held that some types of forum state interests cannot be taken into account in determining whether the court should exercise jurisdiction because the courts lack the resources and the ability to determine what influence they should have. In *Oceanic Sun Line Special Shipping v Fay*, Deane J held that the court could not take into account questions of public interest convenience, such as the costs associated with and delays created by entertaining international disputes, in deciding whether to exercise jurisdiction.[6] This was so even though he thought these factors were cogent. Deane J wrote that: 'The costs of the administration of justice are high and judicial resources are limited. In this country...court lists in many jurisdictions are congested, most judges are overworked and justice is far too often delayed.'[7] These factors were excluded from consideration because His Honour thought that judges should not determine how they should be reflected in the principles. Deane J suggested that if they are to be taken into account, this should be undertaken by parliament,[8] a sentiment later endorsed by members of the New South Wales Court of Appeal in *James Hardie v Grigor*.[9]

5 *Regie National des Usines Renault SA v Zhang* (2002) 210 CLR 491 at 550–51.

6 *Oceanic Sun Line Special Shipping Co Inc v Fay* (1988) 165 CLR 197 at 255. Lord Hope agreed in *Lubbe v Cape plc* [2000] 1 WLR 1545 at 1567.

7 *Oceanic Sun Line Special Shipping Co Inc v Fay* (1988) 165 CLR 197 at 253.

8 *Oceanic Sun Line Special Shipping Co Inc v Fay* (1988) 165 CLR 197 at 255.

9 *James Hardie Industries Pty Ltd v Grigor* (1998) 45 NSWLR 20 at 41 and 43.

Foreign state interests

In most cases, the courts are even more wary of avoiding an indication that they are denying or giving effect to the interests of foreign states. The nature of international litigation is such that a foreign state is always likely to have an interest of some kind in the resolution of the litigation. In very rare cases, that interest is so patent that the court must acknowledge it. Having acknowledged the foreign state's interest, the blunt response of the common law is to refuse to entertain the dispute, on the basis that it is beyond the court's competence to make decisions which may affect international political relations.

In a case known as *Spycatcher*, named after the book which was the subject of the dispute, the Attorney General for the United Kingdom applied for an injunction to restrain publication of this book which was a memoir written by a former officer of the British Security Service. The High Court of Australia held that the Australian courts did not have jurisdiction to deal with the claim, on the ground that the relief sought would require the courts to enforce the governmental interests of a foreign state.[10] The reason was that 'the very subject matter of the claims and the issues which they are likely to generate present a risk of embarrassment to the court and of prejudice to the relationship between its sovereign and the foreign sovereign'.[11]

The issue of the existence of jurisdiction is generally concerned with the court's personal jurisdiction over the defendant. There are relatively fewer rules which establish subject-matter jurisdiction, which refers to the court's competence to deal with a dispute by reference to its subject matter. The foreign governmental interest exception established in *Spycatcher* is an example. The courts also lack subject-matter jurisdiction to deal with disputes essentially concerning title to and possession of foreign land and other 'immovable' property under the *Moçambique* rule.[12] Lord Wilberforce thought this rule clearly must involve 'possible conflict with foreign jurisdictions' and 'political questions of some delicacy'.[13] For this reason, he opposed judicial reform of the rule.

The *Moçambique* rule is consistent with the general allocation of authority between states according to public international law, which is based on the relationship between physical territory and political power. Generally speaking, in public international law, extraterritorial assertions of authority are impermissible. Opinions are divided on the relevance of public international law to the law of jurisdiction in private international disputes. Mann has argued that the extent of legitimate judicial authority is prescribed by public international law (1984: 32, 67–77)[14] but others disagree (see Bowett, 1983: 3–4; Yntema, 1957: 733).

10 *Attorney-General (UK) v Heinemann Publishers Australia Pty Ltd* (1988) 165 CLR 30.

11 *Attorney-General (UK) v Heinemann Publishers Australia Pty Ltd* (1988) 165 CLR 30 at 44.

12 *Companhia de Moçambique v British South Africa Co* [1893] AC 602; *Potter v BHP Co Ltd* (1906) 3 CLR 479. In Australia, this rule applies to some forms of intellectual property, such as patents and trademarks.

13 *Hesperides Hotels v Muftizade* [1979] AC 508 at 537.

14 Kirby J takes the same view: *Regie National des Usines Renault SA v Zhang* (2002) 210 CLR 491 at 528.

According to Akehurst (1974), it is irrelevant as jurisdiction is frequently asserted on the basis of very weak connections between the state and the litigation, and this very seldom led to international political repercussions.

Whether the forum is obliged to recognise the foreign state's interest, perhaps the court might recognise as a matter of comity the forum state's interest in preserving harmonious relations with other states. This should lead to recognition of the foreign state's interests in some cases. As noted above, the court treats itself as jurisdictionally competent in some cases where the connection between the forum and the dispute is trivial so this consideration seems not to have influenced the rules on the existence of jurisdiction. One might expect that comity would certainly be a relevant consideration in the exercise of jurisdiction. According to the High Court, 'considerations of comity and restraint, to which reference has so often been made in cases concerning [the existence of] jurisdiction, will perhaps be of the greatest relevance in considering questions of forum non conveniens'.[15] This is a fine sentiment, but in fact the Australian principle of *forum non conveniens* which was endorsed in that case is extremely chauvinistic, conducive to ignoring the valid concerns of other states and provides no incentive to restraint in the exercise of jurisdiction. The principle requires a defendant to persuade the forum that it is 'clearly inappropriate' for the resolution of the dispute – a task which is not surprisingly difficult to discharge. In my study of the Australian courts' practices in the exercise of jurisdiction, in the cases in which there was no enforceable jurisdictional agreement between the parties, the Australian courts held that they were clearly inappropriate in only 22.5 per cent of decisions (Keyes, 2005: 168).

Balancing forum and foreign state interests

Most international disputes implicate the interests of both the forum and at least one other state. In such cases, the courts generally give priority to local state interests. This problem most clearly arises when the court has to decide whether it will exercise its jurisdiction. The principle of *forum non conveniens* which is applied to resolve this question requires the court to consider the availability and relative virtues of litigation in alternative forums. In England, the defendant must establish clearly and distinctly that there is another available court which is more appropriate to hear and determine the dispute than the courts of the forum.[16] In Australia, the defendant must show that the local court is clearly inappropriate. The Australian test gives substantially less weight to the possible interests of foreign courts than to the interests of the local court. There is no compelling justification for this discrimination. The English test is more accommodating of foreign forums, although it does not expressly admit the relevance of foreign state interests.

The rules as to existence of jurisdiction permit the assertion of jurisdiction on the basis of limited connections between the forum and the dispute (e.g., on the

15 *Agar v Hyde* (2000) 201 CLR 552 at 571.

16 *Spiliada Maritime Corporation v Cansulex Ltd* [1987] AC 460.

basis that the subject-matter of the dispute is a contract which was 'made' within the jurisdiction). This shows that the rules give more weight to local interests than to foreign interests. The principles demonstrate no sensible justification for doing so.

Why are state interests suppressed?

The main reason that the courts avoid an overt responsibility for discussing, weighing and applying state interests is because of perceived constitutional restraints on the courts' functions. International litigation, like its domestic counterpart, is treated as a highly practical subject and therefore is under-theorised. This is so particularly in England and Australia. The assumptions about the role of the courts in an adversarial system also influence the court's view about the propriety of acknowledging the existence of any state interests which might influence the court's responsibility in resolving in international jurisdictional disputes.

Constitutional restraints

The doctrine of the separation of powers prohibits the courts from exercising 'political' functions, which are the concern of the political arms of government. The courts are therefore likely to attempt to avoid the perception that their decisions are motivated by a consideration of state interests. This is particularly manifest in the court's lack of subject-matter jurisdiction to enforce foreign governmental interests, as expressed in *Spycatcher*. This approach closely resembles the government interest analysis approach to choice of law first proposed by Brainerd Currie (1963). Currie wrote that 'assessment of the respective values of the competing legitimate interests of two sovereign states, in order to determine which is to prevail, is a political function of a very high order' which 'should not be committed to the courts in a democracy' (1963: 182). This is almost identical to the reasoning of the High Court in *Spycatcher.* The majority held that to enforce the foreign government's interest in that case may 'require an Australian court to resolve an issue which it could not appropriately entertain or competently determine, namely what was, on balance, in the public interest of the foreign State'.[17]

The majority of the High Court in *Voth v Manildra Flour Mills*, which established the modern Australian principle of *forum non conveniens*, specifically relied on the court's incompetence to address matters of foreign governmental interest as a justification for the chauvinism of the Australian principle. They wrote that the same kind of 'powerful policy considerations' as those which prevent the courts from adjudicating disputes involving the enforcement of foreign governmental interests precluded the Australian courts from determining

17 *Attorney-General (UK) v Heinemann Publishers Australia Pty Ltd* (1988) 165 CLR 30 at 45.

whether a foreign court should hear a dispute.[18] The Australian courts invariably do conduct a comparative evaluation of the merits of litigation in the local as well as available foreign forums (Keyes, 2005: 138–40). The courts therefore do assume the responsibility of determining the suitability of foreign litigation relative to local litigation – it is just that they give foreign interests little weight.

Judges have occasionally stated that judicial reform of jurisdictional principles is inappropriate where questions of state interest are concerned and that legislative reform is required. This is seen both in Deane J's refusal in *Oceanic* to consider questions of public interest convenience from the Australian court's perspective and in Lord Wilberforce's remarks concerning political impediments to judicial reform of the *Moçambique* rule. In Australia, such reforms have not been forthcoming.[19] Responsibility for developing the jurisdictional rules is left entirely to the courts.

The doctrine of parliamentary sovereignty also leads the courts to suppress the valid interests of other states. In some recent Australian cases, the courts have explicitly relied on this doctrine in resolving international jurisdictional disputes. In refusing to enforce a contractual agreement to submit to the exclusive jurisdiction of the English courts, because to do so would mean that Australian legislation would not be applied, Kirby P stated that 'it is the duty of this Court to give effect to the *Act*'.[20] The usual conflict of laws principles, which are designed to determine which of two competing legal systems ought to provide the forum and the applicable law for international disputes in which both forums can claim that they ought to hear the case and that their law ought to be applied, can thus be out-manoeuvred by a combination of clever pleading by the plaintiff and a zealous court. This may do offence to the interests of other states, not to mention the position of the defendant.

Pragmatic formalism

In the English conflict of laws, which has heavily influenced the Australian doctrine, pragmatism is dominant. Theoretical analysis is eschewed in a subject which is widely considered to be fundamentally practical and procedural. A leading English text asserts that 'the most striking feature of the English common law rules relating to competence in actions in personam is their purely procedural character' (North and Fawcett, 1999: 285). According to this approach, the resolution of each international dispute is a practical matter which does not require a theoretical framework. In *Adams v Cape Industries*, the English Court of Appeal stated that the existence of jurisdiction is determined as 'a question of

18 *Voth v Manildra Flour Mills Pty Ltd* (1990) 171 CLR 538 at 559.

19 The only exceptions are enactment of legislation in New South Wales and the Australian Capital Territory reforming the *Moçambique* rule: *Jurisdiction of Courts (Foreign Land) Act 1989* (NSW), *Civil Law (Wrongs) Act 2002* (ACT) s 220.

20 *Akai v The People's Insurance Co Inc* (1995) 8 ANZ Ins Cas 61–254 at 75,389.

fact' and not 'by reference to questions of justice'.[21] The rules of jurisdiction 'have developed on an ad hoc basis, dependent on the exigencies of procedure, and the common law has failed to create a consistent theory of jurisdiction' (Sykes and Pryles, 1991: 20). Most analysis of jurisdiction is descriptive rather than critical or theoretical.

The doctrine of the separation of powers is linked to formalism, a school of jurisprudence which holds that judges do not or should not, for lack of qualification, concern themselves with issues of politics. Formalism has been particularly influential in the English and Australian conflict of laws. Jurisdictional rules are generally regarded as being policy neutral. In 1972, Pryles wrote that 'the courts evinced no general conception of the whole area of adjudicatory competence', and this remains true today (1972: 79–80).

The impact of the adversarial system

It is certainly no surprise that an explicit recognition of state interests is hard to find in international litigation, given the general attitude to this issue in the adversarial system of dispute resolution. In the adversarial system, according to Jacob (1987: 8):

> ...the basic assumptions are that civil disputes are a matter of private concern of the parties involved...though their determination by the courts may have wider, more far-reaching, even public repercussions, and that the parties are themselves the best judges of how to pursue and serve their own interests in the conduct and control of their respective cases, free from the directions of or interventions by the court.

According to this model, the state lacks any substantive interest in litigation which arises independently of the interests of the parties. Its role is merely facilitatory. Recent reforms to the rules of civil procedure in England and Australia have not had a substantial effect on the parties' control over litigation or on the general perceptions about the relative roles of the parties and the courts. They seem in particular to have had a negligible impact in international litigation (Collins, 2000: xvi).

With several important exceptions, international litigation is not differentiated from domestic litigation. Assumptions of the adversarial system of litigation have presumably unintended consequences in international litigation. For example, the principle of party autonomy, which applies in domestic litigation, is generally unchecked in international litigation. This means that a plaintiff can unilaterally invoke the application of mandatory forum legislation, which may well lead the court to decide that the court must exercise its jurisdiction.

21 *Adams v Cape Industries Plc* [1990] 1 Ch 433 at 519.

Why state interests ought not to be suppressed

I suggested in the introduction to this chapter that failure to acknowledge the role that state interests play in influencing the relevant legal principles and their application makes the law unnecessarily complicated, and impedes analysis of and debate about the legitimacy of those interests. This in turn undermines the legitimacy of the principles and of decisions made in this area, and adds to private and public costs of international litigation. It also undermines other local state interests, including the need to ensure certainty and predictability in the application of the law and to accommodate the valid interests of other states.

Failure to expressly acknowledge the role that state interests play in international litigation is likely to do the most damage to foreign state interests. Von Mehren and Trautman observed that 'conduct that is overly self-regarding with respect to the taking and exercise of jurisdiction can disturb the international order and produce political, legal and economic reprisals' (1966: 1127). It is undesirable that private international law should flout the requirement of public international law that a state should only exercise its jurisdiction over cases which have a reasonably close connection to it. Whether public international law imposes an enforceable limitation on the courts' jurisdiction is beside the point. Excessive claims of jurisdiction lead to unnecessary and wasteful overlaps, so that more than one state may well provide a forum for the same dispute which obviously creates needless costs and may result in inconsistent judgements from those different forums. The consequence is likely to be that the dispute is not satisfactorily resolved.

Neither the doctrine of separation of powers nor the doctrine of parliamentary sovereignty were designed with the specific features of international private litigation in mind. It is questionable whether either doctrine is particularly relevant to this area of law. These are domestic constitutional doctrines designed to regulate arrangements between the arms of government, to safeguard the internal superiority of the parliament, and to guard the courts against interference by the political arms of government. While it may be accepted that there are some extraordinary cases in which a dispute necessarily involves international political ramifications for which it is desirable that the political arms of government should take responsibility, this exceptional situation should not be exaggerated. This should certainly not be tolerated as a justification for the unacceptably parochial principle of *forum non conveniens* applied in Australia.

The recent judicial tendency to rely on the doctrine of parliamentary sovereignty in order to justify the retention of jurisdiction because the plaintiff has relied on local mandatory law fails to appreciate the whole purpose of the conflict of laws. It is basic to this area of law that more than one legal system may provide a forum and the substantive law to resolve a dispute. The jurisdictional principles and choice of law rules are intended to resolve the competing claims of the respective legal systems to do these things. The fact that some judges are avoiding the conflict of laws' rules by relying on the mandatory nature of forum law indicates that perhaps it is time for a revision of the jurisdictional principles and choice of law rules specifically to account for the modern awareness of the mandatory nature of some laws. While the enthusiasm of some judges to do their duty according to local law is impressive, it is essential to bear in mind that one legal system cannot isolate itself and its mandatory rules from the rest of the world.

Conclusion

Jurisdiction is an important area of law, whose importance is only likely to increase with the explosion of global and internet-mediated trade, commerce and communication (Bell, 2003: 3–5). Muchlinski, commenting on *Lubbe v Cape*, doubted whether 'the English courts can indefinitely refuse to address public interest issues, and hide behind the apparently apolitical doctrine of forum non conveniens, while at the same time coming to decisions that are doubtless informed by such considerations' (2001: 24). The same is true of Australian courts in relation to jurisdiction in international litigation. It is facile to maintain that state interests have no relevance to this area of law, and insulting to the courts for them to have to continue to pretend that these factors play no part in their decisions. It is high-time commentators, parliaments and courts set about articulating those state interests, explaining how they should be taken into account and resolved in the case of inconsistency.

References

Akehurst, Michael (1974) 'Jurisdiction in international law' 46 *British Yearbook of International Law* 145

Bell, Andrew (2003) *Forum Shopping and Venue in Transnational Litigation*, Oxford: Oxford University Press

Bowett, DW (1983) 'Jurisdiction: Changing patterns of authority over activities and resources' 53 *British Yearbook of International Law* 1

Collins, Hon Lawrence (general editor) (2000) *Dicey and Morris on the Conflict of Laws*, 13th edn, London: Sweet & Maxwell

Currie, Brainerd (1963) *Selected Essays in the Conflict of Laws*, Durham: Duke University Press

Fawcett, JJ (1989) 'Trial in England or abroad: The underlying policy considerations' 9 *Oxford Journal of Legal Studies* 205

Jacob, Jack IH (1987) *The Fabric of English Civil Justice*, London: Stevens & Son

Keyes, Mary (2005) *Jurisdiction in International Litigation*, Sydney: The Federation Press

Mann, FA (1984) 'The doctrine of international jurisdiction revisited after twenty years' 186-III *Recueil des Cours* 9

Muchlinski, Peter (2001) 'Corporations in international litigation: Problems of jurisdiction and the United Kingdom asbestos cases' 50 *International and Comparative Law Quarterly* 1

North, PM and Fawcett, JJ (1999) *Cheshire and North's Private International Law*, 13th edn, London: Butterworths

Pryles, Michael C (1972) 'Adjudicatory competence in private international law' 21 *International and Comparative Law Quarterly* 61

Sykes, Edward I and Pryles, Michael C (1991) *Australian Private International Law*, 3rd edn, Sydney: Law Book Company
Von Mehren, Arthur T and Trautman, Donald T (1966) 'Jurisdiction to adjudicate: A suggested analysis' 79 *Harvard Law Review* 1121
Whincop, Michael and Keyes, Mary (1998) 'Statutes' domains in private international law: An economic theory of the limits of mandatory rules' 20 *Sydney Law Review* 435
Yntema, Hessel (1957) 'The objectives of private international law' 35 *Canadian Bar Review* 721

Cases

Adams v Cape Industries Plc [1990] 1 Ch 433
Agar v Hyde (2000) 201 CLR 552
Akai v The People's Insurance Co Inc (1996) 188 CLR 418
Attorney-General (UK) v Heinemann Publishers Australia Pty Ltd (1988) 165 CLR 30
Compagnie des Messageries Maritimes v Wilson (1954) 94 CLR 577
Companhia de Moçambique v British South Africa Co [1893] AC 602
Hesperides Hotels v Muftizade [1979] AC 508
James Hardie Industries Pty Ltd v Grigor (1998) 45 NSWLR 20
Lubbe v Cape plc [2000] 1 WLR 1545
Oceanic Sun Line Special Shipping Co Inc v Fay (1988) 165 CLR 197
Potter v BHP Co Ltd (1906) 3 CLR 479
Regie National des Usines Renault SA v Zhang (2002) 210 CLR 491
Spiliada Maritime Corporation v Cansulex Ltd [1987] AC 460.
Voth v Manildra Flour Mills Pty Ltd (1990) 171 CLR 538

Legislations

Civil Law (Wrongs) Act 2002 (ACT)
Federal Court Rules 1979 (Cth)
Insurance Contracts Act 1984 (Cth)
Jurisdiction of Courts (Foreign Land) Act 1989 (NSW)
Trade Practices Act 1974 (Cth)
Uniform Civil Procedure Rules 1999 (Qld)

Part IV

Technologies

8 Mapping territories

Shaunnagh Dorsett

> ... it is ... the map that precedes the territory ... that engenders the territory.
>
> (Baudrillard, 1994: 1)

> [He's] got a thing about em, says Menzies. Just trouble, maps. You can't really blame him. Like they suck everythin' up. Can't blame a blackfella not likin' a map ... Go on the country, says the boy ... not on the map.
>
> (Winton, 2001: 312)

Introduction

Picture two images, both of a native title claim area. The first is a map of the claim area, demarcated by latitude and longitude. The areas that cannot be claimed are marked with hatching. There are Crown reservation numbers, and a scale in kilometres – in fact, all the things we expect in a tenure map.[1] The other image is a painting on canvas, in a form that westerners have labelled 'dot painting'. Yet both address similar concerns, albeit expressed through different cultural lenses: in Western legal terms, jurisdiction, territory and ownership; for the Pila Nguru – the creators of the painting – the Tjukurrpa.[2]

In 1995, the Spinifex people lodged a native title claim with the Native Title Tribunal. As part of the native title process, an art project was established to

1 The visual representation of the map is supported by the following written outline of the claim area: 'Commencing at the westernmost north western corner of Yowalga Location 7 as shown on Land Administration plan 20992 and extending east along the northernmost northern boundary of that location and east and south easterly along boundaries of Milyuga Location 20 to the Western Australian–South Australian Border; Then southerly along that border to latitude 29.500000 South; Then west to the south eastern corner of Delisser Location 9; Then west and north along boundaries of that location and north along the western boundary of Delisser Location 8 to the south western corner of Yowalga Location 7 and then generally northerly along boundaries of that location to the commencement point': *Mark Anderson on Behalf of the Spinifex People v State of Western Australia* [2000] FCA 1717 (28 November 2000).

2 For Westerners, it is impossible to precisely define the term 'tjukurrpa'. It encompasses both spiritual and other aspects, including notions of law, ownership, etc.: see Cane (2002: 16).

record and document ownership of the Spinifex area. Two paintings were produced initially, one painted by the men and one by the women (Cane, 2002: 16–17). These are described as 'native title paintings'. In 1998, the Spinifex people entered into a framework agreement with the Western Australian Government which was ratified by parliament. The paintings were formally included in the preamble of the agreement (Cane, 2002: 16). For the Spinifex people, the paintings are part of mapping territory.

This chapter examines mapping and surveying as technologies of jurisdiction.[3] The main concern here is with the way in which a jurisdiction is inaugurated through the mapping of physical space. The practice of mapping makes possible the existence of the legal concept of territory. Maps and territory are mutually supporting. The map is not the territory but it does, to paraphrase Chase, represent a particular spatial embeddedness of authority and jurisdiction (Chase, 1998: 59). As a technology of jurisdiction, mapping allows space to be reconceptualised as place, allows the assertion of jurisdiction over far-flung horizons and – along with its counterpart technology, surveying – allows the legal space of jurisdiction to be mapped on to the physical space of the land and sea. As a concern of jurisdiction, territory mediates between sovereignty and the physical earth. Once mapped, space becomes associated or identified with a sovereign and becomes a territory. Thus mapping is a jurisdictional device, a practice through which jurisdictions are embodied as territories and through which (as a result) people, places and events in that territory become juridified. One particular example of that juridification is the way in which the relationship of Indigenous Australians to their country becomes transformed to the legal construction of native title.

This chapter will proceed in the following way: the first section very briefly considers the shift from jurisdiction based on status to territorial jurisdiction. This is followed by a description of the history and process of graticulation through which early cartographers were able to impose a grid across the known and unknown world, imposing a mathematical regularity across the globe. The third part of this chapter examines how the process of graticulation supported the assertion by early explorers of sovereign jurisdiction over the new world, looking particularly at the assertion of British jurisdiction over the North American and Australian continents. The following section considers the relationship of the map to the physical earth and sea. On one level, that relationship is abstract, mathematical and incommensurate. The abstract nature of the map means that it will never map precisely to the earth. Thus territory can never match the physical. On another level, therefore, law must be simultaneously regrounded through the inscription of law in the landscape by the use of physical markers. A particular example of the juridification which results from territorial jurisdiction is then presented, together with an argument

3 For the purposes of this chapter, I am adopting Rush's definition of jurisdiction. As Rush (1997: 150) states: jurisdiction is literally to speak the law. Jurisdiction is a site of enunciation: 'It refers us first and foremost to the power and authority to speak in the name of the law and only subsequently to the fact that law is stated – and stated to be someone or something.'

that the embodiment of jurisdictions through Western, Cartesian mapping practices facilitates the assertion of common law jurisdiction over native title and renders indigenous understandings of country incommensurable with the legal doctrine of native title.

From status to territory

The predominant model of jurisdiction today is based on territory. However, this has not always been the case. In medieval England, jurisdiction was effected through attachment to a number of modes, the most common of which was status. Status is a concept familiar from Roman law: the filius families, the married woman or the soldier. Similarly, in the medieval common law, certain ranks, groups or classes occupied a special legal position of their own – for example, the ecclesiastic, the lunatic, the married woman, the villein, the Jew, the person attainted, the infant, the leper and most interestingly the monk, who was considered to be legally dead (Pollock and Maitland, 1968: 416). At this time, the status of these groups cut across the developing rules of the common law.

The lunatic, for example, held a special position in medieval law. Jurisdiction over those of unsound mind originally vested in the lunatic's Lord but was later transferred to the Crown. As this jurisdiction was a valuable right, it was vested in the Exchequer. Later, however, as it became a duty – and one from which no profit could be made – the jurisdiction passed to the Chancellor, who appointed a committee to oversee the property of the lunatic (Holdsworth, 1922–1972: 474). A second example is that of the Jew. The Jew was under the wardship of the King and all that he had belonged to the King. Thus, if the interests of the Crown were at stake, he was under his protection; if not, he was dealt with as a gentile (Pollock and Maitland, 1968: 469). Interests of the Crown generally meant the business of money-lending. In the twelfth century, a department of the Royal Exchequer, the Exchequer of the Jews, was organised for the supervision of this business. According to Pollock and Maitland, it was 'both a financial bureau and a judicial tribunal' (Pollock and Maitland, 1968: 469). When property was involved, the Exchequer acted as a judicial body determining disputes between gentile and Jew in both criminal and civil causes. Civil matters purely between Jews were left to the custom of the Jews and their own tribunals.

Jurisdiction was territorial in some contexts. While some local divisions, such as the shire and the hundred, as well as the manor and the borough, clearly operated on a territorial basis, they did not have exclusive jurisdiction in that territory. Even in these cases, however, territorial jurisdiction was often secondary to status. It was a person's status as villein or freeman which primarily determined jurisdiction, rather than the strict notion of a manor as a territorial entity. As Ford (1999: 881) points out, even those divisions which operated on a territorial basis had few of the qualities we associate with territorial jurisdiction today. Most notably, they had no definite territorial boundaries.

The concept of territorial jurisdiction is a relatively recent phenomenon. The 'modern', Westphalian order of states arose in the context of the erosion of the institutional centrality of religion and the colonisation of the new world. The simultaneous 're-spatialisation' of Europe and expansion by first the Spanish and Portuguese, then the Dutch and English, into the new world led in part to the new sovereign territorial state. 'State' became synonymous with bounded territories and specifiable populations. Sovereignty involved the assertion of independence: sole rights to jurisdiction over a particular people and territory.

The rise of the concept of territorial sovereignty is not in itself the reason for the loss of status as a primary method of organisation. In many cases, that was simply a by-product of the growth of the common law and legal centralisation, as well as the disappearance of certain persons who occupied a particular status as the result of social, religious and economic changes (Holdsworth, 1922–1972: 3). Nevertheless, by the time of the colonisation of the new world, jurisdiction based on territory was becoming the dominant form of jurisdiction and is now a normalised construct which obscures earlier and alternative modes of organising jurisdiction.

In order to support territorial jurisdiction, there must be a precise delimitation of territorial boundaries. Ford calls this the 'bright line' rule (Holdsworth, 1922–1972: 853). While the precise location of a boundary may be arbitrary, in jurisdictional terms it functions as an uncrossable barrier (Ford, 1999: 850). One entity's jurisdiction ends precisely at the boundary, where that of another begins. One set of governing laws end and another takes over. Without such a bright line, we are, according to the courts, left with a jurisdictional 'No Man's Land',[4] a neutral place to which 'bad characters' may resort,[5] knowing that jurisdictional uncertainty will render them safe from the interference of the authorities.[6]

The technology of mapping made possible the shift from jurisdiction based primarily on status to the modern, familiar, territorial jurisdiction by making it possible to define territory. The result of defining territory was that it was possible to uniformly 'impose the same institutional and administrative arrangements and laws over [that] territory', a project of the later Enlightenment (Hobsbawm, 1990: 80). Thus one of the effects of territorial jurisdiction is that it eliminates differences based on concepts such as status. All those who are within the territory become subject to that jurisdiction. By virtue of being within the territory, all people, places and events become juridical objects. Even where the remnants of an earlier mode of jurisdiction can be seen – the minor, for example, still has a special status at law – that status is overlaid by territorial jurisdiction. It is the courts of the state within which the minor is located that one must apply to for relief.

The graticulation of space

In early modern Europe, to the extent that jurisdiction was territorial in nature, the reference point for dealings with such jurisdictions – as with land – was local memory and customs. Law was embedded in local life, and in the particularities

4 *State of South Australia v State of Victoria* (1914) 18 CLR 115 at 139 (PC).
5 *State of South Australia v State of Victoria* (1914) 18 CLR 115 at 123 (PC).
6 *State of South Australia v State of Victoria* (1911) 12 CLR 667 at 682 (HC).

of local knowledge and circumstance. Boundaries and communities were amorphous, lacking in physical and geographic distinction. What distinctions existed were maintained by customary practices rather than by geographic 'bright lines'.

One echo of this time exists in the perambulation – the practice of walking the physical markers of the property or jurisdiction. An example is the practice of 'beating the bounds':

> The parson and parish old-timers would lead the rest of their neighbours around the boundaries of the parish. This village parade went over every stile, past every marker, along every hedgerow, providing the community with a 'mental map of the parish' that could be drawn upon in cases of property dispute.
>
> (Bushaway, 1982: 84)[7]

Similarly, the boundaries of manors were defined by markers. Local topological and human-made features – stone walls, levees, hedges, boundary stones – marked the limits of ownership and/or jurisdiction. Remnants of such practices still survive and many US state statutes still refer to boundary surveys as perambulations.[8]

In the absence of 'rational' and 'objective' qualities of spatial order, what mapping there was reflected the physicalised nature of communities' relationships with land and jurisdiction. The tradition of medieval mapping typically emphasises the sensuous rather than the rational and objective (Harvey, 1990: 243). In other words, 'the medieval artist believed that he could render what he saw before his eyes convincingly by representing what it felt like to walk about, experiencing structures, almost tactilely, from many different sides, rather than from a single vantage point' (Edgerton, 1979: 9).

Medieval Europe saw only 'odd pockets of map-making [and] the occasional individual who drew maps'. Society 'simply did not think in cartographic terms when confronted with the need to record or communicate topographic information, whether it concerned half a field or half a continent' (Harvey, 1980: 155–56). Those 'odd pockets' that did exist consisted largely of portolan maps, zonal maps and the medieval *mappae mundi*.[9] There was also some recognition of the benefits of an improved system for locating places, including by reference to coordinate systems. For example, in his thirteenth century *Opus maius*, Bacon had already proposed the use of coordinates of latitude and longitude to map the Earth (Woodward, 1991: 83). However, as Woodward notes, 'neither the data nor

7 To check no one was encroaching on their land, the congregation would walk once a year from one boundary 'mark' to the next, shouting 'Mark, Mark, Mark' at each and beating it with sticks, or a stripped willow branch known as a wand.

8 See, for example, Title 15 (*Cities and Towns*) – Wyoming State Statutes – Chapter 1, Article. 4.

9 Portolan maps or charts were Mediterranean Sea charts. Zonal maps divided the Earth into five climactic zones. Like the *mappae mundi*, they were circular, and often maps combined elements of the two.

the demand were ready for the concept' (1991: 84). No one had yet been able to project such a reticulated surface on to a flat chart (Edgerton, 1979: 98–100).

In 1400, Ptolemy's *Geographia* arrived in Florence from the Byzantine East, apparently brought by scholars who were attempting to obtain texts for the purposes of learning Greek.[10] Its arrival in Europe – and particularly in Florence – at a time of intellectual flowering 'spawned an unprecedented excitement about the *Geographia*' (Edgerton, 1979: 114). Its spread was increased by the translation of the work into Latin in the first decade of the fifteenth century, and its emergence in print around 1475.

Rather than the maps and empirical knowledge of the world contained in them, it was the methods of mapping the world that made the *Geographia* so important. The *Geographia* included three alternative cartographic methods. While all three methods were intended to allow the mapping on a plane surface of the longitudes and latitudes of the globe, it was the third method, contained in Book Seven, which was to revolutionise map-making. Ptolemy explained that his scheme enabled the mapping of places, preserving the proportion of individual locations (chorography) in relation to the whole (geography):

> The end of chorography is to deal separately with a part of the whole, as if one were to paint only the eye or ear by itself. The task of geography is to survey the whole in its just proportion, as one would the entire head. For in an entire painting we must first put in the larger features and afterwards those detailed features which portraits and pictures may require, giving them proportion in relation to one another so that their correct distance apart can be seen by examining them, to note whether they form the whole or part of the picture.
>
> (quoted in Edgerton, 1979: 111)

By using a grid system of longitude and latitude:

> We are able therefore to know the exact position of any particular place; and the position of the various countries, how they are integrated in regard to one another, how situated in regards to the whole inhabitable world.
>
> (quoted in Edgerton, 1979: 111)

The advantage of the Ptolemaic system of cartography was that the grid system reduced the world's surface to geometrical and mathematical uniformity. Further, at a time when an increasing amount of information was becoming known about the outside world, it made clear that the *oikoumene* (the known world) occupied only part of the whole sphere of the Earth (Edgerton, 1979: 113, 115). Ptolemy's projections did not show the entire globe (only 180°), but the map frame slowly

10 An interesting account of the arrival of the *Geographia* in Florence can be found in Edgerton (1979). Note that other authors place the date for the arrival of *Geographia* earlier: see Turnbull, (1996: 14).

expanded to encompass the globe. By 1514, Ptolemy's projection had been extended to cover the entire world – known and unknown.

By locating the *oikoumene* on only one part of a grid of latitude and longitude, the *Geographia* not only changed the way maps were structured but also the perception of space itself (Brotton, 1997: 32). The dominant form of map until this time had been the *mappae mundi*, a form of T-O map, in which purported to show the entire world, divided into three continents: Asia, Europe and Africa. These were often seen as representing the world 'as divided among the three sons of Noah – Shem, Ham and Japheth – and thus to illustrate the three great races of the world – the semitic, hamitic and japhetic' (Woodward, 1991: 83). These maps 'emphasised the spiritual rather than the physical world'; they were a projection of Christian truths on to a geographical framework (Woodward, 1991: 83). The Psalter *Mappae Mundi*, for example, shows Christ standing above the world, with outstretched arms,[11] while Christ sits in judgement above the Hereford *Mappae Mundi* and the map revolves around Jerusalem which is at the exact centre of the world (see further Harvey, 1996). The maps therefore show a world structurally dependent on Christ and his earthly institution, the Church (Ryan, 1997: 104), reflecting the dominance of the Church in medieval life.

By contrast, Ptolemy's *Geographia* made it clear that the known world, the *oikoumene*, occupied only one part of the globe. The graticulation system changed the map fundamentally: not only did it replace the structure and technique of the T-O map with a system of coordinates, confining the *oikoumene* to a part of the globe but also in so doing it undermined the Christian symbolism on which the T-O map was in part dependent (Brotton, 1997: 32). As Brotton states:

> Ptolemy's impact on the world of geography was to revolutionize a certain perception of space itself, which was no longer charged with religious significance but was instead a continuous, open terrestrial space across which the monarchs and merchants who had invested in copies of his *Geographia* could envisage themselves conquering and trading regardless of religious prescription.
>
> (1997: 32)

The graticulation of the globe meant that all known places could be located, and distances and directions between them established. Furthermore, new routes to known destinations could be hypothesised. In the sixteenth century, there was a proliferation of maps, due to their obvious uses in trade and commerce. Maps became highly valued for the access they promised to territories and commodities (Brotton, 1997: 85).

Graticulation not only produced geometrical, abstract space, but also empty, homogenous space. The result of graticulation was a 'movement away from local

11 The Psalter map is reproduced in Whitfield (1994: 19).

topological concepts toward those of a finite, spatially referenced spherical earth, a *tabula rasa* on which the achievements of exploration could be cumulatively inscribed' (Woodward, 1991: 85). The outlines of the southern continent, for example, were progressively mapped on to the grids of longitude and latitude. Through this, geographers created a blank southern continent – a textual space on a map, on to which could be projected a construction of the continent as either empty and uninhabited (Ryan, 1997: 101) or as populated by fantastic creatures and people. The construction of the southern continent as a *tabula rasa* had important consequences. The colonial moment of widespread appropriation, effected by the physical arrival and taking of jurisdiction over the continent, was preceded by a symbolic assertion of jurisdiction through mapping. Mapping rendered the new territory knowable, open to appropriation, even prior to arrival.

Mapping territory

It was not simply mapping, but the form of that mapping which supported jurisdiction. Graticulation meant that unknown spaces could be given coordinates. The vast parts of the globe beyond the *oikoumene* could be assigned locations by latitude and longitude. Despite never having been seen by Europeans, the new world could be mapped: the unknown became knowable and, more importantly, claimable. The place of territorial jurisdiction could be created out of the space of the unknown.

Dividing the globe

The linking of law to the emerging concept of national territory through mapping and geography was given impetus by Columbus's voyage and the 'discovery' of the 'new world'. One of the results of Columbus's voyage was a reinvigoration of previous Castilian and Portuguese disputes concerning the demarcation of their relative spheres of authority in what Schmitt (1996: 30) has termed the 'free space' of the emerging new world. This free space, open to European appropriation through land seizures, 'made necessary certain divisions and distributions' (Schmitt, 1996: 31). It required a delineation of spheres of authority – of the territories of various European princes.

Since the early mid-1300s, Castile and Portugal had competed for trade with, and possession of, newly discovered lands – the Canary Islands, Guinea, Morocco. Alfonso of Portugal sought aid from the Pope in order to bolster his claims. By his 1452 Bull *Dum diversas*, 'Nicholas V granted King Alfonso general and indefinite powers to search out and conquer all pagans, enslave them and appropriate their lands and goods' (Davenport, 1917: 12).[12] Three years later, the Bull *Romanus Pontifex* settled the dispute between the two in

12 The following short account draws on this work.

favour of Portugal by confirming *Dum diversas*, specifying where it applied and granting it:

> The acquisitions already made, and what hereafter shall happen to be acquired [which] do belong and pertain, to the aforesaid king and to his successors and to the infante, and that right of conquest which in the course of these letters we declare to be extended from the capes of Bojador and of Não, as far as through all Guinea, and beyond towards that southern shore.[13]

Importantly, these belonged to the King and 'not to any others' (Davenport, 1917: 24).

After Columbus's voyage, Pope Alexander VI assigned Castile the exclusive right to acquire territory or trade in, or even to approach, the lands lying west of the meridian situated 100 leagues west of any of the Azores or Cape Verde Islands.[14] The line was confirmed and moved westward by the Treaty of Tordesillas in 1494.[15] The Treaty described the demarcation as follows:

> A boundary or straight line [shall] be determined and drawn north and sought, from pole to pole, on the said ocean sea, from the Arctic to the Antarctic pole. This boundary or line shall be drawn, as aforesaid, at a distance of three hundred and seventy leagues west of the Cape Verde Islands, being calculated by degrees, or by any other manner as may be considered the best.
>
> (Davenport, 1917: 95)

Davenport notes that the Spanish and Portuguese 'evidently considered that the line established by the Treaty of Tordesillas passed around the earth' (Davenport, 1917: 2). Problematically, although the idea of the meridian had become commonplace, the ability to match the ideational to the physical surface of the globe lagged behind. Nevertheless, despite the continued problems involved in locating the line of demarcation, or agreeing on the distance represented by a degree, the treaty constituted an attempt to divide the globe in two – to demarcate and underpin spheres of authority by reference to the new technology of mapping. Importantly, this evidences a shift in the means of establishing political–territorial limits. Rather than the physical landmarks that defined the limits of medieval territorial units, the intangible, mathematical line of latitude demarcated the boundaries between one sovereign authority and another.

The practice of delineating jurisdiction by reference to 'objective' map coordinates became a feature of new acquisitions. For the Portuguese and Spanish, the two leading maritime nations of the fifteenth and early sixteenth

13 The Bull *Romanus Pontifex*, 8 January 1455, as reprinted and translated in Davenport (1917: 23–24). The Bull was confirmed in *Inter Caetera*, 13 March 1456, by Calixtus III.

14 Papal Bull *Inter Caetera*, 3 May 1493, cited in Davenport (1917: 56).

15 Treaty of Tordesillas, 7 June 1494, ratified by Spain on 2 July 1494, ratified by Portugal on 5 September 1494. Reprinted in Davenport (1917: 84).

centuries which were exploring at a time when territories in the new world were not even yet discovered, mapping, navigation and astronomy were the key technologies which facilitated jurisdiction and appropriation.

As Schmitt notes, the lines themselves only acted as an internal division between different sets of European powers of zones of authority in which land appropriation could take place (Schmitt, 1996: 35). Despite their often-contested nature, such zones functioned internally as a justification and demarcation of sovereign jurisdiction. While such divisions did not constitute a jurisdictional 'carving up' of the globe (e.g. Spain and Portugal's attempts to divide the new world between themselves were ignored by other European powers), internally to each power it constituted a grand exercise of sovereign jurisdiction, to set in motion the impulse of appropriation.

In the specific case of the English, there was no grand division of the globe. Rather, by the time English commercial activity had fuelled the impulse for appropriation, attention in the new world of the Americas had shifted to the carving up of the land mass of the continent: the creation of bounded places from space.

Creating new territories: mapping British Colonies

The internal medium through which jurisdiction was asserted by the English (later British) Crown in the new world of America was the Royal Charter, a legal/administrative document which produced a new colony as English territory 'by creating jurisdictions in bounded space' (Tomlins, 2001: 316). Royal Charters defined the newly created territories by a mixture of the new techniques of mapping and the 'old' technology of physical landmarks. There was never a complete shift between the localised technology of the perambulation and the abstract technology of mapping. Rather, the two came to be mutually supportive in defining the new territories.

In the first charter of the Virginia Company (1606), James I:

> Vouchsafe[d] unto [the company] our licence to make habitation, plantation and to deduce a colony of sundry of our people into that part of America commonly called Virginia, and other parts and territories in America either appertaining unto us or which are not now actually possessed by any Christian prince or people, situate, lying and being all along the sea coasts between four and thirty degrees of northerly latitude from the equinoctial line and five and forty degrees of the same latitude and in the main land between the same four and thirty and five and forty degrees, and the islands thereunto adjacent or within one hundred miles of the coast thereof.[16]

The second and third charters of the Virginia Colony, in which the jurisdiction of the colony was extended, described the territorial jurisdiction according

16 For the Virginia Charter, see www.yale.edu/lawweb/avalon./states/va01.htm. For a similar example, see also the Charter of the Massachusetts Bay Company, 4 March 1629, reproduced in Jensen (1969: 72).

to more conventional reference points: (recently named) landmarks – 'Cape Comfort' – and physical features – 'the sea coast'.[17]

The Charter of Pennsylvania (1681) combines the two technologies. It also demonstrates the specificity with which territorial jurisdictions could be defined: the precision of the bounded spaces which they created. Under the Charter, Charles II granted:

> Unto the said William Penn, his heirs and assigns, all that tract or part of land in America, with all the islands therein contained, as the same is bounded on the east by the Delaware River, from twelve miles' distance northwards of New Castle Town unto the three and fiftieth degree of northern latitude, if the said river doth extend so far northwards; but if the said river shall not extend so far northward, then by the said river so far as it doth extend; and from the head of the said river, unto the said three and fortieth degree. The said land to extend westwards five degrees in longitude, to be computed from the said eastern bounds; and the said lands to be bounded on the north by the beginning of the three and fortieth degree of northern latitude, and on the south by a circle drawn at twelve miles distance from New Castle northward and westward unto the beginning of the fortieth degree of northern latitude, and then by a straight line westward to the limit of longitude above-mentioned.[18]

In the Charter of Pennsylvania, Penn is granted full power over an area of land, the topography of which is unknown. Two alternative methods of determining the northern boundary of the territory are given – depending on how far the Delaware River 'doth extend', something unknown to Europeans at the time. The abstract divisions of meridians of longitude and latitude allowed the British Crown to assert territorial jurisdiction over a territory whose size and boundaries had not yet been fully established and whose interior was almost completely unknown to it.[19]

Similarly, Governor Phillip's instructions with respect to New South Wales confirmed the boundaries or limits of his jurisdiction – not only by subject-matter but also by geographical scope. His jurisdiction was confined to 'our territory called New South Wales'[20] which was defined as:

> Extending from the northern cape or extremity of the coast called Cape York, in the latitude of 10°37' south, to the southern extremity of the said territory of New South Wales or South Cape, in the latitude of 43°49' south, and of all

17 See the Third Charter of the Virginia Company, 12 March 1612, www.yale.edu/lawweb/avalon/states/va01.htm

18 Charter of Pennsylvania, 4 March 1681, reproduced in Jensen (1969: 93–94).

19 Much of the mapping of the coastline which had occurred had been by the Dutch, French and Portuguese.

20 Governor Phillip's First Commission, King George III to Arthur Phillip, 12 October 1786, (Watson, 1914: 1). The subject-matter of Phillip's jurisdiction is outlined in his Second Commission and Third Commission, dated respectively 2 April 1887 and 25 April 1887. These are reproduced in Watson (1914: 2, 9).

> the country inland to the westward as far as the one hundred and thirty fifth degree of longitude, reckoning from the meridian of Greenwich, including all the islands adjacent in the Pacific Ocean, within the latitude of the aforesaid of 10°37' south and 43°39' south. [21]

The limits of Phillip's territorial jurisdiction were reiterated in his Second and Third Commissions. Although Phillip and the First Fleet had not yet departed for New South Wales, Britain was claiming territorial jurisdiction over half a continent. At the time of Phillip's commission, the entire coastline of the territory of New South Wales was still unclear. In particular, the coastline of the Gulf of Carpentaria was incomplete, as was the Great Australian Bight (Lines, 1992: 16).

Under international law, symbolic acts of possession, such as raising the flag, were insufficient to confer sovereignty. Rather, a mere inchoate title was acquired which required actual possession or occupation in order to confer territorial sovereignty. The position under international law was recognised by the British Government (Smith, 1932–1935: 1). Despite this, the Commission appointing Captain Phillip as Governor conferred upon his jurisdiction to the eastern half of the continent, an area considerably larger than that claimed by Cook, including parts of the coastline and islands not yet seen by Europeans. Similarly, the 1787 Charter of Justice, by which courts of civil and of criminal jurisdiction were established, also appears to have given jurisdiction to these bodies over a wider area than that so far occupied.[22] Thus jurisdiction was asserted although sovereignty had not yet been acquired. As the settlers pushed out from Sydney Cove towards the Blue Mountains and beyond, sovereignty followed in their wake.

Once appropriated, the systematic measurement and surveying of the new territory would become an essential aspect of European colonisation and the consolidation of European control. The administrative measuring and ordering of the territory underpinned the initial exercise of jurisdiction over the new land. Most commonly, in English colonies, this was achieved through cadastral surveying.

In early modern Europe, space was not precisely defined as it is today by modern surveying. Rather, measurements were fluid and approximate (Ford, 1999: 881). Measurement of land was understood in terms of everyday life. As Darby notes, units were often measured by reference to a day's journey, or a morning's ploughing and surveying (insofar as practices could be given that name), and there was marked confusion between units of measurement – for example, customary or statutory acres (Darby, 1933: 530). However, new

21 Notably, the westernmost boundary of the colony was 135°E latitude, which equated to the line of demarcation declared between Spain and Portugal in the Treaty of Tordesillas. Lines comments on this coincidence, noting that 'the reasons for the British Government's choice of the 135 meridian of east latitude as the western boundary of Governor Phillip's jurisdiction are not evident', and are 'the subject of much speculation'. He does not, however, advance any hypothesis as to a possible relationship between the two demarcation lines: Lines (1992: 11–12).

22 See *Charter of Justice*, 2 April 1787 (UK).

techniques in cadastral surveying, made possible in part by the rediscovery of Euclidean geometry, allowed the land mass of the kingdom of Great Britain to be demarcated and ordered with increasing accuracy (see generally Darby, 1933). Cadastral surveying arose in the context of land valuations. In the sixteenth and seventeenth centuries, however, its use moved from the private context to being predominantly used in state-sponsored surveys. By the second half of the nineteenth century, it was an axiomatic adjunct to effective government control of land (Kain and Baigent, 1992: xvii). As with mapping, cadastral surveying projects a regular, ordered grid upon the blank landscape of the new territory. Slowly, and unevenly, surveys filled the blank, unpopulated interior of the new colony of New South Wales, allowing for the extension of imperial control and jurisdiction, and creating a multitude of jurisdictional spaces, public and private.

Abstracting territory and grounding law

Techniques of mapping facilitate the abstraction of territory from the physical earth and allow the concept of territory to act as a mediator between sovereignty/jurisdiction and the physical. At the same time, however, law is also regrounded through the inscription of law in the landscape by the use of physical markers.

The problems of definitively pegging the abstract of latitude and longitude to the physical arose with respect to the boundaries between the colonies, later states, of South Australia and Victoria. The boundary between New South Wales (later Victoria) and South Australia was by the *Act* 4 & 5 Wm IV c 95 and Letters Patent issued under it, defined to be the 141st meridian of East Longitude. According to the Letters Patent:

> We do hereby fix the Boundaries of the said Province [of South Australia] in manner following (that is to say). On the North the twenty sixth Degree of South Latitude On the South the Southern Ocean – On the West the one hundred and thirty second Degree of East Longitude – And on the East the one hundred and forty first Degree of East Longitude including therein all and every the Bays and Gulfs thereof together with the Island called Kangaroo Island and all and every the Islands adjacent to the said last mentioned Island or to that part of the main Land of the said Province.[23]

In addition, s 1 of that *Act* provided that on the partitioning of the territory of South Australia from that of New South Wales, the laws of New South Wales would not, as might be expected, apply in the new province. Rather, the new province was to be treated 'in law (as it was in fact) as new territory acquired by settlement, with the consequence that the settlers would take with them the Common and Statute Law of England so far as applicable'.[24]

23 Letters Patent reproduced in *State of South Australia v State of Victoria* (1914) 18 CLR 115 at 118–20.

24 *State of South Australia v State of Victoria* (1911) 12 CLR 667 at 677.

Thus the border would demarcate the different legal regimes applicable in each jurisdictional entity.

The Letters Patent were issued on 19 February 1836. However, the border remained undefined for some time, not least because of the acknowledged difficulty of ascertaining the location of the 141st meridian of East Longitude in relation to the physical Earth for the purposes of marking the boundary. By 1846, the boundary problem had created a zone of lawlessness, in which murder had been committed and revenues could not be collected.[25] Different surveyors placed the 141st meridian in different physical locations. In the end, 'a mean was struck between the calculations' of the two surveyors.[26] A third surveyor, on the basis of these two earlier attempts, finally produced a survey result acceptable to the Governors of both South Australia and New South Wales. In March 1849, both Governors finally proclaimed the boundary and physical markers were made along the line. From that time until 1911, the line marked in that process was the de facto boundary between South Australia and Victoria, despite the realisation soon after the boundary was marked that it was approximately 2 miles to the west of the 141st meridian. In 1911, South Australia brought an action for recovery of what it alleged was 2 miles of its territory.

Both the High Court and the Privy Council recognised the impossibility at the time of both the fixing of the boundaries and commencement of the action of determining the exact location of the 141st meridian. Yet, for the purposes of jurisdiction, some definite bright line was needed. The 'rights and liberties of the inhabitants of the country' were at stake.[27] If the border were to be the 141st meridian, in the strictest sense, then the relationship of the border to the physical Earth would forever remain indeterminate. If this were so, then the consequence would be:

> . . . that neither at the date of the Order in Council nor at any subsequent time was it possible to fix with accuracy a line on the surface of the earth representing the meridian; he also submitted that the degree of accuracy with which this could be done had increased with the progress of knowledge and would probably increase still further in the future, and that therefore the boundary, however carefully fixed, could never be said to be the legal boundary or to warrant the claim of either colony to exercise jurisdiction up to it in view of the possibility that a redetermination of greater accuracy might shift its position.[28]

In contrast to the Privy Council's statement, however, it could be contended that there is a legal boundary, the 141st meridian, but that that legal boundary could never directly map to the physical.

25 *State of South Australia v State of Victoria* (1911) 12 CLR 667 at 683.
26 *State of South Australia v State of Victoria* (1911) 12 CLR 667 at 686.
27 *State of South Australia v State of Victoria* (1914) 18 CLR 115 at 140.
28 *State of South Australia v State of Victoria* (1914) 18 CLR 115 at 136–37.

In contemporary times, surveying and mapping in Queensland are undertaken within the framework of the Geodetic Datum of Australia 1994 (GDA94). GDA94 is the coordinate reference system which provides a correlation between surveys, maps, charts and the physical of the Earth's surface.[29] Prior to GDA94 coming into use in 2000, the reference system used was GDA84. One of the results of the new standard is that:

> Coordinates related to the current Australian Geodetic Datum (AGD84) will differ from those related to the proposed Geocentric Datum of Australia (GDA94) by about 205 metres.[30]

In consequence, maps and charts which pre-date July 1998 are issued with a 'warning note' as to their inaccuracy.[31] Just as with the Spanish/Portuguese *rayas*, and the problems of defining the relationship between the 135° East meridian and the physical Earth, as well as the delineation of the South Australian–Victorian border, the implementation of new standards for geodetic data also points to the relativity of the relationship between maps and the physical: Australian' Geodetic Datum 1994 (AGD94) connects maps and charts to different physical points than AGD84 – they are 205 metres apart.

Underneath this layer of abstraction, however, lies an older technology – delineation by the physical: the boundary marker, the perambulation. In definition of territorial entities, the new technologies of mapping and survey are layered on top of the older sediments of local memory and the physical. There has never been a clear shift from one resource of delineation to another. The localised of the boundary markers and familiar physical features of the landscape survive as basic tools in modern surveying, albeit in a different and new form. As the High Court observed in *State of South Australia and Victoria*, some kind of physical demarcation is needed for a boundary:

> The word 'boundary' imports, from the very nature and purpose of the thing described, a line of demarcation capable of being marked on the ground as the visible and permanent delimitation of separate independent adjoining jurisdictions.[32]

Or, according to the Privy Council in the same case: 'To define a boundary for such purposes it is necessary that the boundary line should be described or ascertainable on the actual surface of the earth.'[33] Such visible delimitation was

29 See Department of Natural Resources and Mines, Queensland Government, www.nrm.qld.gov.au/property/surveying/geocentric_datum.html

30 Department of Natural Resources and Mines, Queensland Government, www.nrm.qld.gov.au/property/surveying/geocentric_datum.html

31 Department of Natural Resources and Mines, Queensland Government, www.nrm.qld.gov.au/property/surveying/geocentric_datum.html

32 *State of South Australia v State of Victoria* (1911) 12 CLR 667 at 712.

33 *State of South Australia v State of Victoria* (1914) 18 CLR 115 at 140.

to 'be marked upon the ground by a double row of blazing upon the adjacent trees, and by mounds of earth at intervals of one mile where no trees exist'.[34]

The original marking of the intercolonial boundary between Queensland and New South Wales occurred in 1865. The boundary was marked with human-made and physical features: rocks, trees marked with symbols (≠ and Δ) and with steel pins, 1 inch in diameter and 2 feet long. Cairns and posts were also used (*Redefining*, 2001: 4–5). In 1879, the part of the boundary formed by the 29 parallel of East Meridian was resurveyed and marked by 'well squared posts at every mile, concrete obelisks at the extremities of the initial five mile chords, east and West and two brick obelisks at Hungerford, and permanent marks at all important points' (from an account by William Campbell 1895 quoted in *Redefining*, 2001: 6). A one-ton post was placed on the West Bank of the Barwon River. It marked the end of the survey and 'was marked "QL" on the north side, "NSW J Cameron GS" on the South Side and "≠Lat 29" on the west side' (*Redefining*, 2001: 7). Despite the acknowledged lack of precision in the location of the 29th meridian of Latitude East, according to both the Queensland and New South Wales Governments, 'the border as originally marked... defines the true position of the Queensland–New South Wales border' (*Redefining*, 2001: 14).

The marking is the physical act 'required to locate [the] position [of the meridian] with reference to the earth'.[35] But it also harks back to the perambulation, the marking of trees, the insertion of posts – to an earlier time, to an earlier way of knowing and dividing the Earth, when territory was more directly grounded in the physical and law was local. The marking grounds the law in the earth, attaching the legal and ideational of territory to the Earth's surface. Thus law, through the jurisdictional places and spaces of the colonisers, becomes inscribed in the landscape, visible in trees and fences, cairns and posts. In 1993, the Queensland and New South Wales Governments remarked the original boundary posts on the border. In the intervening century, almost 90 per cent of the original mileposts had disappeared. The governments searched for physical evidence of the markers, and mathematically modelled the probable location of the remainder. Recovery marks were placed for the mileposts that were found. The states reinscribed the jurisdictional limits of the state in the physical and reinstituted the bright line on which territorial jurisdiction depends.

Jurisdiction is facilitated and supported by the technologies of surveying and mapping. These technologies mediate a relationship between the law and the physical earth through the concept of territory. Territory has no absolute relationship to the physical earth because it relies in part on technologies which have no absolute relationship to the Earth. Mapping, surveying and charting are themselves mediated. They rely on coordinate reference systems – longitude and latitude in all their complexity – to mediate their relationship to the physical. Such reference systems are never ultimately pegged to the physical, but constantly redefined with increasing scientific precision by the use, for example,

34 *State of South Australia v State of Victoria* (1911) 12 CLR 667 at 689.
35 *State of South Australia v State of Victoria* (1911) 12 CLR 667 at 723.

of satellite imaging and mapping. However, law has never escaped the physical. It is still grounded in the physical – through its markers and stones, inscribed and reinscribed in the landscape.

Mapping native title

The Pila Nguru, or Spinifex people, live in the Tjuntjuntjara, the Great Victoria Desert in Western Australia. The Spinifex people remained largely untouched by the arrival of Europeans until the 1950s when their country was the site of British nuclear testing, requiring the removal of many of them to camps hundreds of kilometres away. They slowly returned to their lands in the 1980s. Some of the Pila Nguru did not leave their country in the 1950s and remained uncontacted until 1986.

Western Australia was formally claimed by the British in 1829. In that year, Fremantle raised the flag at the mouth of the Swan River and took possession of the area, founding the colony of Western Australia, and claiming 'all that part of New Holland which is not included within the territory of New South Wales'. The English, aware that under international law possession was required to confirm title, were concerned to settle in the area to bolster their claim as the French, in particular, had also 'discovered' the west of New Holland. Despite the settlements in Western Australia being confined to a small section in the south west, it was taken that this was enough to confirm possession of the territory.

While the boundaries of the territory and its internal topography remained unknown, long before the arrival of the colonists the continent had been placed on maps and its shape and character hypothesised. Prior to taking physical possession, geographers created an outline of Australia as a blank, inhabited only by fanciful creatures, on to which could be projected a construction of the continent as empty and uninhabited, awaiting a new order. The continent could be brought within imperial jurisdiction by the imposition of a new textual regime. The construction of the continent as a *tabula rasa* set the preconditions for the later legal construction of *terra nullius*, which justified the assertion of jurisdiction, both sovereign and common law, on the grounds of the uninhabited state of the continent, and the subsequent transformation from empty land to sovereign territory (Dorsett and McVeigh, 2002: 300).

As a consequence of the acquisition of territorial sovereignty over the west of New Holland, the common law was introduced to the colony. In *Mabo (No. 2)*, Brennan J considered the introduction of the common law into New South Wales. In the context of that colony, he noted that, as there was considered to be no law in the new colony, the common law was imported not merely as the personal law of the colonists but as the law of the land. Brennan J put the matter thus:

> The view was taken that, when sovereignty of a territory could be acquired under the enlarged notion of terra nullius, for the purposes of the municipal law that territory (though inhabited) could be treated as a 'desert uninhabited' country. The hypothesis being that there was no local law

> already in existence in the territory ... the law of England became the law of the territory (and not merely the personal law of the colonists) ... The indigenous people of a settled colony were thus taken to be without laws, without a sovereign and primitive in their social organization.[36]

The majority in *Mabo (No. 2)* proceeded on this understanding, despite confirming that the colony had not been uninhabited.[37] Thus, in Western Australia – as in New South Wales – the common law became not only the law of the land, but of the entire territory. The result is that, as the common law is the law of the land, it binds not only the colonists but also the Indigenous inhabitants. The consequence of the acquisition of territorial sovereignty was the uniform application of common law jurisdiction across that territory. All those who are within the territory become subject to that jurisdiction. By virtue of being within the newly acquired territory, the Spinifex people, and their relationship to country, are liable to become juridical objects. On making their claim for native title, their relationship to country becomes juridified as native title. As part of making a claim, it is necessary to outline precisely the boundaries of country. In the bureaucratised system which regulates applications for a determination of native title, this requirement is fulfilled by mapping country through the provision of geospatial data, and in so doing by the imposition on to traditional country of Western, Cartesian ways of understanding.

Section 62 of the *Native Title Act 1993* (Cth) prescribes that, in order to register a claimant application for a determination of native title, certain information must be provided. The information required includes a map of the claim area and a detailed written description outlining the boundaries of the area covered by the claim area. As a result of this, the issue of mapping native title claim areas has become a complex one, requiring access to sophisticated geospatial data.

The Geospatial Analysis & Mapping Branch of the National Native Title Tribunal produces geospatial technical guidelines for the preparation of maps to be used in claims. According to the guidelines, an adequate map will 'contain a geographic or grid reference system, together with the map zone (where applicable) and reference datum, such as GDA94, AGD66'. It will also 'depict and label (if scale permits) areas or features mentioned in the written description; clearly depict areas excluded (if applicable and possible); where other detail is used as a spatial reference (e.g., cadastral parcels), include the currency date pertaining to that information [and] include a locality map' (National Native Title Tribunal, 2001).[38]

36 *Mabo v State of Queensland (No. 2)* (1992) 175 CLR 1 at 36.

37 *Mabo v State of Queensland (No. 2)* (1992) 175 CLR 1 at 43 per Brennan J, at 78 per Deane and Gaudron JJ, at 182 per Toohey J.

38 The map is appended to the claim application as Sched B. The claim is lodged on Form 1 as prescribed by the Native Title (Federal Court) Regulations 1998, reg. 5(1)(a).

The guidelines provide that the accompanying written description of the claim area may define the external boundaries in a number of ways:

> ... by way of reference to physical features such as watercourses and roads, together with the location on such... by reference to administrative boundaries (for example, local government areas), other native title claimant applications or areas publicly notified (for example, land acquisition notices)... by metes and bounds description or a series of coordinate points or combination of each. If coordinates are used, the map zone (where applicable) and reference datum must be identified.
>
> (National Native Title Tribunal, 2001)[39]

For a native title claim, the requirements of the *Act* may amount not only to a map and a written description of the claim area but also pages and pages of detailed geographic coordinates: points of longitude and latitude in accordance with GDA84 or GDA94. These coordinates are required to pinpoint the exact boundaries of the claim area. For the claimants, however, the precision of Western mapping denies the complex nature of interrelations between families, clans and other groups. Western mapping practices reinforce the idea of the 'tribe' as a homogenous entity with clearly bounded borders and culture. Yet, for some claimants, the boundaries of their land may be incapable of such precise delineation – they are porous and negotiated. For the Spinifex people, for example, there is no 'bright line' of territory or territorial jurisdiction. Rather, there is a complex set of interconnected personal and communal associations which 'form the basis upon which [they] recognise this country as theirs as distinct from that of their neighbours' (Cane, 2002: 54). According to Cane:

> That recognition is enumerated through a constellation of sites related to an individual's birth, parents, grandparents, brothers and sisters and Tjukurrpa, which together give shape to a geographic area associated with their community.
>
> (2002: 54)

Rather than bright lines, boundaries are:

> To a degree, arbitrary, drawn as a measure of cultural convenience around the area within which a given group has known associations and primary responsibility: 'in the desert proper boundaries lose their significance and the focus is unequivocally on sites and the tracks (dreaming) that link them together'.
>
> (2002: 56, quoting from Peterson and Long, 1986)

For some groups, territorial boundaries may be firm, while for others territorial boundaries are flexible and dynamic – to Western eyes, ambiguous. Yet for both

39 The written description of the claim area is appended to the claim application as Sched C.

Indigenous and non-Indigenous, visual representation is a way of demonstrating territory. Just as mapping demonstrates the bright lines of territorial jurisdictions, visual representations – paintings, maps if you will – represent for indigenous groups their ownership and jurisdiction.

Conclusion

Mapping has been described as the 'midwife' of the nation state (Ford, 1999: 870) and of territorial sovereignty. Along with the technology of surveying, mapping defined the globe as blank space into which imperial and common law jurisdiction could be projected, and in so doing obscured indigenous jurisdictions and ways of seeing and understanding country. The native title paintings of the Pila Nguru are representations of their country, beliefs and kinship systems, and demonstrate profound connection to the land. They provide an older way of understanding spatial order, reflecting the physicalised nature of communities' relationships with, and jurisdiction over, country. Ironically, as a technology of jurisdiction, mapping has never entirely replaced earlier pre-Cartesian ways of representing local environments. Territory still requires attachment to the Earth through markers and cairns. Despite this, the two ways of seeing seem incommensurate. While relationships to country can be – and are – represented on Western maps, something seems lost in the translation. As legal practice, the process of mapping for a native title claim juridifies the relation to country and recreates it as 'native title'. At the same time, the process of mapping for the claim reinstitutes sovereign and common law jurisdiction by reimposing the ordered grid of the Western map on the landscape.

References

Baudrillard, J (1994 [1981]) *Simulacra and Simulation*, Ann Arbor, MI: University of Michigan Press

Brotton, J (1997) *Trading Territories: Mapping the Early Modern World*, Ithac, NY: Cornell University Press

Bushaway, B (1982) *By Rite: Custom, Ceremony and Community in England, 1700–1880*, London: Junction Books

Cane, S (2002) *Pila Nguru: The Spinifex People*, Fremantle: Fremantle Arts Centre Press

Chase, J (1998) 'Porous boundaries and shifting borderlands: The American experience in a new world order' 26 *Reviews in American History* 54

Darby, H (1933) 'The agrarian contribution to surveying in England' 82 *Geographical Journal* 529

Davenport, F (1917) *European Treaties Bearing on the History of the United States and its Dependencies to 1648*, Washington, DC: Carnegie Institution of Washington

Dorsett, S and McVeigh, S (2002) 'Just so: The law which governs Australia is Australian law' 13 *Law and Critique* 289

Edgerton, S (1979) *The Renaissance Rediscovery of Linear Perspective*, New York, NY: Basic Books

Ford, R (1999) 'Law's territory (a history of jurisdiction)' 97 *Michigan Law Review* 843

Harvey, D (1990) *The Condition of Postmodernity: An Enquiry into the Origins of Cultural Change*, Cambridge and Oxford: Blackwell

Harvey, P (1980) *The History of Topographical Maps*, London: Thames and Hudson

Harvey, PDA (1996) *Mappae Mundi: The Hereford World Map*, Toronto: University of Toronto Press

Hobsbawm, E (1990) *Nations and Nationalism Since 1780: Programme, Myth, Reality*, Cambridge: Cambridge University Press

Holdsworth, WS (1922–1972) *A History of English Law*, London: Methuen

Jensen, M (ed) (1969) *English Historical Documents, Vol. IX: American Colonial Documents to 1776*, New York, NY: Oxford University Press

Kain, R and Baigent, E (1992) *The Cadastral Map in the Service of the State: A History of Property Mapping*, Chicago, IL: University of Chicago Press

Lines, J (1992) *Australia on Paper: The Story of Australian Mapping*, Melbourne: Fortune Publications

National Native Title Tribunal (2001) *Geospatial Technical Guidelines for the Preparation of Maps and Area Descriptions*, available at www.nntt.gov.au/nntt/infokit.nsf/area/homepage

Peterson, N and Long, J (1986) *Australian Territorial Organisation* 30 *Oceania Monograph* 1

Pollock, F and Maitland, F (1968) *The History of English Law Before the Time of Edward I*, Vol. 1, 2nd edn, Cambridge: Cambridge University Press

Redefining the Queensland–New South Wales Border: Guidelines for Surveyors (2001) Brisbane: Queensland Department of Natural Resources and Mines and New South Wales Department of Information Technology and Management

Rush, P (1997) 'An altered jurisdiction: Corporeal traces of law' 6 *Griffith Law Review* 144

Ryan, S (1997) *The Cartographic Eye: How Explorers Saw Australia*, Cambridge and Melbourne: Cambridge University Press

Schmitt, C (1996) 'The land appropriation of a new world' (trans. of Ch. II, 'Die Landnahme einer neuen Welt' in *Der Nomos der Erde im Völkerrecht der Jus Publicum Europeaeum*, 1950, 2nd edn, Duncker & Humblot, Berlin, 1974) 109 *Telos* 29

Smith, H (ed) (1932–1935) *Great Britain and the Law of Nations: A Selection of Documents Illustrating the Views of the Government in the United Kingdom Upon Matters of International Law*, Vol. II, London: King

Tomlins, C (2001) 'The legal cartography of colonization, the legal polyphony of settlement: English intrusion on the American mainland in the seventeenth century' 26 *Law & Society of Inquiry* 315

Turnbull, D (1996) 'Cartography and science in early modern Europe: Mapping and the construction of knowledge spaces' 48 *Imago Mundi* 5

Watson, F (ed) (1914) *Historical Records of Australia, Series 1: Governor's Despatches to and from England,* Sydney: Library Committee of the Commonwealth Parliament.

Whitfield, P (1994) *The Image of the World: 20 Centuries of World Maps*, San Francisco, CA: Pomegranate Art Books

Winton, T (2001) *Dirt Music*, Sydney: Picador

Woodward, D (1991) 'Maps and the rationalization of geographic space', in J Levenson (ed), *Circa 1492: Art in the Age of Exploration*, New Haven, Washington: Yale University Press and National Gallery of Art

Cases

Mabo v State of Queensland (No. 2) (1992) 175 CLR 1
Mark Anderson on behalf of the Spinifex People v State of Western Australia [2000] FCA 1717 (28 November 2000)
State of South Australia v State of Victoria (1911) 12 CLR 667 (HC)
State of South Australia v State of Victoria (1914) 18 CLR 115 (PC)

Legislation

Native Title Act 1993 (Cth)

9 Placing jurisdiction

*Leslie J Moran**

Introduction

'Jurisdiction', the *Oxford English Dictionary* reveals, is a complex knot of meanings. It refers to institutional, organisational and functional aspects of law and its (judicial) administration, and more specifically to their 'power'. 'Jurisdiction' is also described as a term that refers to the 'extent', 'range' and 'territory' of those judicial and administrative institutions and operations of power (*Oxford English Dictionary*, 1991: 904). 'Extent', 'range' and 'territory' denote and connote the institutional, organisational and functional aspects of law (its power, authority, rule, monopoly of violence) by way of its limits, its boundaries and its bounded operation. As such, 'jurisdiction' is a term that characterises law and legality as spatial and geographical phenomena. There is a growing body of work that analyses the interface between the spatial and the legal. Some work has drawn attention to the juridical significance of key spatial terms such as 'frontier', 'map', 'territory' and 'nation', while other work has examined the spatial dimension of legal terms, such as 'sovereignty' and 'property' (Blomley, 1994; Cooper, 1998; Goodrich, 1990, 1992; Holder and Harrison, 2002; Johnston, 1990; Nedelsky, 1991; Sarat, Douglas and Umphery, 2003). Both approaches point to the intimate connection between the legal and the spatial. This chapter offers a critical reflection on jurisdiction as a geo-jurisprudential term.

I begin with a word of warning about the use of spatial terms, and more specifically about terms which denote and connote 'edge' and 'limit' such as 'jurisdiction'. Smith and Katz (1993) emphasise the need to carefully examine the relationship between space and language. In particular, they warn of the way spatial terms connote fixity and stability, thereby erasing the contingency of space and the political struggle by which different spaces and spatial

* I would like to thank the Law School at Griffith University for its financial assistance, making my participation in the seminar on jurisdiction at Griffith University possible. Thanks also to Bruce Carolan and the College of Law, Stetson University, Florida who were responsible for organising a visiting fellowship in March–April 2004. The final stages of research and writing were undertaken during the course of this fellowship.

categories come into being and function. For example, 'boundary' is a term that not only refers to an edge, a limit as a line that divides, separates and distributes, but also one that has clarity, is impermeable, stable and fixed. Smith and Katz point to the ways in which all these connotations about the nature of the boundary are problematic. They threaten to erase the contingency, mobility and plurality of experiences (and thereby locations) of edges and limits. Boundaries are neither always (nor only) located and experienced literally as spatially remote in relation to a literal centre. They also may be experienced at the physical core and the heart of a place as well as in a multitude of other more or less physically remote locations. This multiplicity of locations of the experience of a bounded space highlights the way 'limit', 'edge', 'boundary' and 'jurisdiction' operate at the level of metaphor, by way of connotation. Bammer (1992) notes that, as metaphors, these terms have an 'indeterminate referential quality', being capable of constituting experiences of a specific location and place in many different contexts and settings. Any encounter with the spatial dimensions of jurisdiction needs to proceed with these points firmly in mind.

Ingram, Bouthillette and Retter (1997: 7) suggest that one of the effects of this depoliticisation is that, while spatial themes proliferate, the different spaces remain under-documented, analysed and theorised. In response to these dangers, Berlant and Freeman (1993) argue that spatial themes demand detailed consideration. Inspired by these concerns, this chapter explores the borders and boundaries of the institutional, organisational and functional aspects of law and its (judicial) administration in a very specific political and spatial context, in relation to homophobic violence and claims for citizenship being fabricated in demands for and in practices of safety and security in Manchester's 'Gay Village' in the north-west of England.

This particular political context draws another dimension of spatial/legal politics into the frame: the significance of bodies in general and sexual bodies in particular. Elizabeth Grosz (1995) offers a useful insight into the importance of the space–body interface. Spatial categories as metaphor and metonym, she suggests, play a key role in making the sense (the intelligibility) and the non-sense (the unintelligibility) of the corporeal, the body. As de Certeau (1984) notes, the idea of the boundary plays a particularly important role. The body is articulated and defined, he suggests, by way of delimitation (1984: 139). Bodies are imagined as bounded and limited entities. For example, the skin connotes the boundary *par excellence* – between inside and outside, between one person and another (Ahmed and Stacey, 2001). In turn, Grosz notes, the body works as a metaphor and metonym of space. The body as limit and boundary is place personified. The body as place may be both positive and negative, imagined both as the place of good order and its apotheosis. The (male)[1]

1 For work that explores the interface between sexuality and gender by way of lesbian sexuality, see Jagose (1994); Wittig (1992); Mason (2001).

sexualised body has long been one context in which the body as the spatial metaphor of good/bad order has been produced (see, for example, Boswell, 1980). The case studies explored in this chapter examine two proximate contexts in which the sexual body is a space–body interface through which political struggles that make up the institutional, organisational and functional boundaries of law's force take place.

Spatial themes have been a long-standing dimension of a body politic concerned with same-sex desires and identities. Sexual and cultural geography and work informed by urban studies (Adler and Brennan, 1992; Bell and Valentine, 1995; Castells, 1983; Castells and Murphy, 1982; Valentine, 1993a,b,c, 1996) and architectural studies (Betsky, 1997; Sanders, 1996) have begun to document and analyse the rich diversity of spatial categories through which the sense and non-sense of sexualised intimacy and sexual belonging may be made. This work suggests that a diverse spatial language is at play in the generation of the contours of social exclusion and social belonging in general, and the body politics of sexual belonging in particular: place, site, environment, the urban, suburban and rural, queerscapes, locality, liminality, utopia and heterotopia, ghetto, region, neighbourhood, building and home.

The most pervasive spatio-corporeal theme is the distinction between 'the public' and 'the private'. In many respects, the dominance of this particular spatial dichotomy in the context of genital intimacy (between men) is unsurprising. Eve Sedgwick (1990) has pointed to the cultural importance of these spatial terms. The public–private binary, she has argued, does phenomenal cultural work in Western liberal democratic societies. This is realised through an extensive metonomic chain of associations condensed within the public–private binary – for example, as a relation of the impersonal–personal, inauthentic–authentic, danger–safety and insecurity–security, to name but a few. Such is the range of meanings produced through the public–private distinction that it threatens, she warns, to make it difficult to not only differentiate it from, but also imagine, alternative spatial categories. It is therefore not surprising that, in the context of same-sex intimacy, the public and the private have been dominant spatial themes closely connected with matters of the reach of law and its limits, its jurisdiction. From the nineteenth century, they have been a prominent feature of attempts to fabricate and govern the space–body interface according to the particular requirements of law's limits (Lauristen and Thornstad, 1974; Moran, 1996).[2]

However, the public–private distinction does not exhaust spatio-corporeal themes within this body politics. Perhaps most familiar are the spatial–political categories of 'community', 'nation' and 'state' (Altman, 1982; Cooper, 1994; Kinsman, 1987; Moran, 1991). Deployed in various legal contexts, such as demands for civil and human rights (Stychin, 1998, 2003; Waaldijk and Clapham, 1993; Wintermute, 1995), and more recently formulated in terms of sexual

2 Lesbian scholars have challenged the importance of the public–private relation: see Majury (1994); Mason (1995, 1997).

citizenship (Bell, 1995; Binnie and Bell, 2000; Evans, 1993; Phelan, 2001; Stychin, 2003), different geographical categories have been deployed in the figuration of the space–body interface, such as 'the international', 'the supranational' and 'the global' – thereby imagining alternative (and competing) locations of belonging. These particular space–body relations are never far away from the spatial themes that seek to imagine a different limit, creating new juridical locations of belonging (Ford, 1999).

A powerful image in which the spatial, the corporeal and the legal are woven together is the phrase the 'body of law'; another is 'the sovereign' and 'sovereignty'.[3] In 'the sovereign' and 'sovereignty', law may be embodied and thus personified in the corporeality of the reigning monarch, or in a more abstracted image of Leviathan, or in a republican image of a body politic as 'the people'. Common to all is resort to the image of the human body in the representation of law and the good order that law stands for. In the bounded body of the sovereign, law and the legal order are totalised and rendered coherent in the ideal corporeality of that (king's/queen's) body (Kantorowicz, 1957). At the same time, that body works as a visualisation of law as a limited and a located practice and power. The sovereign's body as a corporeal metaphor of law and order (of good order) also gives form to the ideal body of the individual made subject/citizen, both subjected to and the model subject of good order (Cheah and Grosz, 1996). So how does homophobic violence fit into this scheme of things?

The idea and practices of safety and security that constitute the body politic are central to political initiatives focusing on homophobic violence. They seek to draw attention to the pervasive operation and impact of homophobic violence, and make demands that the state intervene to punish this form of violence and bring it to an end. As Shane Phelan (2001) notes, within the Western liberal democratic model, the state plays a key role in the provision of safety and security (cf Moran and Skeggs, 2004). Through its monopoly of legitimate violence, the state is the ultimate provider and guarantor of safety and security. In turn, safety and security are a fundamental dimension of the relationship between the state and the citizen. It is a particularly important context and location through which a politics of belonging (which Fraser, 1995 has characterised as a politics of recognition) is forged.

This particular relationship between the state and the individual has long been informed by heterosexist assumptions. Homophobic violence, rather than being a sign and a practice of a disorder that has no place within the state, threatening both individual, and state safety and security, has long been a characteristic of good order and state safety and security policies and practices. Same-sex genital acts have, in this context, been characterised as disordered and disorderly, as acts out of place. Homophobic violence has been actively pursued though state institutions and, even when not a formal part of these institutions, has been

3 Richard Ford (1999) suggests that the spatial aspect of sovereignty is of recent origin and is particularly associated with geo-political changes in Europe.

characterised as a legitimate (state-sanctioned) private activity, as exemplified in the continuing viability of the 'homosexual panic defence' (Howe, 1997, 1998; Tomsen, 1994, 1998).

Thus safety and security, as the heart of citizenship, have long been informed by heterosexist assumptions. Rosga (2001) argues that demands that the state in general, and its agents of criminal justice in particular, now imagine homophobic violence as a form of disorder, as a threat to community safety and security, represent a political project that seeks to turn the state against itself. This, I would suggest, involves a jurisdictional reconfiguration – a transformation of the nature and form of the boundaries of law. The political struggles that produce and change the boundaries of law are the focus of the following analysis.

Political and spatial contexts

I want to examine the terms of the state's jurisdiction over internal safety and security in two different contexts that are both temporally and spatially proximate. The first is a set of criminal proceedings which have come to be known as the case of the 'Bolton Seven'. The second is gay and lesbian perceptions and practices of safety and security in the 'European gay Mecca' of Manchester's Gay Village.[4]

The case of the 'Bolton Seven' involved criminal proceedings against Norman Williams, Jonathan Moore, David Godfrey, Terry Connell, Gary Abdie, Mark Love and an 'unnamed minor'.[5] All were friends, friends of friends or lovers. The incidents occurred in Bolton, a medium-sized town in the north-west of England. Bolton lies a mere 16 kilometres north of Manchester's Gay Village, which has been described as 'a European gay Mecca' (Healthy Gay Manchester, 1998). It is arguably the largest, most concentrated and thereby the most public commercial gay space in the United Kingdom.

The proceedings against the 'Bolton Seven' arose out of investigations conducted by officers of the Greater Manchester Police Service. Two 'home-made videos' recorded on a camcorder owned by Connell were found during the course of a police search of the home of Williams. The videos were central to the proceedings providing key evidence of the wrongful acts. All of the defendants were charged and found guilty of the offence of gross indecency involving consensual acts of mutual masturbation and oral sex. Three were charged and found guilty of buggery, which involved consensual anal penile penetration. All these acts were performed 'behind closed doors', in the homes of two of the accused. It was

4 The analysis of Manchester's Gay Village draws upon data produced in the course of an empirical research project funded by the Economic and Social Research Council entitled 'Violence, Sexuality, Space', ESRC research award No. L 133 25 1031. That project was undertaken by the author with Beverley Skeggs and research assistants Paul Tyrer, Karen Corteen and Lewis Turner. The research used a multi-method approach: surveys, structured interviews and focus groups: see Moran and Skeggs (2004).

5 It is estimated that half a million pounds was spent on the investigation and prosecution.

accepted that the videos had been made for home, not commercial, use. Five of the accused aged between seventeen and a half and 25 (at the time of the acts) were sentenced by the trial court judge to undertake community service and subject to probation orders.[6] The two older men, one aged 33 and the other 55, were sentenced to terms of imprisonment, of two years and nine months, respectively, suspended for two years. These two defendants were also required to register with the local police as 'sex offenders' under Part 1 of the *Sex Offenders Act 1997*.[7] Spatial themes had a high profile in the proceedings and in the controversy surrounding them.

While geographically proximate to the incidents and proceedings in Bolton, Manchester's Gay Village appears to offer a very different political, spatial and legal landscape. The Gay Village is arguably the largest, most concentrated, visible (public) gay identified location in the United Kingdom. It is also the location one of Britain's first police liaison initiatives bringing the police together with lesbians and gay men. More recently, it has been the site of the United Kingdom's first homophobic hate crime initiative. Both the incidents in Bolton, and the police and community initiatives in the 'gay Mecca' of Manchester's Gay Village have a temporal and geographical proximity, being contemporaneous and little more than 16 kilometres apart. Both have jurisdictional proximities, being subject to the same laws and being administered by the same police service, the Greater Manchester Police. At the same time, the sexual citizenship of the men criminalised for consensual sex with men 'behind closed doors' seems very remote from all that is suggested and celebrated in the sexual citizenship being fabricated though gay and lesbian engagements with the police in the same police service that is committed to taking homophobic violence seriously (cf Stanko and Curry, 1997). The proximity and distance between these two proximate events and locations was captured in a report in a gay monthly journal, *Gay Times*, which announced that:

> Greater Manchester Police gay liaison work, thought of as the most advanced and progressive in the country, has suffered a serious set-back following the force's dogged prosecution of the Bolton Seven.
>
> (Tatchel, 1998: 43)

The analysis that follows seeks to examine the complex and problematic relationship between space, bodies and law, that connects and separates the legal landscapes of these two events and locations within the body politic.

The Queen's Peace

Let us begin with the analysis of the case of the 'Bolton Seven'. The most controversial spatial dimension of the proceedings related to a jurisdictional issue: the

6 On appeal, the community service component of the sentences was quashed for each defendant. Moore's sentence was reduced from two years to twelve months' probation. Abdie's sentence, originally 150 hours' community service, was reduced to a one-year conditional discharge.

7 For the following five years, they have a duty to inform the police of any change of name or address.

reach and limit of criminal law and its administration. Defence challenges to the operation and severity of the criminal law deployed spatial distinctions between the public and the private to explain the limits of criminal law, and thereby to intimate the extent of its legitimate reach. The proceedings explored different and contentious meanings of 'private', from the meaning prescribed in the *1967 Sexual Offences Act* and what might be described as more popular meanings. These spatial dimensions of law are also intimately concerned with bodies: the corporeal. The space–body connection is forged in law by reference to the actions named and forbidden by the criminal law: gross indecency and buggery.

Sections 12 and 13 of the *Sexual Offences Act 1956* describe the prohibitions (buggery and gross indecency) that informed the jurisdiction of the law at that time.[8] Section 12(1) provides: 'It is an offence for a person to commit buggery with another person' and s 13 that:

> It is an offence for a man to commit an act of gross indecency with another man whether in public or private, or to be party to the commission by a man of an act of gross indecency with another man, or to procure the commission by a man of an act of gross indecency with another man.

In these two sections, the limit of law is represented in two different ways. In s 13, the theme of jurisdiction appears by way of an explicit spatial reference, 'whether in public or private'. Here a boundary is named in order to erase it. In s 12(1), the limit of the reach of the criminal law appears by way of the absence of any reference to a limit. Common to both is the apparent limitless reach of the criminal law in relation to these forbidden acts. Here the bodies in question are always within reach of the law and its institutions of administration and enforcement.

The archaic collective term for criminal wrongs is 'pleas of the Crown', their political and spatial form being known as the Queen's/King's Peace. While the two offences outlined above represent the borders of Queen's Peace in different ways (respectively explicitly and implicitly), they achieve the same spatial effect. The Queen's Peace is unlimited, and at the same time limited – but only by the greater limits of sovereignty itself.[9] This Queen's Peace is a delimitation constituted by way of a series of binary oppositions: of order against disorder; of rule in contrast to the unruly; of law against violence. Through the prohibitions, the body is read and written according to the requirements of the Queen's Peace. It is

8 Major changes to the law of sexual offences is to be found in the *Sexual Offences Act 2003*. That Act (see Sched 7) repeals these sections. Non-consensual buggery now falls within the definition of rape (s 1) and a new offence of 'assault by penetration' (s 2). The offence of gross indecency has been abolished (Sched 7). A new offence of 'sexual activity in a public lavatory' (s 71) continues to criminalise consensual sexual activities, though the offence is limited to sexual acts performed in a particular place.

9 While this formally suggests the absence of boundaries within the criminal jurisdiction, it does not necessarily preclude the possibility of other simultaneous jurisdictions (juridical spaces), such as ecclesiastical or feudal jurisdictions that have in the past been the other to the Queen's Peace. Ford (1999) also draws attention to the possibility of contemporary local jurisdictions.

made the disorderly body that calls for order. It is the unruly body and the body of escalating violence that threatens the body of law as order, rule, reason. The limit of the Queen's Peace, its beginning and end, is disorder that is always proximate and always elsewhere. By way of acts of buggery and gross indecency, the sexual body is made always already a body outside the law, as outlaw, that is to be subjected to the law. As a technique of locating and governing this body, the Queen's Peace knows no internal limits other than disorder which calls this technique into being. This sexual body is one that is always before the law, always visible to the law. It is within this scheme of things that domestic and intimate space of the home of the accused is within the Queen's Peace and subject to it, not apart from or beyond its reach or its limit. In this scheme of things, all other possible boundaries are made porous, contingent, ultimately incorporated within the limit of the Queen's Peace.

But the Queen's Peace has been subject to certain spatial qualifications in this context. These were first introduced in the *Sexual Offences Act 1967*,[10] which amended ss 12 and 13 of the *1956 Act*. The *1967 Act* qualified the reach of the Queen's Peace by way of a distinction between the public and the private. It is to this public–private divide that I now want to turn.

'In private'

Under the terms of the *1967 Act*, 'in private' is a limit to the reach of the general criminal law. It erects a boundary that has many dimensions. It locates the limit of the Queen's Peace by reference to bodies, to their sex (under that *Act*, only the male body could attain the status of 'in private')[11] and by reference to particular intimate gestures (confined to anal penetration of one man by the penis of another and a range of forms of genital contact and genital display with another man). It is also a boundary found only in relation to a very specific civil society – a society of two – locating those bodies as beyond the law by way of a sentimental domesticity. As with other privileged civil societies, its subjects are required to have particular capacities (of age[12] and mental ability) and to have performed an 'act of consent'. Judicial commentary on this particular process of boundary formation – for example, in the case of *R v Reakes*[13] draws attention to other

10 These provisions have their origin in law reform initiatives inaugurated by the Wolfenden Committee and found in that committee's report (1957). The *Sexual Offences Act 2003* repeals the provisions of the *1967 Act* (see Sched 7). It now appears that, rather than the terms of the *1967 Act* providing an exception to the reach of the Queen's Peace, the private as a limit of criminal law has become a generalised limit in the context of consensual genital relations in private.

11 This resulted in an interesting state of affairs. Buggery between a man and a woman could not be defined as 'in private' and was thereby criminal under the *Sexual Offences Act* at all times, with or without consent. This situation was reformed in the *Criminal Justice and Public Order Act 1994*.

12 Age had a particular importance in the 'Bolton Seven' case, as one of the accused was under 18 (the then age of consent) at the time of the acts. He was seventeen and a half. I have analysed age as a boundary in the context of the reform of the 'age of consent' in detail: see Moran (1997); Waites (1999).

13 *R v Reakes* (1974) *Crim LR* 613.

contingencies: the time of night, the function of the place, lighting and the likelihood of a third person coming upon the scene. Further unarticulated factors are characterised by the pregnant phrase 'surrounding circumstances'.[14]

The sentencing remarks made in the 'Bolton Seven' case by the trial court judge, His Honour Judge Michael Lever QC, provide an opportunity to examine a particular instance in the formation of the boundary, 'in private' in a particular case. Ultimately, in this context, the 1967 qualification, 'in private', was never available to secure the innocence of the 'Bolton Seven'. As the trial court judge explained, the acts 'were committed in full view of several people, and recorded by another on a camcorder'.[15] The presence of 'several people' and the camcorder operator clearly violated the statutory definition of 'in private' found in the *1967 Act*: no more than two people. The judge's reflections on the boundary between the private and the public demonstrate that this boundary is rich in meaning.

The judge, examining various different dimensions to the meaning of the phrase 'in private', explained:[16] 'The word private carries its natural meaning that the act has taken place in the presence of the two participants and nobody else.' At another point in his sentencing remarks, he commented:

> In my judgement, the vast law-abiding majority of homosexuals, like the vast law-abiding majority of heterosexuals, are private people who consider that their sex lives are their own private affair... They have not the slightest desire to be members of a so called community, or pressure group.

Of particular interest here is the way the judge gives the law's spatial category, 'in private', the gloss of 'natural meaning'. Here the boundary marker 'in private', marking the limit of the criminal jurisdiction, is constituted as a division between nature and nurture, nature and culture (cf Ford, 1999). As 'nature', the politics of space both within the legal category and within the trial are grounded, made authentic and made apolitical. In this context, the apolitical dimension of the private (no more than two subjects) is made over against another civil grouping, a 'so called community or pressure group', its political nature being indicated by reference to its investment in what the judge explained is 'sometimes described as Gay Rights'. Any blurring of the division between private and public is also a blurring of the distinctions connoted by reference to that divide.

14 This does not exhaust the criteria that inform the boundary of 'in private'. Others are to be found in the text of the *1967 Act*. On the jurisdictional aspect of some of these limits: see Dempsey (1998).

15 The camcorder provides a context in which the fragility of the boundary between the public and the private is revealed. This recording technology allowed representations of the acts in private to appear in public.

16 Transcript of the Sentencing Remarks of His Honour Judge Michael Lever QC. The judgement of the Court of Appeal (Criminal Division) suggests that this is not correct. One of the accused, Godfrey, pleaded guilty to an 'offence of buggery in which he was penetrated': Transcript of *R v Turner, Godfrey, Abdie and Love*, Case No. 98/1429/X2 at 1. All quotations in this paper are taken from this transcript unless otherwise specified in the following footnotes.

The judge notes that a blurring of this division has damaging consequences. These seem to be twofold: it damages individuals as private subjects, causing them 'grave embarrassment, distress and humiliation'; and it damages the law and the legal process. In the latter context, the damage takes the form of the corrupting effect of politics upon the law. One sign of the damaging effects of this boundary violation is identified by the judge in terms of its impact upon individual defendants, who experience 'far greater anxiety'. Those identified by the judge as raising political issues in the criminal trial, Williams and Connell, were said to have experienced greater anxiety in relation to the proceedings. While the trial judge was willing to recognise that the law may have some connection with the political, by way of its relation to 'democracy' and its particular institutions, 'elected representatives', this interrelationship had to be rigorously circumscribed, confined and located elsewhere to the law. The elsewhere of politics is explained by reference to the court's only concern: the rule of law. The court, the judge explained, 'is a court of law, not of morals'. To bring the political into the private violates the division between law and politics, and thereby violates nature which is divided from culture.

The naturalisation of 'in private' also has another resonance: the private–public divide echoes the boundary of hetero and homo. The implications of these separate but connected divisions are mapped in the case by way of both contrast and analogy between the hetero and the homo. Homos may be 'like' heteros – that is, a civil society of no more than two. As a private relation of two persons, this is civil society as 'nature' personified. It is good order made apolitical. It is in this context that the hetero (and homo) are described by the judge as a 'law-abiding majority'.

Hetero and homo as both clear division and interconnection meander through the judicial commentary. One context in which it is deployed is in the production of a distinction *between* defendants. On the one hand, Williams and Connell are characterised as 'mature men and practising homosexuals', which for the judge denotes more dangerous offenders to be more severely punished. The remaining five defendants are characterised as 'the rest', said by the judge to be more victims than offenders. Williams and Connell give shape and form to the clear division between hetero and homo.

'The rest' is also a category that connects these apparent opposites. First, 'the rest' is a term that names sexual disorder, but one that is subject to relocation. This term of disorder is figured in a number of ways: 'deprived backgrounds', 'broken families', 'ill-educated' and in being 'immature', 'unsophisticated', 'not very intelligent', 'unemployed' and so on. This list provides a rich catalogue of registers of disorder which might valorise and explain their disorderly actions, putting them clearly on the side of the 'bad' rather than the 'good'. Here genital acts are made signs of minor incivilities described as 'crude antics', the acts of 'smutty-minded schoolboys tipsily experimenting with sex', 'nothing to do with affection, let alone love'. Being acts performed with persons of the same sex, these various registers of the distinction between disorder and order are aligned with the 'homo' rather than the hetero; however, at the end of the proceedings, this distribution is subject to a certain transformation. The judge notes that 'at least three of the five ... are now involved in apparently serious relationships with young women, at least to the extent that [they] are actually living with them'. Here the judge points to the fluidity and porosity of the boundary between hetero and homo, and the interpenetration of one with the other. While this shift most surely threatened to disturb the fixity and stability of the sexual dichotomy (of homo and hetero), it also offers to relocate these sexual bodies, making possible a movement from homo to hetero, from bad to 'good' order. In this move, the 'good homo' seems to disappear from the frame of possibilities of signifying orderly society. Within this scheme of things, the 'homo' threatens to be always disordered, always out of place and subject to erasure under the realisation of the Queen's Peace as a space of heterosexual legal order. The case of the 'Bolton Seven' seems to offer a bleak picture of the Queen's Peace as a possible spatial politics of genital intimacy between men as good order.

The Gay Village: in or beyond the Queen's Peace?

As a juridical spatial order limited only by the boundaries of sovereignty jurisdiction, the Queen's Peace is not limited to or by a concern with the particular sentimental domestic locations that occupied the attention of the Bolton Crown Court. It is a spatial politics of law co-extensive with the second location of this study, the 'European gay Mecca', Manchester's Gay Village. As in the case of the 'Bolton Seven', 'in private' has no significance as a limit upon the reach of the power of law characterised as the Queen's Peace in the Village. Nor are the acts that might invoke the forceful imposition of the Queen's Peace limited to buggery or gross indecency. The Queen's Peace might be made manifest by way of a rich diversity of wrongful acts. For example, in the case of *Masterson v Holden*[17] two men standing together on London's main shopping thoroughfare, Oxford Street, rubbing each other's bodies – described in the case as the buttocks and genital area – were found guilty of a breach of the peace. Nor are the spaces of bars and clubs (civil societies), where entry is contingent upon agreement and subject to capacity, beyond this Queen's Peace. In the late 1970s, police raided gay bars and clubs in the then nascent Gay Village.[18] In that instance, the disorder that threatened the Queen's Peace was the spectacle of men dancing with each other, which was said to be in violation of a prohibition of licentious dancing. In relation to the Queen's Peace, the boundaries of civil society are like the limits of domestic space – penetrated by the reach of a power, the limit of which lies elsewhere.

The operation of the Queen's Peace is to be found in the human actions at work in the fabrication of the places that make up this 'European gay Mecca'. A historical study of that space shows that bars and clubs frequented by men who

17 *Masterson and Another v Holden* [1986] 3 All ER 39.

18 These raids were conducted at the time James Anderton was the local police chief constable. He had gained a certain notoriety for the expression of his right-wing fundamentalist views.

desire genital contact with other men have existed in the area for decades (Quilley, 1997; Whittle, 1994). In the past, these bars had to fabricate a certain invisibility in order to satisfy the spatial and aesthetic requirements of the Queen's Peace. They were located in a then run-down and partly abandoned area close to the city centre (a liminal zone) (Moran, 1996; Moran and McGhee, 1998; Shields, 1991), hidden in back streets, underground in basements and cellars, behind always closed, anonymous doors, unmarked (at least) to a heteronormative gaze (Brown, 2000).

Over against this is the Village as a location of resistance to the Queen's Peace. This resistance has taken various forms: demonstrations against the police raids; the establishment of organisations exposing, challenging and negotiating the heteronormativity of the Queen's Peace through HIV/AIDS activism; and initiatives specifically focusing on policing, crime control and criminal law. Healthy Gay Manchester and a Village-based Manchester lesbian and gay police liaison group have produced victim surveys[19] and developed homophobic hate crime initiatives. The documentation of violence against lesbians and gay men – previously absent from official police data – recording lesbian and gay fears of the police and capturing their experiences of homophobia in encounters with the police has been an important activity. Dialogues with the police to change police practice have been another important initiative.

Resistance has also taken the form of aesthetic practices that have changed the physical fabric of the Village. 'New' bars of the Gay Village have a different aesthetic, one now dominated by the requirements of visibility and display. Manto (the first of this new wave of places) has a 10-metre glass frontage that looks on to the Gay Village's main artery, Canal Street. Outside tables and chairs are another common feature. The 'Gay' of 'the Village' is now overtly marked. The 'C' and the 'S' on the Canal Street signs are continually erased, transforming it into 'anal treet'. Street banners, wall posters and high-profile public events – in particular the annual lesbian and gay festival, Mardi Gras – have further contributed to the public gay signification of the locality.

The Queen's other peace: Manchester's Gay Village

These changes, I suggested, mark challenges and changes to a particular idea of the Queen's Peace that have been taking place over an extended period in a particular place: the constitution of a gay public space as a space of good order. Many of the challenges and initiatives seek to have an impact which goes wider than the Village, the jurisdiction of the local police service is Greater Manchester which covers both Manchester and Bolton. The arrest and subsequent conviction of the 'Bolton Seven' therefore suggests that many of the changes focusing on policing and criminalisation had (at that time) at best a very parochial

19 The Manchester Lesbian and Gay policing initiative produced the first UK lesbian victim survey: see Brett (1999).

effect (cf Corteen *et al.*, 2000). This is not to suggest that the Village has not challenged and changed the Queen's Peace, but to point to the importance of its spatial limitations. It is to the detail of the spatial politics constituting that particular location that I now turn.

I want to focus here on the political and spatial context of that change: boundaries. The theme of boundaries was a preoccupation that emerged early in the generation of research data on homophobic violence initially amongst key business and community activists in the Village, but also in focus groups with gay men and lesbians who use the Village. Changes in the use of the Village, and its popularity as an entertainment space, generated much discussion of a 'straight invasion' of the Village. This perception of boundary violation was the immediate context in which boundary talk provided the forum in which discussions and reflections on the nature of a sexualised (gay) public space of good order, a location of safety and security, took place. The remainder of the chapter focuses upon various aspects of this boundary talk: the form of these boundaries, their location and their valorisation.

The Gay Village 1: techniques of boundary formation

Research data from the Village suggests that techniques of boundary formation are various. Boundaries may be formally signified by way of official boundary-keepers, such as doormen located at the threshold of a premises, or informally – for example, by a drag queen who drove round the Village declaiming its boundaries. Other mechanisms of boundary formation and maintenance include a demand for a formal confession at the border: 'I'm queer', followed by a declaration, 'I agree to abide by the [bar's] Rules and only fetch in my gay friends' or are marked by a certificate of passage, a 'passport' such as a 'VIP card' or a keyring. Successive Mardi Gras events have used a 'pledge band' which gives those wearing the band access to nominated bars, clubs and other premises in the Village. Purchasers were told that the band would ensure safety and security. 'John', the manager of a bar in the Village, illustrates another set of boundary marking practices. He explained that the central characteristic of the bar, captured in the slogan 'don't discriminate, integrate', was to be found emblazoned on each menu card. It also informed the design of the bar and was expressed in its music policy. Marking the boundaries of the place in their different ways, all these practices signify the nature of the place. Other research participants commented upon the way that a boundary is inscribed in and marks the body. Examples given relate to ways of dancing, ways of looking, modes and topics of speech and attitude. The bodies of those who use the entertainment space become a locus and sign of the boundaries of that space and the meanings attributed to that space. As spatial and corporeal markers, these boundaries inscribe different domains of a sexualised good order; a bar club or street. These boundary markers/makers also function as mechanisms of surveillance and governance with various degrees of formality and informality (cf Moran and McGhee, 1998).

As each of these boundary practices constitutes the location and governance of good order in formation, so (potential) boundary violations locate disorder and danger. Borders mark sites of potential boundary failure. Gatekeepers fail to patrol and maintain boundaries. Boundaries prove to be unstable, 'a billboard outside said "Integration not Segregation" which I think is a fantastic idea but unfortunately... it has become too top heavy the other way'. Rather than being something that is fixed in space and time, boundaries are not taken seriously, 'a lot of bars are gay but on a very trivial sense'; they are described as 'token', and a 'camouflage' for 'straight businesses'. Bodies are often read as out of place. As one of the gay male focus group participants explained:

> ... a small but very obnoxious group of straight people, unreasonably pissed [were] affecting the whole character of the bar.... they were dancing... and it was done in a particular way that I don't expect in a gay bar... but the aggression that goes with heterosexual people... was self-evident.

Here heterosexual bodies are reduced to a sign of a threatening disorder and perceived as evidence of a boundary violation (located as beings out of place). More specifically, minor incivilities – one of the most common being 'looking' – evidence pending disorder which takes the form of 'sheer lack of respect'.

The Gay Village 2: locating boundaries

An opening mapping exercise with the research focus groups demonstrated that any idea that the limit of the Village is a fixed or stable bounded entity is problematic. While individual maps of safety and danger shared many similarities, each one differed. Comments by 'Terry', a gay men's officer with the local city council, problematise any simple notion of the solidity of boundaries. He explained that, while on the one hand they are clear, at the same time they are 'a bit fuzzy'. Another respondent, 'Lynn', a local activist and voluntary worker, offered an insight into the 'fuzzy' nature of these boundaries. She explained that the boundary is also to be found 'in the middle you know, in between, not even just like down by the side... It tends to be all over'. 'Lynn' challenges the connotations of fixity, stability and permanence associated with boundaries. Her insight draws attention to the way in which the boundary might not have a privileged location. The boundary as outer edge is mobile and multiple. It is at the edge but also at the heart of the space. Its location is produced in its installation and investment. It is known at the moment of its production. This suggests that the boundary is both elsewhere and everywhere. In terms of the boundary of the Queen's Peace of the Village as a different limit of a different good order of safety and security, its limit and its location are perhaps best understood in terms of the moment of its production and the recognition of its violation rather than as a specific, stable or fixed location.

The Gay Village 3: boundaries of meaning

Finally, I want to briefly examine some of the values that inform and invest these boundaries of good order. Norman, one of the research participants, explained:

> I've bought gay clubs and I open gay clubs and I'm keeping them gay clubs, as gay as I can keep them. And nobody's gonna shove me any other way. I want gay . . . no straights. I think you should shoot . . . them all [straights], they do your head in.

Another, Rose, commented:

> . . . because too many straight people are . . . in the Village at the weekend . . . for the [gay] men who traditionally go out, it obviously seems to affect them because their own private space is being invaded in their eyes.

I want to focus on a particular theme found in these extracts: ideas of property.[20] As Blomley has noted: 'To talk of property in legal and political terms is to talk of order . . . ' (1997: 286). Property talk is one intelligibility through which the sense (and non-sense) of boundaries, and thereby formations and locations of this order, can be explored. Jennifer Nedelsky's (1991) work on American constitutionalism draws attention to the cultural and political importance of property and boundaries, and examines some of the meanings that are being generated about these areas in Western liberal democratic contexts.

Norman's observations contain some key characteristics associated with the idea of property. Exclusive possession informs his comments that he will not allow anyone to interfere with his decision to buy, open and run a gay bar, 'nobody's gonna shove me any other way . . . I think you should shoot them all'. Use informs his determination to 'run them gay . . . [keep] them gay'. Alienation is another characteristic to be found in Norman's observation. He makes reference to it by way of his observation 'I've bought gay clubs . . . ', which implies a capacity to dispose of gay clubs.

The juxtaposition of 'gay' and 'club' draws our attention to another aspect of 'property': propriety. As propriety, the property relation is concerned with the particular characteristic or quality of a thing which might be described as its nature or its essence (the proper, the respectable) (Davies, 1994, 1998, 1999; Naffine, 1998). Propriety is also concerned with the realisation and control of the qualities and attributes of the thing. Norman deploys propriety in his use of the particular nomination 'gay club' and in his determination to maintain that characteristic. Propriety works to give the substantive meaning of the boundary, but it also names the nature of the 'good order' that the boundary circumscribes.

20 Other values made in and through boundaries in this location are explored in Moran and Skeggs (2003).

For Norman, the boundary has particular characteristics: it is associated with exclusion – 'no straights'.

Through these ideas of property, the boundary takes the form of a claim (or right), which is not only a claim to secure, preserve and alienate but also a claim to secure, preserve and alienate the very nature of the thing. Here the property relation takes the form of an entitlement. Entitlement is both a reference to 'title', the claim to property (possession, use, alienation), and a reference to propriety: 'title' as superscription or designation that names the nature of the thing – in this instance, 'gay'.

While it might be trite to note the importance of the attributes of property for Norman, a gay man who over the past 20 years has owned and operated businesses (a taxi company, clubs and bars) in 'the Village', it would be premature to reduce ideas of property to the context of legal ownership of private property. This would miss the wider symbolic significance of the particular mentality of property that may not only be connected to property as legal ownership but also separate from it. It is in this context that the second extract, from 'Rose', has particular significance.

'Rose' makes reference to the Village – albeit in the voice of gay men rather than in her own voice as a lesbian – as 'our private space'. This draws our attention to the use of property as metaphor. By way of metaphors, the themes associated with property as an individual and a private form of spatial appropriation, ownership and belonging are used to make sense of other spatial relations that are communal and collective (be they civil society or the state) rather than individual (cf Nedelsky, 1991).

Margaret Radin's work (1993) on the distinction between property as the personal and the fungible is also important here. In the personal–fungible distinction, Radin explores symbolic meanings of property that are produced in the context of property as legal relations. For Radin, personal property is property 'bound up with a person'. It is contrasted with 'fungible property', described as property 'held purely instrumentally'(1993: 37). Radin explains this 'instrumentality' as 'holding an object that is perfectly replaceable with other goods of equal market value' (1993: 37). But Jeanne Schroeder (1998) raises a note of caution and adds an important point of correction to this scheme. It is wrong, she warns, to reduce property to a relation of subject to object (the thing or place). Property is a relation between subjects. This is true of both Radin's categories of property.

The empirical data suggests that the personal–fungible distinction has significance in various contexts. For example, in Norman's opening observation, in the first instance the property relation appears as a relation of the subject (Norman) to the object (a gay club) where the object might be perfectly replaceable by another object of equal value. However, Norman evidences a different type of investment in the property, giving the property a different symbolic significance. This is evidenced in his insistence on a very particular propriety, 'gay'. Furthermore, it is this propriety that conjoins identity, both individual and collective, to themes of property – use, exclusive possession, title, claim.

As personal property, the bar is a nodal point in a set of interrelations with other subjects, constituted in terms of those included and those excluded. The communal and community dimensions of the personal of property are perhaps more apparent in the metaphors of property and propriety used by Rose in her description of the community of the Gay Village as the 'private space' of gay men. Further evidence in support of this conclusion is to be found in wider discussions about different bars in the Gay Village. The personal–fungible distinction informs descriptions of the distinction between gay bars (personal) with lesbian and gay owners and bars owned by 'big firms' (fungible). Through metaphors of property, gay bars as personal property in contrast to straight bars as fungible property draws attention to the symbolic importance of property relations in contrast to thinking of property purely in terms of economic (Knopp, 1994) or more abstract symbolic relations (cf Forest, 1995). At the same time, it suggests that this distinction is unstable. Both in the case of Norman, as the owner of the gay club, and wider discussions about the 'big firm bars' as a vehicle for heterosexual invasion, the economic and symbolic are intimately connected. For example, the lesbian and gay Mardi Gras exposed the fragility of the distinction between a 'community event' and an event reduced to a profit-making enterprise benefiting breweries and bar owners. The fungible–personal relation as an either/or situation needs to be treated with caution. Particular attention needs to be paid to who is making the claims and the particular claims that are made. In our data, the personal–fungible is perhaps best understood in terms of struggle, tactic and strategy (de Certeau, 1984).

This analysis of borders and boundaries in the experience of making the Village a locus of a gay public space of safety and security highlights the impact of ideas of property, propriety and entitlement in relation to the constitution of an alternative Queen's Peace. This is not to suggest that this exhausts the spatial themes through which that peace might be reimagined in that location, nor is it to suggest that they are only to be found in that spatial context. The analysis here has drawn attention to their possible role in a specific spatial/juridical context in the formation of claims of citizenship (Turner, 2000). Finally, we ought not to forget a warning note raised by Naffine and Davies (2001: 39). While the rhetoric of property has had – and continues to have – significant political purchase, having immense strategic value, it may also retard social change.

Conclusions: the limits of a new jurisdiction

This chapter offers an analysis of two different and in many ways opposed but connected manifestations of the Queen's Peace. In their temporal, spatial and substantive proximity and distance, they demonstrate the ways in which the spatial politics of the Queen's Peace as a single bounded space needs to be treated with caution. As a jurisdiction, the Queen's Peace is necessarily limited and bounded; it is always already a particular place, always already parochial. It is important to take that parochialism seriously in order to understand the particular spatial politics that inform it. In this chapter, the contrast between the 'Bolton Seven' and the Gay Village draws attention to the need to be sensitive to the complexity of the parochial. Santos (1989) has noted that within each jurisdiction different juridical imaginaries may be both superimposed and interpenetrated (cf Ford, 1999). This suggests that the locatedness of law needs to be understood as a singularity, a multiplicity and as the space (in)between different spaces. The contrast between Bolton and the Gay Village draws attention to the multiple, mobile and contested nature of what might in the first instance appear to be a singular Queen's peace.

This chapter does not offer the Village (as a micro or sub-jurisdiction) as the final solution to the horrors of the Queen's Peace, as exemplified in the case of the 'Bolton Seven'. The juxtaposition of the case of the 'Bolton Seven' and the Gay Village offers an example of some of the problems of the ghetto or safe haven as a jurisdictional solution. Homophobic violence as a threat to good order is far from being confined to public space or entertainment spaces. Recent research (*Understanding and Responding to Hate Crime*, nd; Moran, Paterson and Docherty, 2004) suggests that the home, neighbourhood and workplace are the main locations of homophobic violence. The safe haven of the Village is relatively remote from these locations. Furthermore, to offer the Village as a solution would also be to assume and demand that the Village be a spatial unity. The juxtaposition of the 'Bolton Seven' case and the 'good order' of the Village does not seem to be, as Rosga (2001) suggests, an instance in which the state is being turned against itself. I would suggest that, through the lens of jurisdiction, while on the one hand the illusion of the unified, totalising body of the sovereign is exposed, the unity of that body as the limit of law and its administration is always at any one point of time fractured and fragmented. At the same time, the two case studies explore the various contexts and ways in which that unity of the law of the sovereignty comes into being and is marked on the bodies of the subjects that the process locates.

Finally, while the Village does offer a haven, a safer space, a different order, in relation to the potential exposure to the violence and exclusions demanded by the legal order as demonstrated in the case of the 'Bolton Seven', as my colleagues and I have argued elsewhere, the geography and politics of the order of the Gay Village also appears to be a geography and politics of exclusion (Moran and Skeggs, 2003; Moran *et al.*, 2001). The Village is a complex space of both protection from hetero-violence for lesbians and gay men and also a space of exclusions for lesbians and gay men. These exclusions produce a 'good order' of the Village based upon violent hierarchies of class, race and ability. However, it may in the final instance remain important to recognise the strategic significance of the Village as the possibility for a different Queen's Peace.

References

Adler, S and Brennan, J (1992) 'Gender space: lesbians and gay men in the city' 16 *International Journal of Urban and Regional Research* 24

Ahmed, S and Stacey, J (eds) (2001) *Thinking Through the Skin*, London: Routledge

Altman, D (1982) *The Homosexualisation of America*, Boston, MA: Beacon Press
Bammer, Z (1992) 'Editorial, "the question of home" ' 11(6) *New Formations* vii
Bell, D (1995) 'Pleasure and danger: The paradoxical spaces of sexual citizenship' 14 *Political Geography* 139
Bell, D and Valentine, G (1995) *Mapping Desire*, London: Routledge
Berlant, L and Freeman, E (1993) 'Queer nationality', in M Warner (ed), *Fear of a Queer Planet: Queer Politics and Social Theory*, Minneapolis, MI: University of Minnesota Press
Betsky, A (1997) *Queer Space: Architecture and Same Sex Desire*, New York, NY: William Morrow
Binnie, J and Bell, D (2000) *Sexual Citizenship*, Cambridge: Polity
Blomley, N (1994) *Law, Space, and the Geographies of Power*, London: Guilford Press
Blomley, N (1997) 'The properties of space: History, geography and gentrification' 18(4) *Urban Geographer* 286
Boswell, J (1980) *Christianity, Social Tolerance, and Homosexuality: Gay People in Western Europe from the Beginning of the Christian Era to the Fourteenth Century*, Chicago, IL: Chicago University Press
Brett, R (1999) *Lesbians' Experiences of Violence and Harassment*, Manchester: Manchester City Council in partnership with Greater Manchester Police
Brown, MP (2000) *Closet Space: Geography of Metaphors from the Body to the Globe*, Routledge: London
Castells, M (1983) *The City and the Grassroots*, Berkeley, CA: University of California Press
Castells, M and Murphy, K (1982) 'Cultural identity and urban structure: The spatial organisation of San Francisco's gay community', in N Fainstein and S Fainstein (eds), *Urban Policy under Capitalism*, Beverly Hills, CA: Sage
Cheah, P and Grosz, E (1996) 'The body of the law: Notes towards a theory of corporeal justice', in P Cheah, D Fraser and J Grbich (eds), *Thinking Through the Body of the Law*, Sydney: Allen & Unwin
Cooper, D (1994) *Sexing the City: Lesbian and Gay Politics within the Activist State*, London: Rivers Oram Press
Cooper, D (1998) *Governing Out of Order: Space, Law and the Politics of Belonging*, London: Rivers Oram Press
Corteen, K, Moran, L, Skeggs, B and Tyrer, P (2000) 'Citizens' Inquiry Reports: Lancaster and Manchester', available at http://les1.man.ac.uk/sociology/vssrp
Davies, M (1994) 'Feminist appropriations: Law, property and personality' 13 *Social and Legal Studies* 365
Davies, M (1998) 'The proper: Discourses of purity' IX *Law and Critique* 147
Davies, M (1999) 'Queer property, queer persons: Self-ownership and beyond' 8(3) *Social and Legal Studies* 327
de Certeau, M (1984) *The Practice of Everyday Life*, Berkeley, CA: University of California Press
Dempsey, B (1998) 'Piecemeal to equality: Scottish gay law reform', in J Moran, D Monk and S Beresford (eds), *Legal Queeries*, London: Cassell
Evans, D (1993) *Sexual Citizenship*, London: Routledge
Ford, RT (1999) 'Law's territory: A history of jurisdiction' 97 *Michigan Law Review* 843
Forest, B (1995) 'West Hollywood as symbol: The significance of place in the construction of gay identity' 13 *Environment and Planning D: Society and Space* 133
Fraser, N (1995) 'From redistribution to recognition? Dilemmas of justice in the "post socialist" age' 212 *New Left Review* 68

Goodrich, P (1990) *Languages of Law*, London: Weidenfeld

Goodrich, P (1992) 'Poor illiterate reason: History, nationalism and common law', 1 *Social and Legal Studies* 7

Grosz, E (1995) *Space, Time, Perversion*, London: Routledge

Healthy Gay Manchester (1998) *Healthy Gay Manchester's Lesbian and Gay Guide to Greater Manchester*, Manchester: HGM

Holder, J and Harrison, C (eds) (2002) 'Law and Geography', in *Current Legal Issues Vol. 5*, Oxford: Oxford University Press

Howe, A (1997) 'More folk provoke their own demise: Homophobic violence and sexed excuses' 19 *Sydney Law Review* 336

Howe, A (1998) 'Green versus the Queen: The provocation defence finally provoking its own demise?' 22 *Melbourne University Law Review* 466

Ingram, GB, Bouthillette, A-M and Retter, Y (eds) (1997) *Queers in Space: Communities/Public Places/Sites of Resistance*, Seattle: Bay Press

Jagose, A (1994) *Lesbian Utopics*, London: Routledge

Johnston, N (1990) 'The territoriality of law: An exploration' 11(6) *Urban Geography* 548

Kantorowicz, EH (1957) *The King's Two Bodies: A Study in Mediaeval Political Theology*, Princeton, NJ: Princeton University Press

Kinsman, G (1987) *The Regulation of Desire: Sexuality in Canada*, Montreal: Black Rose Press

Knopp, L (1994) 'Social Justice, Sexuality and the City' 15 *Urban Geography* 644

Lauristen, J and Thornstad, M (1974) *The Early Homosexual Rights Movement (1864–1935)*, New York, NY: Times Change Press

Majury, D (1994) 'Refashioning the unfashionable: Claiming lesbian identities in the legal context' 7(2) *Canadian Journal of Women and the Law* 342

Mason, G (1995) '(Out)Laws: Acts of proscription in the sexual order', in Margaret Thornton (ed), *Public and Private: Feminist Legal Debates*, Melbourne: Oxford University Press

Mason, G (1997) 'Boundaries of sexuality: Lesbian experience and feminist discourse on violence against women' 7 *Australasian Gay and Lesbian Law Journal* 40

Mason, G (2001) *Spectacles of Violence*, London: Routledge

Moran, LJ (1991) 'The uses of homosexuality: Homosexuality for national security' 19 *International Journal of Law and Society* 149

Moran, LJ (1996) *The Homosexual(ity) of Law*, London: Routledge

Moran, LJ (1997) 'Enacting intimacy' 16 *Studies in Law Politics and Society* 225

Moran, LJ and McGhee, D (1998) 'Perverting London: Cartographic practices of policing' IX(2) *Law and Critique* 207

Moran, LJ and Skeggs, B (2004) *Sexuality and the Politics of Violence and Safety*, London: Routledge

Moran, LJ, Skeggs, B, Tyrer, P and Corteen, K (2001) 'Property, boundary, exclusion: Making sense of hetero-violence in safer spaces' 2(4) *Social and Cultural Geography* 407

Moran, LJ, Paterson, S and Dochetry, V (2004) 'Count Me In: A Report on the Bexley and Greenwich homophobic Crime Survey', unpublished

Naffine, N (1998) 'The legal structure of self ownership: Or the self possessed man and the woman possessed' 25(2) *Journal of Law and Society* 193

Naffine, N and Davies, M (2001) *Are Persons Property? Legal Debates About Property and Personality*, Aldershot: Ashgate

Nedelsky, J (1991) 'Law, boundaries, and the bounded self', in R Post (ed), *Law and the Order of Culture*, Los Angeles, CA: University of California Press

Oxford English Dictionary (1991) 2nd Edition, Complete Text Reproduced Micrographically, Oxford: Clarendon Press

Phelan, S (2001) *Sexual Strangers: Gays, Lesbians, and the Dilemmas of Citizenship*, Philadelphia, PA: Temple University Press

Quilley, S (1997) 'Gay space and the entrepreneurial city', in GI Ingram, A-M Bouthillette and Y Retter (eds), *Queers in Space: Landscapes of Marginalised Sexualities and Communities*, Washington, DC: Bay Press

Radin, MJ (1993) *Reinterpreting Property*, Chicago: University of Chicago Press

Rosga, A (2001) 'Deadly words: State power and the entanglement of speech and violence in hate crime' 12(3) *Law and Critique* 223

Sanders, J (1996) *Stud: Architectures of Masculinity*, Princeton, NJ: Princeton Architecture Press

Santos, SD (1989) 'Law: A map of misreading: Towards a postmodern concept of law' 14 *Journal of Law and Society* 279

Sarat, A, Douglas, L and Umphrey, MM (2003) *The Place of Law*, Ann Arbor, MI: University of Michigan Press

Schroeder, JL (1998) *The Vestal and the Fasces: Hegel, Lacan, Property and the Feminine*, Berkeley, CA: University of California Press

Sedgwick, E (1990) *Epistemology of the Closet*, Hemel Hempstead: Harvester Wheatsheaf

Shields, R (1991) *Places on the Margin*, London: Routledge

Smith, N and Katz, C (1993) 'Grounding metaphor: Towards a spatialized politics', in M Keith and S Pile (eds), *Place and the Politics of Identity*, London: Routledge

Stanko, EA and Curry, P (1997) 'Homophobic violence and the "self" at risk: Interrogating the boundaries', in 'Legal Perversions', a special edition of 6(4) *Social and Legal Studies* 513

Stychin, CF (1998) *Nation by Rights*, Philadelphia, PA: Temple University Press

Stychin, CF (2003) *Governing Sexuality: The Changing Politics of Citizenship and Law Reform*, Oxford: Hart Publishing

Tatchel, P (1998) 'Manchester gay policing in turmoil' April *Gay Times* 43

Tomsen, S (1994) 'Hatred, murder and male honour: Gay homicides and the "homosexual panic defence" ' 6(2) *Criminology Australia* 2

Tomsen, S (1998) ' "He had to be a poofter or something": Violence, male honour and heterosexual panic' 3(2) *Australian Masculinities (Journal of Interdisciplinary Gender Studies* 44

Turner, BS (2000) 'Cosmopolitan virtue: Loyalty and the city', in EF Islin (ed), *Democracy, Citizenship and the Global City*, London and New York, NY: Routledge

Understanding and Responding to Hate Crime (nd) Factsheet on homophobic violence, London: Metropolitan Police.

Valentine, G (1993a) 'Desperately seeking Susan: A geography of Lesbian friendships' 25(2) *Area* 109

Valentine, G (1993b) '(Hetero)sexing space: Lesbian perceptions and experiences of everyday space' 11 *Environment and Planning D: Society and Space* 395

Valentine, G (1993c) 'Negotiating and managing multiple sexual identities: Lesbian time–space strategies' 18 *Transactions of the Institute of British Geographers* 237

Valentine, G (1996) '(Re)Negotiating the heterosexual street: Lesbian productions of space', in N Duncan (ed), *BodySpace: Destabilising Geographies of Gender and Sexuality*, London: Routledge

Waaldijk, K and Clapham, A (1993) *Homosexuality: A European Community Issue*, Dordrecht: Nijhoff

Waites, M (1999) 'The age of consent and sexual citizenship in the United Kingdom: A history', in J Seymour and P Bagguley (eds), *Relating Intimacies: Power and Resistance*, London: Macmillan

Whittle, S (1994) 'Consuming differences: The collaboration of the gay body with the cultural state', in S Whittle (ed), *The Margins of the City: Gay Men's Urban Lives*, Aldershot: Arena
Wintermute, R (1995) *Sexual Orientation and Human Rights: The United States Constitution, the European Convention, and the Canadian Charter*, Oxford: Clarendon Press
Wittig, M (1992) *The Straight Mind*, Hemel Hempstead: Harvester Press
Wolfenden, J (1957) *Report of the Departmental Committee on Homosexual Offences and Prostitution*, HMSO Cmnd 247

Cases

Masterson and Another v Holden [1986] 3 All ER 39
R v Reakes (1974) *Crim LR* 613
R v Turner, Godfrey, Abdie and Love, Case No 98/1429/X2 (the 'Bolton Seven' case)

Legislations

Criminal Justice and Public Order Act 1994
Sex Offenders Act 1997
Sexual Offences Act 1956
Sexual Offences Act 1967
Sexual Offences Act 2003

10 A jurisdiction of body and desire

Exploring the boundaries of bodily control in prostitution law

Lee Godden

> The very contours of 'the body' are established through markings that seek to establish specific codes of cultural coherence. Any discourse that establishes the boundaries of the body serves the purpose of instating and naturalizing certain taboos regarding the appropriate limits, postures and modes of exchange that define what it is that constitutes bodies.
>
> (Butler, 1999: 166)

Introduction

The *Prostitution Act 1999* in Queensland was the latest in a series of Australian laws that decriminalised various forms of prostitution and brought prostitution in brothels within statutory control (Neave, 1994: 67). At the time, the new laws were proclaimed to strike a balance between providing a regulated environment in which safe, controlled prostitution could operate, and maintaining the moral and social interests of the community. This legal reform represented a significant social change in a relatively conservative Australian community where religious groups adhering to 'traditional Christian values' still hold considerable political influence. Moves to decriminalise prostitution in many Australian jurisdictions also run counter to recent policy trends which invoke a return to 'family and community'. In negotiating the balance between the sacred and the profanely 'material', the Queensland laws provide a means to legitimate the activity of prostitution while setting the putative boundaries of 'family and community', as clearly distinct from those bodies that may corrupt such ideals.

Central to any exercise in the setting of 'boundaries' in law is the concept of 'jurisdiction'. Accordingly, this chapter analyses the manner in which law assumes power over prostitution and its associated 'bodies' by reference to changing conceptions of jurisdiction. The more neutral term 'bodies', rather than 'subjects' or 'individuals', is used to emphasise the process by which law, through an assertion of jurisdiction, acts on or through bodies to 'identify' and ascribe legal status to the subject/individual. Consequently, jurisdiction is given a confined interpretation in this context as the ambit of the legal power to act upon or control 'bodies' as a capacity to prescribe 'proper' boundaries in relation to that legal status. Thus jurisdiction is not simply the assertion of bare control over bodies in a territorial compass but also comprehends the manner and form by which law insinuates itself as the indispensable means of control by establishing a necessary nexus between body and 'law'.

Yet the concept of jurisdiction is not static, as its formulation is dependent upon the prevailing conception of 'law' with which it is associated. Changing historical understandings of the relationship between law, power and jurisdiction add further complexity. The first conception, in simplified terms, comprehends a model of law in juridical form. The second is associated with a move to administrative forms of governance. These two models of 'law' have been prominent in the control of prostitution – first, the criminal law associated with a juridical form of law, and second, regulatory or normative control by the administrative and bureaucratic state. Feminist reactions to prostitution control have varied from denouncing the exploitation of women as social victims with no effective choice (Pateman, 1988) to recognising the autonomy of women to undertake the relatively well-paid employment offered by prostitution (Perkins, 1994). Within Australian society, the two models have fluctuated in importance as the pre-eminent mode of controlling the 'bodies' engaged in prostitution. Each mode exhibits a particular configuration of jurisdiction as part of that control.

Within Australian society, conservative religious and political groups have often identified moral laxity with any moves to decriminalise prostitution.[1] Symbolically, prostitution and sin have been associated – even if this link has not always been reflected in more formal policies. In the context of conservative Christian values, prostitution regulation has been characteristically associated with the need for the imposition of criminal law prohibitions. Such sanctions, this view suggests, work upon a body that is 'subject to law'. Jurisdiction becomes the mode for an imposition of boundaries upon the body. Implicitly, this analysis also accepts that a body already 'exists' with a pre-given status as a prostitute – a body that cannot come within law's jurisdiction except as a naturally sinful body that has transgressed moral values prior to law's assertion of a power to punish, and thereby control, such bodies.

With the advent of a more normative framework for law, it is argued here that, through an assertion of regulatory control over prostitution, law simultaneously 'creates' and constrains the bodies that it recognises as being engaged in prostitution. As a form of access to bodies and their sexuality, the regulatory technologies of prostitution laws construct a particular sexed body that is identified primarily in terms of its potential to transgress 'boundaries'. Accordingly, the identification of such a 'body' concurrently establishes the necessity of a jurisdiction for, and of, those technologies of control. In establishing the contours of such a body, its boundaries, the laws marks out their extent (see MacNeil, 1998

1 For example, a prominent aspect of the Queensland National Party policy platform in the state government election campaign following the 'legalisation' of prostitution was the restoration of the criminal status of brothels. The campaign was based around a theme of the decay of moral values introduced by Labor government reforms and the need to return to 'law and order'.

for a discussion of the construction of the body in rights discourse) by setting appropriate limits, postures and modes of exchange. Such limits, postures and modes of exchange are articulated by reference to the norms of family and community, and thereby mark a purported consolidation – but also an erasure of identity (Butler, 1992: 354) for the prostitute, the body known to law primarily as one to be excluded from entering such family and community 'spaces'.

Punishment of the sins of the flesh

Discourses of desire and flesh as sins to be recanted were central concerns of Christian confessional practices in many Western societies, most prominently (but not exclusively) in the pre-capitalist era (Weeks, 1990). These practices and discourses became associated with more formalised 'law' via a model of repressive sovereign power (Foucault, 1988: 23). This association indicates the centrality of sexuality to many religious discourses – and to law. In particular historical periods in Western society, those women not in 'acceptable' heterosexual relationships have been regarded as an embodiment of sin, associated with the devil. Such women have been persecuted by various means, including legal trials and punishments which sought to establish their status as witches (Roper, 1994: Chapter 8). Similarly, the bodies of prostitutes – to the extent that they exist outside familial bounds – also suggest a perceived breach of moral and social order. Accordingly, their legal control has often been accompanied by criminal sanctions and their rigid enforcement, although – perversely – prostitution has just as often been informally tolerated and only indirectly and sporadically prosecuted (see Hunt, 1999: 35–37 for seventeenth- and eighteenth-century English prosecution statistics).

In Western society, bodily control exercised through criminal sanctions is consistent with the formulation of power in terms of 'Law'. Power is exercised in a negative manner: 'Confronted by a power that is law, the subject who is constituted as subject – who is "subjected" is one who obeys' (Foucault, 1988: 85). This theory is a familiar one from positivist analyses, which echo the earlier Kantian position on law and sovereign authority. Sovereign authority in most Western legal systems is no longer explicitly personified but, it is claimed, it still invokes an inner compulsion so that we persist in the habit of obedience (Dworkin, 1983: 527). In simplified terms, this 'model' of power and law is a linear one of domination and reciprocal obedience, prefaced upon a capacity in the sovereign to do 'violence' (Sarat and Kearns, 1992: Introduction). Moreover, this model of subjugation – historically associated with Law in Western societies – has specific ramifications for an understanding of jurisdiction.

Jurisdiction thus inheres in the sovereign–subject relationship as it has its origins in the sovereign's personal power of death or punishment over those persons 'subject' to law (Cover, 1983: 1–5). In a very immediate and direct sense, then, jurisdiction subtends a relationship between sovereign and subject as a scope of power and authority. The ambit of jurisdiction is extensive with an area defined by exclusivity of control, and a corresponding domain of obedience in the sense that the bodies of 'subjects' remain subject to law.[2] As the bodies remain subject, they remain open to punishment as a form of bodily coercion. Since the Middle Ages, this view of jurisdiction which complements the sovereign-juridico model of law and power (Foucault, 1988: 85) has been prevalent in Western society. Arguably, though, the neatness of fit between the concept of personal and territorial jurisdiction and law/power begins to shift with historical movements in the nature of power away from a single sovereign source.

Criminal law as jurisdiction over a sinful body

Nonetheless, an emphasis upon a personal jurisdiction over the subject body remains clearly evident in criminal law. The association has a long historical lineage. The sovereign power of punishment by death [as a taking of life] was the obverse face to the position that the sovereign was the source of life. Western Christian beliefs posit God as the ultimate creator of life (Foucault, 1988: 138). The sovereign as God's representative on Earth thus assumed a power of life, but more significantly a power to take life. In this manner, the notion that violent punishment falls within the preserve of the sovereign forms the ontological grounds of juridical law and marks off its jurisdiction (Sarat and Kearns, 1992: 9). Thus the instrumentality of the law embodies the moral force of the sovereign state via a criminal law that metes punishment and/or death on the body of the corrupt wrongdoer. Boundaries are defined in the negative terms of prohibition (Foucault, 1977: 10–12, 14–20).

If prostitution laws are conceived primarily as a negative prohibition, then consequently the 'body' of the prostitute comes within law's jurisdiction in order to punish it for its transgressions. An association of moral order and punishment as 'desert' reflects a Kantian conception of law, which in turn draws on Christian religious themes. This view presupposes a rational actor who takes responsibility for breaches of moral order (Kant, 2002). Kant's deontological position assumes that, as rational creatures, it is possible for people to discern right from wrong, such choices not being dependent on contingent social standards but on universal values (the right). Punishment, according to Kantian formulations, is predicated upon a retributive notion of individual responsibility (Kant, 1996 [1797]: 332). Applying such an account, law establishes its criminal jurisdiction over a prostitute's body to punish an individual who has willingly contravened moral standards. In effect, it assumes punishment as the necessary consequence to the corresponding jurisdiction to control the bodies. The application of criminal sanctions thus works at a symbolic level to assert a general power to impose violence upon bodies which transgress.

2 Nietzsche argues that the foundation of social order and sovereign power is based on an ability to extract recompense at the ultimate level of the body. Thus the memory of law is inscribed on bodies as one of pain. 'Civilisation comes about only by branding the law on bodies through a mnemonics of pain, a memory fashioned out of the suffering and pain of the body.' For a discussion, see Cheah and Grosz (1996: 13).

Thus the jurisdiction of control exercised by the criminal law acts directly on the prostitute's body to set bounds through physical coercion as a deserved punishment. Pursuant to a negative form of power, such bodies have been physically restrained and subjected to various forms of bodily constraint. However, the hidden partiality of this model of prostitution control is clear. Jurisdiction is asserted only over one-half of the bodies engaged in the exchange relationship of prostitution – that of the incumbent 'body' rather than the user of that body (Sullivan, 1995). As prostitutes are predominately women and young people, and the users of those bodies are predominately older men, the asymmetry of power that operates through this model of jurisdiction that 'attaches' sanction to a sinful body is readily apparent.

The criminal law also constitutes an instrument of 'civic death' in that it provides criminal sanctions for those activities of the body that are deemed 'outside' community and law (Moran and Sharpe, 2002). To be subject to the jurisdiction of law in this sense is to be placed outside 'community' as one is 'outside' law.[3] At various periods, the prostitute was deemed to be 'outside' family and community (see Garland, 2001 for a discussion of the links between criminal law and social order). Thus the body was subject to the exclusionary force of the criminal law,[4] especially where prostitution was associated with disease and contagion (Allen, 1990: 249). The model of prostitution control based on civic exclusion developed most intensely where laws were framed around extended familial relationships (Neave, 1994: 68–69). The body of a prostitute could find no existential relationship within a network of legitimated bonding that followed the 'differentiation into order and caste' that designated societies of 'blood alliances' (Foucault, 1988: 147). Even when not directly outcast, prostitutes, together with the mendicant and wanderer, were dealt with pursuant to statutes such as *Vagrancy Acts* which proclaimed the distance of such bodies from the fixed, productive stability of law and family (see, for example, Mahood, 1990: 50, 51).

Prostitution has long been the focus of public moral campaigns and policing agendas within Australia (Allen, 1990: Chapter 1). Traditionally, the criminal law and its selective enforcement have provided the most overt form of legal control. Yet the dimensions of control have varied. At particular times, prostitution within Australia has been 'prohibited and prevalent, secret and expensive, industrially regulated by policing and prosecution outcomes, professionalized and normalized' (Allen, 1990: 215). More recently, the prohibitions against prostitution set by criminal law and sanction have been far less stringently enforced in many Australian jurisdictions. Further, the bonds of family and community have extenuated over time. Yet, even when prostitution is

3 The explanatory memoranda accompanying the passage of the Queensland prostitution law reforms clearly recognised that prostitutes were not afforded the same access to law and protection as the rest of the community: Prostitution Bill 1999, Explanatory Notes, pp 2–3.

4 Historically, when linked to the suffragette movement there was a strong association with a sexual purity agenda in 'first phase' feminist thought that sought to abolish prostitution. See, for example, Hunt (1999: 122–33).

decriminalised and controlled by reference to regulatory practices, 'family' and 'community' are still proclaimed as 'boundaries' which must be protected from the incursion of unlawful desires and the potentially corruptive bodies of prostitutes.[5] Thus, although much less prominent than in former eras, the criminal law continues to be employed by the Australian 'state' to constrain the bodies of prostitutes through the assertion of a jurisdiction of coercion and exclusion.[6]

By contrast, the recent legislative change to decriminalise prostitution putatively brings prostitution within the 'civic space' of law as a normalised activity. Prostitution and the bodies that perform such practices no longer attract the prohibition and sanction of the criminal law.

Jurisdiction as a power of life

The transformation in the interplay between the criminal law, prostitution regulation and 'bodily control' reflect broader changes in the conception of the relationship between those with the power to impose 'jurisdiction' and those upon whom that jurisdiction is imposed. From the eighteenth century onward, 'it is no longer a matter of bringing death into play but of distributing the living in the domain of value and utility' (Foucault, 1988: 157). No longer is law framed primarily as a negative, personalised threat of violence. Violence and law as negation are increasing displaced by an assertion of power as a control over life. However, the association of law and violence continue in an uneasy tandem in modern regulatory formulations as a more indirect form of coercion.

Thus, 'to say that law's violence is legitimate is, in the modern age... is to claim that law's violence is controlled through the legal articulation of values, norms and procedures and purposes external to violence itself' (Sarat and Kearns, 1992: 5). It is the move beyond negation to a sense of law and jurisdiction as an articulation of 'values, norms, procedures and purposes' – largely, though not exclusively, external to violence – that is the concern of the next section. Such 'values, norms, procedures and purposes' are articulated in terms of a sexuality conceived primarily as a commercialisation of prostitution, a process that distributes bodies 'in the domain of value and utility'.

This purported rationalisation of prostitution as a promotion of 'life', sustaining value and utility, draws on two more pervasive trends. First, the promotion of life manifests as a control over 'populations', and second, there is an overriding concern with 'body' as the point of access to life: 'Broadly speaking at the juncture of the "body" and the "population" sex became a crucial target of a power organised around the management of life rather than the menace of death' (Foucault, 1988: 147).

5 In 2002, Victoria sought to introduce legislation which allowed so-called 'zones of tolerance' where street solicitation for prostitution would be 'tolerated'. The proposed legislation was abandoned by the government due to strong resistance by local residents and small-business operators in the St Kilda district.

6 In Queensland, for example, despite the legalisation of small-sized brothels, individual soliciting for prostitution outside these contained spaces remains illegal.

> Power would no longer be dealing simply with legal subjects over whom the ultimate dominion was death, but with living beings, and the mastery it would be able to exercise over them would have to be applied at the level of life itself; it was the taking charge of life, more than that, it gave power its access to the body.
>
> (Foucault, 1988: 142–43)

The extent to which modern societies have overcome the menace of death is arguable (Butler, 1992). Any transition to a singular promotion of 'life' through access to the body remains partial. In prostitution control, the technologies employed in the management of life exist in the same regulatory 'space' as attempts to counter the menace of death. Indeed, the menace of death in the form of AIDS is an ever-present impetus for tighter regulatory controls that ultimately seek to preserve life (see *Prostitution Act 1999* (Qld), s 91). Nonetheless, even if incomplete, the ascendancy of bio-power marks a transition away from the sovereign model of law. It marks a change towards 'a conception of power which replaces the privilege of law with the viewpoint of the objective, the privilege of prohibition with the viewpoint of tactical efficacy, the privilege of sovereignty with the analysis of a multiple and mobile field of force relations, wherein far-reaching, but never stable effects of domination are produced' (Foucault, 1980: 102). Indeed, the model of law begins to operate 'more and more as a norm'. Ultimately, a 'normalising society, is the historical outcome of a technology centred on life' (Foucault, 1980: 144).

If sex has become a target for the management of life in a normalising society, this objective has not translated to a simple facilitation of all forms of sexuality. The treatment of prostitution remains highly ambivalent within Australian society. Nonetheless, prostitution has been gradually normalised by reference to the changing dimensions of family, economy and gender roles (Allen, 1990: 215). Such normalisation, though, is not reducible to a simple assimilation with dominant 'family values'. To deal with such ambivalence, a technology of inclusion but containment is promoted. For example, only discrete types of prostitution, such as brothel sex work, have been legalised.

To facilitate such simultaneous inclusion but containment, the regulatory technologies for proliferating, innovating, annexing, creating, penetrating and managing bodies are clearly apparent in the legislative reforms to the *Prostitution Act 1999*. Moreover, consonant with the prediction that this normalising power would be most visible in the 'whole continual and clamorous legislative activity' (Foucault, 1980: 144), we find that this normalising framework extends not just to the substantive prostitution legislation, but to the minutiae of delegated legislation: to building codes, to planning codes and to regulations prescribing various matters under the *Prostitution Act* itself. These technologies exist in tandem with a range of other legal instruments, operating primarily through the planning laws, which are aimed at prostitution control at the broader level of a 'population'.

A jurisdictional space of and for 'desired bodies'

If the advent and extensive penetration of a normalising model of prostitution regulation is accepted, what of jurisdiction? Does such a concept have relevance beyond a sovereign-juridico model of law? Arguably, even within a normalising regime there must exist a nexus, a relationship of control effected as a purported cause and effect between 'law' and the 'purpose' or object of such normalising regulation. In this context, it is suggested that the question of jurisdiction becomes conflated with the question of who/what is the subject/body upon which such norms 'operate'. Law, in its assertion of a jurisdiction to control bodies – to make them regular – in effect needs to identify a particular status or norm referent for such a 'body' (Butler, 1993). Such a position ultimately questions the degree to which law acts as an imposition upon a 'body' already subject to law and discretely discernible, apart from 'law'. (Butler, 1987: 218). Thus, at one level there is arguably no inherently sinful individual who acts as a prostitute in breach of moral codes as contemplated by a Kantian notion of law, jurisdiction and punishment. Any 'transgressive' body cannot be identified in isolation from law's assertion of its ability to instate and naturalise 'certain taboos regarding the appropriate limits, postures and modes of exchange that define what it is that constitutes bodies'.

Arguably, law's jurisdiction over prostitutes' bodies is achieved through the institution of a spatial and temporal normative framework[7] in which to situate and regulate the activity of prostitution as a sexual practice of the body. Within the jurisdictional space that is designated by law as coextensive with the activity of prostitution, the body known to law as that of a prostitute can be concurrently 'constructed' but contained. This system is not simply a cultural inscription upon a 'natural' body (Butler, 1987: 215). It confounds the view that the body is 'subjected' to law's jurisdiction as a precultural individual (Butler, 1987: 187). Indeed, the very construction of a body as designating some predetermined, biological or natural entity has been consistently challenged (Padgug, 1979). A corresponding identification of 'body' with a core identity formulated in terms of a sexed or gendered subject has also attracted criticism:

> Such a view necessitates the location of sexuality within the individual as a fixed essence... These in turn involve the enshrinement of contemporary sexual categories as universal, static and permanent, suitable for the analysis of all human beings and all societies.
>
> (Weeks, 1990: 40)

One response to universalism, biological determinism and fixed essences is to suggest that 'bodies' and 'subjects' rely on more shifting, contingent linguistic and/or cultural constructions employed by law as a deployment of sexual discourses.

7 The intention here is to stretch the meaning of normative as something beyond simply informal 'law or rules'. The use of normative is to convey a sense of creating and sustaining rather than the merely prohibitive.

Drawing also on cultural and linguistic constructions, yet another view suggests that the body identified at law as a 'sexed' or 'gendered' body cannot be understood without reference to 'desire' and the repressive law that 'engenders the culturally accessible experience of desire' (Butler, 1987: 215). Perhaps desire and its limits cannot be conceived apart from the law? Is the desired but corruptive body of the prostitute to be understood as socially conceived by reference to the strictures of family order, the Oedipal complex and incest taboo (Butler, 1987: 201)? Such a suturing of body, law and desire has also been criticised. Feminist writers have argued that the seemingly disembodied law that 'constructs' identities for women by reference to rules of desire is already predicated upon the primacy of an idealised male subject. This signification privileges an inherently gendered and paternalistic order (Stacey, 1996), wherein women's bodies can only signify lack, negation. As Irigaray (1985) contends, such discursive formulations that construct women as constituting 'lack' mark an erasure of the feminine in order to 'produce' identities that are readily 'intelligible' within such a dominant male-oriented gender structure. Putatively, therefore, women's bodies are 'always' the subject of cultural prohibition, even when 'desired' (Butler, 1987: 219). The gender orderings that underlie the designation of the prostitute as a body, seemingly desired but ultimately that which is prohibited, are clearly discriminatory. Such discursive significations of gender and body also privilege an understanding of the institution of law and family in terms of primary negative social prohibitions dealing with 'desire' (Foucault, 1980: 109). 'The consequent formulation of desire as a lack requires that we accept this juridical model of the law as the fundamental political and cultural relation informing the structure of desire' (Butler, 1987: 204). Indeed, the implication that such models of law replicate a more fundamental ordering requires careful assessment of its particular gendered assumptions. Therefore, any analysis that accepts that sexuality is 'socially created out of disciplinary power and discourses of knowledge' also must acknowledge that such discourses are not gender neutral (MacKinnon, 1992: 117).

A performative perspective on law, jurisdiction and sexed bodies

Accordingly, this chapter negotiates the various theoretical positions outlined above to develop an alternative perspective about the relationship between law in its regulatory mode, jurisdiction and the control of 'sexed' bodies. Clearly the appeal to a biologically determined 'body' that is inscripted by, and subject to, law as discussed in relation to the criminal control of prostitution largely relies upon a concept of 'natural bodies' and fixed essences (i.e. as the inherently sinful and sexually corrupt). It also represents a model of law and jurisdiction that has been effectively displaced in many regulatory contexts.[8] The following analysis of the regulatory control of prostitution in Queensland accepts that the body identified

8 See MacKinnon's critique of Nietzsche's will to power as a history of the active and striving: a history of desire (MacKinnon, 1992: 117); cf Peah and Grosz (1996: 3) who recognise the relevance of Nietzche's arguments, but are cautious in their adoption.

to law as a prostitute is formed through a process of social construction and that law inscribes a particular status for that body. Yet the process of construction is not a simple imposition of gender-specific, determinate identities and categories. Rather, it is suggested that bodies and sexuality – and hence prostitution when characterized at law as a sexual practice of bodies – can best be understood as 'performative' (Butler, 1993). Performance in this sense encompasses both the bodily activity of the prostitute as a sexual practice and a relationship in which the body is held in discursive and physical tension with a corresponding assertion of a regulatory technology to control that activity. Moreover, performance as an active process always has the potential to transcend boundaries, and thus calls forth a need for a context for, and boundary to, that activity. Accordingly, the practices set by regulation that prescribe the manner and mode of prostitution as sexual 'performance' institute through law's assertion of a jurisdiction of control the very 'essences' and 'identities' that are claimed to exist prior to the law and which are subsequently held to be 'subject to law' (Butler, 1999: 172–73).

In setting the limits of the 'performance' of such practices, law as regulation institutes and defines its own bounds and promulgates its own basis for existence. Thus it is argued that the fixing of the desired, but potentially transgressive, body of the prostitute occurs through a diffuse yet active structuring of a 'space', both metaphoric and physical. This fixing is not gender neutral, as it stylises the body of a prostitute as potentially fluid and corruptive – one requiring containment. Further, if we accept the trend to increasingly identify a subject with body-referenced sexuality, any challenge to a pre-given 'sexed' body must extend also to the 'subject' itself: 'Indeed the "subject" now appears as the false imposition of an orderly and autonomous self on an experience inherently discontinuous' (Butler, 1987: x).

Thus law's jurisdiction to control prostitution may be regarded as existing in a symbiotic relationship that, in identifying a body to control, constructs an identifiable 'subject' for that regulation; ironically, that subject is realised as both 'body' and 'purpose' in relation to discrete regimes of prostitution control (Cheah and Grosz, 1996: 3–5). The fixing in law of a prostitute's body as corruptive implicitly constructs the subject within discriminatory gender frameworks as a corruptive one that must be contained, or sublimated, in order to preserve the boundaries of that framework. Such technologies of jurisdiction as a manifest framework of containment and sublimation are projected through the spatial and temporal dimensions instituted through licensing regimes and local government planning laws, as exemplified by the Queensland *Prostitution Act*.

Prostitution, law and an economy of bodies and pleasures

While the legal character of state regulation of prostitution in Australia has varied over time, its central function in delivering women's bodies for the use of, and enjoyment by men has not altered radically (Allen, 1990: 2). Thus in order to understand the 'functionality' of law, a mediated understanding of bodily 'performance' and 'activity' is engaged. It acknowledges the physical and economic dimensions of prostitution as an activity transcending the immediate focus on the individual body. Any identification at law of a body as an object for regulation does not 'exist' purely in the abstract designation of status. Object and purpose of regulation become congruent in the need to acknowledge the role of regulation in prescribing bounds for prostitution as an activity operating in an economy of bodies and pleasures (Stanton, 1992: 1). Accordingly, a wider approach is required which places the assertion of jurisdiction as a control over specific bodies in the context of controls over populations and their cultures of economy, pleasures and 're-productivity'. Thus there is a need to existentially situate the prostitute's body, as it is designated at law, by reference to the discursive formation of culturally acceptable forms of 'bodily' consumption in Australian society (see Deleuze on forms of cultural consumption, as discussed in Butler, 1987: 212). In this manner, the role of regulatory practices as instituting particular social and economic forms of bodily 'consumption' is maintained (Butler, 1987: 213). Accordingly, the idea of law as simply a repressive measure that directly institutes its jurisdiction in a negative manner through taboos and prohibitions on a given body must be substantially qualified.[9] Rather, the prostitute's body is known to law as a sexually active body, even while law asserts its power to make that body 'regular' and 'productive' by setting the bounds of acceptable sexual 'activity' and 'consumption' against wider social norms.

The regulatory technologies of the Prostitution Act

Queensland provides an interpenetrating model of law, norm and jurisdiction in its models of prostitution control. The criminal law model of personal jurisdiction operating through physical coercion and exclusion continues to exist alongside a legislative and regulatory regime for prostitution control that functions along two pivots of sexuality. On the one hand, this sexuality is tied to a discipline of the body, and a stylising and structuring of its energies. At another level, it operates in a broader economic and social sense, regulating the bodily exchange relationships germane to family and community, and the bodies that threaten to subvert that order. In 'both categories at once, giving rise to infinitesimal surveillances, [there are] permanent controls, extremely meticulous orderings of space, indeterminate medical or psychological examinations, to an entire micro-power concerned with the body' (Foucault, 1980: 145–46).

The Queensland *Prostitution Act* legalises, yet strictly regulates, prostitution in the State of Queensland.[10] The *Act* allows small, licensed brothels[11] and individual sex workers to operate within the brothel, but street soliciting continues to be illegal.[12]

9 The approach here draws extensively on Foucault's discussion of models of law in his *History of Sexuality Vol. 1*. See also the critique by Butler that for Foucault the subject is always subjected (i.e. historically regulated and produced). Nonetheless, Foucault acknowledges that this power is not monolithic and negative but profoundly affirmative, diffuse and productive.

10 See Prostitution Bill 1999 (Qld), Explanatory Notes, p 1.

11 *Prostitution Act*, Part 6.

12 *Prostitution Act*, s 73.

Indeed, there are increased penalties for street solicitation that are designed to 'remove this activity from suburban streets'.[13] The following analysis concentrates on four aspects of the process by which the prostitution reforms simultaneously create and contain the bodies known to law as prostitutes. These aspects are the bureaucratic licensing process which legitimates the bodily activity as economically productive, the system of bodily constraints and surveillances designed to promote health and safety, the spatial and temporal configuration of bodies within the enclosed spaces designated for prostitution and finally the broader spatial ordering that separates the spheres of commercialised desire from the 'pure' spaces of family and community.

Economies of desire

The foundation for the economic productivity of prostitution as a bodily activity of commercial utility and value is to legitimate and license these sexual practices. Accordingly, the *Prostitution Act* institutes a strict system of licensing for brothel owners who manage such activities.[14] Applicants for licences must be of good character and possess the attributes of honesty, integrity, good business sense and sound financial backing. A Prostitution Licensing Authority oversees the licensing process[15] and there is ongoing supervision of the regime by criminal justice authorities.[16] The ostensible objective is the government's concern to ensure that organised crime does not infiltrate the 'legal' prostitution industry.[17] A similar range of screening controls operates for certifying managers for brothels.[18]

A focus on the personal reliability and business acumen of licensees and managers reveals the normalisation of prostitution as a legitimated economic activity. Rather than being the preserve of corrupt flesh, the brothel is now the space of commercial integrity, and its productivity requires sound financial management. This tightly enclosed sexual activity is identified as a legitimated bodily labour that can participate in the civic parameters of market exchange (Scutt, 1986: 399). Indeed, the very application of industrial and commercial terminology in the legislation points to the integration of this space with other industries which 'use' bodily labour and thus are required to be efficiently and effectively managed (Allen, 1990: 168–80). In keeping with the managerial perspective, the bodily coercion is obtuse and indirect, rather than a direct exhortation upon the prostitute's body. It operates through setting parameters for the activities of managers and licensees as supervisors of the prostitute's bodily labour – a common model in many industrial 'workplaces'.

13 Prostitution Bill 1999 (Qld), Explanatory Notes, p 1.

14 *Prostitution Act*, s 10.

15 *Prostitution Act*, ss 10–16.

16 The need for oversight by the Criminal Justice Commission has its genesis in the Fitzgerald Inquiry into Police Corruption in Queensland, 1987–1988. This inquiry revealed the links between prostitution, organised crime and police corruption.

17 Prostitution Bill 1999 (Qld), Explanatory Notes, p 6.

18 *Prostitution Act*, ss 34–38.

Authorised police powers, including powers of entry and inspection, are designated within Part 3 of the *Prostitution Act*. This Part also contains a provision that a licence must be refused where the grant to a particular person would result 'in the area becoming a red light district'.[19] This concern highlights the central paradox in the legislation: prostitution, in its legitimated form, is to be concentrated into certain locales to facilitate surveillance and supervision, yet the presence of such an enclave of difference – a red light district – is not to be made obvious to the wider community. In these seemingly conflicting aims, a double movement of regulatory legitimation but containment of the sexual practices of prostitution is readily apparent. The bodily activity of prostitution, while clearly of exchange value, is not to intrude upon other more respectable forms of commercial activity that might be threatened by a red light district.[20] Such distinctions underscore the extent to which the regulatory technologies of the *Prostitution Act* operate with reference to wider social norms and power differentials, and yet also remain excised from the dominant 'non-industrial' discursive modes of the heterosexual family.

Promoting life: regulating social contagion

Integral to the economic viability of prostitution as an exchange relationship of bodily consumption is the need for a technology that focuses upon accessing 'life'. This access is exercised through a regulatory concern with health and bodily integrity. Indeed, one of the main outcomes of the reform of prostitution legislation across Australia has been to enable more efficient and transparent regulation of the sex work industry (Scutt, 1986: 406). Concomitant with the trends to equate legitimate prostitution with economic productivity has been an enhanced focus on the health and well-being of the workers regulated within that 'industrial' space.

The *Prostitution Act 1999* explicitly imposes public health standards upon the activity of prostitution by requiring periodic medical checks for sex workers and creating offences where persons work as prostitutes when they know they are suffering from a sexually transmissible disease.[21] While there has long been a public health rationale for the control of prostitution, this emphasis is enhanced in the prostitution law reforms. Even the very decision of when and where and how to 'perform' the sexual practice of prostitution is configured by reference to broader communal concerns that evince an apprehension about the need to ensure the well-being of populations.

The intricacy of the relationship between the body and its disciplining within the parameters set by public health standards are clearly evident in a range of

19 *Prostitution Act*, s 16. See also Prostitution Bill 1999 (Qld), Explanatory Notes, p 6.

20 A similar situation occurred in Victoria where small-business operators in the St Kilda area vociferously denounced proposed reforms to street solicitation laws.

21 *Prostitution Act*, ss 89 and 90.

duties imposed on licensees by the Prostitution Regulation. Section 13 of the regulation provides that a licensee must ensure that each room in the brothel has enough lighting to enable prostitutes to check for clearly visible signs of sexually transmissible disease – on other bodies![22] The regulatory technology that prescribes controls by reference to the lighting of rooms simultaneously thus sets the mode of performance for bodies as a sexual practice. Moreover, such regulatory constraints, while offering protection for sex workers, simultaneously also seek to contain and enclose a social contagion.[23]

Indeed, the state regulatory apparatus assumed by the licensee in controlling the bodily activity of prostitution is detailed, intimate and constricting. Its reach extends from the intimacy of guaranteeing that no prostitution takes place without the constraint of a prophylactic device[24] to ensuring that prostitution is only available within a properly enclosed building.[25] The licensee is the intermediary of a regulatory technology that surveys the body at work, subjecting it to a series of public health criteria and occupational health standards. Accordingly, the bodies engaged in prostitution are not just passive recipients of externally imposed rules. Instead, such 'bodies' represent a realisation of prostitution as a life-energy of bodily consumption and bodily exchange.

Spatial regulation of desired bodies

The *Prostitution Act* implements a range of measures that effect a precise detailing of prostitution as a spatially organised performative practice.[26] Part 6 of the *Act* imposes a number of spatial compliance norms. For example, the activity of prostitution authorised under a licence is only permitted to take place in the premises for which a licence is issued, and this building must be properly enclosed.[27] Although the licence requirements attach to the person of the licensee or manager, they have a wider compass in controlling the spatial and temporal limits of the bodily activity associated with prostitution. A licensee or manager must be personally present during brothel opening times thus imposing a personal obligation of supervision. Indeed, surveillance is one of the primary regulatory technologies employed under the *Prostitution Act*. The bounds of surveillance institute a jurisdiction of bodily control. Imposition of surveillance often requires enclosure – the specification of a place, different to others, and closed in upon itself (see Foucault, 1977: 141–44 for an argument that discipline requires enclosure).

22 Prostitution Regulation 2000 (Qld), s 13 (b).

23 Prostitution Bill 1999, Explanatory Notes, p 2.

24 A licensee must take reasonable steps to ensure that a person does not provide or obtain prostitution involving sexual intercourse or oral sex unless a prophylactic is used. In addition, it is an offence to actively discourage the use of prophylactics. See *Prostitution Act*, s 91. A separate offence is created for the individual prostitute who fails to use a prophylactic in the provision of prostitution.

25 'A building means a fixed structure that is wholly or partly enclosed by walls and is roofed, and includes a floating building and any part of a building': see *Prostitution Act*, s 79.

26 For example *Prostitution Act*, s 29(1).

27 *Prostitution Act*, s 19(3).

Within such enclosed, differentiated space, an individual body can be noted in terms of its presence and absence, its classification and its merits. Mechanisms for the allocation, disciplining and indeed classification of the body are clearly evident in the legislative regulation of prostitution in Queensland. For example, licensed brothels must have: a maximum of five 'working rooms';[28] a maximum of one sex worker per room at any one time; and a maximum of ten workers allowed on site at any one time.[29] The combination of spatial allocation mechanisms, together with the intimate surveillance of prostitutes' bodies, reveals the extent of the access to the body and its energies that is provided by the process of normalisation of prostitution. Regulatory technologies which set the bounds of acceptable activity subtend the prostitute's body in a space imbued with distributive functions that contribute to its 'utility'.

Indeed, law as 'norm', in its delimitation of these regulatory practices, shapes the confines and functions of the social space in which prostitution takes place. To the extent that prostitution now takes place in a 'safe controlled environment', a subtle derivative form of panopticism is instituted. It is a privatised panopticism, exercised not by the state itself, but in a more diffuse manner through its agent, the brothel licensee. This intermediary promotes the productivity of the prostitute's body while simultaneously subjecting it to a series of spatial and temporal compliance norms that define appropriate limits, postures and modes of exchange for the prostitute's body. This new mode requires the assertion of law's jurisdiction to control the 'body', but within an attenuated framework of spatial and public health parameters set by bureaucratic state. It is a regime of bodily styling that simultaneously creates the desired, productive body of the prostitute while providing evidence of the need for such technologies to effect surveillance and containment. Thus the 'physical' dimensions of jurisdiction are not simply prohibitory, but also 'productive' of a construct of a specified body and therefore the purpose for the regulation itself. Yet, potentially, the prostitute's body is seen as corruptive of broader patterns of bodily productivity at the level of the 'population' or community.

Planning the spaces of economy and desire

In Queensland, the personal licence system and the regulatory technologies of the *Prostitution Act* operate in conjunction with development and building controls exercised by the local government planning authorities. The mechanisms of access to, and control over, the body manifests therefore not only in the licensing system, but also in laws directly controlling physical spaces. The *Prostitution Act* made consequential changes to the *Integrated Planning Act 1997* (Qld) so that a legal brothel must undergo planning approval.[30] Once again, the technologies of spatial fixity are evident. It is a mandatory requirement that brothels must be located well away from residential areas. Indeed, there are precise instructions on

28 *Prostitution Act*, s 64(1)(d).

29 *Prostitution Act*, Part 6.

30 See definition of development, *Integrated Planning Act 1997*, Sched 10.

how this distance is to be calculated.[31] In one sense, prostitution is no longer beyond the bounds of respectable society, as technically it occurs within the public spaces regulated by the bureaucratic state. Yet in another sense it remains a space of difference, to be kept a safe distance of 200 metres from a 'place of worship, hospital, school, kindergarten, or any other place regularly frequented by children for recreational or cultural activities'.[32] Prostitution must retain its distance from the labour of love that is family. In addition, a brothel must have no identifying street signage.[33] Brothels must have discrete, unobtrusive lighting and their design must reduce noise levels for neighbouring premises, especially when 'clients' are entering or leaving the premises. These design requirements highlight the extent to which brothel activity is equated with other forms of nuisance or pollution – an intrusion into the legitimate and privileged activities of family and community.

In Queensland, a regulatory technology model that incorporates a personal licence system with broader planning approval processes is used to regulate industries that produce environmental pollution.[34] Given analogous regulatory treatments, it suggests prostitution is now viewed as a form of social or moral pollution. The potential pollution of prostitution is an undesirable 'by-product' of an activity that the state regulates as part of its broader compass to promote and mange 'life'. Such pollution is seen to emanate primarily from the perceived fluidity of women's bodies (Grosz, 1994: 192). The association of prostitution with moral pollution is not surprising given that much of the present environmental and planning laws had their genesis in moral reform discourses of the late- to mid-nineteenth century. These discourses sought to impose middle-class family and community values through an amelioration of both the physical and the moral condition of the working classes (see Hunt, 1999: 185).

The necessity of protecting family and community values from potentially harmful incursions manifests very clearly in the converging aims of the *Prostitution Act* and the *Integrated Planning Act*. Typically, planning legislation posits a desired model of community that forms a baseline against which to assess a diverse range of spatial activities. The incorporation of brothel development within the integrated planning assessment framework means that brothels are to be assessed against the normative standards set out in the planning laws which posit a set of 'desired environmental outcomes' for a given area. The desired environmental outcomes articulate a range of natural, social, cultural and economic environmental goals to be achieved by reference to set 'performance objectives' of the industry or development that is regulated.[35]

31 *Prostitution Act*, ss 64(1)(a) and 64(2).

32 *Prostitution Act*, s 64(1)(b).

33 *Prostitution Act*, s 93.

34 See the *Environmental Pollution Act 1994* (Qld) and *Integrated Planning Act 1997* (Qld).

35 The definition of environment includes 'ecosystems, natural and physical resources, qualities and characteristics of places that contribute to . . . amenity, harmony, and a sense of community, and the social, economic and cultural conditions . . . ': *Integrated Planning Act 1997*, Schedule 10.

The normative planning standards of the *Integrated Planning Act* envision a particular type of community.[36] Arguably, this community signifies an ordering of society that enshrines the model of middle-class respectability and the heterosexual reproductive contract that underlines many aspects of this respectability.[37] Moreover, this discourse of community is strongly assimilative, and it provides the rationale to quarantine or sublimate elements that do not conform. Accordingly, brothel development must assimilate its external characteristics and its spatial and temporal forms to this vision. A brothel design must contain any disparate, potentially polluting elements within the building itself by a procedure of spatial compliance, and bodily containment and disciplining.[38] The jurisdiction to control prostitution as sexual activity thus extends to the spatial configuration of the very buildings where such activities are to be performed.

Imposition of 'performance criteria and standards' upon the activity of prostitution, and ultimately thereby upon the bodies so engaged, reveals a sophisticated, if largely unacknowledged, regulatory jurisdiction of bodily construction and 'performance'. Prostitution regulation, which proceeds on the basis of licensing and planning performance standards, metaphorically and existentially also locates the prostitute's body within a wider network of legitimated activities. These activities are codified and legitimated by reference to criteria designating acceptable 'spatial' activities and modes of performance for activities. The body so identified becomes the subject/object to be regulated through the very laws that determine its performance and thereby instantiate its 'being'. Yet this body is not neutrally constructed in its relationship with the regulatory technologies that prescribe and proscribe its 'essence'.

Women's bodies as a source of transgression

The regulatory technologies of prostitution law effect a space for the prostitute's body in its sexual practice, with reference to other 'spaces' which assume a particular normative – and indeed spatial and temporal – reference point for that body. For prostitution, that reference point is that of the heterosexual, normative order of family and community. Law asserts its jurisdiction over prostitution through regulatory practices which maintain the separate spheres of family and proper community and the physical and metaphorical 'spaces' where prostitution takes place. Moreover, law, in its assertion of a spatially configured jurisdiction over a prostitute's body, operates to give material and cultural value to a 'framework' that purports to provide a truth about bodies and sexuality by

36 *Integrated Planning Act*, s 1.3.3.

37 Hunt (1999) notes a similar identification between middle-class 'respectability' and the urban reform agendas that focused on the control of prostitution in the late nineteenth century in the United Kingdom and United States. The promotion of this ideal of organic community serves to ostracise all those who do not conform to prevailing models of community values.

38 On this point of the coercive function of space see generally Bracken (1991).

prescribing their ultimate limits. Within this framework or jurisdiction, 'bodies' can only be 'known' to law and hence subject to its jurisdiction through a consideration of their sex and the practices of that sexuality (Foucault, 1980: 68–72). Yet there is a subtle 'slippage' and tension, as the Queensland prostitution reforms reveal. The 'subject' of law's jurisdiction as a fluid, sexed body is one that has the potential to transgress and threaten the very spaces of family and community that are its reference point of sexual 'truth' and spatial differentiation.

The identification of women's bodies with corruption and contagion is prominent in many social contexts (Grosz, 1994: 202–06). In anthropological terms, various social taboos (laws) institute the boundaries of the body in regard to what should not be mixed or *joined* (Douglas, 1969: 113). Indeed, it can be suggested that the very contours of the body are established through cultural codes of activity that institute interiors and exteriors and the boundaries in between (Douglas, 1969: 4). Women's bodies are seen as corruptive in that their perceived fluidity presupposes a potential for transgression of boundaries (Butler, 1999: 169–70). Pollution or contagion in this sense becomes a crossing of boundaries, a joining of that which should not be joined. As noted, the identified association between fluidity and transgression is integral to the manner in which women's bodies are identified as sexed or gendered bodies and thus arguably constructed as potentially polluting or corruptive. Thus the limits set for the bodily activity of prostitution provide a boundary but also a point of transmission. Such bodies threaten to pollute by transgressing beyond the legitimated modes and performance limits set by prostitution laws.

Conclusion: the boundaries of prostitution as a sexual practice of bodies

The parameters of the regulatory technologies of the *Prostitution Act* and the *Integrated Planning Act* form a boundary between legitimate, reproductively oriented sexuality and economically productive, but illicit sexuality. But boundaries are also a source of danger. Dangerous 'bodies' and sexual practices ostensibly cross into the interior spaces of family and community through the legislative regime that legalises prostitution. On the other hand, such bodies and the associated practices must still remain distinct from that community and family order to preclude defilement of these 'spaces' (Kristeve, 1980: 65). Accordingly, the purpose and object of prostitution law and regulation become integrally linked to setting the limits for the performance of prostitutes' bodies, the extent of their 'legitimate' activity and the maintenance of a separate realm of family and community.

Given the highly ambiguous objectives of prostitution reform in Queensland, it is hardly surprising that regulatory controls should so clearly institute regimes of surveillance, disciplining and containment while simultaneously legitimating and promoting the activity of prostitution. What is perhaps less obvious is the manner in which such laws also simultaneously identify and construct the subject and purpose for that surveillance, delimitation and containment – the desired but corrupting body of the prostitute. It is a body known to law only through its engagement in a sexual activity that, by its very designation as potentially corruptive, calls into being a need for regulation. Regulation of the boundaries of this activity and bodily 'performance' are then instituted through the practices of law as a regulatory jurisdiction. In this manner, the body of the prostitute and the activity of prostitution cannot pre-exist their regulation or the assertion of law's jurisdiction to regulate given forms of sexuality. Conversely, though, law as a regulation of prostitution in turn cannot have meaning except in the context of the relationship of control over such bodies and activities.

Again, this particular manifestation of the dynamic between regulatory technologies, jurisdiction and bodily control has parallels in broader trends in the management of 'life' through recourse to a control over sexuality. Sexuality as a pervasive discourse institutes a fictitious unity and causal principle for the assertion of control over bodies. As 'the notion of sex made it possible to group together in an artificial unity, anatomical elements, biological functions, conducts, sensations and pleasures . . . it enabled one to make use of this fictitious unity as a causal principle, an omnipresent meaning' (Foucault, 1980: 54). Thus, if the prostitute's body when subject to law's jurisdiction can only ever have meaning as a sexed body requiring containment and control of its activity, then arguably this institutes 'a fictitious unity and causal principle'. Disparate elements such as restrictive building design, locational constraints and bodily elements are unified by the asserted need to control sexual bodies and their performance – and this unity is in turn dependent on the assignment of a particular status in law. Thus it is the imposition of jurisdiction as a form of control over the mode and limit of sexual performance which constructs the fictitious unity of purpose that is the perceived subject of prostitution regulation. If the fictive character of such unity is accepted, it indicates why the earlier model of jurisdiction as primarily the imposition of a negative prohibition upon a body already 'subject' to law is not sustainable under a regulatory form of prostitution control. The older model of the criminal law also assumed a status for the prostitute's body. However, that status arguably was regarded as pre-existing any imposition of a jurisdiction of punishment and bodily coercion. The model of jurisdiction controlling prostitution through the criminal law 'attaches' sanction to a body that it deems as already having a status of being subject to, or outside of, the law.

By contrast, in a regulatory mode, the parameters of jurisdiction as an assertion of a space, time, body and activity to be 'controlled' are not simply inhibitory but also 'productive' of such status (Butler, 1993: 117). The prostitute's body under the Queensland laws is constituted as 'productive' within the normative framework that accords 'proper' spaces for commercial sexuality, family and community. Any putative neutrality in that construction is undermined by the concurrent designation of the prostitute's body as potentially corruptive of that ordering. As a potential source of pollution, this body must be regulated, contained and made safe even as it is normalised against the dominant, familial-based ordering. The manner and form of the symbiotic relationship through which law simultaneously asserts jurisdiction to control prostitution and identifies the sexed yet fluid body subject to that regulation is predicated upon setting the performative limits that act to maintain the 'division' between the bodily exchange relationships that constitute legal prostitution and those which exemplify the traditional virtues of family and community. Jurisdiction in a regulatory regime exists as a setting of boundaries for the prostitute's body and sexual activity by 'identifying' the concurrent necessity for such bounding.

References

Allen, J (1990) *Sex and Secrets: Crimes Involving Australian Women Since 1880*, Oxford: Oxford University Press

Bracken, C (1991) 'Coercive spaces and spatial coercions: Althusser and Foucault' 17 *Philosophy and Social Criticism* 229

Butler, J (1987) *Subjects of Desire: Hegelian Reflections in Twentieth-Century France*, New York, NY: Columbia University Press

Butler, J (1992) 'Sexual inversions', in D Stanton (ed), *Discourses of Sexuality: From Aristotle to AIDS*, Ann Arbor, MI: University of Michigan Press

Butler, J (1993) *Bodies that Matter: On the Discursive Limits of 'Sex'*, New York, NY: Routledge

Butler, J (1999) *Gender Trouble: Feminism and the Subversion of Identity*, Rev. edn, New York, NY: Routledge

Cheah, P and Grosz, E (1996) 'The body of the law: Notes towards a theory of corporeal justice', in P Cheah, D Fraser and J Grbich (eds), *Thinking Through the Body of Law*, Sydney: Allen & Unwin

Cover, R (1983) 'The Supreme Court, 1982 Term – Foreword: Nomos and Narrative' 97 *Harvard Law Review* 1

Douglas, M (1969) *Purity and Danger*, London: Routledge

Dworkin, R (1983) 'Law as interpretation' 60 *Texas Law Review* 527

Foucault, M (1977) *Discipline and Punish*, London: Penguin

Foucault, M (1988) *The History of Sexuality Vol 1: An Introduction*, trans R Hurley, New York, NY: Vintage Press

Garland, D (2001) *The Culture of Control: Crime and Culture in Contemporary Society*, Chicago, IL: University of Chicago Press

Grosz, E (1994) *Volatile Bodies: Toward a Corporeal Feminism*, Sydney: Allen & Unwin

Hunt, A (1999) *Governing Morals: A Social History of Moral Regulation*, Cambridge: Cambridge University Press

Kant, I (1996 [1797]) *Metaphysics of Morals*, trans and ed M Gregor, Cambridge: Cambridge University Press

Kant, I (2002) *Groundwork for the Metaphysics of Morals*, ed and trans A Wood, with essays by JB Schneewind, New Haven, CT: Yale University Press

Kristeve, J (1980) *Desire in Language: A Semiotic Approach to Literature and Art*, ed L Roudiez, trans T Gora, A Jardine L and Roudiez, Oxford: Blackwell

Kristeve, J (1986) *The Kristeva Reader*, ed T Moi, Oxford: Blackwell

MacKinnon, C (1992) 'Does sexuality have a history?', in D Stanton (ed), *Discourses of Sexuality: From Aristotle to AIDS*, Ann Arbor, MI: University of Michigan Press

MacNeil, W (1998) 'Law's Corpus Delicti: The fantasmatic body of rights discourse' 1X *Law and Critique* 37

Mahood, L (1990) 'The Magdalene's friend: prostitution and social control in Glasgow, 1869–1890' 13 *Women's Studies International Forum* 49

Moran, L and Sharpe, A (2002) 'Policing the transgender/violence relation' 13 *Current Issues in Criminal Justice* 269

Neave, M (1994) 'Prostitution laws in Australia: Past history and current trends', in R Perkins and P Garret (eds), *Sex Work and Sex Workers in Australia*, Sydney: University of New South Wales Press

Padgug, R (1979) Sexual matters: On conceptualising sexuality in history' 20 *Radical History Review* as discussed in L Hunt, 'Foucault's subject in the history of Sexuality' in D Stanton, *Discourses of Sexuality: From Aristotle to AIDS*, Ann Arbor, MI: University of Michigan Press

Pateman, C (1988) *The Sexual Contract*, Stanford, CA: Stanford University Press

Perkins, R (1994) 'Female prostitution', in R Perkins and P Garret (eds), *Sex Work and Sex Workers in Australia*, Sydney: University of New South Wales Press

Roper, L (1994) *Oedipus and the Devil: Witchcraft, Sexuality, and Religion in Early Modern Europe*, London and New York, NY: Routledge

Sarat, A and Kearns, K (1992) *Law's Violence*, Michigan, MI: University of Michigan Press

Scutt, J (1986) 'The economic regulation of the brothel industry in Victoria' 60 *Australian Law Journal* 399

Stacey, H (1996) 'Legal discourse and the feminist political economy: Moving beyond sameness/difference' 6 *Australian Feminist Law Journal* 115

Stanton, D (ed) (1992) *Discourses of Sexuality: From Aristotle to AIDS*, Ann Arbor, MI: University of Michigan Press

Sullivan, B (1995) 'Commercial sex and the law: A case for decriminalisation' 14 *Social Alternatives* 23

Weeks, J (1990) 'Sexuality and History Revisited', in L Jamieson and H Corr (eds), *State, Private Life and Political Change*, London: Macmillan

Legislations

Environmental Pollution Act 1994 (Qld)
Prostitution Act 1999 (Qld)
Integrated Planning Act 1997 (Qld)

11 Subjects of jurisdiction

The dying, Northern Territory, Australia, 1995–1997

*Shaun McVeigh**

Blessed are the dead that die.

(Beckett, 1974: 115)

This chapter considers the emergence of a jurisdiction over dying under medical supervision in the Northern Territory of Australia between 1995 and 1997. It does so to explore a number of ways in which the technologies of jurisdiction have been used in the production of an account of dying well subject to the interests of the state or the public interest.[1] In this context, two questions – not altogether distinguishable – will be considered: 'How might a jurisdiction over dying under medical supervision be exercised?' and 'What might amount to dying in a humane and dignified manner?' These questions back into a question asked of jurisdiction: if one of the functions of law is to institute human beings and lead them, so to speak, to their death, what form of life can be instituted through contemporary jurisdictions over dying?

The immediate subject-matter of this chapter is the Northern Territory's *Rights of the Terminally Ill Act 1995* (NT) and the subsequent litigation and legislation.[2] The *Act* briefly permitted, in certain circumstances, a registered medical practitioner to assist a patient to 'die in a humane and dignified manner' without thereby being subject to prosecution for unlawful killing.[3] In juridical terms, this rendering of assistance in dying without legal impediment was achieved by suspending the operation of the criminal law and rendering any such assistance non-justiciable. The validity of the legislation was unsuccessfully challenged in the

* Thanks to Shaunnagh Dorsett, Piyel Haldar, Jeffrey Minson and Peter Rush.

1 On the relationship between interests of state and public interest, see Hunter and Saunders (2003). Hunter and Saunders link the difference in terminology to the reception of Pufendorf's natural law jurisprudence into England in the seventeenth century. In contemporary Anglo-Australian discourse, interests of state are generally restricted to security and the public interest relates to the public good. However, in civil jurisprudence the state also has an interest in the public good.

2 The legislation can be viewed at www.nt.gov.au/lant/parliament/committees/rotti/rotti95.pdf

3 The terminology of 'dying in a humane and dignified manner' is taken from Sched 7 of the *Rights of the Terminally Ill Act 1995* (NT).

Northern Territory Supreme Court in *Wake and Gondarra v NT and Asche* (1996) 109 NTR 1 before it was rendered ineffective by the *Euthanasia Laws Act 1997* (Cth). While it is unlikely that this legislation will ever become a model for future legislation, the *Rights of the Terminally Ill Act 1995* (NT) stands as the first assisted suicide legislation enacted in a common law jurisdiction.[4] However, the *Act* remains instructive in the way that it draws on a civil jurisprudential tradition to establish the legal personality of the terminally ill person as well as in the way its jurisdictional devices establish the horizons of the concerns of civility and civil government.

An initial indication of what might be in dispute by way of dying in a dignified manner can be taken from the work of Dr Philip Nitschke. Dr Nitschke was instrumental in lobbying for the passage of the legislation and was the only doctor to act under the provisions of the legislation. He also developed a device to aid with the giving of assistance in dying in a dignified manner. It consisted of two elements. The first was a machine that, once activated, would inject sufficient drugs to end the life of the recipient; and the second was a computer software program designed to offer a step-by-step approach to the self-administration of the same.[5] The working of this machine evokes two images. The first image is of a proper death: the computer software program provided a way to manage the demise of an individual patient with the minimum intervention from the medical practitioner. The second image is of judicial and medical murder: the machine bears an uncanny resemblance to the chemical injection devices employed in the United States to inflict the death penalty. In this light, it is tempting to consider Dr Nitschke's machine as a device or emblem of judicial and elective self-execution.

The use of such images in political and ethical polemics is well known. On the one side are those who would insist that the significant features of euthanasia are concerned with freedom of choice (autonomy) and the duties of health care provision. On the other side are aligned those who equate the use of the machine, and euthanasia in general, with judicial and moral murder. Both dispute euthanasia as an issue of moral personhood. However, in this chapter, the polemical representation of Dr Nitschke's machine is re-cast as disputing the exercise of a jurisdiction – literally the power to state the law but also, in this case, a power of life and death over the subject. The image of dying and the uncertain institutional status of the ethical arguments over the meaning of assisted suicide and euthanasia mirror the interaction of the medieval order of spiritual and temporal jurisdictions of church and state (Goodrich, 1996: Chapter 1).

4 However, see Lord Joffe's Assisted Dying for the Terminally Ill Bill that was presented to the UK legislature in 2004.

5 A simulation of the program can be found at www.geocities.com/CapitolHill/Lobby/1921/resources/software.html (last viewed October 2004). More recently, Dr Nitschke has been involved in developing a 'suicide pill' to be manufactured by the user from readily available substances. Here dying was to be removed from the medical and legal spheres altogether. See Nitschke and Stewart (2005: Chapter 5) for a general account of the development of the technologies of assisting suicide.

Both the proponents of autonomy and of the sanctity of life lay claim to the authority of what would once have been a spiritual jurisdiction. In contemporary terms, since these jurisdictions have been enfolded into the jurisdiction of the State, they might be distinguished in terms of a jurisdiction over the subject and a social jurisdiction. The former responds to questions of the filiation (authentification and attachment) of the subject as belonging to law and the latter to the governmental inscription of the person within legitimated social forms (Legendre, 1997a: 169–72). In this chapter, the analysis of the *Rights of the Terminally Ill Act 1995* (NT) tracks the representation of these aspects of jurisdiction and their intersection with the state-centred civil jurisprudence that informs the legislation.

As with much contemporary state regulation of dying under medical supervision, in the *Rights of the Terminally Ill Act 1995* (NT), the jurisdiction over dying in a dignified manner was elaborated through an array of procedural, administrative and classificatory devices that focused on questions of the status and role of legal persons. Against an autonomous or sanctified form of dying, it established an *ars moriendi*, or preparation for death, that referred to an ethic and practice of civility, particularly social honour, suitable for medically assisted suicide and euthanasia. These concerns were met as matters of state or public interest. Yet it is far from clear how this state-centred *ars moriendi* can be related to the jurisdictional tasks of instituting the legal person and of ensuring social legitimacy.

In responding to the questions that opened this chapter, two lines of elaboration will be followed. First, largely by way of re-description, the *ars moriendi* established by the *Rights of the Terminally Ill Act 1995* (NT) will be considered in relation to the tasks of jurisdiction. Second, in a more critical manner, consideration is given to the form of life, or courting of death, that can be ordered through a contemporary practice of jurisdiction. To do this, the *Act* is considered in terms of a dogmatic staging of a form of life appropriate to a state-centred civil jurisprudence – that is, in terms of its institution, judgement and address. Briefly, questions of institution are taken up here as referring to the means by which the grounds of law are established as an order or grammar of legal actions; those of judgement direct attention to the individuation achieved in the judgement or performance of law both within and outside the legal order; and questions of address consider the transmission of law as both the end or destination of law – its purpose and audience – and as a mode of interrogation (McVeigh and Rush, 1997). What is circulated amongst these terms is a form of legal life that addresses both a political–legal concern with cruelty, compassion and suffering, and a concern with the formation of a citizenship 'project' of dying properly under medical supervision – whether referenced to a social domain of health or a biological one of suffering (Rose and Novas, 2005).

As the image of Dr Nitschke's machine suggests, the institution of legal life established by the *Rights of the Terminally Ill Act 1995* (NT) was not unequivocal in the manner of attachment it offered. In particular, it could be argued that the way in which the *Act* circumscribed its jurisdiction threatened the collapse of the subject of the jurisdiction it sought to establish. By suspending aspects both of the criminal law relating to homicide and of the power to determine the cause of death, the *Act* could be said to have confused or threatened both the possibility of representing the authority of law and of instituting a suffering terminally ill person as a legal subject. Since the institution of a new form of state-authorised killing remains the scandal or trauma of assisted suicide or euthanasia laws, the last part of this chapter addresses what might be held in contemporary jurisdictions over dying. Finally, in elaborating the civil prudence of the *Act*, an attempt is made to stage the question of jurisdiction as the idiomatic practice of law.

Address

Within a dogmatic order, an opening to questions of jurisdiction can be phrased in terms of the address of law as a procedure of transmission and a mark of destination. At the outset, the *Rights of the Terminally Ill Act* 1995 (NT) answered its question of address in terms of what was instituted – as if the law had already arrived. The preamble simply states that the *Act* is enacted:

> . . . to confirm the right of a terminally ill person to request assistance from a medically qualified person to voluntarily terminate his or her life in a humane manner; to allow for such assistance to be given in certain circumstances without legal impediment to the person rendering the assistance; to provide procedural protection against the possibility of abuse of rights recognised by this *Act*; and for related purposes.

Rather than turn immediately to the order of law instituted by the *Act*, an opening for its address can initially be offered in terms of the interests of the state or the public interest. These interests are diverse and could include the preservation of the life of its citizen-subjects, the project of the government and self-government of the health of its citizen-subjects, the protection of the vulnerable, the protection of the dignity of the medical profession and the management of scarce resources. The legal practice of dying in a dignified manner that the *Act* sought to inaugurate could be viewed as engaging with a number of these interests. However, its form as *ars moriendi* – or preparation for death – suggests a citizenship ‘project’: how to die properly under medical supervision. Some reconstruction is required to bring out the civil form of this address.

The literatures of the *ars moriendi* have been both religious (spiritual) and secular (temporal). Manuals for preparation for death, mourning and the conduct of funerals can be taken here as emblematic. In Christian theologies, preparedness for natural death is as for transformation, and has two aspects – one doctrinal and the other dialectical. The doctrinal arguments established the Christian meaning of death; the dialectical exercises establish a form of spiritual training that has an other-worldly concern, that of separation of the spirit or immortal soul from the mortal body. Many contemporary non-religious guides to dying and death share both a desire for transformation in death and the practice of spiritual exercises. It is through the development of the 'inner' aspect of conscience or spirit that a person prepares themself for death, often as the final stage of 'growth' in life (Elias, 1985; Lavi, 2003; Nuland, 1994).

In the context of the present chapter, it is the more worldly modes of instruction in the *ars moriendi* that are of interest. These are concerned as much with relations between the dying and the living as with questions of conscience. A state-centred *ars moriendi* could be understood as establishing the repertoires of meaningful dying – that is, as an interest of government and government of the self (Elias, 1985: 33; Hockey, 1990; Jacob, 1988; Lawton, 2000: 17–20).[6] To bring out the juridical form of this *ars moriendi*, it is necessary to make a link between civil jurisprudence, civility and civil conscience.

Civil jurisprudence can be considered as a state, or public, interest-centred prudence that responds to a situation where the requirements of moral perfectibility create irreconcilable conflict. It seeks a de-sacralised understanding of the state that could be viewed as a response to the fallible conditions of political and social life. A civil jurisprudence in this respect might be considered in terms of deliberation about contingent and contested matters.[7] Two aspects of prudence will be taken up here: the formation of a de-sacralised jurisprudence of a state with limited interests in government; and the government of value through the institution of office. The latter feature will be considered as a practice or means of institution. The civil jurisprudence that was developed in seventeenth-century Europe was mainly concerned to displace sectarian or confessional religious dispute from the centre of politics and government. For the natural law jurisprudence of the German 'state jurisprudence' of Samuel Pufendorf and, to a lesser degree, the civic humanist jurisprudence of the Scottish and English enlightenments, the key component of this task was the construction of an ethics and jurisprudence that responded to questions of political order more so than to questions of ethical redemption or fulfilment.[8] To do this, it was necessary to develop accounts of the state and of jurisdiction in which there was no need for transcendental or superior justification. These accounts revolved around civilising power and making the sovereign state the sole authority of law.

6 In the *Loneliness of Dying* (1985), Norbert Elias argued that these repertoires were largely concerned with the management of fear and the maintenance of propriety and status. Their meaning was to be found in the statuses and roles that enable dying to be practised rather than in any natural ontological arrangements.

7 To find assisted suicide and euthanasia a non-contingent wrong would remove it from the domain of prudence.

8 See Hunter (2001) for details of the German civil jurisprudence; Pocock (2003) for civic republican accounts; and Phillipson (1993) for accounts of politeness and civic humanism in eighteenth-century England and Scotland.

Redescribed in jurisdictional terms, the development of a state-centred civil jurisprudence sought to produce an account that concentrated on relations within an instituted state juridical order. It gave priority to the external forum of the government of social relations rather than the internal forum of filiation of the subject. The address of this jurisprudence was the behaviour of the citizen – or rather, the conduct or 'form of life' necessary to behave as a citizen subject to the authority of the state. What was suspended or separated from the juridical–political domain was the confessional jurisdiction of the Church – and the internal forum of conscience. It was this domain, as Legendre has succinctly put it, that 'authenticated the subject' by binding or attaching it to the institutional order of truth (Legendre, 1997a: 171). In the contemporary order of jurisdiction, the question of the authentication of the subject remains, but the question of how it is enfolded into a state-centred jurisdiction is subject to dispute (Goodrich, 1996; Saunders, 2004).

Institution

The *Rights of the Terminally Ill Act 1995* (NT) was as brief in its description of modes of institution as it was in its address. Section 4 confirmed a right to request assistance in dying in a dignified; ss 6 and 7 set out a number of requirements that had to be fulfilled before a doctor could give assistance in dying in a dignified manner without criminal prosecution.

To draw out the manner of this institution, it is necessary to develop a second feature of civil jurisprudence: the management of the interests of the state through the institution of offices and the practice of role as a specific prudential ethic. For civil jurisprudence, questions of value were to be related to an office, and an ethic of office or status, rather than a generalised practice of virtue, right or principle (Minson, 1993: Chapter 2). The particular inflection of this jurisprudence made in eighteenth-century Scotland and England was to mediate the interest of the state through the public interest and manners (Pocock, 1995: 35–50). What civil jurisprudence offered to eighteenth-century legal thought – and continues to offer in a more diffuse way – was a way to develop an institutional account of ethical and prudential judgement governed through a range of jurisdictional devices relating to office, legal status and the administrative delimitation of role. It is this account that is developed in the *Rights of the Terminally Ill Act 1995* (NT).

The *Rights of the Terminally Ill Act 1995* (NT) addressed the rights of the terminally ill along two distinct registers, one in the language of rights and the other in terms of legal immunity. The patient was represented as a petitioner before the medical practitioner and the medical practitioner was considered in relation to the Northern Territory (the state). In the *Act*, a patient could initiate proceedings by petitioning the medical practitioner for assistance to die in a dignified manner (s 4) by using a standard form found in Sched 7 of the *Act*. The relation between the doctor and the state was established by the suspending of the laws relating to unlawful killing (s 16(1)) and establishing an immunity from prosecution (ss 20(1) and (2)).[9] Should the medical practitioner have elected to assist the petitioner, then the requirements of capacity, good practice, good faith and due process set out in ss 6 and 7 would have had to be met.

The legal relations enacted in the *Rights of the Terminally Ill Act 1995* (NT) did not then, as might be expected, express an exclusive ethical relation between the doctor and the patient. What bound a person to a practice of dying in a dignified manner was not an ethical relation as such, but a series of documentary exchanges. (This is not to say that there was no ethical relation between the doctor and patient but from the viewpoint of a civil jurisprudence the legal arrangements carry the weight of any ethical ordering.) Central to this was the link made between institution and status. Section 6 established the proper comportment and behaviour of the medical practitioner, and s 7 did the same for the patient. Section 6 confirmed that the medical practitioner should not be influenced by any reward or advantage, other than reasonable payment for medical services. Section 7 set out the conditions under which the medical practitioner may assist the patient. In summary terms, the medical practitioner must be satisfied that:

- the patient has the requisite capacity to decide to die in a humane and dignified manner;
- the patient is suffering from an illness that will, without extraordinary measures, lead to death, and whose only reasonable treatment is palliative with the aim of providing a comfortable death;
- the patient's illness is causing severe pain and suffering;
- all alternative treatments that might be available to the patient have been rejected;
- the patient has considered all the implications of the decision for their family; and
- a period of seven days has elapsed since the appropriate documentary formalities have been completed.

The status established by the legislation is hardly classical in form. It did not refer to a tenurial relation or to an office of state. It had only limited legal effect and its conditions of assumption were voluntary. However, in other respects it was typical

9 Section 16(1). Notwithstanding s 26(3) of the *Criminal Code*, an action taken in accordance with this *Act* by a medical practitioner or by a health care provider on the instructions of a medical practitioner does not constitute an offence against Part VI of the *Criminal Code* or an attempt to commit such an offence, a conspiracy to commit such an offence, or an offence of aiding, abetting, counselling or procuring the commission of such an offence.

Section 26(3) of the Northern Territory *Criminal Code* states: 'A person cannot authorize or permit another to kill him or, except in the case of medical treatment, to cause him grievous harm.' Part VI of the *Criminal Code* deals with offences against the person and other matters. Division 1 of Part VI outlines duties relating to the preservation of human life. A death that had occurred in accordance with the *Rights of the Terminally Ill Act 1995* (NT) would not be in breach of a duty to preserve human life, but it would have remained the case that this death was not authorised or permitted by the deceased.

of a common law legal status: it did not address the whole legal person so much as make a status out of an exception to the (natural) legal person (Graveson, 1953: 5). In doing this, it might be analogised to the status of a child at common law.

The mutability of the status developed in the *Rights of the Terminally Ill Act 1995* (NT) also suggests that the language of office needs more specificity to bring out what is being instituted. To do this, it is necessary to reinscribe the language of office and status in the idiom of common law regulation. Three broad legal concerns dominated early modern law in relation to dying: one relating to inheritance and estate management; a second to sumptuary law; and a third to the treatment of the dead. Of these, it is sumptuary law that is of interest here since it establishes the governmental form of the management of dying. At their broadest, sumptuary laws regulated the proper place and appearance of the divine and social order. They did so primarily through the regulation of consumption and dress – including that of funeral ceremonies and the laws of mourning (Hunt, 1996). Sumptuary law not only produced and protected an institutional order of offices and images, but it also regulated the domains of conscience and the household (Goodrich, 1998). Such laws might be considered as contributing to the licit representation of divine and temporal authority. In the context of the common law tradition, sumptuary laws joined the discourse – and war of images – on the true meaning of the ecclesiastical and later secular polity (Hunt, 1996: 312). Much of the contemporary debate surrounding the legal status of euthanasia can be situated within this polemical domain.

In narrower civil prudential terms, sumptuary law was involved in establishing and governing the hierarchies and status of the temporal social order and of daily life (Goodrich, 1998: 725). Funerals and preparations for death were thus ready objects of regulation.[10] Whilst sumptuary law ceased to be of direct legislative importance in the seventeenth century, sumptuary concerns can be discerned in the domains of both police and health care (Hunt, 1996: 373–92). The *ars moriendi* instituted by the *Rights of the Terminally Ill Act 1995* (NT) might be viewed not so much as an archaic revival of a sumptuary law but as a continuation of a concern with the dignity of the offices of dying.

Judgement

If questions of institution represent the form of jurisdiction, then those of judgement represent its performance. Where questions of institution refer to questions of validity, those of judgement relate to questions of value. It is at the level of judgement and historical particularisation of a form that life gets to be represented in law.

The administrative requirements of judgement suitable for the conduct of dying in a dignified manner were outlined in the legislation, although to substantiate

10 Hunt (1996: 18) has argued that the first 'European' sumptuary laws were funerary. Hocart (1970) argues the same for the practice of administration.

them it is necessary to treat a number of administrative measures as establishing attributes of personality. (This reworking of the parts of legal speech is taken up in the last part of this chapter.) First, someone making a request would have needed to show a demonstrable capacity to understand the purpose of killing oneself in social, ethical and clinical terms. Second, they would have had to possess a set of competencies in the management of one's affairs in relation to kin. Third, if Dr Nitschke's machine was to have been used, it would also have been necessary to master the discipline of using the computer-generated program to inject a lethal dose of drugs.

In terms of the evaluation or judgement of the performance of roles, the *Rights of the Terminally Ill Act 1995* (NT) drew attention to the capacity to conduct ethical arguments and the ability to direct regulatory practices to carry out identifiable procedures and achieve particular ends. The emphasis of manners and civility in the performance of role established the conduct necessary to sustain a status within an institutional and ethical milieu (Minson, 1993: 37). While Dr Nitschke's machine offered one polemical representation of dying in a dignified manner, the requirements of status suggested that a more elaborate set of decisions and responses would have been required of both patient and doctor in order to fulfil their roles. In formal terms, both the doctor and patient were required to conduct themselves in a way appropriate to medical treatment. This might be characterised in terms of a certain practice of restraint or disinterest (*adiaphora*) to give it a stoic inflection.[11] It involved the medical practitioner taking a distance from their ethical beliefs or conscience in order to adopt the appropriate 'professional' manner – for example, the setting aside of personal beliefs in order to carry out medical treatment. The same was required of the patient.

If this reads as an impoverished description of dying in a humane and dignified manner, this in itself should be no surprise. In descriptive terms the *Rights of the Terminally Ill Act 1995* (NT) was primarily concerned with establishing the legal conditions of the conduct of dying under medical supervision. More prosaically the *Act* was only one source of information about the appropriate conduct of doctors, patients and the state. Other sources of guidance as to conduct might be

11 This is one aspect of a more general link between manners and law that can be made through the Stoic literatures of dying and natural law jurisprudence. In the early modern period, it was Stoicism and Epicureanism that provided the first established temporal (de-sacralised), or at least not entirely Christian, discourse on the conduct of both government and dying in Western and Northern Europe (Houlbrooke, 2000; Marshall, 2002; Oestreich, 1982; Warren, 2004). The virtues of uprightness and restraint, and the ability to conduct one's life according to the exigencies of office, have their counterparts in the Stoic literatures on the conduct of dying. Seventeenth- and eighteenth-century common law jurisprudence not only took manners and honour as a subject-matter of law, but also took the practice of jurisprudence and government as a training in personality (Boyer, 1997). The specifically Christian and humanist contexts of fifteenth- and sixteenth-century writing on manners and spiritual exercises, exemplified by Erasmus (1988), were transformed in the eighteenth century into that of the cultivation of politeness, civic humanism, civic virtue and in the process became a discourse of propriety (sensibility and sentiment) (Porter, 2003: 21–26).

found in the documentation of the practice of palliative care, professional ethics, and choices of the patient and their kin. However, this description of the regulation that permits dying in a dignified manner is 'thin' for another reason: the performance of dying well is studiously left out of the governmental account, as is the role of the doctor whether as health care provider or judge. These questions are met by the consent procedures. There were two judgements to be made in the *Act*, the first by the patient or terminally ill legal person and the second by the doctor. For the terminally ill, the question is not whether the *Act* is to be 'applied', since the decision is made from within the legislative regime, but whether a liberty is to be exercised. For the doctor, the decision to assist the patient is described in terms of treatment rather than judgement. How these actions are represented within the symbolic order of law will be considered in the next section.

In civil prudential terms, taking issues of civility and manners as a starting point for the regulation of death and dying under medical care has a number of attractions. Civility and manners establish (or attempt to establish) the conditions in which disputes over the significance of assisted suicide and euthanasia are to be conducted. This takes on importance both with the negotiation of health care provision and in considering the civil prudential framing of the task of legislation in areas of moral controversy. In establishing something like a legal status for the terminally ill legal person, the *Rights of the Terminally Ill Act 1995* (NT) also marked the conditions and limits of the exercise of a jurisdiction and the interests of the state (Saunders, 2004). What has been described here is an account of dignity that is tied to the *dignitas*, or legal ordering of office and role, rather than that of fundamental human dignity (Kantorowicz, 1957). Dignity when associated with office concerns questions of the duties of rank and authority. What is presented in the *Act* is a legal account of dignity delimited by a range of concerns relating to honour (Margalit, 1996: Part 1; Nussbaum, 2004: Chapter 4).

Jurisdictional devices

The first part of this chapter placed the exercise of a jurisdiction over dying within a domain of civil jurisprudence cast in terms of the conduct of manners. Central to this was the delimitation of a relation between institutional order and judgement framed in terms of the sovereign address to the citizen. Here attention is turned from examining jurisdiction as a scene or context for civil jurisprudence to the understanding of jurisdiction as a legal action or device that sustained the civil prudential form of life inaugurated in the *Rights of the Terminally Ill Act 1995* (NT). The particular concerns taken up here lie with what could be considered the function and idiom of jurisdiction: establishing the relation of a subject to a founding order or Reference of law that makes it possible to exist with legal meaning and securing the manner of the government of the legal subject (Legendre, 1997b: 147–50). Or, in an older language of jurisdiction, what is of interest here is the relation between the confessional–penitential (spiritual) jurisdiction of the internal forum that authenticates the subject of law and that of the (temporal) governmental jurisdiction of the external forum that is concerned with exchanges between subjects. In the earlier parts of this chapter, jurisdiction was considered in relation to the formation and delimitation of something like legal status. Here the jurisdictional devices will be figured as delimiting rival formulations of the jurisdictional ordering of law as well as determining the address of law.

The typical gesture of civil jurisprudence has been to accentuate the importance of the external forum of government. The risk, as critics have pointed out, is the loss of a subjective attachment to the normative structure of law and of the means of government.[12] This situation is brought into relief in the *Rights of the Terminally Act 1995* (NT) through its legislative strategy of suspending reference to established jurisdictions in order to produce its legal effects. No doubt this particular formulation of the suspension of laws was designed to minimise opposition to the enactment of laws permitting assisted suicide and euthanasia. However, on its face, it proceeds without reference or attachment – and so, it might be argued, without civil prudence. In different ways, the problematisations of jurisdiction presented here are concerned with the potential of the abandonment of the subject of law.

At the outset, the jurisdiction established by the *Rights of the Terminally Ill Act 1995* (NT) imposed a number of limits to the way that questions of value could be represented. Questions concerning the provision of health care services that shorten life, of ethics and of the representation of dying only indirectly form the subject-matter of the regulatory scheme established by the *Act*. Some of these jurisdictional limits were quite general: questions of justification were restricted to those of the validity of the legislation (see *Wake and Gondarra v NT and Asche* (1996) 109 NTR 1), and those of substantive law were addressed by a number of administrative procedures. Others, however, were more specific to the genre of assisted suicide and euthanasia legislation.

The *Rights of the Terminally Ill Act 1995* (NT) accommodated dying in a humane and dignified manner in relation to the jurisdiction of criminal law by pursuing three approaches. First, in s 16 the *Act* established that there was no crime committed by a doctor who assisted a patient in dying in a dignified manner. Section 16(1) stated that acts in accordance with the legislation would not be in breach of Part VI of the *Criminal Code* – laws relating to the preservation of human life (murder, manslaughter, assisted suicide and so forth). Section 16(2) stated that, for legal purposes, 'assistance given in accordance with this *Act*... is taken to be medical treatment for the purposes of the law'. From this it might be inferred that there was no jurisdiction of criminal law because there was no crime. What was at issue was the manner of dying, not the *mens rea* of the killer (Rush, 1997: 275). Another approach taken in the *Act* was to suspend the operation of the criminal law. Section 20 granted immunity from prosecution if a death complied with the terms of the legislation. However, the general criminal law relating to the authorisation of killing was not repealed or amended

12 These issues have been more fully canvassed in social theory than in jurisprudence (see, for example, Gellner, 1994).

in any way. Section 26(3) of the *Criminal Code* (NT) remained in force: 'A person cannot authorise or permit another to kill him or, except in the case of medical treatment, to cause him grievous harm.' The provisions prohibiting assisted suicide also remained in place (*Criminal Code* (NT), ss 167 and 168). The criminal courts had jurisdiction, but it was not to be exercised. Finally, s 13(2) stated that a death that resulted pursuant to the act need not be reported to the Coroner as unexpected, unnatural or violent. No criminal investigation need be initiated.

In jurisdictional terms, two features stand out in the formulation of the address of the legislation. First, the status of the terminally ill person was given meaning by creating a domain of law apart from the criminal law. Assisted suicide and euthanasia were to be considered as medical treatment, but the relation between medical treatment and criminal law was suspended. Second, s 16 of the *Rights of the Terminally Ill Act 1995* (NT) figured a terminally ill legal person who could be killed without the attribution of legal responsibility. From the viewpoint of the civil jurisprudence already elaborated, the suspension of the law, or the suspending of a law within a legal order, is most comfortably viewed as addressing a number of discrete concerns about the relation between the exercise of sovereign power and the practice of government. The most notable of these was to establish the technology and limits of a jurisdiction.

As a question of institution, the suspension of law might be viewed in relation to two aspects of jurisdiction – one relating to the authority of the external forum of the government of social relations and the other to the confessional–penitential jurisdiction of the subject. In terms of the external forum, the suspension of laws seems to displace the office of the judge and the legal categories through which institution proceeds. In the *Rights of the Terminally Ill Act 1995* (NT), the doctor was required to take up the structural position of the judge without direct recourse to the jurisdictional arrangement of the social meaning of dying in a dignified manner. In s 20 of the *Act*, the intentional killing of the terminally ill patient was given criminal legal significance but the operation of the law was suspended in advance. This suspension links government through law to a generalised system of administration that operates alongside and apart from law.[13] In juridical terms, the decision that was to be made within this excepted domain joined the sovereign act of making die or letting live to the governmental concern, in the field of the health of the population, of making live or letting die. It did so in terms of making survive or letting perish (Agamben, 1999: 82–83, 155). One consequence of this was that the *Rights of the Terminally Ill Act 1995* (NT) did not direct regulation to issues of legal personality; instead, the force of law was handed over to the administration of the medical profession and directed to the question of the

13 Even the document that initiates procedures, the standard form request for assistance in dying in a dignified manner contained in Sched 7 of the *Act*, refuses juridical form. While this form might usefully have been viewed as a 'prayer for relief', the part of a writ requesting relief for a wrong suffered, it reveals no cause of action. Instead, it provides a certification of compliance with the requirements of the *Act*.

biological and social survival of the terminally ill patient. The doctor, however, was required only to make a professional decision about medical treatment.

While the doctor's decision was set apart from the judicial tribunal in the *Rights of the Terminally Ill Act 1995* (NT), it was still judicial in function insofar as it related to the determination of questions of life and death. Viewed from the position of the external forum of government, the problem is not so much the fact that a doctor is putting a patient to death but that the juridical character of the action is not acknowledged. More generally, the administrative arrangements within the *Act* render the dogmatic ordering of the public and social limits of law opaque. No doubt one of the purposes of the suspension of law was to lessen the impact of the institution of a new judicial and medical relation to life. The question here is whether this suspension can be separated from a more general displacement of law into administrative procedure and information exchange – and with this a loss of the institutional substrate necessary to secure social attachment through jurisdictional means (Legendre, 1997c: 106–07).

Much the same point can be made about the institution of the subject of law. Here, however, the suspension of laws invokes another jurisdiction either displaced or lost. What might have been recognised in the suspension of the general law is the authority of a penitential–confessional jurisdiction. At issue in this domain is not so much the government of public conduct but of the institution of the subject into an order of legal meaning. In contemporary terms, since this jurisdiction has been enfolded in the common law, the suspension of laws might be taken as a partial recognition of another jurisdiction in which the subject is brought to their proper end. The doctor in this jurisdiction would take up a confessional role. Alternatively, far from creating a new legal status, the suspension of laws could also indicate that the terminally ill person had lost all their important legal attributes. The terminally ill person had been suspended from both the external and internal forums of jurisdiction. What was instituted was a situation where it was possible to elect to be treated as a 'bare', or suffering, life (Agamben, 1998: 136–43).[14]

Turning to the performance of judgement, the suspension of law can be viewed as bringing law into relation with an anomic element (whether political or ethical). This relation might be situated either as a state of exception – an event outside of the jurisdiction of law but still belonging to it – or as belonging to a penitential jurisdiction – an event staged inside the law but not (or no longer) belonging to it. As a state of exception to sovereign civil authority, the decision on life is made in terms of the interests of the state – it is a decision on the political value or non-value of life (Agamben, 1998: 139–40, 153). If taken as part of a confessional–penitential jurisdiction, the decision is taken in terms of the norms of subjective life: the management of guilt (interdiction) (Legendre, 1997a: 165–69).

14 Agamben does not develop an account of jurisdiction. In *State of Exception*, he provides a brief historical account of states of exception in terms of jurisdiction (2005: 11–22) and in *Remnants of Auschwitz* an account of authority and enunciation in language is given that corresponds closely to his understanding of law (1999: 137–45).

In either account, it marks a decisive threshold where the relations between law and life are fatally blurred. In this light, the *Act* could be viewed not as an exercise in de-juridification, or as a loss of jurisdiction, but as a de-subjectivation and a de-legitimation.

Set against these strong claims for the loss of the social and subjective jurisdiction of law, civil jurisprudence seems to offer a rather fragile position from which to institute and sustain relations between law and life. The problematisation of the institutional staging of the subject and the performative limits of social exchange runs against the claims of a civil prudence to enact and stay within established state jurisdictions. The purpose here is not to return these critical formulations to a proper assertion of the authority of state law, but to give some brief indication, by way of re-description, of how a civil jurisprudential account of jurisdiction might respond and attend to the limits that have been posed.

In Legendre's formulation of the institutional aspects of jurisdiction, the greatest difficulties arise in terms of sustaining a relation to the founding order of law. In Agamben's account of the performance of jurisdiction, the legal subject is abandoned and held in a state of exception (where it is possible to be killed without legal responsibility). Where Legendre takes the internal forum of the penitential jurisdiction to be prior to that of external forum of social government, civil jurisprudence has typically been conducted through the external forum. The gesture of de-sacralisation that has characterised state-centred civil jurisprudence has operated by establishing a number of demarcations between the two jurisdictions (Saunders, 2004). With the enfolding of jurisdictions within common law, the function of filiation has not so much been abandoned as viewed indirectly from the external forum as a concern of the government of social relations and as a particular mode of legal and civil association (Oakeshott, 1991: 165–69). The question, then, is what form of life can be sustained in the absence of, or without a clearly organised, penitential jurisdiction.

In the *Rights of the Terminally Ill Act 1995* (NT), it is the statuses established through sumptuary order of dying in a dignified manner that must institute a de-sacralised authority of law and hold out a form of legal life. Whether or not such a jurisdictional device is capable of so doing is questionable. It has been argued that the great normalisation of government and law in the nineteenth and twentieth centuries has abstracted the medium of status and manners of its meaning and significance (Murphy, 1997). Government, through regimes of statistics, insurance and psychology – that is, through management and administration – has required only a general account of social action and moral responsibility, rather than a substantive jurisdiction of law, in order to secure a form of life (McVeigh and Rush, 1997). The issue here is whether the government of conduct through manners and social honour can secure a mode of transmission sufficient to sustain a legal form of life. The work of Norbert Elias (1972, 1978, 1985) has given centrality to the place of manners and social honour in institutionalising modern forms of living and dying. However, it is also necessary to consider the intransitive aspects of institution – the institutional substrate of a legal speech capable of inscribing or giving ground to normative effects. In the context of the jurisdictional arrangements of the *Rights of the Terminally Ill Act 1995* (NT) this would depend on whether the *Act* was considered as a juridification or de-juridification of dying in a dignified manner.

Agamben's emphasis on the performance of law draws attention to the manner in which the jurisdictional structures of inclusion and exclusion complicate older distinctions between life and law. In the first part of the chapter it was suggested that the status of the terminally ill person depended on an available account of a natural person. However, it is questionable whether nature, or the suffering body, can be figured any longer as being a deeply embedded substrate capable of supplying the divisions necessary to establish a difference between a dignified or undignified death. For Agamben, government through a state of exception has meant that life has become a product of law (Agamben, 2005: 88). Agamben's ontological concern with de-subjectivation is directed to the effects of the 'biopolitical' struggle for life (Being).[15] By contrast, civil jurisprudence proceeds with an artefactual account of the (legal) person and with the means by which life is, or is not, brought within a jurisdiction. It gives priority not to the ontological status of the subject but to the limits of the government of biological life. This requires both a degree of institutional positivity (a status must be describable in terms of positive effects) and some sustainable distinctions between law and life.

In the *Rights of the Terminally Ill Act 1995* (NT), the performative relation of life and law was managed in two ways: the first was by not formally delineating a legal status for the dying; and the second was through making the distinction between law and life a matter of choice. In terms of the questioning of jurisdiction presented here, these devices passed over the problem of the political–legal delimitation of life. Whatever the status established, and the choice made, the linking of the killing of another without responsibility to the governmental management of dying takes place. For a civil jurisprudence to succeed, it must be capable of coming to judgement without encompassing or confronting the generality of these questions. Just as the institutional ordering of civil jurisprudence depends on not capturing all of life, the performance of the *Act* does not judge a whole life (even if the end of life is its sole point). What is performed is not a de-subjectivation so much as a narrow subjectivation, one that is left partially determined by the *Act*. One consequence of this is that dying in a dignified manner, and the status attributes that organise it, emerge from within the legal field. Life – or at least dying in a dignified manner – becomes a matter of legal convention (second nature). What is actualised in legal judgement is not a natural life but a set of legal relations. The effectiveness of such a judgement depends on sustaining a legal address.

15 Loosely, the 'biopolitical' is concerned with the exercise of power over the population in general by means of biology. Agamben develops Foucault's accounts of the government of populations through the investment in life and returns it to a juridical order and of government through the state of exception (Agamben, 1998: 5–10).

As indicated, a strong account of the suspension of law in the *Rights of the Terminally Ill Act 1995* (NT) would suspend the relation of both sovereign and subject to law. The sovereign would act without law and the citizen-subject without attachment – a civil jurisprudence would proceed without a recognisable legal address or authority. This is not solely a question of the authority to make law, a matter considered in *Wake and Gondarra v NT and Asche* (1996) 109 NTR 1 and the *Euthanasia Laws Act 1997* (Cth). It is also one of authorisation and transmission: the relationship of a sovereign and a subject to a jurisdiction.

Viewed as an action of civil jurisdiction, the suspension of the address of law can be considered in two aspects: first, in terms of the pluralisation of jurisdictions over dying under medical supervision; and second, in terms of the audience of law. In relation to the former, it can be noted that the suspension of laws continued both to maintain the jurisdictional authority of law in relation to other discourses of homicide and other practices of suicide and euthanasia. In the *Act*, state law was represented as being subordinate neither to a higher ethical law – for example, the ethic of relieving suffering or of medical necessity – nor to an administrative regime that departs fully from legal normativity.[16] The form of rights represented in the *Act* was also specific to a particular jurisdiction. The *Act* did not make statements of general rights (natural, human or constitutional), but established a specific set of rights and immunities within a legal-administrative structure. It proceeded, that is, by attributing a specific status (the terminally ill patient in unbearable pain) for a particular purpose (dying in a dignified manner), rather than by elaborating a general status (the bearer of human rights or subjectivity). In short, the *Act* provided another juridical manner of dying. It was concerned more with de-moralising and de-politicising disputes about assisted suicide and euthanasia than with a desire to de-juridify dying under medical supervision (this has also been the case in the Netherlands – see Griffith, 1998; Keown, 2002).

In relation to the audience of the address, the suspension of law appeals to a form of prudence. The suspension of law is to be recognised as a (temporary) solution to a conflict that takes place both without and, it has been argued here, within the law. What is suspended is adherence to the representation of law in terms of a direct alignment between sovereign power, statutory authority and legal personality. Formally, what was invoked in its place was left open, but insofar as the address of the *Rights of the Terminally Ill Act 1995* (NT) is prudential, it would involve, it might be imagined, both a recognition of the trauma or scandal of permitting assisted suicide and euthanasia, and a need for it to be addressed indirectly as an *ars moriendi* (van Oenen, 2004: 153–55). In short, the suspension of law invoked – wrongly, as it turned out – the possibility of its addressees accepting the conflict of legal ordering. With this, a return is made to the civil prudential ordering of sovereign–citizen relations.

16 The state of exception is without representation. See also the *Euthanasia Laws Act 1997* (Cth), which rendered the *Rights of the Terminally Ill Act 1995* (NT) ineffective. This legislation contains no substantive sections.

Jurisdiction has been cast here in terms of the authorisation of a number of responses both to the dogmatic order of law and to questions of government. What has been recognised or misrecognised in a civil prudential account of jurisdiction is the limits of the authorisation (or guarantee) of the grounds of institutional life, of the performance of judgement, and of the destination of address. It is this that allows for the characteristic civil prudential reasoning with and through the instruments found in the *Rights of the Terminally Ill Act 1995* (NT). Civil jurisprudence begins with the suspension of confessional truths in favour of a state-centred re-description of interests. The suspension of laws both recognises the trauma or scandal of the laws enacted and suggests a way of living with it without forgoing legal responsibility in its entirety.

Concluding comments

This chapter has followed the work of jurisdiction in establishing a legal domain for providing medical assistance in dying in a dignified manner. The analysis of the *Rights of the Terminally Ill Act 1995* (NT) presented here has drawn out the ways in which a contemporary jurisdiction over dying in a dignified manner might be understood through a state-centred civil jurisprudence. At the centre of the civil prudential understanding of dying in a dignified manner were a number of technical jurisdictional delimitations that organised the authentification of the subject and the government of social relations. Focusing on the dogmatic ordering of law, dying in a dignified manner allowed for an examination of the way in which questions of jurisdiction can be understood as continuing to structure and perform an ethical–prudential arrangement of 'dying in a dignified manner'. More broadly, the assemblage of legal materials considered was used to draw out the way in which questions of civil prudence might be viewed as bringing into relief the relationship between sovereignty and jurisdiction.

To close briefly with the image that opened this chapter: Dr Philip Nitschke's representation of computer-assisted suicide. Initially, it was stated that the rival ethical theories of autonomy and sanctity of life could both be viewed jurisdictionally as occupying, or attempting to occupy, a confessional–penitential jurisdiction. As such, they remain somewhat eccentric to the concerns of a civil jurisprudence that is articulated from another jurisdiction, that of government. In dealing with sovereign–subject relations, the network of concerns of civil jurisprudence is more easily cast in terms of cruelty, compassion and suffering than in terms of autonomy and the sanctity of life. The image of assisted suicide might be understood as representing the exercise of a compassionate or cruel state interest in dying in a dignified manner. The claim of a civil jurisprudence is that it is still possible to reason within law about such concerns and to direct them to a number of citizenship projects – whether viewed in terms of civility, social health or biology. The place of jurisdiction has been rendered here as the idiomatic device of such a prudence, both as the site of enunciation of the law and as an instrument of actualisation.

References

Agamben, G (1998) *Homo Sacer*, Stanford, CA: Stanford University Press

Agamben, G (1999) *Remnants of Auschwitz: The Witness and the Archive*, New York, NY: Zone Books

Agamben, G (2000) *Means Without End: Notes on Politics*, Minneapolis, MN: Minnesota Press

Agamben, G (2005) *State of Exception*, Chicago, IL: University of Chicago Press

Bayertz, K (1996) *Sanctity of Life and Human Dignity*, Dordrecht: Kluwer Academic

Beckett, S (1974) *Mercier and Camier*, London: Caldar and Boyars

Berns, S (2002) 'Regulating the national livestock: An experiment in human husbandry' 4 *University of Notre Dame Australian Law Review* 1

Boyer, A (1997) 'Sir Edward Coke, Circeronianus: Classical rhetoric and the common law tradition' 10 *IJSJ* 3

Elias, N (1978) *The Civilising Process, Volume 1: The History of Manners*, Oxford: Blackwell

Elias, N (1982) *The Civilising Process, Volume 2: Power and Civility*, Oxford: Blackwell

Elias, N (1985) *The Loneliness of Dying*, Oxford: Blackwell

Erasmus, D (1988) 'Preparing for death' (De praeparatione ad morten), in J O'Malley (ed), *Collected Works of Erasmus, Vol. 70*, Toronto: University of Toronto Press

Foucault, M (2000) ' "*Omnes et Singulatim*": Toward a critique of political reason', in D Faubion (ed), *Michel Foucault Power: Essential Works of Foucault 1954–1984*, London: Penguin Books

Foucault, M (2003) *Society Must be Defended*, New York, NY: Penguin Books

Gellner, E (1994) *Conditions of Liberty: Civil Society and Its* Rivals, London: Hamish Hamilton

Goodrich, P (1991) *The Languages of Law: From Logics of Memory to Nomadic Masks*, London: Weidenfeld & Nicolson

Goodrich, P (1996) *Law in the Courts of Love*, London: Routledge

Goodrich, P (1998) 'Signs taken for wonders: Community, identity and *A History of Sumptuary Law*' 23 *Law and Social Inquiry* 707

Graveson, R (1953) *Status in the Common Law*, London: Athlone Press

Griffiths, J *et al.* (1998) *Euthanasia and Law in the Netherlands*, Amsterdam: Amsterdam University Press

Hachamovitch, Y (1997) 'The dummy: An essay on malice prepensed', in P Rush, S McVeigh and A Young (eds), *Criminal Legal Doctrine*, Aldershot: Ashgate

Hertz, R (1960) *Death, and the Right Hand*, London: Cohen and West, French Publication 1907

Hocart, A (1970) *Kings and Councillors: An Essay on the Comparative Analysis of History*, R Needham ed, Chicago, IL: Chicago University Press

Hockey, J (1990) *Experiences of Death*, Edinburgh: Edinburgh University Press

Houlbrooke, R (1998) *Death, Religion, and the Family in England, 1480–1750*, Oxford: Oxford University Press

Hunt, A (1996) *Government of the Consuming Passions*, New York, NY: St Martin's Press

Hunter, I (2001) *Rival Enlightenments*, Cambridge: Cambridge University Press

Hunter, I and Saunders, D (2003) 'Bringing the state to England: Andrew Tooke's translation of Samuel Pufendorf's *De officio hominis et civis*' 24 *History of Political Thought* 218

Huntingdon, R and Metcalfe, P (1991) *Celebrations of Death: The Anthropology of Mortuary Ritual*, Cambridge: Cambridge University Press

Jacob, J (1988) *Doctors and Rules*, London: Routledge

Kantorowicz, E (1957) *The King's Two Bodies: A Study in Mediaeval Political Theology*, Princeton, NJ: Princeton University Press

Kaye, JM (1967) 'Early history of murder and manslaughter' 83 LQR 365

Keown, J (2002) *Euthanasia, Ethics and Public Policy*, Cambridge: Cambridge University Press

Lavi, S (2003) 'Euthanasia and the changing ethics of the deathbed' 4 *Theoretical Inquiries in Law (online edition)* Article 10

Lawton, J (2000) *The Dying Process*, London: Routledge

Legendre, P (1997a) 'The judge amongst the interpreters', in P Goodrich (ed), *Law and the Unconscious: A Legendre Reader*, Basingstoke: Macmillan

Legendre, P (1997b) 'Hermes and institutional structures: An essay on dogmatic communication', in P Goodrich (ed), *Law and the Unconscious: A Legendre Reader*, Basingstoke: Macmillan

Legendre, P (1997c) 'The Masters of Law', in P Goodrich (ed), *Law and the Unconscious: A Legendre Reader*, Basingstoke: Macmillan

Levinas, E (2003) *Escape*, Stanford, CA: Stanford University Press

McVeigh, S (1997) 'Cutting our losses', in P Rush, S McVeigh and A Young (eds), *Criminal Legal Doctrine*, Aldershot: Ashgate

Margalit, A (1996) *The Decent Society*, Cambridge, MA: Harvard University Press

Marshall, P (2002) *Beliefs and the Dead in Reformation England*, Oxford: Oxford University Press

Minson, J (1993) *Questions of Conduct*, London: Macmillan

Minson, J (2002) 'Holding on to Office', in D Burchill and A Leigh (eds), *The Prince's New Clothes, Why Australian Hate Their Politicians*, Sydney: UNSW Press

Murphy, T (1997) *The Oldest Social Science?* Oxford: Oxford University Press

Neil, M (1998) *Issues of Death, Mortality and Identity in English Renaissance Tragedy*, Oxford: Clarendon Press

Nelson, S (2003) *Say Little and Do Much: Nursing, Nuns and Hospitals in the Nineteenth Century*, Philadelphia, PA: University of Pennsylvania Press

Nitschke, P and Stewart, F (2005) *Killing Me Softly*, Ringwood: Penguin

Nuland, S (1994) *How We Die: Reflections on Life's Final Chapter*, New York, NY: Knopf

Nussbaum, M (2004) *Hiding from Humanity*, Princeton, NJ: Princeton University Press

Oakeshott, M (1991) *On Human Conduct*, Oxford: Clarendon Press

Oestreich, G (1982) *Neostoicism and the State*, Cambridge: Cambridge University Press

Phillipson, N (1993) 'Politeness and politics in the reigns of Anne and the early Hanoverians', in JGA Pocock, GJ Schochet and L Schwoerer (eds), *The Varieties of British Political Thought, 1500–1800*, Cambridge: Cambridge University Press

Pocock, JGA (1995) *Virtue, Commerce and History*, Cambridge: Cambridge University Press

Pocock, JGA (2003) *The Machiavellian Moment: Florentine Political Thought and the Atlantic Republican Tradition*, Oxford: Oxford University Press

Porter, R (2003) *Flesh in the Age of Reason*, London: Penguin

Pottage, A (1995) 'A unique and different subject of law' 16 *Cardozo Law Review* 1161

Proctor, R (1998) *Racial Hygiene: Medicine Under the Nazis*, Cambridge, MA: Harvard University Press

Rose, N and Novas, C (2005) 'Biological citizenship', in A Ong and S Collier (eds), *Global Assemblages: Technology, Politics, and Ethics as Anthropological Problems*, Oxford: Blackwell

Rush, P (1997) *Criminal Law*, Sydney: Butterworths
Saunders, D (2004) 'Juridifications and religion in early modern Europe: The challenge of a contextual history of law' 15 *Law and Critique* 99
Thurschwell, A (2003) 'Spectres of Nietzsche: Potential futures of the concept of the political in Agamben and Derrida' 24 *Cardozo Law Review* 1193
van Gennep, A (1960) *The Rites of Passage*, Chicago, IL: Chicago University Press
van Oenen, G (2004) 'Finding cover: Legal trauma and how to take care of it' 15 *Law and Critique* 139
Warren, J (2004) *Facing Death: Epicurus and His Critics*, Oxford: Oxford University Press
Weber, M (1958) 'Science as vocation', in HH Gerth and C Wright Mills (eds), *From Max Weber: Essays in Sociology*, New York, NY: Oxford University Press
Wheeler, S (1996) 'The corporate way of death' 7 *Law and Critique* 217

Websites

http://dying.about.com/od/euthanasia/
www.nt.gov.au/lant/parliament/committees/rotti/rotti95.pdf

Case

Wake and Gondarra v NT and Asche (1996) 109 NTR 1

Legislations

Rights of the Terminally Ill Act 1995 (NT)
Euthanasia Laws Act 1997 (Cth)

Part V

Dictions

12 Embracing jurisdiction

John Ford's *The Man Who Shot Liberty Valance*

Bill Grantham

The critic Georg Lukács wrote:

> The genuine categories of literary forms are not simply literary in essence. They are forms of life especially adapted to the articulation of great alternatives in a practical and effective manner and to the exposition of the maximal inner potentialities of forces and counterforces.
>
> (Lukács, 1970: 21)

Lukács, whose major work included a study of the historical novel (Lukács, 1962), might have had the cinema's major counterpart of historical fiction, the western film, in mind. Often dismissed, in the famous 'slanguage' of the film trade paper *Variety*, as 'oaters' – because of the omnipresence of oat-eating horses – the Western, in part because of its permanent witness to American life and its simple, persistent generic forms, was often a powerful vehicle for articulating the 'great alternatives' contemplated by Lukács.

On the other hand, the master director of Westerns, John Ford, insisted on the empiricism of his narrative approach. He claimed that he was driven only by what actually happened, telling one interviewer: 'I am not trying to make a legend live. I simply recall historic facts. Because it is based on American history, on people who existed, the Western moves me' (Mott, 2001: 95).

Ford was famously resistant to critical engagement with his films. 'I hate the cinema,' he once said, adding: 'But I like making Westerns' (Leguèbe, 2001: 73). One reason for making Westerns, he told the future director Bertrand Tavernier, was that they offered 'a chance to get away from Hollywood and the smog', which partly meant getting away somewhat from the pressures and interferences of the Hollywood studio system (Tavernier, 2001). Ford rejected not only critical readings of his own westerns but also theoretically driven forms of cinematic practice – for instance, telling the French critic Eric Leguèbe:

> What I like in filming is the active life, the excitement of the humming of the cameras, and the passion of the actors in front of them, the landscapes on top of that, the work, work, work . . . It takes a huge effort to remain lucid and not fall in the traps of aestheticism and, above all, intellectualism. What counts

> is what one does and not what one says. When I make a western, all I have to do is film a documentary on the West, just as it was: epic. And from the moment that one is epic, one can't go wrong. It's the reality, outside time, that one records on the negative.
>
> (Leguèbe, 2001: 73)

However, Ford made a point of identifying himself with Western films, and the identification carried more than merely factual force. In an often-told story, he began an address to fellow directors attacking the Hollywood blacklist with the introduction: 'My name is John Ford. I am a director of Westerns' (McBride, 2001: 416). And yet, in one 20-year period of his career, between the silent hit *3 Bad Men* (1926) and *My Darling Clementine* in 1946, Ford directed just one Western – *Stagecoach* (1939) – out of some 44 feature-length films (Bogdanovich, 1978: 113–49). Ford's decision to return wholeheartedly to the Western – and, as the winner of six Academy awards for non-Western films (Libby, 2001: 53), to project himself as 'a director of Westerns' – was the product of deliberate reflection on what he sought to achieve as a film-maker following his experiences in the Second World War. As one biographer, Joseph McBride, puts it:

> Ford consciously set out to keep the values of pioneer America alive in the minds of his fellow countrymen... The genre reflected a continued need among the American public for mythic parables of national identity in an age when America was grappling with the disturbing responsibilities of its new–found superpower status.
>
> (McBride, 2001: 417–18)

In his later films, Ford used the Western genre to expose what he saw as America's ills in the postwar world. In *The Searchers* (1956), he probed racism and the taboos of miscegenation. More explicitly, in *Sergeant Rutledge* (1960), he depicted the affair of a black cavalry soldier falsely accused of raping a white woman. Ford had participated in the D-Day landings in Normandy on 6 June 1944 (McBride, 2001: 396–97), and claimed that the experience had changed his views on race in America. 'When I landed at Omaha Beach,' he told Samuel Lachise, the film critic for the French communist daily *L'Humanité*, in 1966, 'there were scores of black bodies lying in the sand. Then I realised that it was impossible not to consider [negroes] full-fledged American citizens' (Tavernier, 2001: 107). A similar revisionism informed his depiction of wronged Indians in another cavalry Western, *Cheyenne Autumn* (1964). As Ford told Peter Bogdanovich:

> [I] wanted to show [the Indians'] point of view for a change. Let's face it, we've treated them very badly – it's a blot on our shield; we've cheated and robbed, killed, murdered and massacred and everything else, but they kill one white man and, God, out come the troops.
>
> (Bogdanovich, 1978: 104)

Although Ford's meditations on postwar American were not limited to Westerns – his depiction of machine politics in *The Last Hurrah* (1958) and of the travails of women in *7 Women* (1966) lay outside the genre – he nonetheless persistently revisited the conventions of the Western to explore the national and social themes that stirred him in the later part of his career. In *The Man Who Shot Liberty Valance* (1962), Ford's treatment of his themes is possibly the most complex and nuanced of his late films, a meditation both of historical consciousness and contemporary ideologies, of foundation myths and modern legends and, above all, of the developing role of the law in a society reaching the end of its frontier state. This latter theme is, of course, a staple not only of the Western genre but also of American consciousness itself, and one which Ford had touched upon previously. In *Stagecoach* (1939), two protagonists of the story – a prostitute and a drunken doctor – are banished from their town by the emerging forces of law, religion and civilisation and cast out into the desert in the company of, among others, a louche gambler, a corrupt banker and an outlaw. The banishment theme is an echo of one of the earliest successful Western stories, Bret Harte's *The Outcasts of Poker Flat* (1869) (filmed by Ford in 1919 in a now-lost version), in which the eponymous frontier town experiences 'a spasm of virtuous reaction, quite as lawless and ungovernable as any of the acts that had provoked it' and duly casts out a gambler, a drunk and two prostitutes (1869: 12).

But the issues of law in *Liberty Valance* go far beyond these generic commonplaces; the film contains layers of searching and sophisticated meditation upon a number of areas of jurisdiction which are significant both as an exercise of historical memory and as a contemplation of the America of the early 1960s in which the film was made.

In *The Man Who Shot Liberty Valance*, Ransom Stoddard (James Stewart), a senator and former governor of an unnamed American state, returns by train to the small town of Shinbone with his wife Hallie for the funeral of Tom Doniphon (John Wayne), a forgotten man who has died a pauper, leaving only his black servant, Pompey, and the town's former marshal, Link Appleyard, to mourn him. Stoddard's trip piques the curiosity of the local newspaper editor, who demands to know why so distinguished a man would attend the funeral of so obscure a figure as Doniphon. In flashback, Stoddard relates his arrival by stagecoach in Shinbone many years earlier, as a young lawyer from the East who has determined to make his fortune on the frontier. Stoddard's stagecoach is held up by a group of desperadoes headed by Liberty Valance, a cruel and violent thug who beats Stoddard viciously and desecrates his law books. Stoddard is rescued by Doniphon and Pompey, and brought to Shinbone, where he is nursed by Hallie, whom Doniphon loves, and her Scandinavian immigrant parents, the Ericsons, who own a restaurant. Stoddard, faithful to the legal principles that have formed him, wants Link Appleyard to arrest Valance and his men for robbing the coach, but Appleyard, clearly afraid, claims that he has no jurisdiction over criminals outside the town's boundaries. Doniphon mocks the young lawyer's scruples, explaining that his vision of the law does not prevail on the frontier.

Stoddard takes a job washing dishes and serving in Hallie's parents' restaurant. He also opens a school for the town's children and adult illiterates, where the pupils include Hallie herself, who has become attracted to Stoddard, Pompey and Appleyard's children by his Mexican wife. The students not only learn to read but are also inculcated in the virtues of America's Declaration of Independence and Constitution. These values provide a link to a back story of the film, the efforts of the territory in which Shinbone is situated to become a state of the Union. Stoddard becomes involved in Shinbone's efforts to elect representatives to the territorial convention that will vote on statehood.

Liberty Valance, who turns out to be in the pay of wealthy ranching interests determined to block statehood, attempts unsuccessfully to intimidate the Shinbone townspeople into electing anti-state representatives to the convention and, having failed, determines to be rid of Stoddard for ever. Valance challenges Stoddard to a shootout. Stoddard, who has earlier been shown to be an incompetent gunman, appears for the challenge and during the gunfight Valance is killed. Stoddard becomes a hero, 'The Man Who Shot Liberty Valance', goes to the territorial convention and is swept on a wave of popularity into a lifetime of public office. He also wins Hallie, who becomes his wife. But Doniphon reveals to Stoddard that it is he, Doniphon, who killed Valance in order to save Stoddard's life, even though he knew that he would lose Hallie as a result.

Back in the present, Stoddard completes his confession that his entire political life was based on the lie that he shot Liberty Valance. The newspaper editor, however, decides to 'spike' the story. 'When the legend becomes fact', he comments, 'print the legend'. Stoddard and Hallie, clearly bereft at Doniphon's death, leave Shinbone – one surmises for ever.

This rather bald summary does not do justice to the richness of *The Man Who Shot Liberty Valance*. But it is sufficient to illustrate the three aspects of jurisdiction, as reflected in the film, which are discussed in this chapter. First, there is the willingness – or unwillingness – of the state to assert jurisdiction over the person, as reflected by the inability of the inhabitants of Shinbone, most notably the cowardly Marshal Appleyard, to bring Liberty Valance and his men to justice. Second, there is the back story of the territory's campaign for statehood – in effect, its desire to embrace the jurisdiction of the US Federal Government. And third, there is the way in which the film is a mirror of the period when it was made, the early 1960s, when the expansion of federal jurisdiction brought about a social revolution in the United States that is still, 40 years on, one of the essential fault lines in American life.

Criminal jurisdiction over the person

The fulcrum upon which the plot of *The Man Who Shot Liberty Valance* turns is the inability of the inhabitants of Shinbone to bring Valance and his violent gang to justice. The clear reason is fear. The ostensible reason, however, is that the authorities in Shinbone, such as they are, do not have jurisdiction over Valance for acts committed outside the town. Valance's very presence on his trips into Shinbone terrorises the natives, but his acts fall short of arrestable offences. The territorial government, which apparently does have jurisdiction over Valance's crimes, is invisible in the film. Accordingly, Valance operates with impunity and, until the arrival of Stoddard, is unchallenged. In *Liberty Valance*, Marshal Link Appleyard is played by the reedy-voiced Andy Devine, a member of John Ford's extended repertory company of leading and character actors. Devine is always a comic figure in the director's films, 'Ford's broad-beamed Falstaff' (Sarris, 1975: 177), who was sometimes typed as a person who bridged the Anglo and Latino cultures of the West: he once claimed in an interview that every time he worked with him, Ford 'saw to it that I had a Mexican wife and nine kids' (Anderson, 1999: 217). In Liberty Valance, Appleyard is a comic coward, an inept, Dogberryish constable who would rather eat free food in the Ericsons' restaurant than pursue Liberty Valance and his men. Terrified of enforcing the law, he declares that, as far as Liberty Valance's crimes committed outside town are concerned, 'I ain't got no jurisdiction. What Liberty does out on the road ain't no business of mine.' (It later turns out – at least according to Stoddard's law books – that Appleyard *does* have jurisdiction to arrest Valance. This, naturally, makes no difference at all.)

The idea of jurisdictional limitations on police action recurs in the American western, Ford's included. The cavalry led by John Wayne in *Rio Grande* (1950), respects the river border between Texas and Mexico, even where the principles of hot pursuit might allow it to cross. In historical re-enactments reaching as late as the 1930s, fugitives are depicted racing for the state line to escape the police whose jurisdiction ends at the border – for instance, the glamorous criminals in Arthur Penn's quasi-western *Bonnie and Clyde* (1967). And, in a moment of homage to Liberty Valance, the sheriff in Lawrence Kasdan's *Silverado* (1985) abandons his pursuit of escaping presumed outlaws when a bullet comes too close. 'Today,' he announces while turning back, 'my jurisdiction ends here'.

But in Liberty Valance, the meditation on this familiar theme is more complex than simple boundary-drawing. Stoddard has been robbed of all of his money and severely beaten. In the power vacuum represented by Link Appleyard, the only choice offered to him by Tom Doniphon is to learn how to use a gun – a suggestion that repels Stoddard, persistent in his attachment to the rule of law. Of course, the law that Stoddard is attached to is the law of the East, the law of the books that have been brought to Shinbone and violated by Liberty Valance. Tom Doniphon follows a different law, in which each person sets his or her own jurisdiction, a concept of law set forth somewhat sentimentally in Walter Prescott Webb's classic study *The Great Plains*:

> The West was lawless for two reasons: first, because of the social conditions that obtained there during the period under consideration; secondly, because the law that was applied there was not made for those conditions. It did not fit the needs of the country, and could not be obeyed... We know, for example, that in the early period the restraints of law could not make themselves felt in the rarefied population. Each man had to make his own law because there was no other to make it... In the absence of law and in the

> social conditions that obtained, men worked out an extra-legal code or custom by which they guided their actions.
>
> (Webb, 1981: 496–97)

This 'code' called for the rough and ready morality that Tom Doniphon represents, again in Webb's words:

> The code demanded what [Theodore] Roosevelt called a square deal; it demanded fair play. According to it one must not shoot his adversary in the back, and he must not shoot an unarmed man. In actual practice he must give notice of his intention, albeit the action followed by the notice as a lightning stroke. Failure to abide by the code did not necessarily bring formal punishment for the act already committed; it meant that the violator might be cut off without benefit of notice in the next act. Thus was justice carried out in a crude but effective manner, and warning given that in general the code must prevail.
>
> (Webb, 1981: 497)

The rule of the gun was a reality in the West. For instance, it has been estimated that some 50 per cent of homicides in seven California counties between 1850 and 1900 were caused by handguns, which were also implicated in 68 per cent of the murder indictments in one Colorado mining community between 1880 and 1920 (McKanna, 1995). Gun rule gave rise to forms of gun-ruled institutions, such as the vigilante movements and committees that proliferated in the West. However, it has been argued that, like Tom Doniphon, these vigilantes were not themselves lawless; they were simply trying to provide an apt form of law where none otherwise existed. As Lawrence Friedman has said:

> Social control, like nature, abhors a vacuum. The 'respectable' citizens – the majority, perhaps? – in Western towns were not really lawless. Quite to the contrary, people were accustomed to the rule of law and order... They were Americans; they were unwilling to tolerate too sharp a break in social continuity; they reacted against formal law which was too slow, or too corrupt, for their purposes, or which had fallen into the hands of the less respectable.
>
> (Friedman, 1985: 369)

Moreover, it has been shown by John Phillip Reid (1980) that the pioneers who travelled West in the nineteenth century had substantial and sophisticated notions of law, taken from their sense of the legal systems that they had left behind, adapted to the new circumstances in which they found themselves, and applied as a form of customary law while they found themselves in places where no palpable apparatus of the law otherwise existed. Once settled, the West generated its own special forms of law, at least divergent from, if not contrary to, English precedents, to meet its own special conditions, whether topological, historical or both – governing, for instance, water rights (Bakken, 2000: 127–204), land tenure (Bakken, 2000: 311–55), mining practices (Bakken, 2000: 205–47) and marital property (Friedman, 1985: 171). Why, then, did the criminal law, represented in *Liberty Valance* by the aspirations of Stoddard, not also develop its own particularities, forged by the special conditions of the West? One possible reason may be that, despite the thoughtful voice given to Tom Doniphon in *Liberty Valance* and more lurid accounts of frontier lawlessness portrayed elsewhere (Shirley, 1957, 1978), violent crime may have been less prevalent and justice may have functioned better in the West than has previously been acknowledged.

But, whatever the reality, the 'code of the West' is portrayed in *Liberty Valance* as having existed as historical fact, and it is embodied in John Ford's perennial hero, John Wayne, who provides easy opposition to James Stewart's stolid and somewhat priggish Ransom Stoddard. The transformation of the West from Doniphon's world to Stoddard's is not questioned: as famously described by Frederick Jackson Turner, by 1890 the West had its own existential sense of a frontier coming to an end (Turner, 1958). When Stoddard and Hallie return to Shinbone, transformed by the railway into a prosperous but dull small town, they are mourning not only the passing of a friend – and, in Hallie's case, a lover – but of a time when, it is suggested, moral people set their own moral compass. At the beginning of *Liberty Valance*, only Stoddard calls on Appleyard to assert the jurisdiction of the state in running down criminals. By the end of the flashback, even Doniphon hectors Appleyard to lock up the remnants of the Valance gang, now deprived of their leader. Paradoxically, and of course ironically, it is Doniphon who is the midwife of this institutional change, by making the last assertion of the code of the West, and murdering Liberty Valance. What is striking is the deep sense of melancholy surrounding this change. Just as the banishment of the incorrigible in *Stagecoach* seems to portend a loss of fibre in the civilisation that can cast out such people, so does the sacrifice of the floating jurisdiction of the old West in *Liberty Valance* suggest a moral loss. Formal institutions may be the inevitable outcrop of growing complexity in societies, but they suggest a system of values that has been externalised and removed from the sphere of action occupied by those who do not look to others to assert jurisdiction over matters and persons that need to be dealt with. It is Doniphon, the moral man who sets his own jurisdiction, who is the heroic centre of the film, while Stoddard – equally moral but defined by the jurisdictional institutions that he embraces rather than by his own character – is the one who takes the spoils and gets the girl.

Federal jurisdiction in historical memory

In *The Man Who Shot Liberty Valance*, we never know where Shinbone is. We are not told in the short story on which the film was based (Johnson, 1953), nor in the novelisation of the movie (Bellah, 1962). The only geographical reference in the film is to the 'Picketwire', or Purgatoire River (Sarris, 1975: 179), which flows in south-eastern Colorado, near the borders of Kansas, Oklahoma, Texas and New Mexico. It could, in other words, be anywhere in the flat plainslands where the five states meet (or elsewhere), and the back story involving the transformation of the territory in which Shinbone is located into a state is, despite

Ford's never-substantiated claim that *Liberty Valance* was 'based on historical fact' (Tavernier, 2001: 108), a work of historical imagination rather than historical reconstruction. The process of transforming the contiguous territories of North America under US rule to full statehood was a major preoccupation of American politics until well into the twentieth century. While some major states, such as California and Texas, became part of the United States following wars, major states of the West, such as Arizona (1912), Colorado (1876), Kansas (1861), Oklahoma (1907), New Mexico (1912) and Wyoming (1890), were territories that became late entrants to the union (*World Almanac*, 2004: 515).

The newly created United States of America took jurisdiction of American territory that had not achieved statehood as early as 1787, when Congress passed the Northwest Ordinance, the template for territorial government that covered the territories – including new territories added by purchase or conquest – for many more years (Eblen, 1968: 1–7). The territories thus created sent representatives to Congress in Washington, DC from 1797 to 1959, when Hawaii became the fiftieth and (so far) last state (Bloom, 1973: 65–75). The territories had appointed governors and often elected assemblies. Their powers to legislate were often subject to quite specific federal interference – for instance, prohibitions on the creation of unapproved banks (Eblen, 1968: 185).

In *The Man Who Shot Liberty Valance*, the benefits of statehood are seen to be twofold. First, the 'ordinary' population of Shinbone – and, by implication, the entire territory – is offered the chance to shake off the influence of powerful vested interests: the cattle ranchers who have hired Liberty Valance. Second, as manifested in the civics lesson that Stoddard gives to his school class, the federal government is presented as the locus and guarantee of fundamental rights. When Phil Ericson dresses in his Sunday best and carries his beribboned and sealed certificate of American citizenship to the saloon to cast his vote for the first time, his is the comic portrayal of a serious point: that the complete embrace of the jurisdiction of the federal government is the highest benefit a citizen can obtain in the American democracy. The reality, of course, is that the impulse to territorial statehood was not as simple as this. Unsurprisingly, the territorial conventions were dominated by special interests, and the concerns of territorial constitution-makers often extended to fundamental rights that were deemed to be less well delineated either in other states or under the federal system (Bakken, 1987). Moreover, some territorial constitutional conventions have been characterised as demonstrating 'a definite and concerted effort to restrict liberty rather than to expand it', particularly in areas such as female suffrage, race and religious freedom (Bakken, 1990). Furthermore, in *Liberty Valance*, the actual expansion of federal power in the years following the Civil War – for instance, improvements in the habeas corpus laws and the recalibration of the jurisdiction of the federal courts (Wiecek, 1988: 237) – is not portrayed as among the benefits of the acquisition of statehood in the film; instead, it appeals to demotic and fundamentally romantic notions of the benefits of American citizenship. In this sense, the film's historical consciousness of jurisdiction – fundamentally, a false or at least highly partial consciousness – can be viewed as an iteration of the 'print the legend' dichotomy, which has been astutely perceived by Christian Delage 'not as a binary proposition between the truth and a lie, but instead as the space between an event and its narrative' (Keller, 2001: 32). The importance of the 'historical' jurisdictional account of statehood accordingly lies not in its depiction of historical fact – which, as we have seen (despite Ford's claims to the contrary) to be simplistic, if not fanciful – but in the telling of the tale, the force with which these essentially precatory elements of the benefits putatively conferred by federal jurisdiction are shown.

So, if the main thrust of the 'historical' *Liberty Valance* presents the benefits of federal jurisdiction merely simplistically, why is this theme of the film nonetheless interesting? The answer lies in the connection of the first theme of this chapter – the replacement of self-validating jurisdiction by the apparatus of the state – with the last, a discussion of how *Liberty Valance*'s historical reflections additionally had contemporary relevance for the audiences of 1960s America living on John F Kennedy's 'New Frontier' (McBride, 2001: 643). This connection is characterised by the sombre, regretful tone of the film's frame, the visit of the Stoddards to Shinbone for Tom Doniphon's funeral. Of this flashback device – itself a manipulation of historical consciousness – Robin Wood has written:

> The Old West, seen in retrospect from beside Tom Doniphon's coffin, is invested with an exaggerated, stylised vitality; in the film's 'present' (still, of course, our past, but connected to our present, as it were, by the railroad that carries Senator Stoddard and Hallie away at the end) all real vitality has drained away, leaving only the shallow energy of the news-hounds, and a weary, elegiac feeling of loss.
>
> (Wood, 2001: 25–26)

The contemporary sense of federal jurisdiction

The observation that Ford drifted politically to the right in his old age is a commonplace of Ford criticism and biography, but as a view of the director it also lacks clarity. It is true that Ford was an uncompromising supporter of American military power, including the Vietnam War, who ended up supporting the neo-conservative 1964 Republican presidential candidate Barry Goldwater and later President Richard Nixon (McBride, 2001: 6). It is also true that, during his lifetime, he described himself as 'a definite socialist democrat – always left' (2001: 271) and, as late as 1966 (to a communist interviewer) as 'a liberal' (Tavernier, 2001: 106). And, as we have seen, his later films included attempts to revise and reconfigure some of the classic figures both of Western film-making and of the American cinema in general. Such reconfigurations are among the most powerful elements of *The Man Who Shot Liberty Valance*.

The Shinbone of the film's pre-statehood flashback sequences is an emblem of an old America that would have been easily recognised in America of the 1960s. The town is segregated – Pompey may not drink in the saloon where Tom

Doniphon goes, and the Mexican community is confined to separate housing and meeting places. The women, of course, do not have a vote in the elections to the territorial convention, and a rather elderly-looking youth is ejected from the hustings for being under age. In the America of 1962, women had had the vote since the ratification of the Nineteenth Amendment to the Constitution in 1920, but were only beginning to give voice to the broader grievances of the women's movement. Eighteen-year-olds would not receive the vote until the passage of the Twenty-Sixth Amendment in 1971. And, of course, the burning domestic political issue then, as it is to a great extent now, was race.

Although the impulse for racial justice in America came from below – from the marchers, bus passengers, lunch counter squatters and others who took a stand against racial discrimination – the key to the dismantling of the formal system of the segregation system was its federalisation. In the nineteenth century, the federal Supreme Court had systematically used jurisdictional and standing arguments to deprive non-white groups of the protections of the law, thereby denying Indians recourse in property cases[1] and blacks in citizenship and equal protection cases,[2] and retreating from applying federal jurisdiction to certain categories of state action that caused the Constitution, in the dissenting words of Justice Harlan, to be 'sacrificed by a subtle and ingenious verbal criticism'.[3] In Ransom Stoddard's manifestly anachronistic classroom, however, the races are mixed as they are taught the virtues of an inclusive constitutional order – one that would have been unrecognisable to the historical participants represented there, had they existed.

But *Liberty Valance* was made at a time when federal power has been in full expansion for a quarter of a century, beginning with Roosevelt's New Deal in the 1930s, continuing through the Second World War in the 1940s, the growth of the military–industrial complex in the 1950s and the ambitions of the New Frontier and, ultimately, the Great Society projects of the 1960s. Federal power had contributed to the end of the Great Depression, helped win a world war (in which Ford was a decorated officer), turned the country into an economic and military superpower and appeared to be ready to tackle the great stain on the country's conscience, the legacy of slavery. The landmark *Brown v Board of Education* case of 1954,[4] outlawing racial segregation in state-run schools, finds its echo in the unsegregated Shinbone schoolroom imagined in 1962.

But, as always in this film, the apparent positive has its discontents. Critics have remarked on Stoddard's condescension to Pompey in the classroom, and there is some evidence that Ford, manipulative with his actors to the point of cruelty, deliberately played on James Stewart's personal discomfort in the

1 *Johnson and Graham's Lessee v M'Intosh* 21 US (8 Wheat) 543 (1823); *Cherokee Nation v Georgia* 30 US (5 Pet) 1, (1831); *Worcester v Georgia* 31 US (6 Pet) 515 (1832).

2 *Scott v Sandford* [Dred Scott] 60 US 393 (1856); *Slaughter-House Cases* 83 US 36 (1872); *Civil Rights Cases* 109 US 3 (1883).

3 *Civil Rights Cases* 109 US at 27.

4 *Brown v Board of Education of Topeka* 347 US 483 (1954).

presence of black people to foster a sense of ambivalence in Stoddard's teaching Pompey about the Declaration of Independence (McBride, 2001: 631). In the 'new' Shinbone, when the Stoddards return for Doniphon's funeral, Pompey – the old black retainer – and Appleyard – the film's indirect connection to Latino America – are melancholy and ineffably alone, in a sense segregated from the new order of feeling. The railway line – another manifestation of federal power (Meinig, 1999: 4–28) – points directly to Washington; the newspaper, produced in the old days by a soused idealist, is now in the hands of slick newshounds; and the undertaker steals the boots off Doniphon's feet before placing the body in the cheap pine coffin of a pauper's funeral. If the 'old' Shinbone is today, so is the 'new' Shinbone. It is not exactly the new Eden.

Conclusion

How many movies even use the term 'jurisdiction'? In *Liberty Valance*, Appleyard has to get Stoddard to remind him of the word and the lawyer, understanding all things, enlightens him. It is a comic moment but, as discussed previously, resonant of the crisis of living within and without jurisdiction. We need the law, and at times yearn for it, but we are not necessarily improved by it. Stoddard, who has had a glittering career among the institutions that he strove to build, leaves Shinbone determined to retire. And Hallie, the one person in the film who seems to have had a choice, and who chose the 'new' Shinbone, leaves with him, haunted by and heartbroken at Doniphon's death. We may need the new jurisdictions of the modern world, Ford seems to be saying – indeed, we must demand and embrace them. But with them comes a longing that is beyond mere nostalgia, an existential regret for what has – as it had to – passed.

References

Anderson, L (1999 [1981]) *About John Ford*, London: Plexus

Bakken, G (1987) *Rocky Mountain Constitution Making, 1850–1912*, Westport and London: Greenwood Press

Bakken, G (1990) 'Constitutional Convention debates in the West: Racism, religion and gender' 3 *Western Legal History* 213

Bakken, G (ed) (2000) *Law In The Western United States*, Norman, OK: University of Oklahoma Press

Bellah, J (1962) *The Man Who Shot Liberty Valance*, New York, NY: Permabooks

Bloom, J (1973) 'Early delegates in the House of Representatives', in J Bloom (ed), *The American Territorial System*, Athens, OH: Ohio University Press

Bogdanovich, P (1978) *John Ford*, Berkeley, Los Angeles and London: University of California Press

Eblen, J (1968) *The First and Second United States Empires: Governors and Territorial Government, 1784–1912*, Pittsburgh: University of Pittsburgh Press

Friedman, L (1985) *A History of American Law*, 2nd edn, New York, NY: Touchstone/Simon and Schuster.

Harte, B (1869) 'The outcasts of Poker Flat', in Reuben H Margolis (ed), *Bret Harte's Gold Rush*, Berkeley, CA: Heyday Books

Johnson, D (1953) '*The Man Who Shot Liberty Valance*', in *Indian Country*, New York, NY: Ballantine Books

Keller, A (2001) 'Generic subversion in the 1990s: Mario Van Peebles' *Posse*', in Janet Walker (ed), *Westerns: Films Through History*, New York, NY and London: Routledge

Leguèbe, E (2001) 'John Ford', in G Peary (ed), *John Ford Interviews*, Jackson, MS: University Press of Mississippi

Libby, Bill (2001) 'The Old Wrangler Rides Again', in G Peary (ed), *John Ford Interviews*, Jackson, MS: University Press of Mississippi

Lukács, G (1962) *The Historical Novel* (A Történelmi Regény, 1937), trans H Mitchell and S Mitchell, London: Merlin Press

Lukács, G (1970) 'Preface', in A Kahn (ed), *Writer and Critic and Other Essays*, London: Merlin Press

McBride, J (2001) *Searching for John Ford: A Life*, New York, NY: St Martin's Press

McKanna, C (1995) 'Death in the Colorado coal country: Homicide and social instability in Las Animas County, 1880–1920' 8 *Western Legal History* 182

Meinig, D (1999) *Transcontinental America, 1850–1915*, New Haven and London: Yale University Press

Mott, M (2001) 'The Old John Ford Talks About Westerns', in G Peary (ed), *John Ford Interviews*, Jacksons, MS: University Press of Mississippi

Reid, J (1980) *Law for the Elephant*, San Marino, CA: Huntington Library

Sarris, A (1975) *The John Ford Movie Mystery*, Bloomington and London: Indiana University Press

Shirley, G (1957) *Law West of Fort Smith: A History of Frontier Justice in the Indian Territory, 1834–1896*, New York, NY: Henry Holt & Co.

Shirley, G (1978) *West of Hell's Fringe: Crime, Criminals and the Federal Peace Office in the Oklahoma Territory, 1889–1907*, Norman, OK: University of Oklahoma Press

Tavernier, B (2001) 'Notes of a press attaché: John Ford in Paris', in G Peary (ed), *John Ford Interviews*, Jackson, MS: University Press of Mississippi

Turner, F (1958 [1920]) *The Frontier in American History*, New York, NY: Henry Holt & Co.

Webb, W (1981 [1931]) *The Great Plains*, Lincoln, NE and London: University of Nebraska Press

Wiecek, W (1988) 'The Reconstruction of federal judicial power, 1863–1876', in M Friedman and H Scheiber (eds), *American Law and the Constitutional Order: Historical Perspectives*, Cambridge and London: Harvard University Press

Wood, R (2001) 'Shall We Gather at the River?', in G Studlar and N Studlar (eds), *John Ford Made Westerns: Filming the Legend in the Sound Era*, Bloomington and Indianapolis, IN: Indiana University Press

World Almanac and Book of Facts (2004) New York: World Almanac Books

Films

Ford, J, *Cheyenne Autumn*, 1964, Ford–Smith Productions–Warner Bros

Ford, J, *3 Bad Men*, 1926, Fox

Ford, J, *7 Women*, 1966, Ford–Smith Productions–MGM

Ford, J, *My Darling Clementine*, 1946, 20th Century–Fox

Ford, J, *Rio Grande*, 1950, Argosy Pictures–Republic
Ford, J, *Sergeant Rutledge*, 1960, John Ford Productions–Warner Bros
Ford, J, *Stagecoach*, 1939, Walter Wanger Productions–United Artists
Ford, J, *The Last Hurrah*, 1958, Columbia
Ford, J, *The Man Who Shot Liberty Valance*, 1962, John Ford Productions–Paramount Pictures
Ford, J, *The Searchers*, 1956, CV Whitney Pictures–Warner Bros
Kasdan, L, *Silverado*, 1985, Columbia Pictures
Penn, A, *Bonnie and Clyde*, 1967, Warner Bros–Seven Arts

Cases

Brown v Board of Education of Topeka 347 US 483 (1954)
Cherokee Nation v Georgia 30 US (5 Pet) 1, (1831)
Civil Rights Cases 109 US 3 (1883)
Johnson and Graham's Lessee v M'Intosh 21 US (8 Wheat) 543 (1823)
Scott v Sandford [Dred Scott] 60 US 393 (1856)
Slaughter-House Cases 83 US 36 (1872)
Worcester v Georgia 31 US (6 Pet) 515 (1832).

13 Jurisdiction and the colonisation of sublime enjoyment

Piyel Haldar

> Lady J is pretty well; a tiger about a month old, who is suckled by a goat, and has all the gentleness of his foster-mother, is now playing at her feet. I call him Jupiter.
>
> (Cannon, 1970: 785)

> The question of the sublime was doubtless first of all an attempt to measure the decline of the Orient.
>
> (Deguy, 1993: 6)

Introduction

This chapter examines the category of the sublime as an essential component in initiating the phenomenon of jurisdiction. As shall be shown, the juridical appeal to the sublime legitimises jurisdiction. In order to extend its sphere of influence, jurisdiction refers to that which is beyond the secular and temporal domain of human beings.

In order to illustrate and analyse this thesis, this chapter focuses on attempts made by lawyers in the eighteenth century to extend the jurisdiction of the common law overseas. In particular, the problems faced by the courts of the East India Company in its Indian factories enabled Western jurisprudence to develop an idea of jurisdiction that was universal rather than territorial. In other words, such an examination places us in a position where we are better poised to understand the universal attachment to the law.

More specifically, this chapter highlights the manner in which lawyers employed by the East India Company during the eighteenth century referred to the idea of an Oriental sublime. As a descriptive category, the Oriental sublime is used to domesticate the East. It rendered the East (as the specific territory over which the East India Company sought jurisdiction) romantic and inhabitable. But the sublime also helped to connect archaic jurisdictions to its modern counterpart. Eastern and Western forms of authority were linked to a sublime time out of mind. It was here in the mists that the jurisprudence of an universal jurisdiction was born.

Asiatic Jones and the sublimation of Oriental scholarship

Under the administration of Warren Hastings, scholars such as Charles Wilkins and Nathaniel Halhed initiated studies into the Indian past. Having established the first printing press in India, Halhed published his *Grammar of the Bengali Language*, and Wilkins published the first translation of the *Bagavad Gita*. Ostensibly, such works were issued both to inform Englishmen interested in India and to 'conciliate the affection of the natives' (Halhed, 1776: xii). But there was more to these works, and the desire for exotic knowledge betrayed a deeper obsession with India that centred around the remoteness of its antiquity and the origins of its culture, religion and laws. Orientalist scholars, spurred on by such discoveries as the ancient cave temples of Elephanta, turned to the East in an attempt to calculate the origins of *all* culture. The caves of Elephanta, for example, were not simply dark, mysterious and terrifyingly colossal. Their sublimity also resided in the suspicion that their antiquity was thought to predate any known culture. The implication was that somewhere in the East existed the cradle of civilisation and that the clues as to its precise location was to be found in ancient Sanskrit texts (Drew, 1998: 199). Contained in this literature was a history that went further back in time than Christianity or even English time immemorial:

> I, who cannot help believing the Divinity of the Messiah, from the undisputed antiquity and manifest completion of many prophesies, especially those of Isiah, am obliged of course to believe the sanctity of the venerable books to which that sacred person refers as genuine (the books of Moses); but it is not the truth of our national religion, as such, that I have at heart – it is truth itself; and if any cool unbiased reasoner will clearly convince me that Moses drew his narrative, through Egyptian conduits, from primeval fountains of Indian literature, I shall esteem him as a friend for having weeded my mind from a capital error, and promise to stand among the foremost in assisting to circulate the truth which he has ascertained . . . I am persuaded that a connexion subsisted between the old idolatrous nations of Egypt, India, Greece and Italy.[1]
>
> (Jones, 1804a: 280–81)

Nature and the antiquity of the Orient are simply two forms of excess that excited the Oriental scholar. As Voltaire suggested, the Brahmin had 'sublime ideas' about the supreme being and the peculiar theocracy of Hinduism thus prompted Orientalist speculation on the sublime location of divine power.

These appropriately disparate forms of the sublime stimulated the work of the Welshman Sir William Jones, who was regarded perhaps as the most obsessed of all early scholars and about whom a few biographical points are apposite. Details about

1 See also Jones (1799a). It is interesting to note the range of eighteenth century English works suggesting the influence of Brahminism on ancient religious life in Britain. For a discussion, see Drew (1998: 50–51).

the life of William Jones (*c*. 1746–1794) suggest that his was one almost completely devoted to Eastern scholarship. Even before travelling to the East, he had published his *Grammar of the Persian Language* (1771) and *Poems, Consisting chiefly of Translations from the Arabic Languages* (1772). Any residual scholarly commitments outside this exotic field were dedicated only to the more mundane study and practice of law as a judge on the Welsh circuits (see Franklin, 1995).[2] Even so, it was the recognition of Jones' talents as an Orientalist by Warren Hastings which earned him an appointment as a puisne judge in the presidency of Bengal.

In Calcutta, the judge devoted much of his time to the study of various Oriental cultures: 'My daily studies are now, what they will be for six years to come, Persian and law, and whatever relates to India.'[3] His enjoyment of Oriental scholarship is expressed in hymn-like prose: 'as the thirsty antelope runs to a pool of sweet water, so I thirsted for all kinds of knowledge, which was sweet as nectar'.[4] It is sometimes expressed as 'infinite pleasure':

> If envy can exist with an anxious wish of all possible entertainment and reputation to the person envied, I am not free from that passion, when I think of the infinite pleasure which you must receive from a subject so new and interesting [as Sanskrit]. Happy should I be to follow you in the same track.[5]

Even the justification for his studies was Orientalised and his scholarly appetite was determined by, and surrendered to, a more despotic cause: 'The *Mahomedans* have not only the permission, but the positive command, of their law-giver, *to search for learning even in the remotest parts of the globe*' (Jones, 1804: 280–81). However, this compulsive obsession with studying as many things Oriental as he could commanded a certain price: 'I do not expect, as long as I stay in India, to be free from a bad digestion, the *morbus literatorum*, for which there is hardly any remedy, but abstinence from too much food, literary and culinary.'[6] Jones was to die in Calcutta from an inflammation of the liver.

In addition to his judicial tasks, Jones founded the Asiatic Society of Bengal in 1784. Modelled on the Royal Society, its aims were to 'furnish proof to our posterity, that the acquisition of [Indian wealth] did not absorb [our] attention, and that the English laws and English Government, in those distant regions, have sometimes been administered by men of extensive capacity, erudition and application' (Jones, 1799b: 205). Jones himself, the gentleman scholar-administrator, undertook full scale studies in the history, religions, customs, manners, geography, chronology, zodiac, mystical poetry and pastoral drama of

2 Although Franklin does suggest that Jones may have also initiated the society of the 'Druids of Cardigan'.

3 L 362, to Viscount Althrop 1783, pp 13–14. 'By rising before the sun, I allot an hour every day to Sanscrit, and am charmed with knowing so beautiful a sister of Latin and Greek.' (L 449).

4 L 464, 2nd Earl Spencer, p 747. The lines are in fact Jones' translation of a stanza from a Sanskrit poem.

5 Letter to Charles Wilkins, 24 April 1784.

6 L 382, to Patrick Russel, p 632.

India, and is recognised as having founded modern philology. He assiduously gathered a portfolio of icons, drawing images of Hindu Gods and symbols that would later haunt the Gothic imagination of those such as Thomas de Quincey. Broad and eclectic though his research was, its determining influence on imperial manners should not be under-estimated. It shored up respect for a fundamentally inaccessible set of cultures, and informed policy on the treatment of Muslims and Hindus. Yet such an obsessive and zodiacal inquiry, in order to at least be in touch with all forms of Oriental knowledge, betrayed a desire to accumulate a different type of wealth to that sustained by company officials. It may be that, as Edward Said has already argued, early Orientalism laid down a cultural foundation that enabled the establishment of colonial power. Information was to be managed so as to be understood and controlled. It ought to be remembered that the acquisition of knowledge was always already implicit in the idea of imperialism. In classical terms, the colonised world was to be understood as that which had 'fallen under inquiry', and the antecedents of Roman law implied the *imperium* to be a source of knowledge (Polybius, cited in Pagden, 1995: 19).

A distinction has to be drawn between the pleasure of study and the affective quality of the object studied:

> When I was at sea last August, on my voyage to this country, which I had long and ardently desired to visit, I found one evening, on inspecting the observations of the day, that India lay before us, and Persia on our left, while a breeze from Arabia blew nearly on our stern. A situation so pleasing in itself, and to me so new, could not fail to awaken a train of reflections in a mind, which had clearly been accustomed to contemplate with delight the eventful histories and agreeable fictions of this eastern world. It gives me inexpressible pleasure to find myself in the midst of so noble an amphitheatre, almost encircled by the vast regions of Asia, which has ever been esteemed the nurse of sciences, the inventress of delightful and useful arts, the scene of glorious actions, fertile in the productions of human genius, abounding in natural wonders and infinitely diversified in the forms of religion and government, in the laws, manners, customs, and languages, as well as the features and complexions of men. I could not help remarking, how important and extensive a field was yet unexplored, and how many solid advantages unimproved, and when I considered, with pain, that in this fluctuating imperfect, and limited conditions of life, such inquiries and improvements could only be made through the united efforts of many, who are not easily brought, without some pressing inducement or strong impulse, to converge in a common point, I consoled myself with a hope, founded on opinions, which it might have the appearance of flattery to mention, that if in any country or community, such an union could be effected, it was among my countrymen in Bengal, with some of whom I already had, and with most desirous of having, the pleasure of being intimately acquainted.
>
> (Jones, 1799d)

The phrases and metaphors used by Jones consciously engage with the themes of romantic sublime. The 'inexpressible pleasure' in the face of unexplored territories directly transferred on to the Orient the Burkean idea that ignorance incites the sublime passions. Typical of romantic sensibilities, the sublime Orient is expressed through the feminised descriptions of Asia ('nurse of the sciences, inventress of the delightful arts') and Jones directs our attention to the formlessness and excesses of femininity. Elsewhere, Jones is more explicit and suggests that 'the [mythology of] the Hindus and Arabs are perfectly original; and to my taste their compositions are sublime'[7] for the Indians are those 'who receive the first light of the rising sun' (Jones, 1799c: 51). That the study of the Orient produced such an 'infinite pleasure' was due not to the nature of study *qua* study but to the nature of the object of those studies. What is interesting about the above passage, however, is that there is a shift away from the feminine and unexplored sublime to the more mundane descriptions of a society of acquaintances. The thirst for knowledge, and the pleasures of Oriental scholarship, were rooted in the very idea of the sublime East. And, vice versa, 'inexpressible pleasure' turns into expressible pleasure as Jones seeks artistic reward by means of sublimation. The hidden, undiscovered and excessive forms of the East provided the initial motor propelling 'the delightful and glorious arts' and became the condition of the tamer pleasures of societal research, and of mastery through knowledge.

This simultaneous attraction and utilisation of the sublime can be traced over all the disciplines that form objects of Orientalist study. The architectural ruins of India, for example, were a key motif in the sublime imagination (Hodge's images stress the ruins and gloom of India, its supernatural atmosphere, the terror of *suti* and its landscapes):

> the remains of architecture and sculpture in India, which I mention here as mere monuments in antiquity, not as specimens of ancient art, seem to prove an early connection between this country and Africa; the pyramids of Egypt, the colossal statues described by PAUSANIAS and others.
>
> (Jones, 1799i: 221)

Indeed, India itself was characterised as the ruins of ancient and sublime civilisations (a common argument in contemporary literature was that the Indian civilisations had been ruined by Moghul mismanagement). Yet the architectural remains, and the ruin of India, were an excuse to dominate and rebuild the land. The suspicion that the Oriental despot embodied a limitless capacity of enjoyment, coupled with the unpredictable nature of alien manners, provoked the need to reconstitute a sense of order fashioned according to prim European standards. It was by controlling the mysterious sublime of the Orient that colonialism was to install jurisdictional control.

The category of the sublime provided the pivot around which both romantic speculation and imperial mastery revolved. This irresolute attitude towards the sublime was expressed time and again over different fields. Jones' position was

7 L 445 to Robert Orme, p 716.

not unique, and artists and philosophers were drawn to the East in search of romantic inspiration and those elements that lent themselves to sublime feelings. Yet, at the same time as submitting to it, this aspect of Orientalism, this process of sublimating the excess, yielded and mythologised British authority and was crucial to the extension of common law jurisdiction in the East.

The sublime antiquity and force of the law

> Menu sat reclined, with his attention fixed on one object, the Supreme God; when the divine sages approached him.
>
> (Jones, 1799e: 91)

The colonisation of the Oriental sublime must be understood, above all, as a symptom of jurisprudential thought. The process is, after all, the transference, or reassignment, of excess enjoyment into something more socially acceptable, and so it operates as a form of prohibition. Given this, it is not surprising to find the same jurisprudential concerns centred on William Jones' projects to translate Hindu laws. Just as he found 'infinite pleasure' in the study of Sanskrit and Hindu mythology, so too the study of Indian laws became an equally romantic pastime. 'Do you not agree', he wrote to Schultens as early as in 1774, 'that nothing should be more pleasant or noble than the study of native and universal law?'[8] Yet again, it was the object of study itself that satisfied the romantic desire for, and submission to, the sublime. As Jones observed, 'a spirit of sublime devotion...pervades the whole work [of Hindu law]'. On a more mundane level, however, these translations differed significantly from others such as his translation of Kalidasa's plays. In being directly applicable, this was a form of Orientalism which constituted the text as an object of knowledge, while also creating of the 'Indian' a subject of law. The totality of this exercise would have included 'six or seven law books believed to be divine with a commentary on each of nearly equal authority; these are analagous to our Littleton and Coke, next Jimut Bahur, the best book on inheritances; and above all a digest of Hindu law in twenty-seven Volumes precisely in the manner of the original digest'.[9] The project was never completed by Jones in its entirety; what survives are the Laws of Manu, translated in 1794 as *The Institutes of Hindu Law: Or, the Ordinances of Menu*.

What was so sublime, to Jones' mind, about the Hindu laws of Manu was that they were revealed and written down rather than composed and invented:

> It was not MENU who composed the system of law, by the command of his father BRAHMA, but a holy personage or demi-god, named BHRIGU who revealed to men what MENU had delivered at the request of him and other saints or patriarchs.
>
> (Jones, 1799f: 344)

8 Vol. I l.93 to Henry Albert Schultens, 1774, p 167.
9 L 447 to CW Boughton Rouse, p 722.

Menu, or Manu, was not simply the hand, or the amanuensis – he was, as it were, the first hand and the holiest of amanuenses! The law descends, having been promulgated 'in the beginning of time by MENU, son of BRAHMA, or, in plain language, the first of created beings, and not the oldest only, but the holiest of legislators'.[10] So old are these laws ('the laws [of menu] are considerably older than those of SOLON or even LYCURGUS')[11] that Jones declares himself to be 'lost in an inextricable labyrinth of imaginary astronomical cycles, *yugas, mahayugas, calpas, and menwantaras*, in attempting to calculate the time when the first MENU, governed this world, and became the progenitor of mankind'.[12]

While clearly interesting from an Orientalist point of view, it is unclear why, *as a lawyer*, Jones would wish to allocate any legal authority to a high Hindu text such as Manu. A number of reasons, simultaneously practical and ideological, are given by Jones, his contemporaries and modern commentators. It is important to analyse these given reasons in order to reveal the way in which they hang on the idea of the sublime and on the process of sublimation.

A 'best practicable system of judicature'

At one level of analysis, the codification of the original texts of Indian laws arranged according to scientific method simply eased the process of decision-making by judges of the Calcutta Supreme Court. Apart from Jones, judges were unwilling to learn Sanskrit and were consequently ignorant of the laws they were applying to Indian subjects. Instead, they had to rely on the 'written opinion of native lawyers', and translations of particular laws were provided only when required. The inefficiency of this process of discovering and applying Hindu, or Muslim, law was increased by the lack of trust afforded to the relevant court officials: 'Pure integrity is hardly to be found among the Pandits and Maulavis.'[13] Copies of the work enabled British judges to avoid relying on these intermediaries and to detect any misinformation that these *pandits* and *maulavis* may have provided in the courts. In this sense, Jones' attempt to translate the law was symptomatic of the training of all common lawyers. The process of translating the Hindu and Muslim laws might be regarded as equivalent to that of legal education in the Inns of Courts, and simply provided direct access to what was hidden in the depths of an esoteric language. The secular lawyer assumed the mantle of the priest as guardian of a sacred text and of its meaning. Whether written in a 'strange tongue' or in English, a training into legal priesthood was, and remains, necessary in order to unlock the mysteries of legal knowledge (*arcana juris*) (see Goodrich, 1986). The hieroglyphic nature of law was regarded as universal. Translation provided the opportunity for the

10 Preface, p 76.

11 Preface to the *Hindu Laws of Manu*, p 78.

12 Preface, pp 76–77.

13 L 447 to CW Boughton Rouse, p 720. (It is pertinent that Boughton Rouse was then secretary to the Board of Control for India.)

lawyers of the Supreme Courts to have access to legal wisdom without the intermediation of the *pandits* and *maulavis*.

In strict doctrinal terms, however, the idea that a translation of indigenous laws would ease the judicial process of determining rules to be applied somewhat elides a more substantial point. It remains unclear as to why Hindu laws should be used in place of the common law, given that in 1608 the English courts had stated firmly that 'if a Christian king should conquer the kingdom of an infidel . . . the laws of that kingdom are abrogated'.[14]

On this point, a number of reasons were given for keeping intact the laws of the 'native' subject. For Nathaniel Halhed, it was a matter of following the antecedents of Roman imperialism:

> [The Romans] not only allowed their foreign subjects the free exercise of their own religion and the administration of their own civil jurisdiction, but sometimes, by a policy still more flattering, even naturalized parts of the mythology of the conquered, as were in any respect compatible with their own system.
>
> (Halhed, 1776: ix)

The following reason provided by Forbes, however, recognised the limits of imperial authority:

> It is impossible to separate the political tendency of laws from the genius of government from which they emanate. The spirit of the English constitution assigns to the mass of the people an extensive control over the exercise of public authority; and deems the executive government to be the representative of the public will. This spirit pervades the whole body of its laws; these laws necessarily reflect back and reproduce the principles from which they spring; and it is a matter of grave reflection should, that if this species of reaction should ever be produced in India, from that moment it is lost to this country for ever. The efficient protection of our native subjects in all the rights which they themselves consider to be essential to their happiness is certainly the most sacred and Imperious of all our duties . . . It is not the question, whether the English or the Hindu code of religion and jurisprudence be entitled to the preference; but whether the Hindu law and religion . . . are, or are not to be, maintained, or whether we are at liberty to invade both.
>
> (Forbes, 1988: 317)

According to Forbes, the 'invasion' of Indian law, and its replacement with the common law, did not form part of British imperialism. As Jones continually emphasised, such an agenda would have compromised the spirit of liberty that

14 *Calvin's Case* 1608. In *De Laudibus Legum Anglicae* (1773 edn), Sir John Fortesque remarks: 'I am convinced that our laws of England eminently excel, beyond the laws of all other countries.' (cited in Goodrich, 1990: 212)

was essential to the jurisprudence of the common law. In his recommendations to Edmund Burke for the 'Best Practicable System of Judicature', Jones observed that the replacement of Indian laws would have entailed a violent imposition of one institution upon another and would have implied that the English assume the despotic attributes of intolerance to which they were necessarily opposed: 'A system of *liberty*, forced upon a people invincibly attached to opposite *habits*, would in truth be a system of cruel *tyranny*.'[15] The *spirit* of liberty implied that the very system and set of institutions on which it depended could not be transferred to, and imposed upon, other cultures. However, the real paradox and irony of this sentiment was that, for these Hindu and Muslim subjects, the enjoyment of their own laws had to be sanctioned and determined by a foreign system, a foreign institution and foreign legislation:

> A legislative act [is needed] to assure the Hindu and Musselman subjects of Great Britain, that the private laws, which they severally hold secret and a violation of which they would have thought the most grievous oppression, should not be superseded by a new system, of which they could have no knowledge, and which they must have considered as imposed on them by a spirit of rigour and intolerance.[16]

This rhetoric of liberty, in other words, disguised the constitutional theory that there was *posited* a non-Indian geographical location of authority; the seemingly autonomous survival, existence and application of Indian laws hung upon a set of instructions relayed from London to Calcutta. And it should not be forgotten that behind this legislative authority lay an obvious ulterior imperial motive that involved buying the respect and affection of the Bengalis. These additional and superficial reasons for the preferential use of Hindu and Muslim laws, given by Jones in his letter to Burke, point to mercantile interests and the importance of maintaining good relations between the English (or, in Jones' case, the Welsh) and the subjects of Bengal:

> Any system of *judicature* affecting the natives in *Bengal*, and not having for its basis the old *Mogul* constitution, would be dangerous and impracticable... The natives must have an *effective* tribunal for their protection against the *English*, or the country will soon be rendered *worse than useless* to Britain.

Holding back the application of the common law was part of an established code of behaviour that sought to ensure the happiness and respect of 'the natives [who] are charmed with the idea of making their slavery lighter by giving them their own laws'.[17]

15 'Best Practicable System of Judicature' (L 387, to Edmund Burke).

16 L 485 to the Marquis of Cornwall, p 794.

17 L 558 to 2nd Earl Spencer, p 885. Consider, too, his remark that the 'three excellent things, which the ancients feigned to be the daughters of their supreme God, a good system of laws, a just administration of them, and a long peace will render this country a source of infinite advantage to Great Britain': L 397 to William Pitt the Younger, p 664.

Jones' reification of the spirit of liberty thus masks a motive for maintaining imperial authority through the judicial system: 'The Hindus are incapable of civil liberty; few of them have any idea of it; and those who have do not wish it. They must (I deplore the evil, but know the necessity of it) be ruled by an absolute power.'[18]

It might be argued further that the translation of a sacred Hindu text into English ensured the manipulation of that text. Sanskrit texts had their untranslatable words, and contained forms of signification and meaning unthinkable in an English idiom. Indeed, all projects of translation put signification and the status of the original into question. Translation necessitates mistranslation and glosses over the remnants of enigmas and puzzles which are impossible to solve. Where, to subvert Spivak's original argument (in Derrida, 1997), did Sanskrit end and English begin? Translating a legal text into English in order that its rules may be enforced in a court of law simply erases the ability of that text to speak in its own language, in a language other than that of the British court system. Hindu or Mohammedan laws were translated and tailored to fit British conceptions of justice. John Strawson makes the claim in relation to Jones' project of translating the *Al Sirajiyyah*. Islamic law, he suggests, was given legitimacy only 'by reference to European criteria which are taken almost as fact' (Strawson, 1995). Legal Orientalism thus denied and obscured the diverse literary traditions of both Hindu and Islamic jurisprudence.

What is at stake at this level of analysis is the use of the courts and the process of translation to manouevre and contain the law. It might be supposed, therefore, that Hindu law, for example, was to be kept as a mark of difference. Nations might be defined according to their laws, and their systems of interdiction, and so a Hindu was to be kept in his place and differentiated according to the law to which he appealed. The Hindus are Hindus by virtue of their laws. Certainly, the point is implied by Forbes in criticising early attempts by the English to abolish the practice of *suti*: 'If we are to govern Hindoos by their own laws, why do we tear them up by their roots, they are no longer Hindoos if they are subject to innovation.'[19]

The sublime universality of laws

But there was more to this process of translation than the control and manipulation of positive laws, and the 'staging of difference'. For Jones – and here his attitude was symptomatic of contemporary jurisprudential concerns – there was a genuine recognition of the spirit of Hindu law that actually refers him to similarities and connections between Eastern and Western notions of legality. Or, put slightly differently, the spirit of Hindu law refers to the other face of European legality that Jones and common lawyers such as Blackstone had been trying to recuperate throughout the eighteenth century. In what seems like a typical piece

18 L 443, pp 712–13.
19 Forbes (1988: 318).

of apologia, linking a system of laws to the manners and civilisation of its people, the following passage introduces Jones' recognition and obsession with the idea of legal sublimity:

> It is a maxim in the science of legislation and government that *laws are of no avail without manners*, or, to explain the sentence more fully, that the best intended legislative provisions would have no beneficial effect even at first unless they were congenial to the disposition and habits, to the religious prejudices, and approved immemorial usages, of the people, for whom they were enacted; especially if that people universally believed that all their ancient usages and established rules of conduct had the sanction of an actual revelation from heaven.[20]

While this idea of antiquity and sublime revelation is a feature of Hindu law, it also resonates with the reflections on the originary time and place of the common law that had been rattling around the minds of its own lawyers. It was common for eighteenth century doctrinalists to use the category of the sublime to describe the complexity, disorder and obscurity of the common law. For Blackstone in particular, this irregular form of the law was founded in an idea of nature from which England was to derive the law of the land. Like the sublime ruins of Gothic castles, churches and abbeys, the law was magnificent, venerable, winding, difficult, inspiring and at times neglected. Far from rendering common law defunct, the idea of neglect simply meant that it contained latent, undiscovered perfections. It was because of its sublime nature that the law was capable of evolving new and 'beautiful' solutions to problems: 'My system is formed; and I did not carry it *to* the law, but found it *in* the law.'[21] A second level of analysis, beyond the practical concerns of authority, has to be considered, and at this level the focus is on similarity rather than difference. That both Hindu and common law shared ideas about their beginnings, and celebrated their obscurity in similar ways, might seem like weak comparison, but to Jones and other Orientalists of the Asiatic society it implied that both systems may well have emerged from the mists of a common time immemorial, and a common place. It is at this mystical and sublime moment, whose precise time was lost in the labyrinth of astronomical cycles, that Jones saw the familial connection between Eastern and Western sources of law: 'The Hindus believe [their law] to be almost as old as creation. It is ascribed to MENU, the MINOS of India, and like him, the son of JOVE.'[22]

In this respect, eighteenth century jurisprudential claims that English law was to boost its legitimacy if it 'conformed to the norms of a community of legal systems' have to be remembered (Boorstin, 1996: 45). Familial connections were essential to the iconic and jurisdictional unity of the English law. As Jones himself

20 Preface to the *Institutes of Hindu Law*, p 75.

21 L 383, to 2nd Earl Spencer, p 634.

22 L 440 to Patrick Russell, p 706. See also L 464 to 2nd Earl Spencer where he describes Menu as 'the first created man, many millions of years old' (p 747).

puts it: 'The great system of jurisprudence like that of the Universe, consists of many subordinate systems, all of which are connected by nice links and beautiful dependencies.' (Jones, 1781: 173) In this sense, correspondences were even sought and found between the laws of Manu and Justinian's *pandectae* (1485):

> If we had a complete digest of Hindu and Muhammedan laws, after the model of Justinian's inestimable Pandects, compiled by the most learned of native lawyers, with an accurate verbal translation of it into English; and if copies of the work were reposited in the proper offices . . . of the Supreme Court, that they might occasionally be consulted as a standard of justice, we should rarely be at a loss for principles at least and rules of law applicable to the cases before us . . . The great work, of which *Justinian* has the credit, consists of texts collected from law-books of approved authority, which in his time were extant at Rome; and those texts are digested according to a scientifical analysis; the names of the original authors, and the titles of their several books, being constantly cited with references even to parts of their works, from which the different passages were selected; but although it comprehends the whole system of jurisprudence . . . that vast compilation was published, we are told, in three years; with all its imperfections, it is a most valuable mine of juridical knowledge; it gives law at this hour to the greatest part of Europe; and though few English lawyers dare make such an acknowledgement, it is the true source of nearly all our English laws that are not feudal in origin. It would not be unworthy of a British government to give the natives of these Indian provinces a permanent security for the due administration of justice among them, similar to that which Justinian gave to his Greek and Roman subjects. The labour of the work would also be greatly diminished by two compilations already made in Sanscrit and Arabick, which approach nearly in merit and in method, to the Digest of Justinian . . . The *Vivadarnava* [*Bridge over the Sea of Litigation*] consists, like the Roman Digest, of authentick texts, with the names of their several authors regularly prefixed to them, and explained where an explanation is requisite, in short notes taken from commentaries of high authority.
>
> (1804b: 796–97)

Even at the mundane level of individual rules of contract or inheritance, familial connections between the common law and other legal systems had to be sought and found. As Boorstin, commenting on Blackstone, notes: 'The ancient or foreign rule is first used to explain, and then to justify the English institution.' An example of this is provided by Jones:

> That the Hindus were in early ages a *commercial* people, we have many reasons to believe; and in the first of their sacred law-tracts, which they suppose to have been revealed by MENU many *millions* of years ago, we find a curious passage on the legal *interest* of money, and the limited state of it in different cases, with an exception, which the sense of mankind approves, and which commerce

> absolutely requires, though it was not before the reign of CHARLES I that our own jurisprudence fully admitted it in respect of maritime contracts.
>
> (Jones, 1799g: 42–44)

There was, then, no clear discrimination against this foreign legal order. The word 'foreign' simply meant 'ancient', and 'ancient' meant the possibility that at some time – beyond the time of memory – Hindu, Roman and common law systems were conjoined, or even identical to one another.

Furthermore, what was to prove beneficial to the imperial enterprise was that this universal law had universal jurisdiction and applied across the whole human race, irrespective of differences. That the Hindu code of laws was comparable to the *corpus iuris civilis* points to the place of the legal text in classical ideas of imperialism. These comparisons and connections appealed to the policy of the Roman *imperium* according to which the essence of legal authority devolved from the textual body of its laws. Similarly, Manu was to take the place of the Pandects as law's *ur*-text, and thus transfer its authority right across the globe. After all: 'Legislative provisions have not the individual for their object, but the species; and are not made for the convenience of the day but for the regulation of ages.' (Jones, 1799h: 3) Even in this age of reason, law was to be considered universal, beyond mere geography, and as deriving from and revealed by the gods. For Jones: '[Hooker's] idea of heavenly law is just and noble; and human law as derived from it, must partake of the phrase as far as it is perfectly administered.'[23]

The universality of law – so crucial to the idea of Empire – did not derive from differentiating Western from Eastern jurisprudence. It was, rather, based on their similarities – or at least a similarity insofar as both posited a mysterious and sublime cause at the centre of their institutional organisation.

The dread force of law

In the context of imperial jurisdiction, the sublimity of Hindu laws offered the English further advantages. The sublime was connected with power, and control over the sublime would be control over power: 'I know of nothing sublime,' states Burke, 'which is not some modification of power' (Burke, 1999: 69).[24] Or, as Jean-Luc Nancy puts it: 'In the sublime, enjoyment touches, moves, that is also commands.' (Nancy, 1993: 52) For Burke, and for later romantics such as Jones and Forbes, the sublime was rooted in objects obscured from sight; darkness, confusion, ignorance and terror are what excited romantic passions. As Nietzsche later put it, legal authority rests on 'the assumption that the rationale of every law is not human in origin, that it was not sought and found after ages of error, but

23 L 516 to John Shore, p 835. The text Jones refers to is 'of law there can be no less acknowledged, than that her seat is the bosom of God, her voice the harmony of the world'.

24 The same, incidentally, is to be said of the Kantian sublime, which commands and turns imagination into an instrument of reason.

that it is divine in its origin, completely and utterly without a history, a gift, a miracle, a mere communication' (Nietzsche, 1991: xv). To reveal the origins of law as something positive, as opposed to divine, would be to obviate its imperative tone. The original cause of law, in other words, had to act like the Oriental despot. Just as, for Burke, the dread of night and the fear of ghosts lay in their obscure forms, similarly the despot was one who exercised his form of justice in private: 'Those despotic governments, which are founded on the passions of men, and principally upon the passion of fear, keep their chief as much as may be from the public eye' (Burke, 1999: 836).

In evoking the sublime, it was to be the law, with its origins obscured among the labyrinths of a mystical and different temporality, that was to exercise power and replace the 'dread majesty' of the sultans. In terms of its power to declare the law, jurisdiction simply occupies the place vacated by the (deposed) sultans. Its power lay hidden beyond the call of its subjects.

The law-givers: Manu, Solon, Tribonian, Jones

The effect of sublimation thus converted the exclusive enjoyment of the sultans, and the obscene excesses of religious idolatry, into more acceptable and useful forms of control. The sublime allows power to emerge and to be 'posited' as legitimate force. However, just as super-abundant enjoyment is what distinguished the despot from his subjects, so too sublime power conferred a similar, but more acceptable, status on the legislator. As Deleuze and Guattari (1983) observe, the machinery of despotism is driven by the one who establishes a filial link between his subjects and a superior deity. The Oriental despot held a particular place as a mediator and messenger of the gods. According to Grosrichard, the despot had to submit to the law because to do so was to endow the law with universal characteristics (Grosrichard, 1998: 92–93) And, simultaneously, because the law was regarded as universal, it empowered him to act and speak imperatively. The law created the despot and the despot created the law. That the despot was simultaneously subject to the law, and in a unique position to create the law, might be characterised in terms of a split. This being so, it may be argued that this split is what allows the charisma of authority to emerge.

This same split economy of power, and of jurisdiction, is discernable if we analyse Jones' own position in relation to the law. In typical fashion, and throughout his writings, Jones maintained his submission before the law. In a letter to Earl Spencer, he declares his refusal to take sides in the battle between Burke and Hastings in the run-up to the latter's impeachment. Jones declared that his allegiances were only to aspects of the law. Thus he has 'an equity-*side*, a common-law-*side*, an ecclesiastical *side*, and an admiralty-*side*, but I am quadrilateral by act of parliament'. Jones' quadrilateral nature involves his submission to a higher cause: 'it is my sole duty to convey law as though a channel' (Grosrichard, 1998: 92–93).[25]

25 L 383, p 634.

Jones' subservient relationship to the law conformed to the correct manners demanded of its institution. Yet this passive position within the dogmatic structure of the law assigned Jones to a particular place that distinguished him from those other (pre-)colonial subjects of law over whom he held authority. He was not merely a passive recipient of the law, but a messenger and conduit of an already established truth. Jones himself recognised the power conferred upon him by power over his subjects. It was a power, he freely admitted, that made him tremble: 'All the police and judicial power, therefore, of this settlement, where at least half a million of natives reside, are in my hands: I tremble at the power, which I possess.'[26]

The simultaneity of passivity and authority is more pertinently discernable in relation to the translations of the legal codes. For here Jones was more than a judge: 'I speak the *language of the Gods* as the Brahmins call it, and am engaged in superintending a *Digest* of Indian law for the benefit of *twenty-four millions* of black subjects in these provinces.'[27] Jones conferred upon himself the status of a law-giver, and continually referred to himself as occupying the same position as that of Solon. Indeed, in the following passage, Jones admits to a position that Solon would have envied:

> I have the delight of knowing that my studies go hand in hand with my duty, since I now read both Sanscrit and Arabik with so much ease, that the native lawyers can never impose upon the courts, in which I sit. I converse fluently in Arabick with the Maulavi's, in Sanscrit with the Pandit's, and in Persian with the nobles of the country; thus possessing an advantage which neither Pythagoras nor Solon possessed, though they must ardently have wished it.[28]

Given that the sublimity of law renders it universal, the law-giver need not be Greek. And so, on occasions, Jones described himself as a reincarnation of Manu himself who, 'having written the laws of BRAHMA in a hundred thousand couplets, arranged under *twenty-four* heads in a *thousand* chapters presented them to the primitive world' (Jones, 1799e: 84). What Manu presented to the primitive world, the modern day amanuensis, Jones, was to present to the civilised world of European judges and governor generals.

But Solon's was not the only position he sought to occupy. In a private letter sent from Calcutta to London in 1786, Jones expressed his plans for the systematic translation and compilation of Hindu and Mohammedan laws. Here Jones likened himself to Tribonian, the compiler of the Justinian code, and declares that the mantle of Justinian himself was to fall upon his patron, Lord Cornwallis, the Governor-General of Bengal. The Maulavy Mujdudden is given the title *omni exceptione major* taken from Justinian's institutes.[29]

26 L 372, to 2nd Earl Spencer, p 623.
27 L 558, to 2nd Earl Spencer, p 885.
28 L 742; Teltscher (1995).
29 L 409, to John Macpherson.

The category of the sublime thus clears a space to be occupied by a mediating figure. As Pierre Legendre puts it: 'In theology, the power of God or absolute place of the mythical Third must always pass through a mediating figure – that of the pope, the emperor or the priest – before it becomes an object of subjective attachment.' (Goodrich, 1997: 262) Similarly, in Jones' imperial jurisprudence, it is the law-giver – Manu, Solon, Justinian or Jones himself – who occupies that charismatic position as mediator between the gods and his subjects.

Conclusions

Jones' translations of the codes of Manu illustrate that colonial legality was based on more than the desire to use law in the interests of colonialism. His projects and those of other Orientalists were built on a desire to master the origins of law. The attempt to extend the jurisdiction of the common law exposes a void at the origin of legal authority. For Jones, it was a matter of colonising this void so as to occupy it. The sublime provided that terrifying yet empty space from which to instruct and colonise the subject. It allowed the development of a rational legal system within the colonies.[30]

Yet, aside from the specific imperial concerns of the eighteenth century, these conclusions also illuminate a more general point about common law jurisprudence. The translation of Manu was not an attempt to recreate an alternative history of the law, but to ascertain the origins of law and the essence of jurisdiction. This project was not so much the reinvention of the history of law, but a rediscovery of the roots of all law. Similarly, these translations tell us more than the idea that the translated text was a product of discursive construction. The text (that which remains untranslatable) betrayed an order of legal dogmatism and hierarchy which Western legal institutions, in spite of their modernity, failed to successfully exclude. Colonialism – rather than being, as Marx had thought, a measure of modern industrial statecraft – marked the immediate demise of modernity.

Jones' failure to translate the whole of the ordinances might be regarded as symptomatic of the failure of the mind to grasp the sublime origins of the law; it is the failure to return to an experience that the mind cannot grasp. Nevertheless, this does not negate the importance of the sublime in understanding the relationship between the question of jurisdiction and the governance of (colonial) subjectivity.

References

Boorstin, D (1996) *The Mysterious Science of the Law: An Essay on Blackstone's Commentaries*, Chicago, IL: Chicago University Press

Burke, E (1999) 'A philosophical enquiry into the origins of our ideas on the sublime and beautiful', in I Kramnick (ed), *The Portable Burke*, London: Penguin

30 '[Science] embraces the whole circle of pure and mixed mathematics, together with ethics and law.' (Jones, 1799d: 6) Thus, in a letter to Edward Hay (L 584, p 916), Jones states that the 'laws of the ancient legislator are obscure when detached, yet clear when connected'. It is this process of connection that rationalises the Oriental sublime spirit of Oriental law.

Cannon, Garland (ed) (1970) *The Letters of William Jones*, 2 Vols, Oxford: Oxford University Press

Deleuze, G and Guattari, F (1983) *Anti-Oedipus: Capitalism and Schizophrenia*, Minneapolis, MI: University of Minnesota Press

Deguy, Michel (1993) 'The discourse of exaltation', in JS Librett (ed), *Of the Sublime: Presence in Question*, Essays by Jean-François *et al.*, Albany, NY: State University of New York Press

Derrida, Jacques (1997) *Of Grammatology*, trans Gayatri Chakravorty Spivak, Baltimore: Johns Hopkins University Press

Drew, John (1998) *India and the Romantic Imagination*, New York: Oxford University Press

Forbes, John (1988) *Oriental Memoirs, Selected from a Series of Familiar Letters Written During Seventeen Years' Residence in India*, Vol. II, New Delhi: Gyan Publishing

Franklin, Michael J (1995) *Sir William Jones*, Cardiff: University of Wales Press

Goodrich, Peter (1986) *Reading the Law: A Critical Introduction to Legal Method and Techniques*, Oxford: Blackwell

Goodrich, Peter (1990) *Languages of Law: from Logics of Memory to Nomadic Masks*, London : Weidenfeld and Nicolson

Grosrichard, Alain (1998) *The Sultan's Court: European Fantasies of the East*, trans Liz Heron, with an introduction by Mladen Dolar, London and New York, NY: Verso

Halhed, Nathaniel (1776) *A Code of Gentoo Laws, or Ordinations of the Pundits*, London: np

Jones, William (1781) *An Essay on the Law of Bailment*, London: Hatchard

Jones, William (1799a) 'Ninth discourse on the origin and families of nations', in John Shore (Lord Teignmouth) (ed), *The Works of Sir William Jones*, Vol. III, London: Hatchard

Jones, William (1799b) 'Presidential address', in John Shore (Lord Teignmouth) (ed), *The Works of Sir William Jones*, Vol. III, London: Hatchard

Jones, William (1799c) 'Third Anniversary Discourse', in John Shore (Lord Teignmouth) (ed), *The Works of Sir William Jones*, Vol. III, London: Hatchard

Jones, William (1799d) 'A discourse on the institution of a society, for inquiring into the history, civil and natural, the antiquities, arts, sciences, literature of Asia, by the president', in John Shore (Lord Teignmouth) (ed), *The Works of Sir William Jones*, Vol. III, London: Hatchard

Jones, William (1799e) 'Preface to the Institutes of Hindu Law; or the Ordinances of Menu according to the gloss of Culluca comprising the Indian system of duties, religious and civil', in John Shore (Lord Teignmouth) (ed), *The Works of Sir William Jones*, Vol. III, London: Hatchard

Jones, William (1799f) 'On the gods of Greece, Italy and India', in John Shore (Lord Teignmouth) (ed), *The Works of Sir William Jones*, Vol. III, London: Hatchard

Jones, William (1799g) 'Second anniversary discourse', in John Shore (Lord Teignmouth) (ed), *The Works of Sir William Jones*, Vol. III, London: Hatchard

Jones, William (1799h) 'Charge to the Grand Jury', in John Shore (Lord Teignmouth) (ed), *The Works of Sir William Jones*, Vol. III, London: Hatchard

Jones, William (1799i) *Asiatic Researches*, Vol. 1, London: Hatchard

Jones, William (1804a) 'On the divine inspiration of the Jewish scriptures', in John Shore (Lord Teignmouth) (ed), *Memoirs of the Life, Writings and Correspondence of Sir William Jones*, London: Hatchard

Jones, William (1804b) 'Letter to the Marquis of Cornwall', in John Shore (Lord Teighnmouth) (ed), *Memoirs of the Life, Writings and Correspondence of Sir William Jones*, London: Hatchard

Nancy, Jean-Luc (1993) 'The sublime offering', in JS Librett (trans. and ed.) *Of the Sublime: Presence in Question*, Essays by Jean-Francois Courtine *et al.*, Albany, NY: State of New York Press

Nietzsche, Friedrich (1991) 'The Anti-Christ', cited in Wendy Doniger (ed), *The Laws of Manu*, London: Penguin

Pagden, Anthony (1995) *Lords of All the World: Ideologies of Empire in Spain, Britain and France, c.1500–c.1800*, New Haven, CT: Yale University Press

Strawson, John (1995) 'Islamic law and English texts' 5 *Law and Critique* 21

Teltscher, Kate (1995) *India Inscribed : European and British Writing on India, 1600–1800*, Delhi: Oxford University Press

Index

For Product Safety Concerns and Information please contact our EU representative GPSR@taylorandfrancis.com Taylor & Francis Verlag GmbH, Kaufingerstraße 24, 80331 München, Germany